ENGAGING QUESTIONS
A Guide to Writing

Second Edition
MLA Updated Edition

Carolyn E. Channell *Southern Methodist University*

Timothy W. Crusius *Southern Methodist University*

Mc
Graw
Hill
Education

Engaging Questions: A Guide to Writing, Second Edition, MLA Updated Edition

Published by McGraw-Hill Education, 2 Penn Plaza, New York, NY 10121. Copyright © 2017 by McGraw-Hill Education. All rights reserved. Printed in the United States of America. Previous edition © 2013. No part of this publication may be reproduced or distributed in any form or by any means, or stored in a database or retrieval system, without the prior written consent of McGraw-Hill Education, including, but not limited to, in any network or other electronic storage or transmission, or broadcast for distance learning.

Some ancillaries, including electronic and print components, may not be available to customers outside the United States.

This book is printed on acid-free paper.

1 2 3 4 5 6 7 8 9 0 LCR 21 20 19 18 17 16

ISBN 978-1-259-98828-8
MHID 1-259-98828-7

Senior Vice President, Products & Markets: *Kurt L. Strand*
Vice President, General Manager, Products & Markets: *Michael Ryan*
Vice President, Content Design & Delivery: *Kimberly Meriwether David*
Managing Director: *David Patterson*
Director: *Kelly Villella*
Brand Manager: *Claire Brantley*
Lead Product Developer: *Lisa Pinto*
Senior Product Developer: *Scott Harris*
Lead Digital Product Analyst: *Janet Smith*
Senior Marketing Manager: *Brigeth Rivera*
Marketing Manager: *Marisa Cavanaugh*

Director, Content Design & Delivery: *Terri Schiesl*
Program Manager: *Jennifer Gehl*
Content Project Managers: *Lisa Bruflodt, Samantha Donisi-Hamm*
Buyer: *Susan K.Culbertson*
Designer: *Debra Kubiak*
Content Licensing Specialists: *Shawntel Schmitt, Deanna Dausener*
Cover Image: *Egzon Shaqiri*
Compositor: *SPi Global*
Printer: *LSC Communications*

All credits appearing on page or at the end of the book are considered to be an extension of the copyright page.

Library of Congress Cataloging-in-Publication Data

Channell, Carolyn E.. author.
   Engaging questions : a guide to writing / Carolyn E. Channell, Southern Methodist University ; Timothy W.Crusius Southern Methodist University. — Second Edition.
      pages cm
   Includes bibliographical references and index.
   ISBN 978-0-07-803622-4 (alk. paper)
   1. English language—Rhetoric—Handbooks, manuals, etc. 2. English language—Grammar—Handbooks, manuals, etc. 3. Report writing—Handbooks, manuals, etc. I. Crusius, Timothy W., 1950– author. II. Title.
   PE1408.C3963 2017
   808´.042—dc23
                                                                        2015036288

The Internet addresses listed in the text were accurate at the time of publication. The inclusion of a website does not indicate an endorsement by the authors or McGraw-Hill Education, and McGraw-Hill Education does not guarantee the accuracy of the information presented at these sites.

mheducation.com/highered

DEDICATION

For James L. Kinneavy

ABOUT THE AUTHORS

Carolyn E. Channell taught high school and community college students before joining the faculty at Southern Methodist University, where she is now a senior lecturer and a specialist in first-year writing courses. She has served as a writing program administrator and is currently coordinator of computer-assisted instruction. Her research interests involve literacy in the digital age. She resides in Richardson, Texas, with her husband, David.

Timothy W. Crusius is professor of English at Southern Methodist University, where he teaches beginning and advanced composition. He is the author of books on discourse theory, philosophical hermeneutics, argumentation, and Kenneth Burke. His long-standing interest in the relation between dialogue and rhetoric has led in recent years to a fascination with the art of questioning, his current research focus. He resides in Dallas with his wife, Elizabeth.

BRIEF CONTENTS

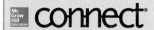
Comprehensive digital handbook is available in **Mc Graw Hill Education connect**

CONTENTS

PART III

Researching Writing 319

connect

Comprehensive digital handbook is available in

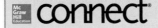

The Learning Support System to Accompany *Engaging Questions*

Connect Composition

McGraw-Hill Education's *Connect Composition* offers:

- **Mobile access.** Students can now access powerful *Connect Composition* learning resources directly from their tablets and phones.
- **SmartBook.** SmartBook is the first and only adaptive reading experience designed to change the way students read and learn. *Engaging Questions* will be offered in the SmartBook format.
- **Power of Process.** This tool guides students through performance-based activities that require them to apply active reading and writing strategies.
- **Simple LMS integration.** *Connect Composition* seamlessly integrates with any learning management system. Instructors can quickly access registration, attendance, assignments, grades, and course resources in real time in one location.
- **Tegrity.** Students can view recordings of instructor lectures with this lecture-capture tool.
- *Connect Insight.* This analytics tool provides a series of visual data displays—each framed by an intuitive question—to provide instructors with at-a-glance information regarding how their classes are doing based on indicators of engagement and performance.
- **Outcomes-Based Assessment for writing assignments.** Instructors and administrators can incorporate their own custom learning outcomes into *Connect Composition,*

creating a grading rubric for specific course outcomes and generating detailed reports for students, sections, or departments.

- **Writing assignments.** Instructors can choose from a wide variety of customizable writing assignments, with intuitive instructor commenting and annotating capabilities.
- **Four years of student access.** Students benefit from this dependable writing and research resource throughout college, at a fraction of the cost of traditional textbooks.

Flexible Text Format

- McGraw-Hill's CREATE allows instructors to build their own course material to perfectly match their course by selecting specific chapters from *Engaging Questions*. Instructors may also add readings from a wide range of collections or include their own content, such as syllabi, assignments, and course information. Finally, instructors may choose to offer their students a print or electronic version of their customized version of *Engaging Questions*.

© Caia Image/Glow Images, RF

WHY ENGAGING QUESTIONS?

The Spirit of Writing as Discovery

Engaging Questions is dedicated to the spirit of writing as discovery, encouraging students to interact—with the texts they read and write, as well as with peers, teachers, and others involved in a writing project. By emphasizing interaction and critical thinking, *Engaging Questions* transforms passive learners into active learners empowered to ask their own questions and pursue these questions wherever they lead:

- **In reading and thinking before writing,** to interpret texts and assignments and to evaluate the credibility of sources.
- **In planning and organizing,** to investigate the writing situation, to find a topic, and to anticipate audience concerns.
- **In drafting,** to consider choices of style, voice, and genre and question the effectiveness of the choices made.
- **In revising and editing,** to anticipate a reader's experience with the text and see where changes could make the text more readable and effective.

With *Engaging Questions,* students will learn to see writing as essential to thinking, discussing, and reading, all of which develop around the questions they pose and pursue. These key questions are built into each assignment chapter, guiding students through a process that is both creative and critical, inviting genuine engagement, and preparing students to become skilled thinkers and confident writers.

Teaching Students—An Inquiry-Based Approach

The *Engaging Questions* SmartBook is an adaptive reading experience that enhances the inquiry-based approach of the text. SmartBook questions students on their current knowledge and adapts constantly to what they know and don't know, assisting students in long-term knowledge retention and preparing them for active in-class participation.

> ■ **Writing** Because writing requires us to express our ideas completely and precisely, it is central to both college and career. Lab reports, essay exams, and research papers are common tools used to measure whether students have absorbed facts, mastered concepts, and become engaged enough to think critically and creatively about what they have learned. Writing does not end with graduation. In our knowledge-based economy, people spend up to 50 percent of their time at work composing e-mails, reports, proposals, letters, and so on.[1] Even in community and personal activities, from writing letters to the editor to updating a Facebook page, writing is how we represent ourselves. Most importantly, writing our thoughts down helps us examine them; writing is a tool for questioning what we think and read and discuss.
>
> Thinking, discussion, reading, and writing are too deeply intertwined to describe fully; Figure 1.1 will help you envision how intertwined they are.
>
> 1. Deborah Brandt. *The Rise of Writing: Redefining Mass Literacy.* Cambridge: Cambridge UP, 2015. Print.

SmartBook identifies and highlights content students have not yet mastered.

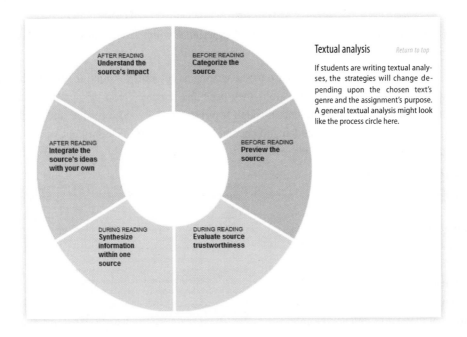

SmartBook adapts based on what students know and what they do not know, focusing study time on critical material.

Power of Process is a learning technology that pushes students to become active readers and writers by guiding students through the critical reading and writing process and having them ask and answer questions throughout the entire assignment.

With Power of Process students move through a step-by-step approach designed to improve reading comprehension; students highlight, annotate, respond, and directly engage with the material. Instructors using *Engaging Questions* can utilize the easy-to-read Power of Process breakdown report to see exactly where students understood or struggled with the material and provide individualized feedback where appropriate.

Power of Process transforms the readings from *Engaging Questions* into highly engaging assignments that help students read and annotate texts strategically and critically. The second edition of *Engaging Questions* offers the following readings as part of the rich library of works enhanced by Power of Process:

"Apparently, Facts No Longer Mean What They Once Did" by Leonard Pitts

"Notes of an Alien Son: Immigration Paradoxes" by Andrei Codrescu

"Where My Writing Came from and Where It Went" by student Allison Griffin

"The Disappearing Neighborhoods" by student Julie Ross

"A Dark, Skinny Stranger in Cleveland Park" by Stephen L. Carter

"Writing with the Master" by Joel Achenbach

"We're Losing the Raw Human Part of Being with Each Other" by Catherine de Lange

"Major Survey Challenges Western Perceptions of Islam" by Agence France-Presse

"What Is Civility?" by P. M. Forni

"Open Your Ears to Biased Professors" by David Fryman

"Building a Better Life through Greenways and Trails" by Trails and Greenways Clearinghouse

"The Case against Grades" by Alfie Kohn

"2011 Motor Trend Car of the Year: Chevrolet Volt, A Car of the Future You Can Drive Today" by Angus Mackenzie

"Review of *Water for Elephants*" by Sara Gruen

"Is Climate Disaster Inevitable?" by Adam Frank

"The Wonder of Ordinary Places" by Julian Hoffman

"New Hampshire Professor Pushes for Return to Slow Reading" by Holly Ramer

"The Benefits of Slow Reading Lost on Our Fast-Paced Culture," sample research paper by student Kyle van Buskirk

"A Proposal to Enact a 'Smoke-Free Campus' Policy" by Santa Clara University

"Popularity's Downside: Valuing Quality over Quantity in Friendship" by student Audra Ames

"Driving Away" by student Katherine Krueger-Land

"The Monday Omelette" by student Molly Tilton

"Tomorrow, I Love Ya!" by Eric Hoover

"The Supreme Chutzpah" by Jack Achiezer Guggenheim

"Being Nice Is Good Business" by student Amie Hazama

"The Human Cost of Animal Suffering" by Mark Bittman

"Eating Well vs. Being Good" by David Katz

"The Ethics of Eating Meat" by Paul Schwennesen

"Reciprocity: A Foundation for Balance" by Clara Sue Kidwell, Homer Noley, and George E. "Tink" Tinker

"Why Sherry Turkle Is So Wrong" by Tom Stafford

"'Precious' Mettle" by Ann Hornaday

"Rhetorical Analysis of the Section on the Church in 'Letter from Birmingham Jail'" by Ginny Norton

"Exploring the Concept of Gender" by student Jamie Cummins

"Indoctrination Is Not Education" by student J. R. Solomon

"Multitasking: A Poor Study Habit" by student Noelle Alberto

"Is Too Much Pressure Healthy?" by student Natsumi Hazama

"Is Classic Status Out of Reach?," example of an evaluation by student Collin Dobmeyer

"Civility in the Workplace," example of a research proposal by student Amie Hazama

"How to Do the Heimlich Maneuver," example of instructions by Deaconess Heimlich Institute

"Transpiration," example of a lab report by student Deborah A. Smith

"Where Sweatshops Are a Dream" by Nicholas D. Kristof

"The Factories of Lost Children" by Katharine Weber

"Mr. Santa Claus" example profile by student Molly Tilton

Engaging Questions in Your Course

Part I of *Engaging Questions: A Guide to Writing,* assists students in developing a set of highly transferable skills that they will return to again and again whenever critical thinking, reading, and writing are in play. Students will learn to ask fundamental questions about their own writing as well as that of others, such as:

- What is the rhetorical situation?
- What is critical reading?
- What could I write about?

Parts II and III introduce students to the specific questions that apply to each genre of writing and to such related activities as doing research, avoiding plagiarism, and giving effective oral presentations. For example:

- How do writers make a case?
- How do I decide if a source is reliable?
- How do I deliver an oral presentation?

The result is an innovative, comprehensive, and coherent approach to writing instruction.

© KidStock/Blend Images LLC, RF

CONNECT COMPOSITION TOOLS

Connect offers four years of access to comprehensive, reliable instruction in writing and research. The following tools and services are available as part of Connect:

Feature	Description	Instructional Value
Simple LMS Integration	• Seamlessly integrates with every learning management system.	• Students have automatic single sign on. • *Connect* assignment results sync to the LMS's gradebook.
LearnSmart Achieve	• Continuously adapts to a student's strengths and weaknesses, to create a personalized learning environment. • Covers the writing process, critical reading, the research process, reasoning and argument, multilingual writers, grammar and common sentence problems, punctuations and mechanics, and style and word choice. • Provides instructors with reports that include data on student and class performance.	• Students independently study the fundamental topics across Composition in an adaptive environment. • Metacognitive component supports knowledge transfer. • Students track their own understanding and mastery and discover where their gaps are.
SmartBook	• The first and only continuously adaptive reading experience *available for rhetorics.* Identifies and highlights content students have not mastered. • Provides instructors with reports that include data on student and class performance.	• The text adapts to the student based on what he or she knows and doesn't know and focuses study time on critical material. • Metacognitive component supports knowledge transfer. • Students track their own understanding and mastery and discover where their gaps are.
Power of Process	Guides students through the critical reading and writing process step-by-step.	• Students demonstrate understanding and develop critical thinking skills for reading, writing, and evaluating sources by responding to short-answer and annotation questions. Students are also prompted to reflect on their own processes. • Instructors or students can choose from a preloaded set of readings or upload their own. • Students can use the guidelines to consider a potential source critically.

Feature	Description	Instructional Value
Writing Assignments (with Peer Review)	• Allows instructors to assign and grade writing assignments online. • Gives instructors the option of easily and efficiently setting up and managing online peer review assignments for the entire class.	• This online tool makes grading writing assignments more efficient, saving time for instructors. • Students import their Word document(s), and instructors can comment and annotate submissions. • Frequently used comments are automatically saved so instructors do not have to type the same feedback over and over.
Writing Assignments with Outcomes-Based Assessment	• Allows instructors or course administrators to assess student writing around specific learning outcomes. • Generates easy-to-read reports around program-specific learning outcomes. • Includes the most up-to-date Writing Program Administrators learning outcomes, but also gives instructors the option of creating their own.	• This tool provides assessment transparency to students. They can see why a "B" is a "B" and what it will take to improve to an "A." • Reports allow a program or instructor to demonstrate progress in attaining section, course, or program goals.
Connect eBook	• Provides comprehensive course content, exceeding what is offered in print. • Supports annotation and bookmarking.	The ebook allows instructors and students to access their course materials anytime and anywhere.
Connect eReader	Provides access to 31 additional readings that are assignable via *Connect*.	Sample essays provide models for students as well as interesting topics to consider for discussion and writing.

Insight for Instructors	• A powerful data analytics tool. Insight's visualizations are framed by questions and provide users with knowledge that they can act upon.
	• For instructors, Insight provides a quick view of student and class performance with a series of visual data displays that answer the following questions:
	  • How are my students doing?
	  • How is this student doing?
	  • How is my section doing?
	  • How is this assignment working?
	  • How are my assignments working?
		Instructors can quickly check on and analyze student and class performance.

Feature	Description	Instructional Value
Insight for Students	• A powerful data analytics tool that provides at-a-glance visualizations to help students understand their performance on *Connect* assignments. • Insight provides a view of the student's progress and performance in a series of visual displays that answer the following questions: • "How am I progressing?" which for classes larger than 10 students will show the student's individual assignment scores vs. the class average on that assignment. • "How am I doing?" which shows assignments across all courses the student is taking on Connect, allowing the student to spot assignments and even courses that may be particularly challenging.	Student Insight offers the student details on each *Connect* assignment. When possible, it offers suggestions for the student on how he or she can improve scores. These data can help guide the student to behaviors that will lead to better scores in the future.
Instructor Reports	• Allow instructors to review the performance of an individual student or an entire section. • Allow instructors or course administrators to review multiple sections to gauge progress in attaining course, department, or institutional goals.	• Instructors can identify struggling students early and intervene to ensure retention. • Instructors can identify challenging topics and adjust instruction accordingly. • Reports can be generated for an accreditation process or a program evaluation.
Student Reports	Allow students to review their performance for specific assignments or the course.	Students can keep track of their performance and identify areas they are struggling with.
Pre-and Posttests	Offers precreated nonadaptive assessments for pre and posttesting.	Pretest provides a static benchmark for student knowledge at the beginning of the program. Posttest offers a concluding assessment of student progress.
Tegrity	• Allows instructors to capture course material or lectures on video. • Allows students to watch videos recorded by their instructor and learn course material at their own pace.	• Instructors can keep track of which students have watched the videos they post. • Students can watch and review lectures from their instructor. • Students can search each lecture for specific bites of information.

SPOTLIGHT ON THREE TOOLS IN CONNECT

LearnSmart Achieve

LearnSmart Achieve helps learners establish a baseline understanding of the language and concepts that make up the critical processes of composition—writing, critical reading, research, reasoning and argument, grammar, mechanics, and style, as well as issues surrounding multilingual writers.

UNIT	TOPIC	
THE WRITING PROCESS	The Writing Process Generating Ideas Planning and Organizing	Drafting Revising Proofreading, Formatting, and Producing Texts
CRITICAL READING	Reading to Understand Literal Meaning Evaluating Truth and Accuracy in a Text	Evaluating the Effectiveness and Appropriateness of a Text
THE RESEARCH PROCESS	Developing and Implementing a Research Plan Evaluating Information and Sources	Integrating Source Material into a Text Using Information Ethically and Legally
REASONING AND ARGUMENT	Developing an Effective Thesis or Claim Using Evidence and Reasoning to Support a Thesis or Claim	Using Ethos (Ethics) to Persuade Readers Using Pathos (Emotion) to Persuade Readers Using Logos (Logic) to Persuade Readers
GRAMMAR AND COMMON SENTENCE PROBLEMS	Parts of Speech Phrases, Clauses, and Fragments Sentence Types Fused (Run-on) Sentences and Comma Splices Pronouns Pronoun-Antecedent Agreement	Pronoun Reference Subject-Verb Agreement Verbs and Verbals Adjectives and Adverbs Dangling and Misplaced Modifiers Mixed Constructions Verb Tense and Voice Shifts
PUNCTUATION AND MECHANICS	Commas Semicolons Colons End Punctuation Apostrophes Quotation Marks Dashes	Parentheses Hyphens Abbreviations Capitalization Italics Numbers Spelling
STYLE AND WORD CHOICE	Wordiness Eliminating Redundancies and Sentence Variety Coordination and Subordination	Faulty Comparisons Word Choice Clichés, Slang, and Jargon Parallelism
MULTILINGUAL WRITERS	Helping Verbs, Gerunds and Infinitives, and Phrasal Verbs Nouns, Verbs, and Objects Articles	Count and Noncount Nouns Sentence Structure and Word Order Verb Agreement Participles and Adverb Placement

Outcomes-Based Assessment of Writing

Writing assignments with Outcomes-Based Assessment provide a way for any instructor to grade a writing assignment using a rubric of outcomes and proficiency levels. The Council of Writing Program Administrators (CWPA) outcomes are preloaded; however, instructors may adapt any of these outcomes with other instructors or the whole department. Writing assignments with Outcomes-Based Assessment offer a range of clear, simple reports that allow instructors or course administrators to view progress and achievement in a variety of ways. These reports may also satisfy department or college-level requests for data relating to program goals or for accreditation purposes.

Connect Composition Reports

Connect Composition generates a number of powerful reports and charts that allow instructors to quickly review the performance of a specific student, an entire section, or various sections. Students have their own set of reports (which include only their individual performance) that can demonstrate at a glance where they are doing well and where they are struggling. Here are a few of the reports that are available:

- **Assignment Results Report**—shows an entire section's performance across all assignments.

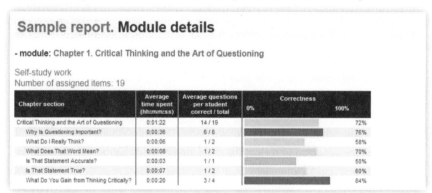

- **Assignment Statistics Report**—provides quick data on each assignment, including mean score as well as high and low scores.
- **Student Performance Report**—focuses on a specific student's progress across all assignments.

Sample report. Practice quiz progress

Student	Time spent (hh:mm:ss)	Quizzes	Questions	Average score
Student, 1	00:24:32	11	71	65%
Student, 3	00:44:47	6	91	81%
Student, 6	00:28:58	6	64	94%
Student, 10	00:23:29	5	71	53%
Student, 11	00:17:41	3	43	76%
Student, 15	00:25:29	8	76	75%
Student, 19	00:23:50	7	49	31%
Student, 21	00:46:10	11	164	75%
Student, 25	00:25:11	7	69	63%
Student, 26	00:20:38	3	42	77%
Student, 28	00:29:20	11	60	84%
Student, 32	00:48:59	9	130	85%
Student, 35	00:11:09	3	23	49%
Student, 38	00:11:36	4	41	90%
Student, 39	00:20:03	5	51	93%
Student, 40	00:04:13	3	16	59%
Student, 41	01:01:3645	12	162	50%
Student, 42	00:25:50	7	70	87%
Student, 43	00:27:39	11	67	74%
Student, 46	00:48:15	9	136	99%
Student, 47	00:36:20	13	138	75%
Student, 48	00:28:34	6	85	99%

- **Learning Outcomes Assessment Report**—for instructors who use the Outcomes-Based Assessment tool to grade a writing assignment, this report provides data on student performance for specific outcomes.
- **At-Risk Report**—provides instructors a dashboard of information that can help identify at-risk students on the basis of low engagement levels.
- **LearnSmart Achieve Reports**—focus on student usage, progress, and mastery of the modules contained within LearnSmart Achieve.

CHANGES TO THE SECOND EDITION

The second edition of *Engaging Questions* offers the same meaningful guidance as the first edition, in addition to the following updates:

- Fifteen new readings represent a range of genres
- All forty-three readings available in a Connect eReader and Power of Process
- Expanded discussions of voice and style
- A more consistent approach to writing assignments
- Assignment chapters reorganized to reflect the steps in the writing process and include a new section focusing on the moves a writer can make
- An enriched adaptive ebook experience through SmartBook emphasizes critical thinking skills and provides remediation for all answer choices
- A streamlined design allows for easier navigation of chapter headings and better aligns with the adaptive reading experience
- A refreshed feature program
- A revised and updated treatment of blogging and writing for the Web

Engaging Questions offers a useful, efficient text that promotes writing based on questioning and thinking, a writing guide that is responsive to contemporary students, instructors, and current writing programs. We welcome your suggestions for making it better.

ACKNOWLEDGMENTS

A book like this could never be brought to completion without the work of a host of people, far too many to be recognized in the space we have.

We would like to call special attention to our developmental team on the first edition. Thank you to Cara Labell, whose ideas and expertise greatly impacted the book's focus, visual design, reading selections, and overall readiness for use in the classroom. Dawn Groundwater, with her energy, honesty, and vision, also deserves special mention. We also wish to acknowledge the work of an outstanding research librarian at SMU, Rebecca Graff, who went far beyond professional duty in helping us.

The meticulous work and generous help of Elizabeth Murphy, Scott Harris, Lisa Pinto, and Claire Brantley made possible this second edition of *Engaging Questions,* which includes an improved and expanded SmartBook. A special thanks to Lisa Bruflodt and Debra Kubiak for managing the details of the book's production and design, and to Brigeth Rivera, Nanette Giles, and Marisa Cavanaugh for working tirelessly to introduce *Engaging Questions* to students and instructors across the country. We owe more to the people at McGraw-Hill Education than we can adequately express.

Finally our appreciation goes out to our colleagues who provided feedback on our evolving plans for the project, drafts of the manuscript, and our digital vision. Thank you.

Angelina College
Diana Throckmorton

Arizona State University
Angela Clark-Oates

Baylor University
Jesse Airaudi

Brigham Young University
Brett McInelly

Cedar Valley College
Andrew Anderson
Elsie Burnett (Board of Advisors)

Suzanne Disheroon
Beth Gulley
Rebekah Rios-Harris
Marilyn Senter

Central Michigan University
Jennifer Jeremiah

Central New Mexico Community College Main
Jonathan Briggs

Claflin University
Linda Hill (Board of Advisors)
Peggy Ratliff (Board of Advisors)
Mitali Wong

Clayton State University
Mary Lamb

College of Coastal Georgia
Anna Crowe Dewart
Meribeth Huebner Fell

Community College of Aurora
Susan Achziger

Dutchess Community College
Angela Batchelor

Eastern Washington University
Polly Buckingham
Justin Young

El Centro College
Carrie Sanford

Georgia Southwestern State University
Paul Dahlgren

Hampton University
Shonda Buchanan
Bryan Herek (Board of Advisors)
DaRelle Rollins (Board of Advisors)
Christina Pinkston Streets

Highpoint University
William Carpenter

Indiana University–Purdue University, Fort Wayne
Stevens Amidon (Board of Advisors)
Karol Dehr
Jennifer Stewart (Board of Advisors)

Indiana University–Purdue University, Indianapolis
Scott Weeden
Mel Winniger

Ivy Tech Community College, Indianapolis
Judith LaFourest

Ivy Tech Community College, Terre Haute
Phyllis Cox
Lucinda Ligget
Leslie Stultz

Johnson County Community College
Maureen Fitzpatrick
Sayanti Ganguly-Puckett
Ted Rollins (Board of Advisors)
Matthew Schmeer (Board of Advisors)

JS Reynolds Community College
Beth Bersen-Barber
Marti Leighty

Kansas City Kansas Community College
Jim Krajewski
Kapiolani Community College
Georgeanne Nordstrom

Murray State College
Jeana West

North Central Texas College
William Franklin (Board of Advisors)
Rochelle Gregory (Board of Advisors)

North Dakota State University
Amy Rupiper-Taggart
Joshua Webster

Northwest Arkansas Community College
Audley Hall (Board of Advisors)
Curtis Harrell (Board of Advisors)
Timothy McGinn

Oakland Community College
Subashini Subbarao

Pima Community College
Kristina Beckman-Brito

Pittsburg State University
Lyle Morgan

Purdue University North Central
Jesse Cohn
Bob Mellin
Jane Rose

Queens University of Charlotte
Marion Bruner (Board of Advisors)
Helen Hull (Board of Advisors)

Quinnipiac University
Glenda Pritchett

Rowan-Cabarrus Community College
Donna Johnson Ginn
Shelly Palmer

Sacramento Community College
Jeff Knorr

Salt Lake Community College
Ron Christiansen (Board of Advisors)
Brittany Stephenson (Board of Advisors)

San Jacinto College
Ann Pearson

Santa Fe College
Rhonda Morris

Savanna State University
Emma Conyers
April Gentry (Board of Advisors)
Gwendolyn Hale

Seminole State College
Ruth Reis-Palatiere

Sheridan College
Keri DeFeo

Sinclair Community College
Susan Callender
Kate Geiselman

Southeast Missouri State University
Trishina Nieveen Phegley (Board of Advisors)

Southern Illinois University, Carbondale
Ronda Dively

Southern Illinois University, Edwardsville
Anushiya Sivanarayanan

Spokane Community College
Angela Rasmussen

Tidewater Community College, Chesapeake
Joseph Antinarella (Board of Advisors)

Truckee Meadows Community College
Robert Lively

Truman State University
Monica Barron
Christine Harker

University of California, Irvine
Lynda Haas

University of Idaho
Jodie Nicotra (Board of Advisors)
Karen Thompson (Board of Advisors)

University of Rhode Island
Kim Hensley Owens

University of Utah
Jay Jordan
Susan Miller

University of Southern Alabama
Larry Beason

University of Wisconsin, Stout
Andrea Deacon

Utah State University, Logan
Whitney Olsen

Vance Granville Community College
Maureen Walters

Virginia State University
Michael McClure

Waubonsee Community College
Mary Edith Butler
Gary Clark
Billy Clem
Ellen Lindeen
Jeanne McDonald (Board of Advisors)
Daniel Portincaso
Sarah Quirk

Western Michigan University
Jonathan Bush (Board of Advisors)

Exploring Writing and Reading

Recommended Genres for Further Practice

CHAPTER 1

Critical Thinking and the Art of Questioning

MOST PEOPLE EQUATE INTELLIGENCE AND EDUCATION WITH KNOWLEDGE—that is, having a large store of information in one's head. Of course, knowledge is important. A college education is partly about acquiring more knowledge by taking a wide range of courses. However, what you can do with what you know matters more. You can look up information you lack. You cannot look up the ability to think critically, interpret information, evaluate it, and put it to new uses.

By **thinking critically** we mean *the ability to examine anything you or someone else has done, said, or written to discover how sound or useful it is.* Critical thinking depends on **the art of questioning,** which means *finding, asking, and pursuing the questions that enable you to examine what you or someone else has done, said, or written.* Thinking critically and questioning go hand in hand. Together, they promote genuine engagement with writing and the other language activities essential to success in college, career, and life.

Why Is Questioning Important?

Questioning helps you become engaged when performing any of the following language activities:

- **Thinking**   Thinking underlies everything we do. Without it, any other activity—including discussion, reading, and writing—is meaningless. Critical thinking first begins with questioning what we think, read, observe, or hear. Through critical thinking, we examine and revise our beliefs and opinions.

- **Discussing**   Talking with other people, which means listening to them and asking them questions, not just holding the floor ourselves, has enormous value. It is central not only to forming friendships but also to learning from and collaborating with classmates, colleagues, and others. Discussion allows us to try out and refine first thoughts in response to the thoughts and reactions of other people. Thought nurtures discussion; discussion nurtures thought.

To learn more about reading critically, see pages 13–31.

- **Reading**   Reading is central to both college and career. It fuels our thinking and discussions. Whether the text is a magazine or a book, an e-mail or a report, reading it effectively means not just passing the eyes over the page but going beyond the surface to understand and question what the text says. Like thinking critically, reading critically requires thoughtful engagement.

FIGURE **1.1**

The Circle of Language Activities

What is the common thread in the activities that these people are engaging in?

Top: © Flying Colours Ltd/ Getty Images, RF; right: © Masterfile, RF; bottom: © Laura Doss/ Fancy/Corbis, RF; left: © Ingram Publishing/ Getty Images, RF

■ **Writing** Because writing requires us to express our ideas completely and precisely, it is central to both college and career. Lab reports, essay exams, and research papers are common tools used to measure whether students have absorbed facts, mastered concepts, and become engaged enough to think critically and creatively about what they have learned. Writing does not end with graduation. In our knowledge-based economy, people spend up to 50 percent of their time at work composing e-mails, reports, proposals, letters, and so on.[1] Even in community and personal activities, from writing letters to the editor to updating a Facebook page, writing is how we represent ourselves. Most importantly, writing our thoughts down helps us examine them; writing is a tool for questioning what we think and read and discuss.

Thinking, discussion, reading, and writing are too deeply intertwined to describe fully; Figure 1.1 will help you envision how intertwined they are.

---

1. Deborah Brandt. *The Rise of Writing: Redefining Mass Literacy.* Cambridge UP, 2015.

BEST PRACTICES   The Importance of Informal Writing

Throughout *Engaging Questions,* we will invite you to write in various informal ways. Each Writer's Notebook provides valuable informal writing practice, but the activities can take many different forms, such as online journals, files on your computer, or even old-fashioned notebooks.

Informal writing supports all of the language activities described above. While thinking, people make outlines, flowcharts, lists, and notes. During class discussions and meetings, people write notes to hold onto interesting ideas. While reading, people annotate the margins of books or ebooks with informal notes to themselves. And writing itself usually begins with informal writing, sometimes called freewriting, intended to get early thoughts out where they can be examined. The more you write informally, the easier it will be for you to write in more formal ways.

Thinking, discussing, reading, and especially writing all start with asking questions. The sections that follow demonstrate how focusing on a few crucial questions—such as What do I really think? What does that word mean? Is that statement accurate? and Is that statement true?—can help us become more critical thinkers, readers, writers, and discussion participants. These and other questions will appear throughout this book. We hope you will keep them with you and use them to dig deeper and discover what is important to you and to your readers.

■■■ ACTIVITY 1.1 *Collaborative Activity*

Exploring the Connection between Writing and Discussing

Spend five minutes freewriting (writing nonstop) about a question that interests you, such as a course to take as an elective or the qualities that make a good friend. Then, discuss these questions in groups of three or four. Add to your freewriting any further thoughts that occurred as a result of discussion. Finally, write a paragraph about this process: Did your freewriting stimulate thought about your topic? Why or why not? To what extent did discussion help refine your ideas? ■

What Do I Really Think?

"What do I really think?" is a serious and challenging question. It is serious because critical thinking must be honest, and it is challenging because being honest is not easy. Sometimes students are taught to keep their opinions out of their writing, yet critical thinking cannot begin without opinions. Frequently, we know what we are supposed to think because other people tell us what the "right" opinions are. To get beyond what "everybody thinks," however, we must consider what we really think, as student Tony Lee does in the following blog post.

Steroids for Your Brain

Sunday, October 26, 2008

Coffee. Red Bull. Adderall.

Set for another study session, I am enhancing my focus and ability to stay awake so that I can do better in my classes. The truth of the matter is that with the drugs and energy supplements I can push myself to study longer and work more than someone not taking the supplements can. Basically, I'm taking steroids for my brain to help me achieve a goal. Unlike steroids, however, there are no long-lasting side effects, and my reward is knowledge.

Is using these drugs a form of cheating? Is using them similar to an athlete taking steroids? The thing with steroids is that they don't themselves build muscle; you have to be willing to put time in to lift weights. In the same way, although Adderall or Ritalin helps you stay awake and focus on what you study, you actually have to open a book and learn the material. So is it any different from physical enhancers?

Lee knows what he thinks and has expressed his opinion clearly. The problem is that too often thinking *stops* with stating an opinion, whereas critical thinking *begins* with an opinion. Now we have something to examine, to explore with questions. What questions can we ask?

What Does That Word Mean?

The meaning of even the most ordinary word needs examination. What prevents us from asking, "What does that word mean?" is the assumption that "everybody knows" what it means, and therefore we do not need to ask. The assumption is usually wrong.

For example, what does *enhancement* mean? It means *anything* people can do to improve their ability to perform a task better. Certainly Adderall, a drug used to treat attention deficit disorder (ADD), can increase concentration and therefore enhance Lee's ability to study. However, if Lee takes Adderall on a doctor's prescription to treat ADD, what he is doing may qualify not as enhancement, but only as restoring the normal ability to concentrate.

What does *cheating* mean? It means *violating the rules that all participants in an activity are supposed to observe.* Steroid use is dangerous and unwise for people who train with weights, but it is cheating in professional baseball because the rules governing the game prohibit it.

So what can we say about Lee's question, "Is using these drugs a form of cheating?" The answer is: It depends. It would be cheating if the honor code at Lee's university prohibited the use of brain-enhancing drugs. Otherwise, it cannot be called cheating.

Just by examining what the words *enhancement* and *cheating* mean, we can answer Lee's question and therefore advance the thinking begun in his blog post.

Tony Lee. "Steroids for Your Brain." *Another View, Blogspot,* 26 Oct. 2008.

To learn more about
exploring a concept, see
pages 142–67.

■■■■ ACTIVITY 1.2 *Writer's Notebook*

Reflecting on Key Terms

Return to the question you freewrote about in Activity 1.1 on page 4. In one
or two paragraphs, explore the meaning of a key term, such as *elective* or
friend. ■

Is That Statement Accurate?

What other questions might help us examine Lee's blog post? Just as we can fail to
examine the meaning of words because we think "everybody knows" what they mean,
we can fail to examine statements because "everybody knows" that they are accurate.

Consider Lee's statement that drugs like Adderall have "no long-lasting side effects."
Is this accurate? The answer to the question is a matter of fact. To answer it, we must
locate authoritative information. Perhaps Lee is right, perhaps he is wrong, or perhaps
the long-term effects depend on the individual, how much the person takes, and for how
long. Whatever the case may be, the question needs to be asked and answered, or else we
may assume that a statement is accurate when it is not. Letting inaccurate statements slide
by is another common way critical thinking can go wrong; it is just as common as not
thinking about what words mean.

To learn how to conduct
an effective Internet
search, see pages
344–46.

■■■■ ACTIVITY 1.3 *In Your Own Work*

Checking the Accuracy of Statements

Freewrite for five minutes on an opinion you hold, explaining why you believe that
opinion is correct. Then look over what you wrote. Did you make any statements
that you are not positive are totally accurate? Did you make any statements that
you think are accurate but that someone else might challenge? Do an Internet
search to check the accuracy of any factual statements you made. Then revise
your statements to eliminate inaccuracies and to incorporate information that
improves what you wrote. ■

Is That Statement True?

There are many other questions we could ask about Lee's blog post. A short list of
such questions follows on pages 8–9. First, let's consider a general point: If we are
truly dedicated to critical thinking, then nobody should get a free pass. We have been
considering a student's blog post, but the same process can be applied to the work of
others, no matter who they are. Let's consider the passage below, excerpted from a
book by Michael Walzer, a distinguished philosopher:

> *My subject is toleration—or, perhaps better, the peaceful coexistence of groups of people
> with different histories, cultures, and identities, which is what toleration makes possible.*

I begin with the proposition that peaceful coexistence (of a certain sort: I am not writing here about the coexistence of masters and slaves) is always a good thing.

—MICHAEL WALZER, ON TOLERATION

We value "toleration" and "peaceful coexistence," so we are likely to agree with Walzer's proposition without thinking it through. Nevertheless, we should resist this temptation and ask, "Is peaceful coexistence *always* a good thing?"

Note that we are asking a question that is different from the one we asked about Adderall's long-term side effects. That one—"Is it accurate to say that Adderall has no long-term side effects?"—is a question of fact. This one—"Is peaceful coexistence always a good thing?"—is a question of value. Data, or facts, can answer the first question, but no amount of data can answer the second, because questions about what is good or desirable are questions of *belief* and not of accuracy. The answers to questions of belief must be based on our knowledge and experience.

How, then, can we think critically about Walzer's statement that peaceful coexistence is always a good thing? The sentence in parentheses—"I am not writing here about the coexistence of masters and slaves"—offers one way to think about what he says. Clearly, Walzer does not believe that *everything* should be tolerated. He excludes masters and slaves because he considers slavery intolerable. What other conditions might also be intolerable?

■■■■ ACTIVITY 1.4 *Collaborative Activity*

Thinking through What Walzer Says

In groups of two or three, discuss the limits of toleration. What behavior can we peacefully coexist with and what behavior must we oppose by persuasion, law, or force? For instance, can we tolerate organizations in the United States that promote terrorism and other forms of violent protest? Can we peacefully coexist with Iran when its government seeks the destruction of Israel? Then write one or two paragraphs in which you explore your beliefs about this topic. ■

What Do You Gain from Thinking Critically?

You gain a number of things by devoting time and effort to thinking through a statement like the one Walzer made about toleration and peaceful coexistence:

1. Instead of letting what he says slide by, your mind is engaged with what you are reading.

2. You have something to look for as you read and to talk about. If you go on to read the book that contains the passage quoted above, you will read in part to see if the author deals with the relation between tolerance and peaceful coexistence in a way that answers your questions and resolves your doubts.

3. You become interested in words and the relation of words to reality. You are not only thinking but also *thinking as a writer thinks,* as a person who works with words and their meanings. If you write about tolerance and peaceful coexistence

Michael Walzer. *On Toleration.* Yale University Press, 1997.

When you think critically and respond thoughtfully, you take part in the conversation—a key goal of education.

© Stockbyte/ PunchStock/Getty Images, RF

yourself, you are much better prepared to do so because you thought critically about what Walzer said. Indeed, *the very ability to say something of your own depends on asking questions.* Otherwise you can do little more than repeat what someone else has said.

4. You claim power by asking and pursuing questions. Usually people defer to authority figures like Walzer and let him ask the questions. Asking one yourself can help you claim authority. All it takes is finding a good question, being willing to ask it, and then pursuing it wherever it leads.

5. You take part in the conversation—a key goal of education— by thinking and responding thoughtfully. When you ask a question, you show that you are listening carefully enough to think of a question worth asking.

In sum, from practicing the art of questioning you gain the ability to think critically, to determine what you really think, to challenge what "everybody knows," and to decide for yourself what is really true and why. We invite you to turn the world upside down. Instead of being satisfied with obvious answers, learn to value questions. For only when you pose questions, especially those that challenge the obvious answers, can real thinking begin.

THE ART OF QUESTIONING   Common Critical Thinking Questions

In this chapter we have seen the value of asking four critical thinking questions:

1. **What do I really think?**
2. **What does that word mean?**
3. **Is that statement accurate?**
4. **Is that statement true?**

There are many more such questions. Indeed, *any question that helps you explore what you or someone else has said is a good question.* Here are a few more commonly asked critical thinking questions.

5. What does "x" assume?

Almost every statement is based on assumptions. Asking questions can help us determine whether we should accept or challenge assumptions. For example, consider this statement: "Jane is smart; her IQ is 130." It assumes that the tests purporting to measure intelligence are reliable. Because the reliability of these tests is frequently disputed, we can challenge this assumption.

6. What does "x" imply?

Asking questions about what follows from a statement can help us determine whether we should accept it. For example, if someone says, "Internet privacy should be protected no matter what," then you can ask, "Are you willing to give up free Internet access to protect your privacy?" "Are you willing to protect the privacy of terrorists?" You can ask these questions because the statement implies them.

7. Is "x" a good analogy?

Frequently statements are based on analogies or comparisons. The claim that animals have rights, for example, is based on an analogy, a comparison with people's rights, such as the right to vote or the right to a trial by jury. Obviously animals do not have the *same* rights as human beings, so what rights should they have and why?

8. How many kinds of "x" can we distinguish?

Often a single word or concept has many meanings. *Love* can mean the feelings of a parent for a child or a lover for the beloved. The biblical command to "love thy neighbor as thyself" has nothing to do with emotions. Here *love* means treating others with courtesy and respect. Many concepts are like "love"; they are used to refer to numerous situations or behaviors. We often need to distinguish among the meanings of a word.

9. What is a good example of "x"?

Thinking of concrete examples can often help us understand and think critically about abstract ideas. For example, *peaceful coexistence* may initially seem a wonderful thing. However, when we think about a concrete example of peaceful coexistence, such as Britain and France peacefully coexisting with Nazi Germany in the 1930s, we realize that it may come at a high price.

10. What are the likely consequences of "x"?

With any proposal for action, we should consider what is likely to happen. If someone says, "We should withdraw our troops from Afghanistan as soon as we can," we should ask questions like the following: "If we pull out, will Afghanistan again fall under Taliban control?" "Will the Taliban allow al-Qaeda to reestablish a base of operations there?" "What will happen to women and girls there?"

READING **1.1**

Apparently Facts No Longer Mean What They Once Did

LEONARD PITTS

Leonard Pitts is a journalist and novelist who won the 2004 Pulitzer Prize for news commentary. In this op-ed piece he calls forceful attention to our highly politicized world where even verified facts carry no weight for too many people when the facts don't align with preexisting prejudices.

I got an e-mail the other day that depressed me.   1

It concerned a piece I recently did that mentioned   2
Henry Johnson, who was awarded the French Croix de Guerre in World War I for singlehandedly fighting off a company of Germans (some accounts say there were 14, some say almost 30; the ones I find most authoritative say there were about two dozen) who threatened to overrun his post. Johnson managed this despite the fact that he was only 5 foot 4 inches tall and 130 pounds, despite the fact that his gun had jammed, despite the fact that he was wounded 21 times.

My mention of Johnson's heroics drew a rebuke from a fellow named Ken   3
Thompson, which I quote verbatim and in its entirety:

"Hate to tell you that blacks were not allowed into combat until 1947, that's a fact.   4
World War II ended in 1945. So all that feel good, one black man killing two dozen Nazis,
is just that, PC bull."

In response, my assistant, Judi Smith, sent Mr. Thompson proof of Johnson's heroics: 5
a link to his page on the Web site of Arlington National Cemetery. She thought this
settled the matter.

Thompson's reply? "There is no race on headstones and they didn't come up with   6
the story in tell [sic] 2002."

Judi: "I guess you can choose to believe Arlington National Cemetery or not."   7

Thompson: "It is what it is, you don't believe either . . ."   8

At this point, Judi forwarded me their correspondence, along with a despairing note.   9
She is probably somewhere drinking right now.

You see, like me, she can remember a time when facts settled arguments. This is back   10
before everything became a partisan shouting match, back before it was permissible to
ignore or deride as "biased" anything that didn't support your worldview.

If you and I had an argument and I produced facts from an authoritative source to back   11
me up, you couldn't just blow that off. You might try to undermine my facts, might counter
with facts of your own, but you couldn't just pretend my facts had no weight or meaning.

But that's the intellectual state of the union these days, as evidenced by all the   12
people who still don't believe the president was born in Hawaii or that the planet is
warming. And by Mr. Thompson, who doesn't believe Henry Johnson did what he did.

I could send him more proof, I suppose. Johnson is lauded in history books (*Before   13
the Mayflower* by Lerone Bennett Jr., *The Dictionary of American Negro Biography* by
Rayford Logan and Michael Winston) and in contemporaneous accounts (*The Saturday
Evening Post,* the *New York Times*). I could also point out that blacks have fought in
every war in American history, though before Harry Truman desegregated the military in
1948, they did so in Jim Crow units. Also, there were no Nazis in World War I.

But those are facts, and the whole point here is that facts no longer mean what they   14
once did. I suppose I could also ignore him. But you see, Ken Thompson is not just some
isolated eccentric. No, he is the Zeitgeist personified.

To listen to talk radio, to watch TV pundits, to read a newspaper's online message   15
board, is to realize that increasingly, we are a people estranged from critical thinking,
divorced from logic, alienated from even objective truth. We admit no ideas that do
not confirm us, hear no voices that do not echo us, sift out all information that does not
validate what we wish to believe.

I submit that any people thus handicapped sow the seeds of their own decline; they   16
respond to the world as they wish it were rather than to the world as it is.

That's the story of the Iraq War.   17

But objective reality does not change because you refuse to accept it. The fact that   18
you refuse to acknowledge a wall does not change the fact that it's a wall.

And you shouldn't have to hit it to find that out.   19

▮▮▮ *Writer's Notebook*

Asking Critical Questions

Analyze the reading selection by asking one or more of the ten critical questions listed on pages 8–9 and write a paragraph answering your question or questions. Exchange paragraphs with other students and then, in class discussion, address all the concerns and issues your class found worth discussing. ■

CHAPTER 2

Reading Critically and the Art of Questioning

WHY INCLUDE A CHAPTER ON READING IN A BOOK ABOUT WRITING? Reading is complementary to writing. It provides the raw material for having something to say. It also increases vocabulary, making it easier to think and express ideas. And it develops the art of questioning and critical thinking described in Chapter 1. The habit of questioning when you read carries over to the habit of questioning when you write, allowing writers to see where their writing needs rethinking and revising.

There are many ways to read, depending on your purpose. Skimming may be appropriate when you are looking for bits of information. Slower, repeated reading is needed when your goal is to understand and retain the specialized information in textbooks. When the goal deepens from just gathering information to following an author's train of thought in order to respond to his or her ideas and opinions, then critical reading is necessary. Most of the reading you do in college—and in business—requires this kind of critical engagement.

What Is Critical Reading?

Critical reading is *active and involved interaction with a text, not just reading to find out what it says, but reading to respond to it by asking and answering questions.* Reading critically is like engaging in a silent dialogue with the text and its author. When we read, we seldom think about our dialogue with the text, but we are often unconsciously asking and answering questions like the following:

What does this word mean, based on the words around it?

What is likely to come next?

Is the author being ironic?

Why do I find this part of the text confusing?

Is this a convincing argument?

What do I think about this new idea?

Through questions like these, we not only monitor our comprehension but construct our own ideas about the meaning of a text.

The following passage provides an example of a reader's dialogue with a text. In this excerpt from an *Atlantic Monthly* article, the writer is concerned that his use of the Internet is undermining his ability to read deeply.

Is Google Making Us Stupid?

NICHOLAS CARR

The main source?

Prediction: He's going to talk about McLuhan. "The medium is the message."

For me, as for others, the Net is becoming a universal medium, the conduit for most of the information that flows through my eyes and ears and into my mind. The advantages of having immediate access to such an incredibly rich store of information are many, and they've been widely described and duly applauded. "The perfect recall of silicon memory," *Wired*'s Clive Thompson has written, "can be an enormous boon to thinking." But that boon comes at a price. As the media theorist Marshall McLuhan pointed out in the 1960s, media are not just passive channels of information. They supply the stuff of thought, but they also shape the process of thought. And what the Net seems to be doing is chipping away my capacity for concentration and contemplation. My mind now expects to take in information the way the Net distributes it: in a swiftly moving stream of particles. Once I was a scuba diver in the sea of words. Now I zip along the surface like a guy on a Jet Ski.

Here comes his point.

Digital files. Artificial intelligence an aid to human intelligence.

Clever metaphor to illustrate the point.

A simile describes how he now reads.

Questions for Discussion

1. Do you agree with Carr that using the Internet reduces your ability to concentrate when reading? How would you describe the difference between your experience of reading online and reading a printed book? Are there some kinds of texts for which you prefer one medium over the other?

2. Marshall McLuhan is famous for saying, "The medium is the message." Discuss what this means. Do you think the medium (printed versus online, for example) of your communication affects the message? For example, consider how e-mail messages differ from text messages or posts on Twitter or Facebook.

How Does Critical Reading Work?

What distinguishes critical reading from reading to get the gist is the ability to find underlying meanings, to "read between the lines." Reading between the lines means following complex lines of thought, understanding what is implied but not stated explicitly, and noting how the parts add up to construct the big picture. An important skill for reading between the lines is the ability to draw inferences from evidence in the text.

Nicholas Carr. "Is Google Making Us Stupid?" *Atlantic Monthly,* 1 July 2008.

CONCEPT CLOSE-UP Drawing Inferences

Inferences are educated guesses about what we do not know, based on facts we do know. In a windowless classroom, for example, we may not know whether it has started to rain, but by observing students entering with wet hair and soaked jackets, we would be able to infer that it is raining.

Readers infer meanings of unfamiliar words by looking for synonyms or, better yet, patterns of synonyms in a text. Consider the sentences below from the reading selection on page 13:

Unfamiliar word

Context clue

Synonym for

> For me, as for others, the Net is becoming a universal medium, the conduit for most of the information that flows through my eyes and ears and into my mind. . . . As the media theorist Marshall McLuhan pointed out in the 1960s, media are not just passive channels of information.

If the word *conduit* is unfamiliar, you can infer its meaning because you know that liquids usually "flow" and that "channels" (like the English Channel) are waterways. Putting these pieces of information together, you realize that *conduit* must mean a pipeline or waterway.

Readers also infer meaning by bringing outside knowledge to a text. When Clive Thompson, quoted in the passage on page 13, talks about the "perfect recall of silicon memory," the reader infers that he is talking about information stored on computers. This inference is based on knowledge that computers store data on silicon chips.

▬▬▬ ACTIVITY 2.1 *Writer's Notebook*

Drawing Inferences from a Cartoon

Visual texts also require readers to draw inferences. This is especially true of cartoons. Readers have to use prior knowledge to draw inferences about meaning.

The following cartoon by Mick Stevens appeared in *The New Yorker.*

To infer the point of the cartoon, you have to connect outside knowledge with observations of the text. In your Writer's Notebook, answer the following questions.

- What details tell you where you are?
- How do you know what the newborn child is doing?
- What does the language in the baby's exclamations tell you?
- What are we laughing at? What state of affairs is being called to our attention?

Readers must draw inferences from visual texts such as cartoons, which require knowledge of current events. ■

■■■ ACTIVITY 2.2 *Collaborative Activity*

Interpreting a Visual

Working with a partner, find another cartoon. Bring copies to class or arrange to project the image. In a brief oral presentation, explain what observations you used to draw inferences about the cartoonist's comment on the topic. How would you state the cartoonist's point in your own words? ■

What Questions Guide Critical Reading?

Because critical reading is interacting with a text, you need to be able to focus your attention on it. Begin by finding a place where your friends are unlikely to seek you out, and turn off your BlackBerry or iPhone. Like any serious task or skill, critical reading is more successful if you work methodically by doing the following:

- *Preview the text.*
- *Read* the text slowly to discover the key ideas and the author's angle on the topic.
- *Reread* the text to deepen your comprehension and to evaluate the author's reasoning.

Previewing the Text

Find out what you are getting into before you plunge into reading a text. Besides gauging how long it will take you to read it, you should also ask the following questions about the text and its rhetorical situation. The **rhetorical situation** means *the*

Mick Stevens, The New Yorker Collection/The Cartoon Bank

variables in any writing situation: the author and his or her purpose for writing, the audience to whom the text is addressed, and the decisions the author makes in constructing the text to suit purpose and audience. Chapter 3, Writing and the Art of Questioning, explains rhetorical situation in more detail. (See Figure 3.1 on page 33.) Questions to ask include:

- **What is this text about?** From the title, what can you infer about the *topic* and the author's *angle,* or point of view, on the topic? Skim the subheadings if the text has them; if not, look at the opening of each paragraph. Skim the introduction and the conclusion. Based on your preview, try to predict what questions this text will answer. Make a list of questions about the topic that you expect to find answered in the reading. Looking for answers to these questions will make your reading more purposeful.

- **What do I already know about the topic? What opinions do I have about it?** Before reading, take a moment to recall what you may already know about the topic of the text. Refreshing your memory about relevant facts and issues readies you for thinking about what the text will offer. Reflect as well on your own bias, if you have one, and what the origins of that bias might be.

- **Who wrote this text? When and where was it published?** What can you find out about the author or authors? Biographical details about an author (such as date of birth and level of education) and the author's political or philosophical positions and other writings offer many clues for comprehending the text. The Internet is a good resource for this step.

- **Who is the audience for this text?** The author had a readership in mind while composing. Your comprehension will be better if you consider who this readership was and why the author wrote to those readers. How do you match or differ from the intended readers?

- **What special features does the text contain that might aid comprehension?** Aspects of layout and visual presentation such as photographs and other images, charts or graphs, boxes or sidebars, and subheadings can all aid understanding. Subheadings are especially helpful when sampling a text to predict what it will say.

- **Epigraphs** (from the Greek, meaning "to write on" or inscribe) are another common feature. Epigraphs are usually *brief quotations from some other text, set above and apart, followed by the author's name and sometimes the title of the source.* They set up the theme of a reading. Take a moment to look up the source and author of an epigraph; this information will help you draw inferences about the relevance of the passage.

We will work with a reading titled "Notes of an Alien Son: Immigration Paradoxes" to illustrate the stages of critical reading. Skim the reading on pages 17–19. Then look at our answers below to the questions for previewing a text.

- **What is this text about?** Skimming Codrescu's essay through to the end, we see that he is describing his mother's experience as a Romanian immigrant. It will show the contradictions between her expectations for a better life in America and what she actually found—and why immigrating might have been a "good deal after all."

■ **What do I know about the topic? What opinions do I have about it?** From the title, you might infer that the author is an immigrant, the son of immigrants. Skimming it, you notice that he is describing his mother's difficulties in adjusting to life in America. What do you know about some of the problems people have when coming to the United States from other cultures? What opinions do you have about American customs and culture and why adjusting to it is sometimes difficult?

■ **Who wrote this text? When and where was it published?** The author is Andrei Codrescu, a well-known writer of essays, novels, and poetry. He is the MacCurdy Distinguished Professor of English at Louisiana State University and a regular columnist on National Public Radio. Codrescu was born in Romania and lived there with his family while the country was under communist rule, which ended in a revolution in 1989. The family left in 1966 when Codrescu was twenty. This essay was published originally in 1994 in *The Nation* magazine.

■ **Who is the audience for this text?** Readers of *The Nation* are the well-educated public, people concerned with political and social issues. This essay has been reprinted in numerous anthologies or collections of essays on the immigrant experience.

■ **What special features does the text contain that might aid comprehension?** This is a brief text, without a need for subheadings. However, a closer look reveals that Codrescu uses signal words, like *first* and *second,* to clue the reader to the moves he makes in writing the essay. He speaks of "one" paradox, the two stages of his mother's sense of loss, and the two things she learned. He also uses chronological signal words, such as *at this point,* to help readers see the evolving process of her understanding.

READING **2.1**

Notes of an Alien Son: Immigration Paradoxes

ANDREI CODRESCU

My mother, ever a practical woman, started investing in furniture when she came to America. Not just any furniture. Sears furniture. Furniture that she kept the plastic on for fifteen years before she had to conclude, sadly, that Sears wasn't such a great investment. In Romania, she would have been the richest woman on the block.   1

Which brings us to at least one paradox of immigration. Most people come here because they are sick of being poor. They want to eat and they want to show something for their industry. But soon enough it becomes evident to them that these things aren't   2 enough. They have eaten and they are full, but they have eaten alone and there was no one with whom to make toasts and sing songs. They have new furniture with plastic on it but the neighbors aren't coming over to ooh and aah. If American neighbors or less recent immigrants do come over, they smile condescendingly at the poor taste and the pathetic greed. And so, the greenhorns find themselves poor once more: This time they are lacking something more elusive than salami and furniture. They are bereft of a social and cultural milieu.

My mother, who was middle class by Romanian standards, found herself immensely impoverished after her first flush of material well-being. It wasn't just the disappearance of her milieu—that was obvious—but the feeling that she had, somehow, been had. The American supermarket tomatoes didn't taste at all like the rare genuine item back in Romania. American chicken was tasteless. Mass-produced furniture was built to fall apart. Her car, the crowning glory of her achievements in the eyes of folks back home, was only three years old and was already beginning to wheeze and groan. It began to dawn on my mother that she had perhaps made a bad deal: She had traded in her friends and relatives for ersatz tomatoes, fake chicken, phony furniture. 3

Leaving behind your kin, your friends, your language, your smells, your childhood, is traumatic. It is a kind of death. You're dead for the home folk and they are dead to you. When you first arrive on these shores you are in mourning. The only consolations are these products, which had been imbued with religious significance back at home. But when these things turn out not to be the real things, you begin to experience a second death, brought about by betrayal. You begin to suspect that the religious significance you had attached to them was only possible back home, where these things did not exist. Here, where they are plentiful, they have no significance whatsoever. They are inanimate fetishes, somebody else's fetishes, no help to you at all. When this realization dawned on my mother, she began to rage against her new country. She deplored its rudeness, its insensitivity, its outright meanness, its indifference, the chase after the almighty buck, the social isolation of most Americans, their inability to partake in warm, genuine fellowship and, above all, their deplorable lack of awe before what they had made. 4

This was the second stage of grief for her old self. The first, leaving her country, was sharp and immediate, almost toxic in its violence. The second was more prolonged, more damaging, because no hope was attached to it. Certainly not the hope of return. 5

And here, thinking of return, she began to reflect that perhaps there had been more to this deal than she'd first thought. True, she had left behind a lot that was good, but she had also left behind a vast range of daily humiliations. If she was ordered to move out of town she had to comply. If a party member took a dislike to her she had to go to extraordinary lengths to placate him because she was considered petit-bourgeois and could easily have lost her small photo shop. She lived in fear of being denounced for something she had said. And worst of all, she was a Jew, which meant that she was structurally incapable of obtaining any justice in her 6 native land. She had lived by the grace of an immensely complicated web of human relations, kept in place by a thousand small concessions, betrayals, indignities, bribes, little and big lies.

At this point, the ersatz tomatoes and the faux chicken did not appear all that important. An imponderable had made its appearance, a bracing, heady feeling of liberty. If she took that ersatz tomato and flung it at the head of the Agriculture Secretary of the United States, she would be making a statement about the disastrous effects of pesticides and mechanized farming. Flinging that faux chicken at Barbara Mandrell would be equally dramatic and perhaps even media-worthy. And she'd probably serve only a suspended sentence. What's more, she didn't have to eat those things, because she could buy organic tomatoes and free-range chicken. Of course, it would cost more, but that was one of the paradoxes of America: To eat as well as people in a Third World country eat (when they eat) costs more.   7

My mother was beginning to learn two things: one, that she had gotten a good deal after all, because in addition to food and furniture they had thrown in freedom; and two, America is a place of paradoxes; one proceeds from paradox to paradox like a chicken from the pot into the fire.   8

▮▮▮ *Writer's Notebook*

Practicing Previewing

Choose a different reading and preview it on your own. This might be a reading your instructor assigns, or one of the readings in Chapters 3 through 13. Write answers to the questions that appear on page 16. ▪

Reading the Text

After you have skimmed a text and answered the previewing questions, you are ready to settle in and read the text slowly, straight through. Try to keep moving forward. You can go back over difficult passages, but do not stop reading just because you do not fully understand them. Finishing the text will give you insights that will make the difficult passages more accessible when you go back to them. Have a pen or pencil ready to mark up the reading as described below.

As you read, mark the text with **annotations**—that is, *notes in the margins*. Annotating is essential to reading critically. If you do not want to mark up a book, photocopy the reading or use sticky notes. The important thing is to use a pen or pencil, not a highlighter. You want to preserve your thoughts as you read; you cannot do this with a highlighter.

Annotating helps you preserve your thoughts as you read. This is essential to reading critically.

© Gary Conner/ PhotoEdit

THE ART OF QUESTIONING   Some Questions for Annotations

How should you annotate? Here are some questions your annotations might answer:

- **What words do I not know?** You can look them up now and write the definition in an annotation or circle them and look them up later. Why is it important not just to skip them? In the short run, the more you skip, the less you comprehend. In the long run, looking up the words will help build your vocabulary and enable you to infer the meaning of words in future readings, allowing you more time to engage with the ideas as you read.

- **What are the main points as opposed to subordinate passages?** Mark the main ideas in the margin so you can easily find them later. Use brackets to show which paragraphs go together to develop each main idea.

- **What words signal turns in the author's train of thought?** Words like *however* and *but* show that the author will contradict something just stated. Expressions like *for example* suggest that the author will elaborate on an idea. Circle or underline these words, and note how the author's train of thought shifts.

- **Where does the author introduce viewpoints other than his or her own?** Authors often introduce other people who agree or disagree with their ideas. They may present others' viewpoints as direct quotations but often use paraphrases.

■ **How well am I connecting with this reading?** If you find some parts of a text difficult to comprehend, put a question mark in the margin to tell yourself what you need to return to later. If you can connect any prior knowledge, observation, or personal opinion to something in the text, note it in the margin.

We have reprinted the first two paragraphs of the reading by Codrescu to demonstrate the kinds of annotations a critical reader could make.

My mother, ever a practical woman, started investing in furniture when she came to America. Not just any furniture. Sears furniture. Furniture that she kept the plastic on for fifteen years before she had to conclude, sadly, that Sears wasn't such a great investment. In Romania, she would have been the richest woman on the block.

> In other words, cheap furniture. Tone is humorous, ironic.

> Signals the first major point.

Which brings us to at least one paradox of immigration. Most people come here because they are sick of being poor. They want to eat and they want to show something for their industry. But soon enough it becomes evident to them that these things aren't enough. They have eaten and they are full, but they have eaten alone and there was no one with whom to make toasts and sing songs. They have new furniture with plastic on it but the neighbors aren't coming over to ooh and aah. If American neighbors or less recent immigrants do come over, they smile condescendingly at the poor taste and the pathetic greed. And so, the greenhorns find themselves poor once more: This time they are lacking something more elusive than salami and furniture. They are bereft of a social and cultural milieu.

> Here is the point, the paradox: They have plenty but they are still poor.

> Shifts to the neighbors' point of view.

> An inexperienced person.

> Hard to find.

▨■■ ACTIVITY 2.3 *Collaborative Activity*

Comparing Annotations

Write annotations to the remainder of Codrescu's essay. In small groups, compare your annotations. Did you agree on the main points? Did you have similar questions about any part of the reading? ■

▨▨■■ ACTIVITY 2.4 *Writer's Notebook*

Adding to Your Vocabulary

In your reading journal, make a list of words that you had to look up or for which you had to use context clues to infer the meaning. Write the definition next to each. You might also "flex" your knowledge of a word by writing some other words with the same root:

indignities—indignity—dignity

Then, for each vocabulary word, write an original sentence using the word in a way that demonstrates your understanding of its meaning. Using the word a few times will help you establish it in your working vocabulary. ■

Rereading the Text

When you are preparing to discuss a reading in class or to use it in your own writing, you will want to reread it or at least portions of it. Go back to passages that you marked as difficult. You will understand them better once you have finished the entire reading. Activities 2.5–2.10 help you get the most out of rereading.

Recognizing Shifts in Point of View and Voice

Writers shift point of view more often than you might expect. Attentive readers note where the author is speaking for himself or herself, and where he or she has slipped into someone else's perspective and voice. For example, an author might present an opposing view without signaling the shift with quotation marks or a transitional expression. If you have been paying attention to the point of view established by the author, you can infer where the point of view shifts.

We noted in Codrescu's essay that he briefly shifts in paragraph 2 to the perspective of the American neighbors who might view new immigrants as having "poor taste" and "pathetic greed." You know that this is not Codrescu's own point of view, not his voice, because he sympathizes with his mother and other immigrants who, as he says in paragraph 4, seek out material objects as "consolations."

▨▨■■ ACTIVITY 2.5 *Collaborative Activity*

Identifying Voice

In pairs or small groups, reread the paragraph below and decide in which sentences Codrescu shifts from his own point of view and voice to the point of view of his mother.

My mother, who was middle class by Romanian standards, found herself immensely impoverished after her first flush of material well-being. It wasn't just the disappearance of her milieu—that was obvious—but the feeling that she had, somehow, been had. The American supermarket tomatoes didn't taste at all like the rare genuine item back in Romania. American chicken was tasteless. Mass-produced furniture was built to fall apart. Her car, the crowning glory of her achievements in the eyes of folks back home, was only three years old and was already beginning to wheeze and groan. It began to dawn on my mother that she had perhaps made a bad deal: She had traded in her friends and relatives for ersatz tomatoes, fake chicken, phony furniture. ■

Analyzing Figurative Language

Figurative language (or figures of speech) is *language used in a nonliteral way to convey meaning in a vivid and powerful way.* Two common figures of speech are metaphors and similes. **Metaphors** make *an implicit (or not-on-the-surface) comparison between two things that are not apparently very much alike at all:* "The news story went viral" implicitly compares the spread of news with the spread of a virus. A **simile** also *makes a comparison between two unlike things, but it does so explicitly,* using words such as *like* or *as:* "The news spread like a virus." Other common figures of speech include analogy (an extended metaphor or simile), personification (attributing human qualities to animals, ideas, or objects), and hyperbole (exaggeration for emphasis).

We already noted on page 13 that Nicholas Carr used a metaphor to describe his former reading style ("Once I was a scuba diver in the sea of words") and a simile to describe what has happened to his reading ("Now I zip along the surface like a guy on a Jet Ski"). Figurative language adds voice and angle to writing. The metaphor of the scuba diver suggests depth and silence, while the "guy on a Jet Ski" suggests superficiality and noise.

▨▨■ ACTIVITY 2.6 *Writer's Notebook*

Interpreting Figurative Language

Reread paragraph 4 in Codrescu's essay on page 18. In your Writer's Notebook, discuss the effect of Codrescu's use of death as a simile for the loss experienced by new immigrants. Codrescu also uses the word *religion* metaphorically in this paragraph, but he is not referring to an actual religion such as Judaism or Christianity. How would you interpret the meaning of "religion" in the context of this paragraph? Writers often extend an idea through a series of related metaphors, as Codrescu does here. Highlight or underline all of the references to religion in paragraph 4. How do these assembled religious metaphors contribute to the point Codrescu is making about material objects in the lives of immigrants who are experiencing "a kind of death"? Be ready to discuss your answers to these questions in class. ■

Paraphrasing Difficult Passages

The reading you do in college is sometimes difficult. Paraphrasing can help you make sense of challenging passages. A **paraphrase** is a *restatement in your own words and sentences*. Paraphrasing is like translating the passage into language you can better understand—using shorter, more direct sentences and more familiar vocabulary. It ought to substitute your own language for the author's voice, sentence patterns, and word choices. A paraphrase should be in your own voice, which usually means trading more literal language for any metaphors or similes, unless you put them in quotation marks.

To learn more about paraphrasing, see Chapter 18, pages 365–67.

Below is a passage from Codrescu's reading in which he explains the immigrant's disillusionment with American material goods. Note that the paraphrase, on the right, is approximately as long as the original. A paraphrase is not a summary, and it should contain all of the points in the original passage. As the color coding indicates, all the points in the original appear in the paraphrase.

Original Passage	Paraphrase
When you first arrive on these shores, you are in mourning. The only consolations are these products, which had been imbued with religious significance back at home. But when these things turn out not to be the real things, you begin to experience a second death, brought about by betrayal. You begin to suspect that the religious significance you had attached to them was only possible back home, where these things did not exist. Here, where they are plentiful, they have no significance whatsoever. They are inanimate fetishes, somebody else's fetishes, no help to you at all.	New immigrants to America feel the loss of their friends, family, and culture. Codrescu compares this sense of loss to mourning a death. To console themselves, they turn to material objects such as cars and furniture, things that they could not buy in the old country but could only dream of possessing. They believed in the power of these objects to give meaning to life. But the immigrant discovers, sadly, that the products are cheap and shoddily made. This discovery is a second loss, as the immigrant mourns the loss of hope. Paradoxically, the products had meaning only in the old country, when they were out of reach. Here, they are nothing but junk, and the buyer finds that they are useless in providing any sort of consolation.

■□■■ ACTIVITY 2.7 *Writer's Notebook*

Practicing Paraphrase

Using the advice and the example paraphrase above, write a paraphrase of another passage. More help with writing paraphrase is available in Chapter 18; see pages 365–67. For a passage to paraphrase, you might look at the alternative reading you may have already previewed and annotated, or you may use the passage below, from Codrescu's essay. You will need to go back to see where the passage fits into the text so that you can write a good paraphrase that clarifies what point in time Codrescu refers to here.

> At this point, the ersatz tomatoes and the faux chicken did not appear all that important. An imponderable had made its appearance, a bracing, heady feeling of liberty. ■

Finding the Writer's Moves in a Text

One way of seeing the big picture of any text you are reading is to go behind the scenes and think about how the text was constructed. **What moves did the writer make in creating it?** Groups of paragraphs often work together to perform a function, such as providing an introduction, background information, an opposing view, or an illustration.

Recognizing these universally available moves and distinguishing them from their specific content is a way to analyze any text. A good strategy is to make a descriptive outline showing the major subdivisions. For each subdivision of the reading, a descriptive outline answers two questions:

- What is the move or function of this section? In other words, what is it doing?
- What is the main point or content of this section? In other words, what is it saying?

Writing a descriptive outline requires two skills: analyzing the function of each section and paraphrasing the most important point or points in each section. Following is an example showing the subdivisions of this short reading by Codrescu.

Subdivisions of "Notes of an Alien Son: Immigration Paradoxes"

Paragraphs 1–2

Does: Gives an example of one problem, or paradox.

Says: When Andrei Codrescu's mother emigrated from Romania, she found a better life materially, but she had to accept the loss of her home, friends, and family—her supportive social and cultural environment.

Paragraphs 3–4

Does: Gives an example of another problem, or paradox.

Says: American products turned out to be cheaply made junk that did not last. They had been more powerful as dream than as reality. Realizing their dreams were built on false expectations is an even greater loss for the immigrants than leaving home and family.

Paragraph 5

Does: Sums up the two main points of the essay so far.

Says: His mother suffered two losses: first, the loss of her cultural and social environment, and second, the loss of her belief in products as a consolation for the first loss.

Paragraphs 6–7

Does: Puts the problems into a larger context or perspective.

Says: She realized that going back to Romania would be worse. In Romania, her life was bound by a bureaucracy run by favors and bribes. In America, she had freedom, an amazing discovery.

Paragraph 8

Does: Sums up the main point of the whole essay.

Says: His mother learned that the benefits of emigrating were worth the costs and also that life in America was more complicated than she had envisioned.

▨▦■■ ACTIVITY 2.8 *Thinking as a Writer*

Finding a Writer's Moves in a Different Reading

Analyze the reading selection you previewed, read, and annotated (as instructed on pages 19 and 21). Note the major subdivisions and the main point of each subdivision. Make an outline to show (1) how each subdivision functions (the role it performs) and (2) what it says (the point it makes). Use the example outline above as a model. ■

Summarizing the Text

To learn more about summarizing, see Chapter 18, pages 367–69.

Writing a summary of a reading helps you see the text as a whole, not a series of parts. It is often necessary to sum up the entire content of a reading, such as when you want to explain someone else's argument in a paper of your own or when writing an annotated bibliography to let others know the content of your sources.

To write a summary, you must first sort out the main ideas from the supporting details and then put the main ideas into your own words—that is, paraphrase them. Writing a descriptive outline, as explained above, is an excellent strategy for drafting a summary. Once you have found the major subdivisions of a reading and paraphrased their key points, you have material to work with for a summary.

Simply splicing the paraphrases together, however, may not result in a smooth summary. The biggest challenge is to unite these paraphrases into a coherent piece of writing that reflects the train of thought in the original passage. You will need to add transitions and possibly some additional information from the original text. You may use brief quotations. Bear in mind, however, that a summary should be no more than one-third the length of the original.

An example summary of "Notes of an Alien Son: Immigration Paradoxes" appears below. The original complete text is on pages 17–19.

Summary of "Notes of an Alien Son: Immigration Paradoxes"

When Andrei Codrescu's mother emigrated from Romania she had to accept the loss of her home, friends and family, her social and cultural support. In exchange, she dreamed of a better lifestyle materially, with new furniture and a car. However, she was disappointed by the reality: mass-produced food with no flavor and cheaply made cars and furniture that fell apart. She felt that she had "been had." In her anger, she saw only the bad side of America—the greed, the selfish individualism, people's blasé lack of appreciation for what they have. Realizing that her dreams were built on false expectations was an even greater loss than leaving home and family, because now she had no hope for any kind of consolation.

But then she realized that going back would be worse. In Romania, she had had no rights. Even where she lived could be dictated to her. As a Jew, she had no legal standing. Her life was bound by a bureaucracy run by favors and bribes. In contrast, the freedom in America gave her a "heady feeling of liberty." She could protest, she could even throw things and be confident that the penalties would be light.

Codrescu's mother realized that even if America was a "place of paradoxes" where a good tomato costs more than it would in a Third World country, freedom made emigrating "a good deal after all."

Covers paragraphs 1 and 2

Covers paragraphs 3 and 4

Covers paragraph 5

Covers paragraphs 6 and 7

Covers paragraph 8

▧▨▩▦ ACTIVITY 2.9 *Writer's Notebook*

Summarizing a Reading

After having worked through the critical reading stages for an alternative reading, write a summary of it using the advice on page 26 and the model above. You should also consult Chapter 18 for more advice on how to write summaries; see pages 367–69. ∎

Responding to a Reading

During and after rereading, you should have more extensive responses to a stimulating text, with more thoughts than can fit in a marginal note. That is why serious readers and researchers keep reading response journals for recording thoughts, reactions, and opinions that are more extensive than brief annotations.

You could simply write your thoughts in a spiral notebook or in a file you keep on your computer, or you could follow the suggestion of many reading experts and use a double-entry journal, a notebook, or online document divided into two columns with quotations or paraphrases of the text in one column and your reactions on the right. Following is an example of a double-entry reading journal:

What the text says:	**What I say back to the text:**
Par. 2: Codrescu shows how isolated immigrants can be: "there was no one with whom to make toasts and sing songs."	This passage explains why many new immigrants want to live in neighborhoods with others who share their customs and language. I think as they assimilate, they lose this dependency, but that is sad too because their children often forget about their roots.
Par. 3: "She had traded in her friends and relatives for ersatz tomatoes, fake chicken, phony furniture."	His mother expected American products to be a good part, and they weren't. Why not? Possibly because Americans are more interested in saving money on necessities like food and furniture so they can spend it on other more status-symbol things.
Par. 4: "She deplored its rudeness, its insensitivity, its outright meanness, its indifference, the chase after the almighty buck, the social isolation of most Americans, their inability to partake in warm, genuine fellowship and, above all, their deplorable lack of awe before what they had made."	This is a pretty harsh description of Americans. It shows how an outsider notices the downside of our fast-paced, materialistic lifestyle—things that we might acknowledge if pointed out to us, but that we just accept as how it is. It would be interesting to get other opinions about this, such as from exchange students.

Par. 6: ". . . she had left behind a vast range of daily humiliations."	Romania has changed now that it is a democracy and part of the European Union. She may not even want to leave if she lived there today, but the point of the essay is still relevant because it describes a universal experience for the many who still want to escape to America for freedom and a better life.
Par. 8: "America is a place of paradoxes. . . ."	What does he mean here? What other examples can I think of? An example would be American middle-class women who can choose to eat a healthy diet but are forced by fashion images to eat the calorie intake of someone in a developing country. They are free and yet they are controlled by media messages. That's a paradox.

The advantage of the double-entry journal is that it shows the connection between what you read and what you thought about what you read. The double-entry journal is useful for stimulating your own thinking in response to the text. You can also consult it for citing the passages in the text when writing in response to a reading.

▒▓▮■ ACTIVITY 2.10 *Writer's Notebook*

Double-Entry Journal

Use a double-entry template to make your own notes and responses to Codrescu's text. Is there any connection among the comments you made in the right-hand column? Write two or three paragraphs describing these connections. ■

The Assignment

Just as writing a summary of a reading helps you to see the whole text coherently, writing a personal response essay helps you assess your own thinking in response to a reading. Writing your response helps you examine, revise, and possibly gain new insights into the text. On his blog, the best-selling writer Steven Johnson explains how writing a book review helps him appreciate the book more deeply: ". . . [A]ctually sitting down to write out a response to something makes you see it in a new way, often with greater complexity." For this assignment, write a short essay explaining your response to a text that you choose or that your instructor assigns. Begin by reading the text critically using the process and strategies described in this chapter.

What Could I Write About?

To stimulate your thinking, ask yourself questions like the following:

- What is the central issue raised in the reading? What are the author's views on this issue? Did you have views on the issue before reading? If so, how would you compare your prior thinking with the author's?

- Do your observations and experiences confirm, illustrate, or contradict what the text says?

- Did the reading present any new ideas that had not occurred to you before? Did the reading raise some new questions you had never considered? Did it question some assumption or belief you had been holding?

- If you could ask the author one question, what would it be? Why would this question matter to the line of thought or argument in the text?

- What other writers' views have you read on this topic? How do their views compare with the views expressed in this reading?

- Even if you did not accept all of the views and ideas in this reading, what can you take away from it to add to your knowledge about the topic?

When writing your response, tie your own thoughts to specific passages in the text.

What Is My Rhetorical Situation?

When previewing a reading, readers should ask questions about the rhetorical situation, as explained on pages 32–33. Likewise, when preparing to write, writers should consider the rhetorical situation for their own texts. Consider the rhetorical situation for an essay responding to a reading.

Writer: What Is My Purpose?

The purpose of a response essay is to express the writer's ideas about the text. A response can be an evaluation of the reading or it could simply discuss the ideas that

Steven Johnson. "More on the Shallows." *StevenBerlinJohnson.com*, 2010, www.stevenberlinjohnson.com/2010/06/more-on-the-shallows.html.

the writer found important and worth further thought. See the list of moves in the section below titled Text: What Moves Can I Make?

Reader: Who Is My Audience?

The response essay shares the results of your critical reading with other readers of the same text.

Text: What Moves Can I Make?

Response essays can do some or all of the following:

- **Draw connections between the world of the text and your own world,** things you have experienced, prior knowledge you bring to the text.
- **Offer insights into the meaning of the text,** as revealed by relationships between parts of the text, analysis of the language, style, arrangement, and voice of the author.
- **Evaluate the thinking;** tell why the writing is convincing to you or not.
- **Reflect on the significance of the text,** explaining the degree to which reading it contributed to your understanding of the topic.
- **Make specific and accurate references** to passages in the text while making any of the moves listed here.

CHAPTER 3
Writing and the Art of Questioning

THE KEY POINT IN CHAPTER 1 IS THAT THINKING BEGINS WHEN YOU ASK QUESTIONS. In this chapter we consider the kinds of questions that writing requires. A good way to begin is to think about the act of writing. What are you doing when you write?

What Is Good Writing?

Writing well is not simply writing correctly. It is **communicating effectively.** Good writing, whether a letter, a memo, a report, or a paper in school, sends a message from a writer to a reader. For example:

- We send a text or write an e-mail to a professor to set up a meeting.
- We write letters to customers to explain a new service.
- We write a letter to the editor to tell the community our views on a proposed law or policy.
- We write a paper in a class on popular culture to share our research on how popular music shapes group identity.

Short or long, formal or informal, in school, at work, or in another setting, writing is always communication, and good communication responds appropriately to its *rhetorical situation.*

What Is the Rhetorical Situation?

The relationship among the **writer,** the **reader,** and the **text** forms the **rhetorical situation;** *these are the variables always present when we think about a writing task.*[1] (See Figure 3.1.)

The effectiveness of any piece of writing depends on how well the author has thought about these three basic elements of communication and how they relate to each other. See Figure 3.1 for some questions to consider.

Notice that the categories overlap and interrelate: The context for a piece of writing determines what is appropriate to include in the message. Facebook, for example, is a more public context than a personal e-mail or text message. Audience also influences the text, as writers choose what to put in or leave out depending on how much the audience already knows about a topic.

---

1. In this book **rhetoric** means *the art of writing well*. We learn this art by doing it and by developing knowledge about how to do it better, the purpose of this book and all writing courses.

Writer

Reader

Text

About the Writer

- Why am I writing this text? What is my **purpose** (to inform, to persuade, to entertain, to express my feelings, and so on)?

- What is my **angle,** or **point of view,** on the topic?

- Why do I have my angle? That is, what did I hear, read, or experience that led me to my point of view?

- What does my angle imply about my **voice,** how I want to sound to my readers?

About the Reader

- For whom am I writing this text? That is, who are my **readers,** people I most want to reach?

- Will my readers find my topic and my angle useful, interesting, something they can relate to?

- What **prior knowledge** of my topic do my readers have or what background do they need?

- In what **context** (academic, business, public, personal) will my audience read and talk about this text?

About the Text

- What kind, or **genre,** of text is this, and what **conventions** govern it?

- What **expectations** do readers have for texts of this genre?

- In what **medium** (print or digital, spoken or read) is this genre typically available?

- What **design** features are associated with this genre?

Why Ask about the Rhetorical Situation?

Without a sense of audience and purpose, no one can write well. Inattention to the rhetorical situation results in disorganized memos that employees ignore or misunderstand, public speeches that last too long and make an audience drowsy or restless, and lectures that leave students confused.

When we ask about angle, we are looking for something of our own to say, a key point we will elaborate on shortly. If we find something we want to say, we are more likely to care about saying it well. If we have something to say, we also think about readers we want to reach. Connecting with them suddenly matters to us, so we care about how we sound. That is, we care about *voice*.

What Is Voice?

Voice refers to the writer's presence in a text, *how the writer "sounds."* When we read carefully, we can "hear" a person—a personality—in the words. Once again, the rhetorical situation determines how you want to sound. In informal social writing such as comments on a Facebook page, there is almost no such thing as too much personality. In other rhetorical situations, such as when writing a letter to a customer, the voice will sound more formal and reserved: Impatience, anger, and even humor in excess can be offensive in workplace communications. In some science writing an objective tone is appropriate. Voice varies according to the situation, but in all cases we should hear a person saying something that matters in a way that holds the reader's attention and is appropriate to the context and the genre of the text.

Read to hear the voice in each of the following two passages on the same topic, paleontology.[2] The first is from a museum website at the University of California. The author is not identified. The second is from an essay published originally in the literary magazine *Harper's*. The author, David Quammen, writes with a concern for the environment.

---

2. "Paleontology is the study of what fossils tell us about the ecologies of the past, about evolution, and about our place, as humans, in the world" (University of California at Berkeley website).

R E A D I N G **3.1**

What Is Paleontology?

UNIVERSITY OF CALIFORNIA MUSEUM OF PALEONTOLOGY

. . . [P]aleontology is the study of what fossils tell us about the ecologies of the past, about evolution, and about our place, as humans, in the world. Paleontology incorporates knowledge from biology, geology, ecology, anthropology, archaeology, and even computer science to understand the processes that have led to the origination and eventual destruction of the different types of organisms since life arose.

READING **3.2**

Planet of Weeds

DAVID QUAMMEN

Hope is a duty from which paleontologists are exempt. Their job is to take the long view, the cold and stony view, of triumphs and catastrophes in the history of life. They study the fossil record, that erratic selection of petrified shells, carapaces, bones, teeth, tree trunks, leaves, pollen, and other biological relics, and from it they attempt to discern the lost secrets of time, the big patterns of stasis and change, the trends of innovation and adaptation and refinement and decline that have blown like sea winds among ancient creatures in ancient ecosystems.

▨▩▣ *Writer's Notebook*

Analyzing the Rhetorical Situation

Write one or two paragraphs answering the following questions about the pair of reading selections on paleontology. (Readings 3.1 and 3.2).

1. How do the contexts for each piece of writing determine the authors' choices of what material to include? What information is similar in the two? What is different?
2. How would you describe the difference in purpose for each passage?
3. How would you describe the writer's angle on paleontology in each passage?
4. How would you describe the writer's voice in each passage? How do the elements of purpose, context, audience, and angle affect the writer's decisions about voice? ▪

Why Does Voice Matter?

Learning to control the voice in your writing can increase your satisfaction with a writing project and improve your grade. A former student at the University of Hawaii, Monique Fournier, describes her discovery of the difference voice can make:

> *Six years ago, I dropped out of college after completing my sophomore year.*
> *I assumed that it was because college wasn't for me, that I just wasn't meant for the*

David Quammen. "Planet of Weeds: Tallying the Losses of Earth's Animals and Plants." *Harper's Magazine,* Oct. 1998, pp. 57–69.

classroom. It turns out that I wasn't ready for college writing. I now believe that once a writer finds her voice, she can easily apply it to any college-level writing assignment. Writing those first two years was difficult for me because I was simply plugging chains of words into every paper without any "me" glue to hold them together. Realizing I had a voice, and taking steps to uncover it, has helped me (and my grade point average) immensely.

—MONIQUE FOURNIER, "BEES AND FEARS: WHY I WRITE"[3]

Fournier realized that she had a voice and took "steps to uncover it." That sounds easy, but what steps did she take? Where does voice come from?

To write with voice, we need the following:

- An angle, a point of view toward whatever we are writing about
- The courage to assert it

Writers adjust their voice to suit their purpose, topic, audience, and genre, but the essential question at the heart of writing with voice is, **What stake do I have in my topic?**

What Is an Angle?

What is this "me" that Fournier calls the glue that holds her words together? It comes from personal engagement, having a stake, in your topic. Writers often refer to this as "having an angle." For example, consider the two passages on pages 34–35 on paleontology. On the museum website, the writer's angle is the broad range of knowledge included in the modern study of paleontology. This angle promotes paleontology; it suggests that the reader might want to visit the museum or even take a course.

The other passage shows a darker angle on paleontology as the study of nature's indifference toward the plants and animals that have become extinct. Listing the specific objects that paleontologists study, the author shows his view of paleontology as a study of ancient mysteries. Not everyone would see it that way, but Quammen's angle fits his purpose, which is to interpret what the science means to him. In each case, the author has a point of view that gives voice to the writing.

A good way to think about angle is to compare writing with taking a photograph. Through your camera lens, you decide how to frame a scene or a person. You may try out different angles, with different amounts of background, foreground, and contrast between light and dark. All of these decisions affect how you want to present your subject. Pictures show the photographer's angle on the subject (see Figure 3.2).

---

3. Sidney I. Dobrin and Anis S. Bawarski, editors. *A Closer Look: The Writer's Reader.* McGraw-Hill, 2003, p. 763.

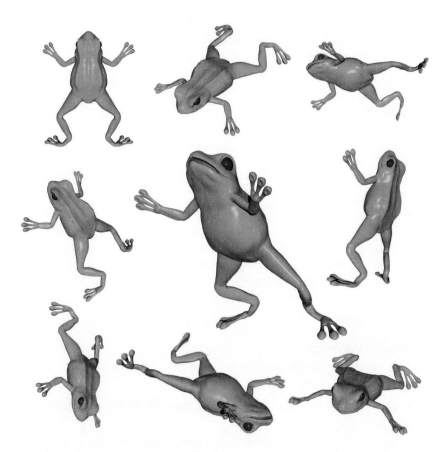

FIGURE **3.2**

**A Writer's Angle
Shows Point of View**

A writer's angle is similar
to a photographer's
angle on a subject.
The angle reflects the
creator's point of view.

© Simone Brandt/
Alamy, RF

Engaging with Topics: How Can I Find an Angle?

Whether you are writing about a social problem like bullying or a scientific topic like climate change, reflecting on your experiences and prior knowledge will help you find an angle. On any topic (represented here by "x"), questions that help to find an angle include the following:

- How does "x" affect me? Why does "x" matter?
- What is my opinion of "x"? What does it mean to me?
- What is the most interesting thing about "x"?
- How is "x" relevant to anything else I have observed or experienced?
- How is "x" relevant to anything else I have read about or studied?
- If I had to put "x" into a larger picture or category, what would that be?

Angle and Rhetorical Situation

A writer's angle on a topic is also influenced by the rhetorical situation, such as the audience, the purpose, and the genre or kind of text that he or she needs to write. Figure 3.3 shows a promotional description of a suburb of Dallas.

FIGURE **3.3**

A Writer's Angle Is Influenced by the Rhetorical Situation

How would you describe the rhetorical situation as related to this promotional material?

about richardson

Discover Richardson!

Richardson is located within minutes of all the amenities of Dallas Fort Worth and enjoys a temperate climate with mild winters and warm summers. Spanning 28 square miles and nestled just to the north of downtown Dallas, Richardson is a City like no other.

Known nationally as the Telecom Corridor® which, is home to over 500 high tech and telecommunications companies, today, Richardson has found its place as a sophisticated, modern suburb featuring award winning family festivals, nationally ranked championship golf courses, 30 beautiful parks, more than 40 miles of hike and bike trails and our cultural gem, the Charles W. Eisemann Center for the Performing Arts.

Because the audience for this description is people interested in finding locations for meetings, this description of the city plays up its proximity to Dallas as well as its many cultural and recreational amenities.

■■■■ ACTIVITY 3.1 *Writer's Notebook*

Changing the Angle

Revise the description of "About Richardson" based on one of the following angles:

- The viewpoint of a zoologist *celebrating the survival of wild animals in suburban areas.*
- The viewpoint of a resident *interested in honoring and preserving the city's history.*
- The viewpoint of a bicyclist *informing other fitness enthusiasts about the city's bike trails.*
- The viewpoint of an environmentalist *opposed to suburban sprawl.*

Be sure to consider how the voice, message, and purpose of this writing would change with the angle. ■

■■■ ACTIVITY 3.2 *In Your Own Work*

Describing Your Hometown

Write a one- or two-paragraph description of your hometown from an angle that interests you. Who would be an appropriate audience for a paragraph written from this angle? To share your description with classmates, post it on an online discussion board or on a blog. ■

The Assignment

The start of a college writing class is a good time to take stock as a writer. What strengths or abilities do you have, and in what areas do you hope to improve? Looking at the learning goals for your course or writing program will help you assess your skills.

For this assignment, you will focus on some aspect of your writing that matters to you. Maybe there is something about writing that you particularly enjoy, or something that challenges you, such as a problem you would like to overcome. Maybe it is an experience you had with writing—in your childhood, in high school, or maybe outside school—that influenced your development. This will be a brief essay, so focus on a specific topic connected with your writing. What might you benefit from thinking more about? How might readers benefit from knowing about your experiences with writing?

What Could I Write About?

Some ideas for topics include:

- A teacher, relative, or other role model of a writer
- Some advice or instruction that helped or did not help
- A book, reading, or author that inspired you or influenced you
- A particular assignment or some writing that you did outside the classroom

What Is My Rhetorical Situation?

As we discussed earlier, the rhetorical situation is a combination of a writer with something to say, a reader the writer wishes to reach, and a kind (or genre) of text appropriate to the writing task.

Writer: What Are My Purpose and Angle, and How Will They Be Reflected in My Voice?

Your purpose is to reflect on some aspect or experience that has influenced you as a writer.

We have been talking about angle because it is what makes your writing matter to you and matter to your readers. If you do not have something you want to say, your writing will be empty. What do you really think about your development as a writer? What point would be worth sharing with your teacher and your classmates? Why would your point matter to them?

All of the elements discussed influence how you sound in your essay. Envision your audience as the real people they are, and speak to them in the same voice you would use in a conversation or class discussion about writing. Your voice and angle grow out of your life, so do not discount the specific details of your experience, such as teachers' comments, books you have read, papers you have written.

Reader: Who Is My Audience?

Your instructor and your classmates are a natural audience for your essay. In your class, you are part of a community focused on developing as writers. Your instructor is your guide, so sharing some experience or reflecting on some aspect of your writing will help him or her get to know you. You and your classmates will share work and helpful critiques. Getting to know each other as writers will make everyone more comfortable exchanging writing and advice.

Text: What Moves Can I Make?

The genre (kind of writing) for this writing project is the **essay.** An essay is *a short composition in which the author expresses his or her personal views on a topic.* The word itself comes from the French *essai,* meaning "to attempt" or "to try or test out." The writing shows the thought processes of the writer. Essays are more polished than journal entries. A main point or central idea gives the essay coherence, and transitions signal the writer's train of thought.

The following short essay was written by a student in response to the activity outlined above. Read through it once just to see what she has to say, and then go back to note her attention to elements of the rhetorical situation discussed in this chapter.

Griffin 1

Allison Griffin

Professor Channell

English 1301

September 10, 2010

Where My Writing Came from, and Where It Went

As a child, I loved to write. I wanted to be a writer. I wrote about anything   1
and everything. I created fictional stories to release my imagination and poems to express my emotions. I wrote down prayers and kept journals that preserved my deepest worries, fears, and moments of happiness, and kept track of my changing

Griffin 2

aspirations. I remember getting lost in my writing time. I would jot down my thoughts and watch them develop into something interesting, to me at least.

I had special places I put pen to paper. My most inspirational times were when I was surrounded by nature; the solitude I found crouched under a tree liberated my thoughts. I also remember turning my closet into a writing sanctuary equipped with pens, paper, and pillows. My mom sometimes worried when I disappeared into my closet for hours, but she also looked forward to my reappearance with a new creation for her to read. I had this pure gratification from writing, the desire to write for its own sake, but also competed successfully in writing contests, which fed my dream to be a writer. I could transform my voice for creative writing prompts, poetry and stories that other people liked. 2

Notice I've been writing in the past tense. I wish it weren't true, but long ago I betrayed my longing to create with words. When did my attitude change, and why? I am studious, and in middle school devoted all my writing time to school assignments. I didn't realize it then, but the formulas and guidelines caused me to lose my appetite for simply expressing myself. Sentences with huge SAT words dominated my writing. I got caught up in writing the ideal essay to please my teachers. Each year a new teacher would offer a "better" formula for the "perfect" paper. 3

Of course, there were occasional essays in high school that I felt good about—and I couldn't wait to share them. Somehow they were different from the rest, but my teachers always seemed to find the parts that broke the rules, diminishing my pride and satisfaction. Gradually I learned to strangle my voice because the more "me" I put in a paper the more I was criticized. 4

My mom has wondered about what happened to that part of me that loved to write. Maybe it was all the formulas and rules that caused me to lose my voice, or maybe during adolescence I became too afraid to reveal myself. After not using my voice for so long, I found this paper hard to write and harder to share with others. But maybe I did find my voice again, or perhaps it was always there, hidden beneath all the rules and formulas for a while. Whatever happened, I realize what I have lost and want to recover my passion for writing. 5

Questions for Discussion

In small groups or as a class, discuss the following questions:

1. What is Griffin's **purpose** for writing?
2. For whom is she writing—that is, what **readers** does she have in mind and how does she make it interesting for them?
3. What is her **angle** or point of view on her past writing experience?
4. How would you describe her **voice,** the way she sounds to you? Point out specific places in the text where you can "hear" Griffin's voice. Is it appropriate for her **purpose,** her **audience,** and her **angle** on the topic?

PART II

Practicing Writing

Recommended Genres for Further Practice **connect**

CHAPTER 4

Claiming Voice

WHEN YOU HAVE TO WRITE SOMETHING, DO YOU SEE YOUR BLANK COMPUTER SCREEN AS A MINEFIELD TO CROSS GINGERLY? Do you creep from word to word, afraid you will do something wrong, rather than thinking about what you want to say and how to connect with a reader? If you do, you are far from alone; many people lack confidence when they write.

This chapter is about gaining confidence as a writer. This means being yourself when you write; as you draft, try using the words and sentences you would choose in conversation or other less formal contexts. Gaining confidence means setting anxiety about grammar aside and focusing first on what you want to say to your readers. You can deal with mistakes later, when you revise and edit. Ultimately, gaining confidence means *claiming voice,* your right to express yourself and communicate with other people.

Do you hear David Treuer's voice?

© Ulf Andersen/Getty Images

What Is Voice?

To a reader, voice is *how a text sounds;* to a writer, it is how he or she wants to sound to readers. Consider the following passage from a book by David Treuer, a Native American writer, about what life is like for his people, the Ojibwe, on the Leech Lake Reservation in northern Minnesota. This passage, which comes from the book's introduction, expresses Treuer's angle and purpose for writing.

I once heard a journalist state that to write a book of nonfiction, a book about the lives of others, the writer had to feel in his gut that his informants owed him something, that he owned a piece of their lives. But I don't think this is true. I think the opposite is true. I don't think my family or my people owe me anything. I feel that I owe my life to them and I set out to write a book that reflects this, reflects the debt I owe them, and does them honor. To understand American Indians is to understand America. This is the story of the paradoxically least and most American place in the twenty-first century. Welcome to the Rez.

How does Treuer sound in this passage? What kind of person is speaking to you? Notice how he uses first person, intentional repetitions, and parallel sentence patterns to show that

David Treuer. *Rez Life: An Indian's Journey Through Reservation Life.* Grove/Atlantic, 2012. Copyright © 2012 by David Treuer.

his topic matters to him and should matter to his readers. All these conscious choices about style depend on the most important aspect of voice: Having something to say.

Now listen to a very different voice. Pragya Lohani is a student writing about the conditions in her native country when she was growing up:

> I remember a little girl standing in front of the mirror in her room, pretending to give speeches like politicians do. She barely knew what a politician was but even then she wanted to be one, as her father would be later. The little girl asked adults questions about her country, Nepal, and she would describe its high mountains, winding roads, fresh air, and peaceful ways to anyone who didn't know about them already. That little girl was me.

> Today I don't stand in front of mirrors pretending to be what I'm not. I still like to describe Nepal's natural beauty to anyone who is interested. But Nepal has changed a lot. The "Peace Zone of the World," as it was once called, is no longer peaceful. Now Nepal weeps tears of blood.

In this passage, you can hear Lohani *talking*. The language is clear, direct, and forceful, just as Treuer's was. But her voice does not sound like his. Her voice is right for her subject, point of view, and audience, just as Treuer's was for his.

That is what voice should be in writing—*the right fit between what you have to say and how you want to sound to your readers.* Voice and style are closely related. Voice is the sound of a personality, and style refers to choices the writer makes that convey that personality. For example, David Treuer says, "I don't think my family or my people owe me anything. I feel that I owe my life to them and I set out to write a book that reflects this, reflects the debt I owe them, and does them honor." His voice, that of a humble and honest man, results from Treuer's style, his choice to use simple sentences with few words longer than one syllable. Style can change when the topic changes. In other parts of *Rez Life,* Treuer is angry, funny, or ironic. Here he is being ironic as he describes the obscurity of his tribe:

> It's a blessing, I suppose. We have largely avoided being written about by others—who prefer to write about the Apache, Comanche, Blackfeet, Nez Perce, and Sioux. And we have avoided being overrun by wannabes and "culture vultures" because, after all, who wants to be an Indian who doesn't own horses and lives in a swamp and traps beavers and didn't evolve striking geometric beading patterns or cool war bonnets?

He slips into an ironic voice to satirize the people who stereotype "real" Indians as the warriors and buffalo hunters of the Western Plains, not the trappers and wild-rice growers of Minnesota. We see a different style, but the voice is still the humble Ojibwe, David Treuer, writing to honor his people.

▨▪■■ ACTIVITY 4.1 *Asking Questions*

Assessing Voice in Writing

Newspapers, both in print and online, both local and national, publish letters from readers. These people usually write to express their opinions on issues in the news or to agree or disagree with the paper's editorial or opinion columns. Sometimes people write in response to other letter writers. The letters may be as short as a few sentences or as long as several paragraphs. Because most of the letters are not by professional writers, they can vary widely in reasoning and writing style, including voice. Thus, the letters pages of any newspaper can serve as a laboratory for studying different voices and evaluating the writers' abilities to use voice effectively. Look at a couple of different papers for a few days and you can gather some examples of good and not-so-good use of voice. Make copies to distribute to the class and be prepared to share your assessments. In making your assessments, consider the following questions:

1. **How does the writing sound?** Describe the voice you hear.
2. Given the subject matter and purpose, **how effective is the voice?**
3. **How formal is it?** Are you drawn in or pushed away by it?
4. **Is the voice consistent or does it change?** If it changes, why does it change? ■

Why Care about Voice?

When you think about writing rhetorically, that is, with a purpose and an audience in mind, you realize that voice can make or break your efforts to communicate. How you sound matters. Mumbling on paper because you do not have your point clear in your own head, expecting readers to follow a fifty-word sentence that is not carefully constructed, or insulting your readers' intelligence by repeating yourself or telling them something they already know—these are just some of the ways voice can work against you. Teachers, as a rule, are more forgiving of such infractions since they have to read your writing. Outsiders will not be so lenient.

Students often do not even consider voice when writing an academic paper. They worry about content and correctness more than how they present themselves as authors. Or they may worry about whether they are making a sufficiently intellectual impression, using long, complicated sentences and an inflated vocabulary. Some academic assignments actually work against developing voice in writing. Students are sometimes discouraged from putting their ideas and opinions into academic writing, which leads them to write a generic, voiceless kind of prose. In Chapter 3, you can find an essay by student Allison Griffin (see pages 40–41) in which she reflects on how teachers' expectations that she use "SAT vocabulary" and follow rigid guidelines caused her to "strangle" her voice and subsequently lose interest in writing. When she realized, in college, that voice does matter, she was able to regain hers.

Writing is always a struggle, but at least it can be an interesting struggle when you put yourself into it. And it can be a more rewarding struggle in terms of grades. Also in Chapter 3, Monique Fournier (see pages 35–36) tells the story of her academic turnaround from failure to success when she discovered that academic writing had to be more than fitting sources together with no voice and angle of her own.

She realized that asserting her angle and voice took some courage. For all writers, claiming voice involves some risk, some self-revelation. Voice is not just a put-on personality, an entertainer's effort to amuse. If a writer doesn't have something to say, personality cannot compensate.

If you don't learn to care about voice in college, you can become a liability in the workplace and a financial burden to employers. When people in business write tone-deaf letters, memos, and e-mails, they can elicit unexpected responses from their intended readers. For example, exclamation points can make a writer sound hysterical, not forceful. Capital letters can make a writer sound angry, not emphatic. Voice matters because readers matter.

The Assignment

Imagine that you have been invited to write a short opinion piece for your campus or local newspaper. You can choose any topic that you care enough about to put your voice into the piece. The great American novelist Kurt Vonnegut wrote a famous column on writing with voice, in which his first and most important tip is to choose a subject that matters to you and that you believe will matter to others. You will have to come up with a thought-worthy topic, find an angle to focus on, ask yourself what you really think, and assert your opinion in a voice appropriate to your purpose, topic, and audience. The goal of the project is to practice claiming your voice.

What Can I Write About?

While you could use an interesting news story for inspiration, you want to arrive at a topic that you know about and care about personally. For example, as we are going to press with this book, the U.S. Supreme Court has just handed down its decision to allow gay couples the same rights to marriage as heterosexual couples. Nearly everyone has an opinion on the decision, but gays who have waited to wed, or their friends and family, might find it easier to write with a voice and angle on the topic and specifics to make their response interesting to readers.

So, in addition to the news, think about experiences or observations that made you ask the critical thinking questions listed in Chapter 1: What do I really think? What does a word (like *marriage*) really mean? Can I question the accuracy of some commonly held belief among my peers or parents, such as how marriage is defined in the Bible? Can I question the truth of some assertion that usually goes unchallenged, such as everyone needs a four-year college degree? (See pages 4–7 for these four questions and more.)

Topics can come from reading opinion columns and asking these questions in response to what you have read. Many op-ed (opinion-editorial) pieces are relevant to college students. Just recently, critic Lee Siegel wrote about why he chose to default on his college loan and feels no guilt about it. Not surprisingly, many graduates who had paid off their loans wrote with strong voices to disapprove.

Topics can come from paying attention, like a reporter, to goings-on right under your nose that most people simply accept as the way things are. For example, in many older neighborhoods, it's common to see older houses, usually small houses, being torn down and replaced with larger, upscale homes. One of our former students, Julie Ross, found a topic for claiming voice when she asked herself, "What is wrong with this picture?" She asked, "What are the consequences to the neighborhood if everyone does this?" Her essay appears at the end of this chapter, on pages 57–60.

What Is My Rhetorical Situation?

As with any writing assignment, this one begins with consideration of the rhetorical situation, as explained and diagrammed on pages 32–33 of Chapter 3. Pay particular attention to the questions in the column "About the Writer." These questions will help you find and engage with an appropriate topic for this project.

Writer: What Are My Purpose and Angle, and How Will They Be Reflected in My Voice?

It's worth noting that finding a topic you care about is not enough; you have to think about *why* you care—what in your background and personal experience has caused you to care and given you the angle or point of view that will inform your writing. For example, Julie Ross was an older-than-average first-year student, living off campus in an older Dallas neighborhood, in a modest-size older home. Her interests run to art and design, not materialistic objects. She is concerned with the environment and other liberal causes. Her angle on the topic of teardowns was formed by these experiences; she wanted to show teardowns as part of the bigger picture of overconsumption as destroying more traditional and modest versions of the American Dream.

Reader: Who Is My Audience?

Since you are likely to share papers with your classmates, they can be one set of readers. It is good to write to peers because you will sound more like yourself if you are not straining to impress unfamiliar readers. However, you should also think of a more narrow audience of people who may have particular interest in your topic, be it a campus issue, a local issue like neighborhood zoning, or an issue that is of special interest to college students.

Text: What Moves Can I Make?

You have many options for genres for this writing project. As with the writing assignment in Chapter 3, you could choose to write a narrative about an experience that mattered to you and that will matter to your readers. For example, Allison Griffin (pages 40–41) wrote about an experience with her writing, but it was more than just a private experience. It was relevant to other first-year college students whose writing might have suffered a similar fate through the high school years, running the gamut of different teachers' advice and admonitions on "correct" writing. Or your genre for this project could be a letter to the editor, an opinion column, or even a blog post. These genres are modeled in How Do I Write an Editorial or Opinion Column? (Chapter 32) and How Do I Write a Blog? (Chapter 28).

The basic moves for all these genres are:

- **The lead:** You will need to open in a way that will catch readers' attention and invite them to read on.

■ **The point and purpose:** The purpose should be persuasive, and you should not leave the readers wondering about your position.

■ **The development:** Claiming voice does not mean that the content of your essay comes completely from your heart. You will need facts and specifics, such as examples and observations. Ross, writing about the trees that were being torn out for new houses, specified the kinds of trees that were native to her area: pecan and magnolia trees.

How Do I Claim My Voice?
Engaging the Writing Process

In order to claim voice in writing, you must know what you are talking about. The word *author* is related to the word *authority,* and for good reason. An author has to be an authority, at least on the topic at hand. The reason much academic writing sounds voiceless and generic is that the student may not know enough, may not have spent enough time researching the topic. Voice is so important that Richard Lanham, author of many books on how to write effectively, offered this simple test to decide how good a piece of writing is: "If you can't read it aloud, with feeling, watch out."[1]

Putting Lanham's point another way, *the difference between how you talk and how you should write is not as great as you may think it is.* When you are composing, imagine you are talking to someone you know—not a close friend, but an acquaintance whose opinion of you matters. Write as you would talk to such a person. You'll write better and more fluently. You might even begin to enjoy writing.

How Do I Use Spontaneous Style?

What happens when you claim or recover your voice? The answer is **spontaneous style,** *how you express yourself in writing when you concentrate on what you have to say and getting it across to a reader.* In Chapter 3, pages 40–41, you will find an essay by former student Allison Griffin, describing her problems with having a voice in her high school writing. In this paper, Griffin shows that she recovered the voice she thought she had lost. What gives this essay voice?

First, and most important, she has an angle, something to say about her topic: What happened to her writing? She lost her love for it, partly as a result of growing up, partly because of school writing.

Second, look at the sentences. Griffin was thinking about what she had to say and tried to say it as simply and directly as possible. The result is the opposite of sentences written to impress rather than communicate.

Third, look at the words. Where are the "huge SAT words" she mentions? There is not a single word she would not use if she were talking to an acquaintance whose opinion of her matters.

---

1. Richard A. Lanham. *Revising Business Prose.* 4th ed. Allyn and Bacon, 2000, p. 63.

■■■ ■ ACTIVITY 4.2 *In Your Own Work*

Recovering Spontaneous Style

Choose something you wrote recently. It can be anything—a letter, a memo, a business report, an essay for a class, a personal statement for a college application, a blog. Assess your voice, comparing how you sound to the examples in this chapter.

Rewrite it until you can hear yourself talking. Read it aloud, with feeling. Does it sound convincing, genuine, like something you would say in a serious conversation? If it does not, or if you find places where it does not, revise it or those places to make your writing more like your speaking voice. ■

How Do I Use Conscious Style?

Spontaneous voice is best for drafting because you turn off the imaginary critic looking over your shoulder, that little internalized English teacher with the imaginary red pen. He or she strangles your voice and makes you second-guess every word of every sentence. However, your style should not end with spontaneous voice. After all, writing is a craft. Good voice is crafted by reworking what spontaneous voice produced.

The world is full of advice for writers about how to write with style. Vonnegut's essay, which we mentioned earlier, offers ten tips, humorously expressed. (You can find his list at www.kmh-lanl.hansonhub.com/pc-24-66-vonnegut.pdf). One of his tips is "Pity the reader." Spontaneous style does not always consider the difficult job that is any reading task. Conscious style invokes the imaginary reader, not a critic looking for errors but simply a regular person making his or her way through your maze of words. There are also books on voice and style. One of the best we've read is William Zinsser's *On Writing Well.* (You can learn a lot about his passion for simplicity in writing by visiting his website at www.williamzinsserwriter.com/).

In this short chapter, we will offer only the most basic advice, some of it quite practical. For example, did you know that longer is not better when it comes to sentences? Journalists advise an average sentence length of eighteen to twenty-five words, with some longer and some shorter. (This advice comes from *The Book on Writing: The Ultimate Guide to Writing Well* by Paula LaRocque.) Did you know that you can use the spelling and grammar checker in Word to find the average length of the sentences in any piece or part of your writing?

But numbers are only part of the story, and the sound of your prose is the real test of whether you have claimed your voice effectively. That is why we advise that you read your spontaneous creations out loud or at least in *sotto voce,* which is Latin for "in a quiet voice." Reading aloud, you will hear:

The sound of monotony when all your sentences are roughly the same length.

The annoying sound of repeated words and expressions.

The places where you have to gasp for breath in the middle of a too-long sentence.

The choppy sound of short sentences in succession that would be smoother if combined.

The overuse of *and* to string ideas together in compound sentences.

Reading aloud is also the best way to proofread for accidentally repeated words or unfinished editing jobs you need to revisit, but we are not asking you to read for voice and errors at the same time. Focus now on how the writing sounds.

An Example: Handling the Overuse of "I"

Look again at the first paragraph of Allison Griffin's essay:

> As a child, I loved to write. I wanted to be a writer. I wrote about anything and everything. I created fictional stories to release my imagination and poems to express my emotions. I wrote down prayers and kept journals that preserved my deepest worries, fears, and moments of happiness and kept track of my changing aspirations. I remember getting lost in my writing time. I would jot down my thoughts and watch them develop into something interesting, to me at least.

As excellent as Griffin's essay is, it might benefit from a little more crafting, a little more conscious voice. She uses "I" because it is appropriate for a personal essay about her experience with writing. However, overuse of "I" can be irritating. Her spontaneous style needs some conscious styling. Here is a revised version:

> As a child, I loved to write and wanted to be a writer. I wrote about anything and everything, creating fictional stories that released my imagination, poems that expressed my emotions. I wrote down prayers and kept journals that preserved worries, fears, moments of happiness, and my changing aspirations. I remember getting lost in my writing time, jotting down thoughts, watching them develop into something interesting—at least, to me.

Her voice remains, but the overuse of "I" and "my" has been reduced. The paragraph flows and sounds better. That is what conscious style should do: *solve a problem while preserving voice.*

Consider these two versions of the opening sentences:

Spontaneous Version

As a child, I loved to write. I wanted to be a writer.

Griffin's first two sentences are simply combined into one:

Conscious Version

As a child, I loved to write and wanted to be a writer.

How would you describe the difference in style in the two versions? Has the voice itself changed?

Spontaneous Version

I wrote about anything and everything. I created fictional stories to release my imagination and poems to express my emotions.

Here, sentences are also combined. The word "created" is turned into "creating," and then it is attached to the first sentence with a comma:

Conscious Version

I wrote about anything and everything, creating fictional stories to release my imagination, and poems to express my emotions.

Writing in—and Editing for—Third Person

For various reasons, sometimes you should not use "I" at all. Some college assignments specify **third person,** *using "he," "she," and "it."* In general, if your reading assignments in a course do not use "I," your writing in that course should avoid it as well. Avoidance of first person is common in scientific writing and in technical and business communication when writers want to sound objective—and when *what* is being done is of more importance than *who* does it.

When you encounter a situation requiring third person, our advice for the first draft remains the same: Let it flow. Keep your attention on saying what you want to say in a way a reader will understand. Often you will write in third person without thinking about it just because it feels right for the kind of writing you are doing. If that does not happen, you can always edit out "I," "me," and "my" in your second draft.

Converting First Person to Third Person, with Voice

Having to write in third person rather than first is no excuse for not claiming voice. The self-referential "I" is not required for a writer to be present in the writing. Consider the example of Julie Ross's essay "The Disappearing Neighborhoods" (pages 57–60). As we explained earlier, Ross got her topic from living in a neighborhood where tearing down was, to her mind, going too far. She originally drafted the essay using first person, but as you see in the following paragraph, she did not overuse "I," "me," and "my." That made converting to third person a small step.

In First Person

My neighborhood in Dallas, known as Lakewood Heights, has been plagued by more than its share of tearing down and building up. Once famous for its 1920's Craftsman and Tudor architecture, my quiet residential street is now marred by rows of McMansions, bustling traffic, and noisy, new construction.

In Third Person

One neighborhood in Dallas, known as Lakewood Heights, has been plagued by more than its share of tearing down and building up. Once famous for its 1920's Craftsman and Tudor architecture, the formerly quiet residential streets are now marred by rows of McMansions, bustling traffic, and noisy, new construction.

Removing the first-person references made the passage longer by a couple of words, but it did not subtract from the voice, which has angle and tone because of word choices like "plagued" and "marred," as well as the specific information about the architectural style of the houses being torn down.

Sometimes converting from first person to third will alter the meaning of a passage, as in the edited version of this passage from a book about luxury spending. There are reasons for using first person when it serves the author's topic, purpose, and desired relationship with his or her readers, as in this passage by James B. Twitchell.

Original Version (First Person)

I must say that I found most of the luxury objects that I've looked at, from Patek Philippe watches to Porsche Turbos to the men's room at the Bellagio Hotel, to be a little over the top. But I am not so oblivious to the world around me that I can't appreciate how important the new luxury has become.

—James B. Twitchell

Edited Version (Third Person)

Most luxury objects, from Patek Philippe watches to Porsche Turbos to the men's room at the Bellagio Hotel, are a little over the top. However, no one in touch with the world around them can fail to appreciate how important the new luxury has become.

The third-person version of this passage leaves out the author's desire to indicate that his views of luxury objects are only his views. That is, the third-person edited version makes something the author wanted us to hear as personal opinion sound like indisputable fact. If you have to write in third person, you will sometimes have to accept meaning changes like these.

■■■■ ACTIVITY 4.3 *In Your Own Work*

Conscious Styling

Select anything you have written recently—the short essay assigned in Chapter 3 about your history with writing might be a good choice. Read it aloud, listening for any problem that might need attention, such as too many "I's," awkward sentences, or sentences that do not say what you mean. Rework your sentences until the problems you detect diminish or go away. ■

How Do I Extend My Voice?

Using conscious style to reduce or eliminate problems with spontaneous style is part of editing, but conscious style also has an important role to play in the never-ending process of learning to write. We call this role "extending your voice." It consists of three steps you can repeat over and over:

1. Become aware of options you have for saying things not yet part of your spontaneous style.

2. Understand how these options work and why they are effective.

James B. Twitchell. "Needing the Unnecessary." *Reason*, Aug. 2002.

3. Use them to express what you want to say so that they become part of your own options for saying things.

You can repeat this process over and over because you will never stop encountering new options in writers you admire and enjoy reading. Do it because *extending your voice is the only way to develop more options for expressing yourself.*

Experimenting with Patterns and Rhythms

Here is a sentence Richard Lanham admired enough to cite as an example of effective style. The writer is discussing bureaucrats in a large company:

> They are not interested in solving the problem; they are interested in keeping the bureaucracy alive, in their pensions, their perks, and their power.[2]

Note the pattern:

X is not _____ (choose your verb) Y.

They are not   interested   in solving the problem

X is _____ (repeat verb) Z.

They   are interested   in keeping the bureaucracy alive

It also has three phrases:

in _____ (choose your noun)   their *pensions*

in _____ (choose your noun)   their *perks*

in _____ (choose your noun)   their *power*

Finally, there is the repetition of the "p" sound: *pensions, perks,* and *power. Repetition of an initial sound in words* is called **alliteration;** you may remember this term from studying poetry, but the device is just as effective in prose.

Here is a pattern you can use to say something else. For instance, we heard a faculty member say this in a meeting:

> Too often alumni aren't concerned with academic quality; they just like the football, the fun, and the folly of being on national TV.

This example is close to the pattern in the sentence Lanham cites. Close is good enough: Try to catch the rhythm and sound that makes the pattern effective.

What have we learned from this sentence? Apparently the negative assertion followed by an affirmative one has power. John F. Kennedy said, "Ask not what your country can do for you; ask what you can do for your country." There is also power in threes. Winston Churchill praised the British pilots that fought the Battle of Britain

---

2. Richard A. Lanham. *Revising Business Prose,* 4th ed. Allyn and Bacon, 2000, p. 35.

in World War II by saying, "Never . . . was so much owed by so many to so few." Abraham Lincoln referred to a government "of the people, by the people, for the people" in the famous *Gettysburg Address.* You do not have to be a Kennedy, a Churchill, or a Lincoln to use similar patterns and rhythms. They belong to everyone because they belong to language.

■■■■ ACTIVITY 4.4 *Collaborative Activity*

Discussing Pattern and Rhythm

Find a short text, or select an excerpt from a longer one written by someone whose writing you enjoy and admire. Write down two sentences that seem especially good to you. Answer these questions for each one:

■ Why is it effective?

■ How is it put together?

Using any subject matter on your mind, compose a sentence similar to the pattern and rhythm of the sentences you selected. Then, in groups of three or four people, share both the sentences from the text and your sentences. Read everyone's sentences aloud and discuss why the sentences are effective and how they are constructed. ■

Using Parallelism

The concept of parallelism is easier to see than it is to define, so let's borrow from Lanham again and display an example as he did:

> They are not interested in solving the problem
> They are interested in keeping the bureaucracy alive
> > in their pensions
> > their perks and
> > their power

As you can see, **parallelism** *repeats word patterns, including verb forms or the constructions of phrases or clauses.* For instance, *the rain **fell,** the thunder **roared,** and the dogs **whined*** is more effective (and clearer) than this construction: *the rain **fell,** there **was** thunder **roaring,** and the dogs **whined.*** You do not have to repeat words or phrases exactly to get the impact. In this example from a celebrated writer, Annie Dillard, the three highlighted phrases are parallel.

> The morning woods were utterly new. A strong yellow light pooled between the trees; my shadow appeared and vanished on the path since a third of the trees I walked under were still bare, a third spread a luminous haze wherever they grew, and another third blocked the sun with new, whole leaves.

Winston Churchill, Wartime Speech, August 20, 1940.
Annie Dillard. *Pilgrim at Tinker Creek.* HarperCollins, 1999.

To see another forceful example of parallelism in action, turn to Leonard Pitts's essay about the loss of respect for facts, on pages 9–11 in Chapter 1. In paragraph 15, in just two sentences, Pitts performs a *tour de force* of parallelism, opening the first sentence with a series of three parallel phrases and closing the second sentence with another series of three.

Usually you will need to style sentences consciously to make them parallel enough to get the effect. It is something to look for in revising and editing your first drafts. Parallelism may seem a small thing, but it offers a powerful extension of voice.

Including Sentence Modifiers

Using sentence modifiers is another way of extending voice. In the examples below, the modifiers are emphasized in italics:

1. It was American writers who first used a vernacular that was both true and lyrical, *true to the rhythms of the working man's speech, lyrical in its celebration of labor.*

2. Socrates questioned the foundations of political behavior, *forcing his fellow citizens to examine the duty they owed to the laws of their gods and to the laws of the state, encouraging young people to question the authority of their elders, maintaining all the while that he was trying in his poor way to puzzle out the truth as best he could.*[3]

Once you understand how they work, sentence modifiers are easy to create and control. For a sentence like the first one above, just repeat a word in your main clause and add modifiers.

A chief advantage of using modifiers is compression, *the ability to say a lot in a few words.*

Original Version

Baseball is a game of numbers. People who love it compile them endlessly. They cite numbers at every opportunity.

In the revision, three sentences become one:

Edited Version

Baseball is a game of *numbers, numbers* that those who love it compile endlessly and cite at every opportunity.

Modifiers are also one way to overcome using too many short sentences in a row. Sentence 2 simply attaches modifiers with commas to the main clause. Here's another example:

Original Version (Modifiers as List)

Many writers—**afflicted by** too many rules, **grammar-obsessed, scared to** spread their wings for fear of falling out of the nest—suffer from red mark anxiety.

---

3. Joseph M. Williams, *Style: Ten Lessons in Clarity and Grace,* 4th ed. HarperCollins, 1994, pp. 174–75.

Sentence 2 uses the same kind of modifier three times in a row (forcing . . . encouraging . . . maintaining), but as this sentence shows, you can also use three or more different ones—or only one or two, some of the same type, some different. You can even move one of the modifiers to the front:

Edited/Alternative Version (Modifier in Front)

Afflicted by too many rules, many grammar-obsessed writers suffer from red mark anxiety, unable to spread their wings for fear of falling out of the nest.

Avoid using too many modifiers up front because in English we expect to get the main clause, the subject and the verb of each sentence, without much delay. Favor the end spot for modifiers, especially if there are three or more and they are long. However, remember to avoid misplaced or dangling modifiers. In the preceding example, it would be confusing to list all of the modifiers after *anxiety* instead of *writers* because they would seem to modify the wrong noun.

There are countless ways to extend voice, but what matters most is *taking the time to notice how the good writing you encounter in college and elsewhere works.* Write down sentences you especially like, and then match them with sentences of your own that imitate or emulate the pattern. In this way you will always be learning more about how rhythm and voice inform the craft of writing.

REVISED STUDENT EXAMPLE

Ross 1

Julie Ross

ENGL 1301, Section 009

Professor Channell

November 20, 2006

The Disappearing Neighborhoods

Home ownership is a significant part of the American dream. Americans take [1] great pride in putting down roots and raising a family in a good neighborhood. And, if a recent boom in residential construction is any indication, more Americans are realizing that dream. In addition to the number of new homes being built, the average home size has also grown significantly. The National Association of Homebuilders reports that the average size of a single-family home has grown from 983 square feet

Ross 2

in 1950 to 2,434 square feet in 2005, "even as the average household shrunk from 3.4 to 2.6 people" (Brown 23). This desire for more living space keeps cities sprawling outward as developers look for open land. In big cities like Dallas, huge new houses are springing up in the outer-ring suburbs like Frisco and Flower Mound.

However, older, urban residential areas are also being impacted by new build-   2
ing. Affluent Americans want super-sized homes plus close-in living. New giant houses are popping up on lots that were once occupied by historic and humble houses. The older houses are now known as "teardowns." In their place, towering "McMansions" dominate the streets. Richard Moe, President of the National Trust for Historic Preservation, reports that teardowns affect over 300 U.S. cities, with a total of 75,000 older houses razed each year. Moe compares the teardown trend to a cancer on the community: "Teardowns wreck neighborhoods. They [destroy] the character and livability that are a neighborhood's lifeblood." The problem is too many people want mansion-size houses in neighborhoods without lots big enough to accommodate them.

One neighborhood in Dallas, known as Lakewood Heights, has been plagued   3
by more than its share of tearing down and building up. Once famous for its 1920's Craftsman and Tudor architecture, the formerly quiet residential streets are now

FIGURE **1**

A super-sized new home towers over its older next-door neighbor.

Courtesy of Carolyn Channell

marred by rows of McMansions, bustling traffic, and noisy, new construction. These colossal residences vary little in outward appearance from one to the next. "Starter mansions," as they are often called, have no particular architectural style and only remotely

Ross 3

resemble Tudor or Craftsman styles. These giants tower over their single-story neighbors, blocking the sunlight and peering into once-private backyards from their tall, garish peaks.

The builders and buyers of these giant homes are callous to community   4
and environmental concerns. Preserving an old Dallas neighborhood's rich architectural history and green landscape is of little importance to them. The original homes in this neighborhood occupied about a third of their rectangular lots, leaving room for a big back yard, a one-car garage, and a front lawn with native pecan and magnolia trees that shaded the houses and sidewalks from the triple-digit, Texas summer heat. By contrast, mega homebuilders rip out the trees and lawns to make space for as much house as possible, raking in more profit with each square foot. Instead of a front lawn, each tall fortress has a wide concrete driveway leading to the grandiose two-Tahoe garage, which itself is nearly equivalent to half the size of the older homes on the street. There is no way the new home owners' landscaping can replace what is lost. The charm of the neighborhood is being destroyed.

Maybe a compromise is possible for those who want to build new in old   5
neighborhoods. One builder, the Cottage Company in Seattle, specializes in "finely detailed" houses of between 1,000 and 2,000 square feet. Linda Pruitt, the co-owner of the company, says their houses "'live as big' as McMansions because they're better designed, with features like vaulted ceilings and abundant built-ins" (qtd. in Brown 24). As in a yacht, the quality of the space is more important than its quantity (Brown 24).

Even Richard Moe of the National Trust admits that responsible new construc-   6
tion has a place in older neighborhoods:

> No one is saying that homebuyers shouldn't be able to alter or expand their
> home to meet their needs, just as no one is saying that older neighbor-
> hoods should be frozen in time like museum exhibits. A neighborhood is a
> living thing, and change is both inevitable and desirable. The challenge is

Ross 4

to manage change so that it respects the character and distinctiveness that made these neighborhoods so appealing in the first place.

This is the challenge that must be met in neighborhoods like Lakewood 7
Heights. If new construction is as architecturally interesting as the older homes and comparable with them in size, preserving what is left of the lawns and trees, the neighborhood can retain some of its unique character.

Works Cited

Brown, Martin John. "Hummers on the Homefront: At 4,600 Square Feet, Is It an Eco-House?" *E, The Environmental Magazine*, Sept.–Oct. 2006, www.emagazine.com/magazine-archive/hummers-on-the-homefront.

Moe, Richard. "Battling Teardowns, Saving Neighborhoods." *The National Trust for Historic Preservation,* 28 June 2006, https://savingplaces.org/news/2006/20060628_speech_sf.html#.Vw-sExMrIdU.

Questions for Discussion

1. Ross's angle on teardowns was to portray the new "McMansions" as, frankly, evil. Look through the essay for examples of word choices that contribute to this idea.
2. How does she portray the houses that are being torn down or that remain standing in between the new construction? What word choices did she consciously use to persuade the readers to care about these houses?
3. How would you describe Ross's personality? What would you expect her to be like if you met her? How would you describe the tone of her voice? How angry does she sound? Does she use any humor or irony?

CHAPTER 5
Interpreting Experiences

WE LEARNED TO LOVE STORIES AS CHILDREN, AND WE CONTINUE TO LOVE THEM AS WE GROW. This chapter is about one kind of story, the **personal narrative,** *an account of something that has happened to us.* It answers two key questions: What happened? Why does it matter? Answering the first question draws readers into your story simply because people are interested in what happens to other people. Answering the second makes what happened an experience, something meaningful, worth remembering.

Experiences are not always major events. The *New York Times* has a weekly feature called "Metropolitan Diary," in which readers share their experiences of city life. Online, an array of travel blogs share the experiences of travelers who enjoy seeing different cultures. The diary entries and blogs like those published by Lonely Planet are effective because they have **angles,** *distinctive points of view or interpretations that make you think.*

What Is Interpreting Experience?

An **experience** is something that stands out in memory, *a departure from the routine.* When we have a memorable experience, we share it with others and talk about how we might understand it. As writers we create **narratives,** *stories based on memorable experiences.* We offer these stories to readers for enjoyment and contemplation, and we interpret them to explore what they mean.

CONCEPT CLOSE-UP Angle in Personal Narrative

All good writing depends on the writer having an angle on his or her topic. In personal narratives, the angle shows that the writer has thought about the experience and developed a point of view on it. The angle does the following:

- Helps the writer decide what details are relevant to include in the story

- Helps the reader see how the story is relevant to people other than the writer

Interpreting Experience

Has a "little" experience struck you as surprising, funny, or thought provoking? It could be a conversational exchange or some other interaction between people; an observation about animal behavior; something you noticed on the freeway, at the mall, in a restaurant. Describe the experience for your readers, making it as vivid as you can. How would you describe your angle on the experience? ■

Why Write to Interpret Experience?

Narratives are among the most common kinds of writing we encounter. People write and read them because human beings enjoy sharing experiences and exploring what they mean. Personal narratives also develop thinking and writing skills applicable to all kinds of writing, among them the following:

- Sharing the meaning of an experience enables you to gain and hold reader attention. The key question is, **"How can you connect your experience with the lives, interests, and concerns of other people?"**

- In narrative genres such as memoirs, travel writing, and blogs, sharing experience provides the opportunity to assert your attitudes, ideas, and opinions. In other genres, such as political speeches or newspaper editorials, narratives can provide evidence and make emotional appeals.

- Interpreting experiences allows you to develop your **voice,** *how you sound to your readers.* Depending upon the purpose of your story, you may sound, for example, serious and sincere or warm and funny.

- Sharing stories about specific events helps you move beyond **stock responses—** *the standard things people say about something that happens.* We all know the typical reaction to a friend's betrayal of trust, but we can get beyond this stock response by posing questions such as the following: Was this person really a friend in whom I should have placed my trust? What role did I play in setting myself up to be betrayed? Critical thinking, which involves asking such questions, matters in all significant writing.

How Do Writers Interpret Experiences?

Narrative essays share five characteristics with fiction. That is, they work as all stories work by pulling together voice, plot, conflict, concrete and relevant details, and shared insight (see Figure 5.1).

Voice

Stories are told by a **narrator,** *the person telling the story.* You are the "I" who is writing about something that happened to you, and therefore your presence contributes to

FIGURE **5.1**

**The Five Features
of Storytelling**

There are five important
elements to successful
storytelling: voice, plot,
conflict, concrete and
relevant details, and
shared insight.

the story's meaning, mainly as point of view. For example, if you are writing about
an event that occurred when you were younger and more limited in your understanding, you might tell the story from your more mature viewpoint but include scenes that
show the viewpoint of your younger self.

Plot and Conflict

Every story has a **plot,** another word for *plan* or *story line.* Most plots begin by setting the scene and providing background information. Then, as the action of the story
builds, the plot develops. The story's action depends on **conflict,** a *problem or source
of tension,* which comes from lack of harmony in desires, ideas, or behavior. It can
exist within a person, between people, or between a person and the circumstances. In
most plots, there is a high point where the action or tension reaches a climax. In an
autobiographical narrative, the plot usually ends by showing the narrator's personal
growth or increased understanding.

Concrete and Relevant Details

Stories contain sensory details: sights, sounds (including dialogue and people's
voices), scents, and the way things feel to the touch or on the skin. Details make experiences vivid. In choosing what to include or leave out, favor details that contribute to
bringing out the point of the story.

Shared Insight

Whether stated or implied by the action, personal narratives reveal the significance of an experience. This significance amounts to *shared insight* because readers come to see how your story relates to their lives and how it might help them interpret similar experiences.

READING **5.1**

A Dark, Skinny Stranger in Cleveland Park

STEPHEN L. CARTER

The following reading is an excerpt from Stephen L. Carter's Civility: Manners, Morals, and the Etiquette of Democracy. *In this passage, Carter describes the experience of moving with his African-American family into a white, upper-class neighborhood in Washington, DC, in 1966. Well-known as a writer of both fiction and nonfiction, Carter is the William Nelson Cromwell Professor of Law at Yale Law School. In the following reading, note especially how well he depicts the limited understanding he had as a boy of the society around him and what a great difference one kind, open-hearted person can make in overcoming fear and alienation.*

> Gives background of family's move to Washington, DC.

n the summer of 1966, my parents moved with their five children to a large house near the corner of 35th and Macomb Streets in Cleveland Park, a neighborhood of Northwest Washington, D.C., and, in those days, a lily-white enclave. My father, trained as a lawyer, was working for the federal government, and this was an area of the city where many lawyers and government officials lived. There were senators, there were lobbyists, there were undersecretaries of this and that. My first impression was of block upon block of grim, forbidding old homes, each of which seemed to feature a massive dog and spoiled children in the uniforms of various private schools. My brother and two sisters and I sat on the front steps, missing our playmates, as the movers carried in our furniture. Cars passed what was now our house, slowing for a look as did people on foot. We waited for somebody to say hello, to welcome us. Nobody did.

1

> Depicts first impression of unwelcoming neighborhood and the children's desire for their old, familiar environment.

> Explains how African Americans living in the North were conditioned to view the Southern world across the river, within the limits of a child's understanding.

We children had no previous experience of white neighborhoods. But we had heard unpleasant rumors. The gang of boys I used to hang out with in Southwest Washington traded tall tales of places where white people did evil things to us, mostly in the South, where none of us had ever lived, nor wanted to. Now and then, perhaps on a Saturday afternoon, we would take a walk to see the evil empire. We would walk up Fourth Street, beneath the highway and the railroad tracks that separated our neighborhood from the federal areas of the city, past the red-brick police station, a half-mile or so up to the Mall. Then, nudging each other with nervous excitement, we would turn west and continue our march. We wanted to see. We would pass with barely a glance the museums that on any other day

2

would keep us occupied for hours. We would circle around the Washington Monument, whose pointed top with twin windows on each side, some of the older boys said, reminded them of a Ku Klux Klan hood, an image that scared me a little, although at eleven years old, raised in the North by protective parents, I was not too sure what the Ku Klux Klan was. We would walk along the Reflecting Pool and continue past the Lincoln Memorial, which, then as now, seemed under constant repair. At last we would reach the shores of the Potomac River which, in those days, exuded the fetid odors of sewage and industrial waste. And we would stand on the bank; a tiny band of dark, skinny children, still growing into full awareness of our race; we would stand there and gaze across the river at the shores of the forbidden land. Mostly what we saw was trees. Sometimes we could pick out a house, perhaps a mansion, including one named for Robert E. Lee. We knew nothing of General Lee except that he had something to do with slavery. On the wrong side. That was enough. We looked, but from our safe distance. There were bridges, but we never crossed them. We had somehow picked up the idea that to go there for more than a short time meant death. Or maybe worse. Emboldened by the river running before us like a moat, we stood our ground and kept looking. A few of the boys claimed to have visited the evil empire, but the rest of us laughed uneasily to show our doubts. We stood, we gazed, we told bad jokes. We poked each other and pointed.

> Refers to familiar landmarks in our nation's capital, singling out both that of Washington, a Virginia slaveholder, and of Lincoln, the Great Emancipator. Note that the Lincoln Memorial "seemed under constant repair," as if the task of overcoming our history of racial trouble is never complete.

> Note the combination of truth, myth, bravado, and nervous laughter among the boys as they contemplate Virginia.

"That's Virginia," we would say, shuddering. 3

Times have changed. Virginia has changed. I have changed. Today I love the state, its beauty, its people, even its complicated sense of history. But in 1966, sitting on the front step of our grand new house in our grand new lonely white neighborhood of Washington, I felt as if we had moved to the fearsome Virginia of the sixties, which, in my child's mind, captured all the horror of what I knew of how white people treated black people. I watched the strange new people passing us and wordlessly watching back, and I knew we were not welcome here. I knew we would not be liked here. I knew we would have no friends here. I knew we should not have moved here. I knew . . . 4

> Transitional paragraph that acknowledges changes since 1966; sets up conclusion featuring the words and actions of Sara Kestenbaum.

And all at once, a white woman arriving home from work at the house across the street from ours turned and smiled with obvious delight and waved and called out, "Welcome!" in a booming, confident voice I would come to love. She bustled into her house, only to emerge, minutes later, with a huge tray of cream cheese and jelly sandwiches, which she carried to our porch and offered around with her ready smile, simultaneously feeding and greeting the children of a family she had never met—and a black family at that—with nothing to gain for herself except perhaps the knowledge that she had done the right thing. We were strangers, black strangers, and she went out of her way to make us feel welcome. This woman's name was Sara Kestenbaum, and she died much too soon, but she remains, in my experience, one of the great exemplars of all that is best about civility. 5

> Clarifies the point of the story: One person's civil behavior does not cancel out how other people behaved, but it did then and does now make a significant difference.

Questions for Discussion

1. Where in the story does the author introduce conflict for the first time? What details in the description of the new neighborhood best reveal the pervasive racial tensions of 1966? Why does Carter devote a lengthy paragraph to his youthful experiences on the banks of the Potomac? Why does the story end with the actions of Sara Kestenbaum?

2. Find examples of *concrete sensory details,* appeals to sight, sound, smell, and so on. How is each example relevant to the interpretation of the experience?

3. Concentrate on the narrator's *voice.* What attitude toward his younger self does Carter imply? How does he show the anxieties he felt as a boy without making the story sentimental?

■ ■ ■ *Thinking as a Writer*

What Is the Rhetorical Situation?

1. What is Carter's *purpose* in writing this essay? What is his *angle* on the topic? How would you describe his *voice*?

2. Who is Carter's intended *audience*? Many of his readers have no experience with racial prejudice as it existed when he was growing up or now. How does the writer help such people understand and connect with his story?

3. Personal narratives offer shared insight into life. What did you learn about the past and present from Carter's narrative? ■

The following narrative, written by a student in a first-year composition course at Southern Methodist University, tells a common story—the struggle with substance abuse—in a compelling way. Note especially how well the author handles dialogue.

READING 5.2

Driving Away

KATHERINE KRUEGER-LAND

The first car I ever owned was a fifteen-year-old, lipstick-red, '91 Ford Thunderbird. 1991: The car was too recent to be cool, but too old to be reliable. Still, I loved it. My parents bought it for me when I got out of rehab and moved down to La Grange, Texas, to live with my Aunt Priscilla and Uncle Kelley.   1

I was lucky that they would take me; I had nowhere else to go. I was considered a serious gamble: no one wanted a relapsed Katherine on their hands. Yet they took me in, helped me get a job waiting tables, and treated me like an adult. I consider them my second family. 2

Apart from having had relatively few options, there was one other enticing reason to choose Texas: Nick Nolan. Although I intended to stay sober and made him swear never to tempt me, it still seemed a good idea to have an old friend around just in case I changed my mind. 3

Nick and I had been running buddies since high school. During our freshman year in college, I spent fall and spring breaks down at A&M partying with him. We had a platonic relationship built entirely around getting as stupidly high as possible and sustaining it until we dropped. 4

Nick Nolan was fun: quick to laugh, quick to anger, cruel and uproarious, dishonest, manipulative and narcissistic, and at times disarmingly self-effacing. He was a violent drunk, an adventurous stoner, and a suicidal, self-harming depressive with the impulsivity of a toddler. In short: perfect. 5

Perfect, that is, if you want to grab an 8-ball and a shotgun and trespass on an airfield to shoot off rounds at your own pants hanging in a tree, drive to the coast but miss the sunrise just to pass out stoned watching cartoons in a motel room, and wake up in time to crash your Houston dealer's family dinner—"watch out for the dogs and don't wake the baby"—where your nose bleeds all over the new couch. 6

But that was before I got sober. 7

I had been in La Grange for two months when I finally heard from Nick. I was working at the Marburger Antique Fair helping out a family friend, Becky Barnsdall, at her stall in Tent D. During my lunch hour I would wander around the nearby fairgrounds and comb through the junk. I was admiring a display of decapitated dolls' heads when he called me. 8

"Hey Nick what's up?" 9

"Dude, I had a freakin' heart attack yesterday!" *A heart attack?* 10

"Wait, what?" 11

"I know, right?" 12

"Are you ok?" 13

"Tommy just picked me up from the hospital with a fifth." 14

"Should you be drinking?" I whispered, self-conscious in front of the dolls. 15

"Probably not," he said. 16

With my cell phone still pinned to my ear, I started tracking across the hay-strewn grounds toward my car, past armless mannequins, old Coca-Cola bottles, wooden toy-wagons, and buckets full of colorful glass beads. On the other end of the line Nick told me his story: the chest pains, the gasping, the ambulance, the hospital stay. 17

"So now that I'm better you have to come celebrate." 18

"I'm working." 19

"Quit." 20

"I need the money. Besides, you're drinking; it won't be any fun for me." 21

"Then you'll just have to drink with us." 22

"You know I can't do that, Nick."   23

He sighed, "I know, I know," and paused. "Krueger, man, I'm not going to make you   24
do anything you don't want to do."

"I know," I answered. And I believed it.   25

* * *

I was at his house on the Tuesday afternoon three months later when Nick was   26
again rushed to the hospital. We were sitting on the couch inside watching South Park
with the dog, JD. Named for James Dean, he was half Dalmatian, half pit bull, and the
sweetest dog you ever met. He liked to sit on top of the sofa back like a giant cat and
lean his sweet warm face on your shoulder.

Nick had gone into the other room to get his guitar; he generally could not watch TV   27
without doing something else at the same time. Several minutes elapsed before I heard
the knocking. I called but he did not answer. All I heard were two more muffled knocks.

I got up from the sofa and peered around the doorframe into the bedroom and   28
there he was, lying on his back, his face turning red, his right hand clutching his left side.
As he struggled to breathe he looked up at me, his eyes wide and pleading. The sight
momentarily shocked me: I'd never known him to be afraid of anything. I bent over him
to see if he was hurt, but I already knew what was happening. I reached for my phone.

"911, what is your emergency?"   29

"I think my friend is having a heart attack."   30

"Is he breathing?"   31

"Yes."   32

"Is he awake?"   33

"Yes."   34

"Is he able to tell you what's wrong?"   35

"No, he's gasping, he can't talk."   36

"What is your location, ma'am?" I didn't know the address.   37

"I'm on McCommas, past Winding, uhh, hold on—"   38

"Are you in a house?"   39

"Yes. Hold on—" I rifled through the papers on his desk, but couldn't find any letters   40
addressed to him.

"And what is the address of the house, ma'am?"   41

"It's his house, I don't know the address, just hold on—" I gave Nick an exasperated   42
look and dashed out of the room, climbing over the dog to keep him from getting out the
front door, and ran to the mailbox. "2389 Alhambra. That's 2-3-8-9 A-l-h-a-m-b-r-a."

In a rush of nylon jackets and plastic gloves, the paramedics came and with cool   43
efficiency swept him off the floor, onto a gurney, into the ambulance, and off to the
hospital. I followed them, and found Nick in a bed divided by curtains from three other
patients in a small holding area. He sat up when he saw me.

"The doctor said I need to quit doing drugs," he smiled weakly.   44

"How do you feel?" He looked small to me. He's tall and strong, but lying down and   45
wearing a hospital gown, he looked frail.

"Bad."   46

"You look like it," I said. He chuckled, and then coughed.   47

"They told me I'd die if I don't quit," Nick said. 48

"So will you?" 49

"Yeah, maybe." 50

I left Nick in the hospital hooked up to an IV watching television and drove home. 51
Being in the hospital had made me claustrophobic. After all, I'd only just checked myself
out of a hospital a few months before. Perversely, I felt a little nostalgic for the insanity of
living life in self-destruct mode. But I didn't want to go back. I didn't want to wear shoes
without laces and have my blood pressure taken at 5:00 a.m. everyday and sit in a group
talking about feeling worthless. *Still,* I thought, *it wasn't all bad.*

* * *

The last time I saw Nick, I was just stopping by on my way up from La Grange to 52
Dallas, where I was soon to move. I was sitting out on his back porch on the sofa we had
once lit on fire (quite by accident) listening to him tell stories, which he's good at, and
make plans, which he's even better at, although he never follows through on anything.
After a few minutes he paused, dug around in the dirty seat cushions for a lighter, and lit
a cigarette for himself, and one for me. He smoked Camel Turkish Golds, the ones with
the pretty blue borders. I smoked Pall Malls, in a soft-pack, back then.

"I need to quit smoking," he said. He meant pot, I was sure. 53

"Yeah, maybe." 54

"I need to quit with the coke, too." 55

"You look thin," I told him. 56

"I'm down to 130 now. I was 175 a couple months ago." 57

Jeez, I thought. *At 6´3˝, 130 pounds isn't much.* 58

"You look really thin," I repeated. And he looked tired, too. And not in a didn't-sleep- 59
last-night way, but in a haven't-really-slept-in-weeks way.

"I don't eat much." 60

"That's the coke." 61

"And the pot." 62

"You look tired." 63

"I know. I haven't been sleeping." 64

"Maybe you should quit." 65

"Yeah, maybe." 66

I was surprised to see him so reflective. Maybe he really would quit, maybe he was 67
finally ready. I got up to leave, sliding open the glass back door—JD bouncing cheerfully
into the house behind me. I grabbed my purse, slipped on my shoes, and was just
trying to open the front door without letting the dog out when I looked up and saw Nick
standing by the back door.

"Hey, wait, if I'm going to quit, then you need to smoke with me one last time." 68

"I can't, Nick, you know that." 69

"Sure you can. I'll even let you roll it, old school." 70

"No, Nick." *But I could.* 71

"Come on." 72

"No, Nick." *But I want to.* 73

"Just one more time, and then we'll both quit together." 74

"I already quit. I quit a year ago." 75

"Exactly, it'll be no big deal." 76

"It *is* a big deal," I said, angrily. He had promised not to pressure me. 77

"No, it's not." *You pathetic fool,* I thought. *You have no idea what I went through. You have no idea how hard it was to leave everything behind.* 78

"You just don't get it, Nick. You can't stick with anything, and you don't understand how anyone else can either. That's why you'll never get sober. That's why the stuff is going to kill you." 79

And with that, I climbed over the dog and squeezed out the front door. I was shaking with anger and fear as I paced down the driveway, and started to climb into my old red T-Bird. I was tempted to turn back, to apologize and have one more good time with my old running buddy, but I was already in motion, the decision already made. *No, I won't do it. I want to, but I won't.* I had passed the test. 80

I glanced back and saw him standing there, one hand holding open the front door, the other firmly grasping JD's collar as he wriggled wildly, desperate to run after the passing cars. 81

We looked at each other, and it seemed to me he was a lot farther away. He was miles away, years away. Already he was part of another time, another life, one I could not go back to. There was a gulf between us and a long narrow bridge: I had driven across, and he had not, and that's all there was to it. 82

"Have a good drive," he called. 83

"Thanks." 84

"Come back soon." 85

"I will," I lied, and drove away. 86

Questions for Discussion

1. Note especially in paragraphs 8, 17, and 26 the use of effective descriptive detail. How do the details contribute to the themes of the story?
2. Conflict is essential to a good narrative. What are the sources of conflict in "Driving Away"? How does the author develop them?
3. Review two instances of conversation in the story. What are the exchanges like? How and why is the writer's use of dialogue effective?

▪▪▪ *Thinking as a Writer*

What Is the Rhetorical Situation?

1. What is Krueger-Land's *purpose* in writing this essay? What is her *angle* on the topic? How would you describe her voice?
2. Who is the writer's intended *audience*? If you have never struggled with addiction yourself, how did the writer help you to understand and sympathize with people who do struggle with it ?
3. The story gives us insight into friends, people we love and need but whose impact on us can be negative as well as positive. How would you describe this insight? How does the insight apply to your friendships? ▪

The Assignment

Write a narrative sharing a personal experience and offering insight into its meaning. The goal is to tell an interesting story that leaves your readers with insight they can relate to their own lives.

What Can I Write About?

Stories that hold the reader's interest involve conflict or tension. Consider experiences that did one or more of the following:

- Resulted in intellectual or moral growth, an increase in maturity.
- Challenged your beliefs, attitudes, or values.
- Allowed you to see your behavior from someone else's perspective.
- Disappointed or surprised you about your own character or the character of someone you thought you knew.
- Led you to see some past event in a new context or category that transformed its meaning.
- Called conventional wisdom about right and wrong into question.
- Created a dilemma, a choice between two paths of action, neither of which is entirely satisfactory.

Remember that the significance of an event is *not in the event itself but in what you make of it,* the angle or point of view you bring to it or discover in thinking or writing about it. Nevertheless, finding the right topic for you does matter. If you are having trouble locating yours, consider the following possibilities:

- **Distinctive people, places, and objects.** Carter focused on just one episode in his experience of moving into a new neighborhood; Krueger-Land focused on one part of her experience with drugs, the temptation to go back to them. Stories about places include journeys to wilderness or foreign places and revisiting places from our past.
- **A troubling memory.** Perhaps you liked a person that others did not like, perhaps even someone you should not have liked. Or you did something unethical, but you would do it again. Or you visited a place meant to stimulate a certain reaction, but you actually responded "inappropriately."
- **Class readings.** The readings in this chapter may remind you of an experience you should write about. Perhaps a concept you encountered in one of your courses gives you a new angle for understanding a past event.
- **Your own or other people's blogs.** Look over your blog for promising topics, such as reunions with friends from high school, something that happened at work or at home with your family, and decisions you have made since starting college.
- **Work or community experience.** Consider times of conflict or tension where you work or the insights you have gained from internships, volunteer work, church activities, attending social events, and the like.

How Do I Interpret Experience?
Questioning the Rhetorical Situation

Begin by picturing a **rhetorical situation** for your writing project, a real-world context for communicating. You should consider the *key variables in any act of communication:*

- A writer with something to say
- A reader the writer wishes to reach
- A kind of text appropriate to the writing task

These three variables will affect many decisions in the composing process.

Writer: What Is My Purpose, and What Impression Should Readers Have of Me?

Autobiographical narratives share an interesting and meaningful experience with an appropriate readership. Because the experience comes from your life, your purpose is self-expression. You are revealing a part of yourself. Because you are sharing a part of yourself with others, you want them to enjoy reading the story and gain from it insight that they will remember.

Your purpose implies your role as a writer for this assignment. Both Carter and Krueger-Land assume the role of the experienced person, someone who is "in the know" from having experienced being a minority in a white neighborhood or being a recovered addict. Your role in writing your story will be much like theirs: No one else knows your life better than you do; no one else is in a better position to say what it means.

Being experienced does not mean that you know everything or have all the answers. You can freely admit to gaps in your knowledge, even to being puzzled about your own motives or the motives of someone else in your story. Just be honest about what happened to you and how well you understand it.

Audience: Who Is My Reader?

Because almost anyone can read and enjoy an interesting story, it is tempting to think of your readers as everyone. However, stories are always told *to someone,* and actual readerships are never everyone. The key question is: Who might gain most from reading about your experience? They should be your readership.

Why is it important to have a definite readership in mind? First, you have to assume a certain level of existing knowledge. Carter, for example, does not explain what a "lily-white enclave" is or what Virginia's "complicated sense of history" means. He has to assume a certain amount of knowledge about Washington, DC, its nearness to the North/South divide, and the prominent role Virginia played in the Civil War, because otherwise he would have to explain too much; likewise, you will not want to clutter your narrative with too much explanation. Second, the readership you choose helps you to decide what to include and what to emphasize in your story. Krueger-Land was writing primarily for people who may not fully understand how hard it is to escape addiction, which is why she emphasized her entanglement with a person from her earlier, drug-dominated life.

Text: What Moves Can I Make?

Readings 5.1 and 5.2 in this chapter and the student example at the end of this chapter make all or some of the following basic moves:

- Establish the time and place of your experience.
- Provide vivid details in descriptions, selecting from everything you could describe only those details that connect with what your story means.
- Share what you said and thought, using some dialogue or conversational exchange when appropriate.
- Zoom in for "close-ups" of important moments in your experience.
- Supply transitional paragraphs to help your readers move from one part of your experience to another.
- Structure your story around a central conflict.
- Imply or state directly what your story means.

How Do I Interpret Experience?
Engaging the Writing Process

No two people compose in exactly the same way, and even the same person may go through the writing process in different ways with different assignments. Nevertheless, because no one can attend to everything at once, there are phases in handling any significant writing task. You begin by preparing to write, generating content and finding your angle.

The next phase is planning and drafting your paper, getting a version, however rough it may be, on paper or screen so that you have something to work with during the next two stages. The first stage is revision, where your attention should be on content, arrangement, and style. The second is editing to take care of problems at the paragraph and sentence level, such as loss of focus and coherence, awkward or unclear sentences, and errors of grammar, spelling, and punctuation.

Preparing to Write

When you have decided what story to tell, explore it by writing informally to generate ideas and material for drafting.

No one else knows your life better than you do. When writing your story, be honest and tell it from your point of view.

© Jupiterimages/Getty Images, RF

■■■■ ACTIVITY 5.2 *Writer's Notebook*

Asking Questions about the Elements of Your Narrative

Using lists, diagrams, and/or a series of notes to yourself, jot down your responses to the following questions:

■ **Characters:** Besides you, what other people played a role in this experience? Of these, who were the most important? Why?

■ **Setting:** Picture a scene from the experience. What sensory details have stuck in your memory? What do you recall seeing, tasting, hearing, smelling, or touching? Ask *why* you recall those details: Perhaps you can discover a pattern in what you remember that will lead to an insight or imply what the story means.

■ **Plot:** What conflict or tension makes this experience interesting for you and for your readers? What was the moment of greatest tension? How was the tension resolved? If it was not fully resolved, what problems or issues remain?

■ **Angle:** Explore possible meanings or interpretations of the experience. What was your point of view when you were living it? As you look back on it, has your interpretation of it changed? What central insight or insights can you offer? ■

▨▨▧■ ACTIVITY 5.3 *Writer's Notebook*

Discussing Your Topic Idea

Post your best ideas for your narrative on your class's discussion board. When everyone has posted, read through the posts and send replies to at least three classmates. In your reply, ask questions to stimulate thought about the event's significance, the conflict or tension that could drive a good plot, and the relevance of the experience to others. ■

Asking Questions: Framing the Plot

Choosing where to begin your story is one of the more important choices you will make. For instance, how much background do you need to provide so your readers will understand the story?

Some narratives open with background material, some with the action itself. Either way, draw your readers in with something specific, such as Krueger-Land's new living situation after rehab or Carter's description of his new neighborhood.

Once you have decided how to open the story, plot out the key scenes. Think of your essay as if it were a video with action, setting, characters, and dialogue. Often one of these elements dominates a particular scene. For example, Krueger-Land's memory of the fun she once had with Nick dominates the early scenes in her narrative.

▨▨▧■ ACTIVITY 5.4 *Writer's Notebook*

Listing Key Scenes

Depict your experience in a series of scenes. If you were making a film, which moments would you show in action, and which would a narrator summarize? In Carter's story, there are two key scenes:

- The new neighborhood
- The view of Virginia from the north bank of the Potomac

List two or three key scenes in your experience. How can each contribute to building the tension, and which one will you use to resolve it? ■

Borrowing a Film Technique: The Storyboard

Some writers of fiction and nonfiction borrow the storyboard technique used in filmmaking (see Figure 5.2 on page 77). Carolyn Coman—author of many acclaimed novels for young people, including *What Jamie Saw*—got the idea of storyboarding from reading comic books with her young daughter. Coman draws a blank square for each main scene in a story and, using stick figures, draws the central action of the scene. Sketching the scene is a kind of visual drafting. As with a rough draft, when you reread it, you discover surprises, clues to meaning. As

Coman says, "The size of the stick figures, the amount of white space around them, the kinds of marks you make . . . all of these have things to tell you about tone, distance, point of view."[1]

It also helps you organize around a main idea. If you write a sentence or two beneath each drawing, the storyboard will help you find connections between scenes and identify the angle or main idea of your narrative. Even a single sentence about the emotion or tension each scene conveys will help you organize and sort the material.

A storyboard made of individual diagram cards offers several advantages. You can do the following:

- Add, delete, or rearrange scenes
- Sketch visually or verbally a scene's setting and characters
- Create dialogue
- Indicate what you will be telling the reader

An alternative is to make a series of boxes on sheets of plain paper, in the style of a comic book, and draw your scenes in sequence.

Student Example: Molly Tilton's Storyboard for a Personal Narrative

Figure 5.2 on the next page shows an example of how one student used the storyboard technique to get her story started and focused. Molly Tilton wrote about an experience she had while working as a waitress in a diner. A regular customer, Frank, was waiting for his daughter to join him for breakfast; as the event unfolded, Tilton gained some insight about her own life. Sketching scenes for her story helped Tilton order the events, including the use of a flashback, and decide which moments to focus on in her narrative.

■■■ ACTIVITY 5.5 *In Your Own Work*

Visualizing Your Story

Using storyboard sketches on index cards, work out a plan for your story. Think about how you might open the essay, how you might work in background information, and how the essay should end. ■

Drafting Your Paper

What should be most on your mind as you are writing your first draft of the narrative? Focus on your voice and on development and organization.

What Voice Is Appropriate in Personal Narratives?

When we say that writing has voice, we mean that readers can sense the human presence in the words. The author's personal interest and angle on the topic are evident in

---

1. Carolyn Coman. "Seeing the Whole Story: Storyboarding." *Highlights Foundation,* www.highlightsfoundation.org.

FIGURE **5.2**

An Example of a Simple Storyboard

Storyboards don't need to be elaborate to be helpful in piecing your story together. Grab a pencil and some paper and try sketching out simple "scenes" that capture critical moments of your personal story.

Courtesy of Molly Tilton

the writing. *Well-chosen details convey your lived experience best* and connect with readers more effectively than general statements.

Consider the scene in "A Dark, Skinny Stranger in Cleveland Park" in which Carter describes his small group of young friends looking across the Potomac at "the evil empire."

> And we would stand on the bank; a tiny band of dark, skinny children, still growing into full awareness of our race; we would stand there and gaze across the river at the shores of the forbidden land. Mostly what we saw was trees. Sometimes we could pick out a house, perhaps a mansion, including one named for Robert E. Lee. We knew nothing of General Lee except that he had something to do with slavery. On the wrong side. That was enough. We looked, but from our safe distance. There were bridges, but we never crossed them.

Carter expresses well the combination of fear and fascination he and his friends had for a place none of them knew firsthand, only by "unpleasant rumors" and a few half-understood facts, like who Robert E. Lee was and the existence of the Ku Klux Klan.

He doesn't say "we were scared and intrigued"; rather he allows his descriptive details to imply what he was feeling.

■■■■ ACTIVITY 5.6 *Thinking as a Writer*

Developing and Organizing Your Personal Narrative

You have many options in writing your story. It can start at the beginning, at the end, or in the middle. You can omit events that do not contribute to your point and zoom in on details that do. You can use flashbacks and flash-forwards.

Begin by writing a central episode or scene. Structure the other scenes around it. Then concentrate on background, transitions, and opening and concluding strategies. ■

■■■■ ACTIVITY 5.7 *Writer's Notebook*

Composing Your Scenes

Concentrate on details of setting, character, and action. Consider posting your scenes on a blog or discussion board or sharing them with other students in some other way to receive feedback. ■

Revising Your Draft

In revising, concentrate especially on the following:

- **Interpretation** Consider what writing about the experience has revealed to you. Perhaps the meaning of it has changed and therefore needs reformulating.

- **Focus** Look for opportunities to add relevant details that come to mind as you revise.

- **Shape** Craft your story into a well-paced narrative. Get to the action as quickly as possible. Keep the story moving. Make statements of your thoughts and emotions short and simple.

Write a brief assessment of your draft. Exchange your draft and assessment with at least one other student and use the revision questions in the Art of Questioning box to help each other decide what needs to improve.

THE ART OF QUESTIONING | Revision Checklist for Interpreting Experiences

1. Make a list of the best images in the draft. Do these words and phrases present concrete, sensory details of the place?

2. What do these images have in common? Do they imply a theme or central idea? If you cannot find a theme or idea emerging *through the details,* review the draft again to locate its best scene. What theme for the whole story might be developed from it?

3. What conflict does the narrator face? Do you encounter the conflict early in the story? How does it build and come to a crisis or point of maximum tension? How is it resolved?

4. What parts of the essay do not contribute to the theme or the conflict? Consider cutting them.

5. Can you make any suggestions for improving the organization? Should events be presented in a different order? Should the story open or end more quickly?

6. Are there any places in the story where the author spends too much time talking about emotions, how he or she feels? Replace with details that convey emotion without having to say what it is.

7. Either to clear up confusion or to satisfy curiosity, what might your reader like to know more about? Consider developing parts of the essay to answer questions your reader might have.

Student Example: Excerpts from Tilton's Draft

The most common revision problem when interpreting experience is underdevelopment, not supplying enough detail for the reader to understand the story. Here is a paragraph from Molly Tilton's first draft of "The Monday Omelette," a story about fathers and daughters, the revised version of which appears on pages 81–83:

> He would ask a lot of questions per usual and tell me how much he missed me that day. I would apologize and say that I would see him tomorrow morning and that we could go to lunch, knowing that the plan would most likely fall through. Then he would drag himself upstairs to bed, without the smile on his face.

Here is the revised version:

> He would ask a lot of questions per usual and tell me how much he missed me that day. He would always assure me it was OK. I would apologize and tell him that I would try to see him the next day. That promise always sounded empty. After the divorce, I couldn't guarantee when I would see him. Alternating between my mother's and father's houses was sometimes too complicated. And then I had my friends. I was busy. I was sorry. After I hung up the phone, I would imagine him turning off the TV and dragging himself upstairs to bed. I pictured the let-down expression on his face. He had been ditched, stood up by his own daughter.

The revised paragraph is not just longer, but better. Note the improvements:

- "After the divorce" adds important information: It explains why father and daughter have to make plans to see each other.

- The details about her own life make standing up her father understandable, even if she is using them as an excuse.

- Because she cannot know for sure how her father reacted when she did not show up, it is better to say "I would imagine" what his response was.
- Taken together, the details she adds give greater support to her feelings of guilt, which readers will then understand and relate to more easily.

Examine your own essay for opportunities to add detail. The key question is: **What do my readers need?** Tilton saw that they needed to know more about the father-daughter situation and why she feels guilty. She added only what she needed to include, and the result was a stronger story.

Editing Your Revised Draft

An important concern in editing is cohesion, whether sentences connect smoothly. People sometimes use the word *flow* to describe cohesion. When writing has cohesion, each sentence picks up on something in the one before it, and readers' expectations about what comes next are rewarded. When writing lacks cohesion, it sounds choppy. Below are some examples to show how editing can improve cohesion. In this passage, student Molly Tilton describes the man in the diner waiting for his daughter:

Before Editing

Frank waited for another forty minutes. With a smile, he told me, "My daughter will be here soon, but I am just going to order anyway."

This point interrupts the point about the phone call.

Then his cell phone rang. He was sitting in the beat-up gray booth, and I felt the room go dark. Something had come up. She would not be able to meet him.

This sentence too abruptly shifts the topic from Frank's daughter to the narrator.

I was a daughter. I had done this. I had broken similar news to my own father before.

After Editing

This point now helps to set up the scene for the call.

Forty minutes later, he was still sitting alone in the beat-up gray booth, waiting. With a smile he told me, "My daughter will be here soon, but I'm just going to order anyway."

Then his cell phone rang . . . I felt the room go dark. Something had come up. She would not be able to meet him.

Adding a transitional sentence helps the reader see the connection that the writer left unstated.

Suddenly, the scene felt familiar to me. I was a daughter. I had done this. I had broken similar news to my own father.

The following two passages follow a flashback scene in which the narrator recalls having "stood up" her father after she had told him she would visit him.

Before Editing

This sentence offers a great image, but it would work better as a transition from the flashback to the present time.

I went into the kitchen to bring out Frank's meal. I was sweating from guilt of being a daughter. When I delivered Frank his omelette, he lifted his face, fake-smiled, and said "Ahh, Miss Molly. Thank you so much!"

After Editing

The image now works as a transition from Tilton's thoughts about her own father to her experience with the other father in the diner.

Sweating from the guilt of being a daughter, I went back into the kitchen to bring out Frank's meal. When I delivered his omelette, he lifted his face, fake-smiled, and said "Ahh, Miss Molly. Thank you so much!"

▨▨▨■ ACTIVITY 5.8 *In Your Own Work*

Editing Your Revised Draft

Every writer has editing problems. Keep a checklist of your editing problems. For instance, list words that you misspelled. If you did not punctuate a sentence correctly, write down the sentence and circle or underline the correct punctuation mark. If you need examples to remember other types of problems—such as editing for flow—take one from your paper. Check your revised draft for your most common problems.

When editing at the sentence-level, try reading your revised draft aloud. Repetitions and wordy passages are easier to hear than to see. Study your instructor's marks and comments on every paper. Add new editing problems to your list as needed. *Always check your next paper for the problems you have listed.* In this way you can reduce your characteristic editing problems. ■

REVISED STUDENT EXAMPLE

Tilton 1

Molly Tilton

Professor Channell

English 1301

May 6, 2011

The Monday Omelette

"Hi! My name is Molly and I will be taking care of you today. Coffee, anyone?"   1

These were the words I spoke daily when working as a waitress at Bacarri's Diner on Cape Cod this past summer.

> Establishes the setting for the story, both time and place.

The weekend people were sometimes tough customers: the grumpy old   2 man whose orange juice was not cold enough, the woman whose bacon was too burnt, and the screaming three-year-old girl who threw her pancakes on the ground. A mother complained about the coffee spills from my hands shaking from nervousness. I apologized, grabbed five napkins, and blamed it on the wobbly tables.

Tilton 2

> Good contrast between hectic weekends and weekday customers.

Serving breakfast on Monday morning always seemed so simple. After a weekend of impatient customers, I was delighted to wait on regulars, who were kind and respectful. 3

The diner was an old-fashioned, low-key place. The light blue walls were hung with Marilyn Monroe photos, and Elvis was almost always playing on the jukebox. The paint was chipped and the white tile floor, although clean, looked dingy. These details only augmented the retro feeling. The older folks said they felt like they were back in the sixties. 4

> Details chosen to imply the generation of people who like the diner—her parents' generation.

All the regulars sat at the off-white countertop. Frank came in everyday, usually twice. He smiled like a child, but his white hair gave away his age. He would wear a collared shirt and khaki pants every morning. In the afternoons, he was more relaxed, usually wearing his beat-up jean shorts. His lunch order never varied: a hot dog and a cup of beans. I never really got to know Frank that well. He did not talk much, but called me "Miss Molly" and said I reminded him of his daughter. 5

> Introduces key character and establishes relation in her mind between Frank and her own father.

> Details indicate the ties between father and daughter in appearance and show how special seeing his daughter is to Frank.

The weekends were special for Frank. His daughter met him for breakfast, and they would sit in one of the booths, chatting about Hailey's busy life. She was in her third year of law school. Hailey had Frank's smile and his delicate face. Her long brown hair perfectly draped over her sundress. She usually ordered French toast or a grilled muffin. When Hailey was there, Frank upgraded his breakfast order to the egg-white, sausage-and-peppers omelette. 6

On this Monday morning, Frank arrived around 8:30 and took a seat in one of the booths instead of his weekday perch at the counter. I poured him a cup of coffee, and he told me he was not going to order at the moment because he was waiting for his daughter to meet him for breakfast. His face was glowing when he told me. I could feel his excitement. He sat there for ten minutes and, still smiling, asked for more coffee. 7

> The narrative tension builds with each reference to the passing of time.

Forty minutes later he was still sitting alone in the beat-up gray booth, waiting. With a smile he told me, "My daughter will be here soon but I'm just going to order anyway." 8

Then his cell phone rang. He answered. "Hi, where are you? Oh, that's OK. I know about Mondays. No, it's OK. We'll do it another day." I felt the room go dark. Something had come up. She would not be able to meet him. 9

Tilton 3

Putting Frank's experience into the context of her own life gives Tilton an angle for interpreting her experience.

Suddenly, the scene felt familiar to me. I was a daughter. I had done this. I had broken similar news to my own father.   10

I pictured my dad, sitting on the brown leather couch on a Friday night watching the news—anticipating my arrival. He was drifting off to sleep. Then his phone rang.   11

"Hi, Dad. It's me. I'm sorry, but I'm going to stay at Courtney's tonight. I'll call you in the morning, OK?"   12

He would ask a lot of questions per usual and tell me how much he missed me that day. He would always assure me it was OK. I would apologize and tell him that I would try to see him the next day. That promise always sounded empty. After the divorce, I couldn't guarantee when I would see him. Alternating between my mother's and father's houses was sometimes too complicated. And then I had my friends. I was busy. I was sorry. After I hung up the phone, I would imagine him turning off the TV and dragging himself upstairs to bed. I pictured the let-down expression on his face. He had been ditched, stood up by his own daughter.   13

Effective understated ending, with no explicit statement of the lesson inherent in the story.

Sweating from the guilt of being a daughter, I went back into the kitchen to bring out Frank's meal. When I delivered his omelette, he lifted his face, fake-smiled, and said "Ahh, Miss Molly. Thank you so much!"   14

CHAPTER 6

Creating Profiles

MOST PEOPLE FIND NOTHING MORE INTERESTING THAN OTHER PEOPLE. That is why we gossip, tell stories about ourselves and others at parties, watch television shows about famous people, enjoy Facebook, and read biographies. The important questions are: Who is this person? What is she doing now? Why does this person and his activities matter? The **profile** answers these questions by *depicting people who matter to us so that our readers will know about them too.*

What Is a Profile?

A **profile** *describes a subject of interest to the writer, such as a person, organization, place, event, or situation.* While some profiles can be purely informative—facts about a corporation or a prominent figure in business—the profile essay, which is the assignment in this chapter, is more subjective. A **profile essay** expresses the *writer's interpretation of the subject; the writer chooses what to include and omit based on the impression of the subject he or she wants readers to have.* This impression comes from the writer's *angle* or point of view, which gives the paper focus and purpose. A profile should show why the subject matters to the writer and should matter to readers as well.

CONCEPT CLOSE-UP   More about Profiles

Profiles depict a person, place, organization, event, or situation. They do the following:

- Provide *snapshots,* not a complete or even necessarily balanced view.
- Seek to create a *memorable impression.*
- *Convey information but not in a detached or objective way:* The interpretation is yours, the writer's, and therefore implies what matters to you.
- Are often *ethical and moral,* concerned with right and wrong, good and bad, the desirable and the undesirable.
- Strive for *lifelike immediacy.*

Mark Zuckerberg, creator of the social networking site Facebook, has been profiled countless times in recent years. Though celebrity profiles can be very satisfying for us to read,
might a profile of the ordinary be more enriching and meaningful to our lives?

© Steve Jennings/Getty Images

Why Write Profiles?

We encounter profiles in many places: in human interest pieces written for magazines,
newspapers, and television shows; online in blog posts and on websites; in speeches
that pay tribute to important people. Profiles are also often part of larger pieces of
writing; for example, a profile of Abraham Lincoln may be included in a book about
the Civil War.

In a world of more than 7 billion people who inhabit nearly all places on our
planet and who come together in an almost infinite number of organizations, events,
situations, and online social networks, why single out this person, or that place, organization, and so on, for attention?

In our media-saturated world, one answer is obvious: because someone or something is famous, and people therefore want to know more. It explains profiles of a
person like Bill Gates, a place like the White House, an organization like Habitat for
Humanity, an event like a basketball team losing a game 100 to 0, and a situation like
the unending conflict between Israel and Palestine.

However, some of the best profiles are about the little known, even the seem-
ingly insignificant. How do we explain these? Such profiles reveal a motive more profound than satisfying media-generated curiosity. They are protests against obscurity, a
struggle for attention and memory. "This person," they say or imply, "no matter how

THE ART OF QUESTIONING | What Matters?

Profiles involve ethics; that is, they always imply questions such as the following:

- What counts most in life?
- How should I treat other people?
- What's the right thing to do?
- How can I maintain integrity amid all the pressures to do what others want me to do or what the immediate situation seems to require?

Writers select subjects for profiles based on their values; how they depict their subjects implies what matters to them. Consequently, the most important question when you read or write a profile is this: **Why does this matter?** Put another way: **Why do you care?**

unknown otherwise, matters." "This place, organization, event, or situation you have never heard of is more important than you think." Such profiles enlarge reader awareness and reveal the value of someone or something that may never make the evening news or even turn up on a Google search.

The questions, "Why does this matter? Why do I care?" are important in writing profiles. Hold them in mind as you read the profiles by Joel Achenbach, Catherine de Lange, and Molly Tilton in this chapter. **What do they value? Do you value the same things? Why or why not?** Keep them in mind also as you move into the assignment. The questions have everything to do with the subject you select and how you treat it. **Why do you care about your subject? How can you get your readers to care about it too?**

How Do Writers Compose Profiles?

Profiles strive for lifelike immediacy, ways to connect readers intimately to the subject. Some of the strategies writers use to compose successful profiles include:

- Vivid description.
- Interesting details from available background information.
- Quotations of what people say and what others say about them.
- Use of dialogue to report conversational exchanges.
- Use of photographs and other visual means of transmitting information, such as maps and drawings.

In the readings that follow you will see how all of these tools work in detail.

READING **6.1**

Writing with the Master

JOEL ACHENBACH

Joel Achenbach is the author of seven books and a distinguished journalist for the Washington Post. His profile of John McPhee, a legendary writer and teacher of writing and a major contributor to the development of literary nonfiction, pays tribute to a mentor, not only for Achenbach but also for several generations of McPhee's students. As you read, pay special attention to what counts as good writing as McPhee practiced and taught it. The virtues he embodied are the virtues of good writing generally, not just in journalism.

This profile appeared in the Princeton Alumni Weekly (November 12, 2014), which explains why the year of graduation from Princeton appears along with the names of people mentioned in the article.

John McPhee '53 has many moves as a writer, one of which he calls a "gossip ladder"—nothing more than a stack of quotations, each its own paragraph, unencumbered by attribution or context. You are eavesdropping in a crowd. You take these scraps of conversation and put them in a pile. Like this: 1

"A piece of writing needs to start somewhere, go somewhere, and sit down when it gets there." 2

"Taking things from one source is plagiarism; taking things from several sources is research." 3

"A thousand details add up to one impression." 4

"You cannot interview the dead." 5

"Readers are not supposed to see structure. It should be as invisible as living bones. It shouldn't be imposed; structure arises within the story." 6

"Don't start off with the most intense, scary part, or it will all be anticlimactic from there." 7

"You can get away with things in fact that would be tacky in fiction—and stuck on TV at 3 o'clock in the morning. Sometimes the scene is carried by the binding force of fact." 8

The speaker in every instance is John McPhee. I assembled this particular ladder from the class notes of Amanda Wood Kingsley '84, an illustrator and 9

© David Johnson

writer who, like me, took McPhee's nonfiction writing class, "The Literature of Fact," in the spring of 1982. In February, McPhee will mark 40 years as a Princeton professor, which he has pulled off in the midst of an extraordinarily productive career as a staff writer for *The New Yorker* and the author of more than two dozen books.

When the editor of this magazine asked me to write something about McPhee's class, I knew it would be the easiest assignment ever, though a little nerve-wracking. It was because most of McPhee's former students have saved their class notes and marked-up papers (Marc Fisher '80: "I've never lived anywhere without knowing where my notes from his class are"). 10

Attention-getting and interesting opening, a collection of memorable statements from McPhee.

After piquing our interest, this paragraph supplies the information we need to know whom the profile is about and the context of the author's experience with McPhee.

11   When I meet Rick Klein '98 at a coffee shop down the block, we examined forensically Rick's class papers and the McPhee marginalia, the admonitions and praise from a teacher who keeps his pencils sharp. McPhee never overlooked a typo, and when Rick (now the hotshot political director at ABC News) wrote "fowl" instead of "foul," the professor's pencil produced a devastating noose.

12   McPhee's greatest passion was for structure, and he required that students explain, in a few sentences at the end of every assignment, how they structured the piece. (McPhee noted on a piece Rick wrote about his father: "This is a perfect structure—simple, like a small office building, as you suggest. The relationship of time to paragraphing is an example of what building a piece of writing is all about.")

13   Rick reminds me that the class was pass/fail.

14   "You were competing not for a grade, but for his approval. You were so scared to turn in a piece of writing that John McPhee would realize was dirt. We were just trying to impress a legend," he says.

15   Which is the nerve-wracking part, *still*. He is likely to read this article and will notice the infelicities, the stray words, the unnecessary punctuation, the galumphing syntax, the desperate metaphors, and the sentences that wander into the woods. "They're paying you by the comma?" McPhee might write in the margin after reading the foregoing sentence. My own student work tended toward the self-conscious, the cute, and the undisciplined, and McPhee sometimes would simply write: "Sober up."

16   He favors simplicity in general, and believes a metaphor needs room to breathe. "Don't slather one verbal flourish on top of another lest you smother them all," he'd tell his students. On one of Amanda's papers, he numbered the images, metaphors, and similes from 1 to 11, and then declared, "They all work well, to a greater or lesser degree. In 1,300 words, however, there may be too many of them—as in a fruitcake that is mostly fruit."

17   When Amanda produced a verbose, mushy description of the "Oval with Points" sculpture on campus, McPhee drew brackets around one passage and wrote, "Pea soup."

18   That one was a famously difficult assignment: You had to describe a piece of abstract art on campus. It was an invitation to overwriting. As McPhee put it, "Most writers do a wild skid, leave the road, and plunge into the dirty river." Novice writers believe they will improve a piece of writing by adding things to it; mature writers know they will improve it by taking things out.

19   Another standard McPhee assignment came on Day One of the class: Pair up and interview each other, then write a profile. It was both an early test of our nonfiction writing skills and a clever way for McPhee to get to know his students at the beginning of the semester.

20   McPhee's dedication to his students was, and is, remarkable, given the other demands on his time. One never got the sense that he wished he could be off writing a magazine story for *The New Yorker* rather than annotating, and discussing face-to-face, a clumsy, ill-conceived, syntactically mangled piece of writing by a 20-year-old.

21   He met with each of his 16 students for half an hour every other week. Many of his students became professional writers, and he lined up their books on his office shelf, but McPhee never has suggested that the point of writing is to make money, or that the merit

---

Note the humor in the word choice: "forensically," as if they were examining the body of a murdered person. Also note the humor in McPhee's noose comment.

Note Achenbach's voice here. He is still speaking as the student anxious about winning McPhee's approval.

Note how Achenbach transitions in paragraphs 19 and 20 from one section of his profile, on typical assignments McPhee gave, to another section, on McPhee's character as a teacher.

In this paragraph Achenbach explores the unselfish depth of McPhee's involvement with his students and his concern for writing well regardless of the circumstances.

of your writing is determined by its market value. A great paragraph is a great paragraph wherever it resides, he'd say. It could be in your diary.

"I think he loves it when students run off and become field biologists in Africa or elementary school teachers," Jenny Price '85 tells me. She's now a writer, artist, and visiting Princeton professor.   22

McPhee taught us to revere language, to care about every word, and to abjure the loose synonym. He told us that words have subtle and distinct meanings, textures, implications, intonations, flavors. (McPhee might say: "Nuances" alone could have done the trick there.) Use a dictionary, he implored. He proselytized on behalf of the gigantic, unabridged *Webster's Second Edition,* a tank of a dictionary that not only would give a definition, but also would explore the possible synonyms and describe how each is slightly different in meaning. If you treat these words interchangeably, it's like taping together adjacent keys on a piano, he said.   23

Robert Wright '79, an acclaimed author and these days a frequent cycling companion of McPhee, tells me by email, "I'd be surprised if there have been many or even any Ferris professors who care about words as much as John—I don't mean their proper use so much as their creative, deft use, sometimes in a way that exploits their multiple meanings; he also pays attention to the rhythm of words. All this explains why some of his prose reads kind of like poetry."   24

Just to write a simple description clearly can take you days, he taught us (once again I'm citing Amanda's class notes): "If you do it right, it'll slide by unnoticed. If you blow it, it's obvious."   25

We had to learn to read. One of his assignments is called "greening." You pretend you are in the composing room slinging hot type and need to remove a certain amount of the text block to get it to fit into an available space. You must search the text for words that can be removed surgically.   26

"It's as if you were removing freight cars here and there in order to shorten a train—or pruning bits and pieces of a plant for aesthetic and pathological reasons, not to mention length," McPhee commanded. "Do not do violence to the author's tone, manner, style, nature, thumbprint."   27

He made us green a couple of lines from the famously lean Gettysburg Address, an assignment bordering on sadism. A favorite paragraph designated for greening was the one in Joseph Conrad's *Heart of Darkness* that begins, "Going up that river was like traveling back to the earliest beginnings of the world, when vegetation rioted on the earth and the big trees were kings. An empty stream, a great silence, an impenetrable forest. The air was warm, thick, heavy, sluggish. There was no joy in the brilliance of sunshine." (McPhee, in assigning this, wrote: "Caution: You are approaching what may be my favorite paragraph in a lifetime of sporadic reading.")   28

One time the young Bob Wright used the word "minced" in an assignment. In their bi-weekly office conference, McPhee challenged Bob to justify the word. Bob offered his reasoning. McPhee looked up "minced" in the hulking *Webster*'s. "You found the perfect word," McPhee declared.   29

Achenbach develops his profile with specific teaching techniques used by McPhee.

30   McPhee's career coincided with the rise of "New Journalism," but he never was really part of that movement and the liberties it took with the material. A college student often feels that rules are suffocating, that old-school verities need to be obliterated, and so some of us were tempted, naturally, to enhance our nonfiction—to add details from the imagination and produce a work of literature that's better than "true" and existed on a more exalted plane of meaning. We'd make things up. McPhee wouldn't stand for it.

31   Amanda remembers being called into his office one day: "I could tell something was wrong because he wasn't his usual smiling self. He had me sit down and glared at me a moment. Then he asked me very sternly whether I had made up the character I had allegedly interviewed for my paper that week about animal traps and snares—I'd talked to an elderly African American friend of my grandparents, whose snare-building skills helped him survive the Depression. Once I convinced him that Oscar was a real person, McPhee sat quietly a moment, then smiled and said it was one of the best papers he had received. Those were some of the finest words I'll ever hear."

32   Perhaps there are writers out there who make it look easy, but that is not the example set by McPhee. He is of the school of thought that says a writer is someone for whom writing is more difficult than for other people. Some people joke about lashing themselves to the chair to get a piece of writing done, but McPhee actually has done it, with the belt of his bathrobe.

33   Here's David Remnick '81, the McPhee student who is now McPhee's editor at *The New Yorker:* "You were working with a practicing creative artist, a writer of 'primary texts,' as the scholars say, but one who was eloquent, detailed, unfancy, and clear in the way he talked about essential things: description, reporting, structure, sentences, punctuation, rhythm, to say nothing of the emotional aspects of writing—anxiety, lostness, frustration. He didn't sugarcoat the difficulty of writing well. If anything, he highlighted the bitter-tasting terrors, he cherished them, rolled them around on his tongue. But behind all that was an immensely revealing, and rewarding, glimpse of the writing life. Not the glamour or the readings or the reviews. No, he allowed you to glimpse the process, what it meant to write alone in a room."

34   Marc Fisher, my *Washington Post* colleague, points out that part of McPhee's magic was getting students to slow down. "He catches adolescents at exactly the moment when we've been racing to get somewhere in life, and he corrals our ambition and raw skills and somehow persuades us that the wisdom, the power, and the mystery of telling people's stories comes in good part from pressing down on the brakes, taking it all in, and putting it down on paper—yes, paper—in a way that is true to the people we meet and the lives they lead."

35   I doubt many of us ever took a class that resonated so profoundly over the years. Part of it was that McPhee felt invested in our later success, regardless of our vocations. You could knock on his door years later and confer with him about your writing, your personal issues, your hopes and dreams. How many teachers are willing to be Professor For Life?

> Note Achenbach's use of testimonials from other former students in paragraphs 31, 33, and 34 to develop his profile with additional specifics.

The profile concludes with a specific experience that relates to Achenbach's angle on his subject.

These are tough times in my business, which the people in suits now refer to as "content creation." Revolutionary changes in how we consume information have created challenges for anyone who is committed to serious, time-consuming writing, the kind that involves revision and the search for that perfect word.

36

But I don't think anyone can obliterate the beauty of a deftly constructed piece of writing. This is particularly the case if you've written it yourself. It's like hitting a great golf shot; you forget the shanks and slices and remember the one exquisite 3-iron.

37

One day in McPhee's class, he praised a sentence I'd written about the Louise Nevelson sculpture "Atmosphere and Environment X," near Firestone Library. He had me read it aloud. The hook was set. I don't always think about it consciously, but that's pretty much what I've been trying to do for more than three decades—write another sentence that might win the approval of John McPhee.

38

Questions for Discussion

1. Note the stress on "putting it down on paper" in paragraph 34. When would such an approach be appropriate for writing something? Do you always compose on a computer screen? If not, when do you use paper and pencil or some other nonelectronic tool for writing?
2. Learning anything that requires a high level of skill and judgment involves mentors, whether they are teachers in schools or not. What mentors have you had? What difference did they make in what you were learning to do?
3. The article singles out for attention what McPhee cared about most in teaching his students to write well. List his emphases. What do you consider most important? What do you consider least important? Why?

■■■ *Thinking as a Writer*

What Is the Rhetorical Situation?

1. What is Achenbach's *purpose* in writing this essay? What is his *angle* on the topic? How would you describe his *voice*?
2. Achenbach's intended audience is obviously Princeton alumni. How might other people respond to his essay?
3. Using Concept Close-Up: More about Profiles (page 84) as a guide, answer the following question: How does Achenbach use the *conventions* for creating a subjective profile? Specifically, how does he use background information about John McPhee? How does he include McPhee's voice, the sort of things he said, and the manner he used in saying them? How does he use detail to give his subject fuller humanity, a view of McPhee from more than one side? ■

Joel Achenbach. "Writing with the Master." *Princeton Alumni Weekly*, 12 Nov. 2014. Copyright © 2014 by Joel Achenbach. Reprinted by permission.

READING **6.2**

We're Losing the Raw, Human Part of Being with Each Other

CATHERINE DE LANGE

Sherry Turkle is a distinguished professor of science and technology at the Massachusetts Institute of Technology and author of many books, including Alone Together: Why We Expect More from Technology and Less from Each Other *(2011). A psychiatrist, she has done extensive research on the impact of technology on our lives. Her controversial work in this area has made her internationally famous.*

The author of this short profile of Turkle is Catherine de Lange, the biomedical features editor for New Scientist *and a freelance journalist who lives in London.*

edraggled from a walk in the rain, Sherry Turkle   1
shows up begging for a latte. She's left her wallet
in her hotel room. She's exhausted, she says, and
could do with a coffee. "You can see it's not my most perky
morning. But I'm really thrilled to be meeting with you."

These aren't just pleasantries—Turkle has a serious   2
point to make. As professor of the social studies of science
and technology at MIT and the founder and current director
of the MIT Initiative on Technology and Self, she has spent over three decades studying
the way people interact with machines, and is growing increasingly worried about the
amount of human interaction people are happy to delegate to robots or carry out over
phones and computers. As a human, within seconds of meeting her in person, I can
interpret the complexities of her mood—the tired part, and the happy to be here part.
"This is a complex dance that we know how to do with each other," she says. A dance
she fears is being forgotten.

Turkle wasn't always this interested in technology. Born in Brooklyn in 1948, she   3
studied in Paris before returning to do her PhD in sociology and psychology at Harvard.
By 1978 she had just written her first book, on French psychoanalysis, when MIT hired
her to study the sociology of sciences of the mind. "I began to hear students talking
about their minds as machines, based on the early personal computers they had.
They'd use phrases like 'debugging' or 'don't talk to me until I clear my buffer.' I'd never heard any of this stuff before."

So Turkle began to   4
study the way that artificial
intelligence was taking hold
in everyday life, at a time
when these interactions with
machines were pretty raw.
She "literally was at the right
place at the right time."

© Pat Greenhouse/Boston Globe/Getty Images

The place being MIT, home to some of the pioneers of artificial intelligence and social robotics, and the birthplace of perhaps the most sophisticated, and endearing, social robots. Turkle tested these anthropomorphic robots on children, "computer virgins." In one study she observed how children would bond with the robots, which were programmed to respond with human-like emotions, in a way they wouldn't with other toys. "This becomes a tremendously significant relationship for the child," she says, "and then it will get broken or disappoint, and the child will go ballistic. My research group went berserk at how much damage we felt we'd done."

5

Turkle was "smitten with the subject and stayed with it for 30 years." In the early days she was labelled as a "cyber diva." "People thought I was very pro-computer. I was on the cover of *Wired* magazine." Then things began to change. In the early 80s, "we met this technology and became smitten like young lovers," she says, but today our attachment is unhealthy. In her latest book, *Alone Together: Why We Expect More from Technology and Less from Each Other,* Turkle says we have reached a point she calls the "robotic moment"—where we delegate important human relationships, in particular interactions at "the most vulnerable moments in life"—childhood and old age—to robots. "We are so worried about Asperger's, so worried about the way we communicate with faces. To me, as somebody who likes technology, this is just playing with fire."

6

Turkle frequently takes calls from journalists seeking comments on the latest story about robots in nursing homes, teacherbot programs or nannybots to look after children. She sees married couples who prefer to have their fights online. "My studies of funerals are hilarious," she says. "Everybody's texting. When I ask them about it, they say, 'Yeah, I do it during the boring bits.' So that's the question: what does it mean as a society that we are there for the boring bits?"

7

She is particularly concerned about the effect on children. "I am a single mum. I raised my daughter, and she was very listened to." Today our phones are always on, and always on us. Parents are too busy texting to watch their kids, she cautions. There's been a spike in playground accidents. "These kids are extremely lonely. We are giving everybody the impression that we aren't really there for them. It's toxic." This is what she means by "alone together"—that our ability to be in the world is compromised by "all that other stuff" we want to do with technology.

8

For many these are inconvenient truths, and lately Turkle has come to be seen as a naysayer, even a technophobe. She is no longer the cover girl for *Wired*. "This time they didn't even review my book." In fact, the initial reviews of *Alone Together,* Turkle says, can be summarised as "everybody likes Facebook, can't she just get with the program?" This, she adds, is unfair to the 15 years of research behind it. "I mean, give me the credit. I didn't do a think piece. I was reporting. People tell me they wish [iPhone companion] Siri were their best friend. I was stunned. You can't make this stuff up."

9

Turkle is optimistic that people will begin to want to reclaim their privacy, to turn back to their relationships with real people. Yet she concedes that the lure of technology is such that it's a tough challenge. "Online you become the self you want to be." But the downside? We lose the "raw, human part" of being with each other. She points to our

10

early morning meeting, for example. She's tired, and we could have done the interview over Skype. "Online I am perfect," she says. "But what's the worst that can happen here? You write a story that says, 'Bedraggled from her walk in the rain, she shows up begging for a latte?' So what? You pretty much see me as I am. And I'm willing to say that's a good thing."

Questions for Discussion

1. In your own words, explain what Turkle means by the "robotic moment" (paragraphs 5–6). As yet, robots do not play a significant role in most people's lives. What do you imagine the future of human-robot interaction will be?
2. Do you see any signs that we are losing the "raw, human part" of face-to-face interaction, good talk without electronic mediation? Do you see any signs that face-to-face interaction is itself changing because so much human communication involves cell phones and computers? How do you evaluate what is happening?
3. All technologies have both up sides and down sides; for instance, antibiotics save many lives, but they also result in so-called superbugs, disease-causing microbes that are antibiotic-resistant. Turkle may have grasped part of the down side of our reliance on the digital world. What other problems can you think of? In your view, how does the downside weigh on the scales against the upside of digital technology?

▣▣▣ *Thinking as a Writer*

What Is the Rhetorical Situation?

1. What is de Lange's *purpose* in writing this essay? What is her *angle* on the topic? How would you describe her *voice*?
2. Who is de Lange's intended *audience*? Is there anything in the article you can cite that implies her target readership?
3. Using Concept Close-Up: More about Profiles (page 84) as a guide, answer this question: How does de Lange use the *conventions* for creating a subjective profile? Specifically, how does she use background information, Turkle's voice and behavior, and detailed description to create a vivid impression of Turkle and her view of the dangers of our attachment to information technology? ▪

The Assignment

Write a profile about a person, organization, place, event, or situation. We recommend writing a single-person profile because it is easier to research and control. We also recommend that you at least be acquainted with the person you choose to profile. Extending and deepening a relationship you already have usually works better than establishing a new one from scratch.

What Can I Write About?

The most important criterion for making your selection is that the subject matters to you. Genuine interest in and involvement with your subject cannot be faked. Here are some possible topics:

- An older family member, a family friend, a mentor (such as a coach or teacher), someone in the community you interact with often, someone you work for or with, or a close, personal friend.

- Profiles in newspapers and magazines are about at least locally well-known people, such as artists, musicians, entertainers, sports figures, politicians, business leaders, and so on. If you happen to know a "high-profile" subject, as journalists call such people, she or he can be a good choice.

- Situations you, your family, or your local community face, such as entering the military, taking your first job, raising children, taking care of older relatives, or coping with illness or injury.

- Places you have lived or visited often, such as a foreign country; places you go to visit family, conduct business, or take vacations; the neighborhood where you grew up or live now.

- Significant happenings or gatherings of people, such as a concert or sporting event; something you witnessed that made the news and/or was a topic of conversation on your campus or in your local community.

How Do I Write a Profile?
Questioning the Rhetorical Situation

Begin by picturing a **rhetorical situation** for your writing project, a real-world context for communicating. You should consider the key variables in any act of communication: a writer with something to say, a reader the writer wishes to reach, and a kind of text appropriate to the writing task. These three variables will affect many decisions in the composing process.

Writer: What Is My Purpose, and What Impression Should Readers Have of Me?

The purpose of a profile is to depict a person, place, organization, or some other suitable subject that you care about, that matters to you. You are informing, telling readers what they need to know to understand your subject. Using your own point of view, your angle, you are also communicating an interpretation of your subject, what it means, the value it has—in short, why it should matter to your readers. Your readers should perceive you as knowledgeable about your subject, consistent in your point of view, and interested in depicting your subject in a memorable way.

Audience: Who Is My Reader?

Profiles often communicate with a broad audience because human beings are social animals and enjoy reading about other people. However, skillful profiles have *particular readerships* in mind. Given the subject you have chosen and the angle you have on it, ask yourself this question: **What group of people will gain the most from reading it?** What do they need to know to understand your subject? What could you tell them that they will find interesting, intriguing, or challenging? How can you get them involved in the ethical issues your subject raises—that is, questions of right and wrong, good and bad?

Text: What Moves Can I Make?

To create a meaningful and memorable impression of the person you are writing about, you can do some or all of the following:

- Include conversational exchanges that you have had with your subject or that were reported to you by someone you interviewed.

- Quote a favorite saying of your subject that reveals his or her character or wisdom.

- Depict an action that shows what matters to your subject.

- Discuss events that you and your subject were part of, especially events that allow you to discuss your subject's values and characteristic commitments.

- Describe your subject's physical makeup and what you have seen him or her wearing if such details are relevant to the central impression you want your readers to have.

- Describe places where you and your subject have interacted, such as your subject's home or work environment.

- Connect your subject to some enterprise that plays a major role in your subject's life, such as what he or she does for a living; the causes he or she supports; games, hobbies, sports, or leisure activities that indicate long-term interests or facets of personality.

People working to accomplish something, such as installing a community garden in your neighborhood, make good profile subjects.

© Tony Anderson/Digital Vision/Getty Images, RF

- Give background about your subject's life history, such as where the subject was born and went to school and whom he or she married, especially when such information helps to explain why your subject became what he or she now is.

- Discuss the impact your subject has had on your life and the kind of relationship you have had with him or her (friend, mentor, business associate, and so on).

- Include a photo of your subject performing some action and comment on its significance.

Remember that these are moves you *can* make, not moves you must make, and that there are many other moves not listed here you could make. What you do depends on your angle, the information you have or can acquire, what you can do to make your subject interesting, and the central impression you want your readers to have.

How Do I Write a Profile?
Engaging the Writing Process

No two people compose in exactly the same way, and even the same person may go through the writing process in different ways with different assignments. Nevertheless, because no one can attend to everything at once, there are phases in handling any significant writing task. You prepare to write by generating content and finding your angle.

The next phase is planning and drafting your paper, getting a version, however rough it may be, on paper or screen so that you have something to work with during the following two stages: revising your draft by making changes to the content, arrangement, and style of your writing; and editing your draft to take care of problems at the paragraph and sentence level, such as lack of focus and coherence, awkward or unclear sentences, and errors of grammar, spelling, and punctuation.

Exploring Your Topic

Most profiles draw on both what the writer knows already about the person profiled—that is, experience with that person—and additional information gathered from research. Start by investigating your experience.

Mining for Details about a Person

It is remarkable what we know about relatives, friends, acquaintances, and colleagues yet do not fully realize that we know. The following questions should help you recover some of what you know about the person you have chosen to profile.

In your writer's notebook or in an electronic file, write down everything that occurs to you in response to each of the following questions:

1. What does the person look like?

2. How does the person dress?

3. What is it like to talk to this person? Are there characteristic facial expressions, qualities of voice, mannerisms, gestures, accent, and so on that you recall?

4. How would you describe the person's character? For instance, how does she or he handle problems and setbacks?

5. What achievements and activities is the person proudest of?

6. How self-aware is the person? Does the person's self-conception match your view of him or her?

7. What does the person most like to talk about? What topics does she or he avoid or say nothing about when others raise them?

8. Where have you talked with the person? What did you notice about the home, office, or other place where the two of you talked?

9. What sort of people does your person have as friends or associates? If you have met some of them, what were your impressions? What did they say about your person?

10. If you were talking with someone else who does not know the person as well as you do, what story or stories would you tell? What stories about your person do you recall others telling you?

■■■■ ACTIVITY 6.1 *Writer's Notebook*

Assessing Your Materials

After you finish brainstorming your topic using the ten questions on page 98, step back and begin looking for *patterns and convergences* in the material. Do you see a dominant theme in your person's life, something that she or he is always concerned with or pursuing? Do you detect fundamental loyalties or commitments, a basic philosophy, outlook, or set of controlling attitudes or values?

Profiles create memorable impressions, and therefore you need to be seeking the impression you want to create for yours. You may not know yet what it will be, but probably somewhere in your first exploration there are clues or intuitions. Write them down, even if you have doubts, even if some of the details do not fit. You are not committing yourself to anything yet, but you need some first ideas for further thought and to help guide the research you will probably need to do. ■

Preparing to Write

You can see from the example profiles at the beginning of this chapter that the amount of research required varies considerably. Achenbach's profile drew extensively on the files of McPhee's students; de Lange drew on what she knew about Turkle combined with her impressions of their meeting. How much you need depends on how long you have known and how well you know the person you have chosen and on your instructor's assignment requirements.

Interviewing is the most common form of research in doing profiles, and we will devote special attention to it shortly. What other ways of acquiring information might be available to you?

BEST PRACTICES   Sources of Information for Profiles

1. Besides interviewing the person you are profiling, talk to people who know your subject as well as or better than you do, such as friends, associates, family members, and other relatives.
2. Find out if your person has written anything that you might gain access to: articles, books, texts for speeches, diaries, journals, blogs, even e-mail exchanges she or he might be willing to share.
3. Ask if you may look at scrapbooks or photo albums your subject might have.
4. Look for information via Google, news stories you can find via your local paper's index or your library's databases (see pages 341–44), Who's Who publications, résumés, bios written by your subject or by someone else, and so on. Ask your subject for help in accessing such information.
5. Arrange to attend meetings or other gatherings of people in which your subject plays a prominent role.

See Chapter 16, Finding Sources, and Chapter 17, Evaluating Sources, for more on using print and online materials.

Conducting Interviews

Interviews are *guided conversations,* and they are guided largely by the questions you ask. On the one hand, you want as natural and free-flowing a conversation as possible, something close to what would happen if you were sitting next to someone on an airplane and just happened to strike up a conversation. On the other hand, there is information you need and questions you have thought of in advance to elicit it, and you do not want the interview to end with too few of those questions asked and answered. Interviews are, therefore, a challenge, a push-pull between *let it flow* and *steer it toward what you need to know.* Following are important considerations when conducting interviews (also see Figure 6.1):

1. **The medium matters.** We recommend face-to-face interviews over telephone interviews, and telephone interviews over online chats or e-mail exchanges. Of course, you conduct interviews any way you can, but as you move down the line in methods of communication, you lose more and more information. Face-to-face interviews give you the full experience of good talk, including gestures, facial expressions, changes in posture, and information from the surroundings. Over the telephone, you have only the interviewee's voice in addition to what is said; with online communication you have only the written text to work with.

2. **Bring a camera with you.** Photographs of your subject and places associated with him or her can help supplement descriptions and confirm the impression you want to create. Many profiles include photographs.

3. **Plan to bring an audio recorder.** Ask your interviewee before the conversation begins whether or not you can use the recorder. Have a notebook with you as well for making quick notes between questions, during a response, and immediately after the interview when your memory is freshest. However, do not allow note-taking to intrude into the conversation—fast jottings are all you will have time for during the interview itself.

4. **Bring with you a set of questions** that are printed out or written on your note-pad and rank ordered from the most to the least important. The questions should address holes in your knowledge detected after recalling what you know already about your person and after pursuing some of the suggestions in Best Practices (page 99) for gaining additional information. They should also fill out what you have learned that you and your readers are likely to find most interesting.

   Often your questions will either not lead to anything interesting or will turn up much more than you anticipated. In the first case, be ready to pose another question as soon as you can; in the second case, let the person talk until you sense the well is going dry, even if it means you do not get to ask a few of your less important questions.

5. Finally, as your interview draws to a close, ask if you may arrange another meeting later and/or pose follow-up questions over the telephone or via e-mail. Also ask about additional sources of information listed on page 99 that you can obtain only if the interviewee is able and willing to supply them—texts of speeches, for instance.

Face-to-face interviewing is an art well worth learning how to do. Start practicing it now, on this assignment, because you will need it for information-gathering on the job or for community-based leadership positions.

FIGURE **6.1**

Things to Remember for an Interview

When conducting an interview, there are a few important things to remember to help you get the most out of it: (1) speak to your subject face-to-face, (2) take the person's picture, (3) record the interview, and (4) have good questions prepared.

Top left: © Brand X Pictures/PunchStock, RF; bottom left: © BananaStock/Jupiterimages, RF; top right: © Thomas Northcut/Photodisc/Getty Images, RF; bottom right: © C Squared Studios/Photodisc/Getty Images, RF

Selecting Details Based on Your Angle

Profiles are always based on far more information than the writer can actually use in the profile itself. If you feel somewhat overwhelmed by all the information you have gathered, that is normal. Here is how to gain a measure of control over it sufficient to write a first draft.

First, remember that profiles are always *partial depictions of your person, and the source of the partiality is your angle or point of view.* Put another way, you need to create a memorable impression, and it can only come from your point of view. It is time to decide on your point of view and commit yourself to it—at least until you see how well it works in a first draft.

Remember also that your point of view is what it is, and so it cannot be wrong. Have confidence in it and suspend judgment until you get the first draft completed. Only then can you assess your point of view according to the only criterion that matters: Did it work? Were you able to write an engaging profile? If not, adjusting your point of view may be one of the keys to revising it.

For Joel Achenbach, John McPhee is the role model for a master writing teacher. For Catherine de Lange, her meeting with Turkle represents the raw, unmediated human contact that Turkle thinks is being lost and de Lange seems to value.

In formulating your point of view, then, ask two questions:

- Why does my subject matter to me?
- How can I connect what matters to me with my readers' concerns and interests?

Answer these questions and you have what you need to select information from all the data you have gathered. If an item relates *directly* to depicting what matters to you and your readers, include it in your plan for the first draft; if not, leave it out.

Drafting Your Paper

As you write your draft, focus on the following concerns.

What Voice Is Appropriate for a Profile?

Profiles are informative, not primarily expressive; thus the focus is on the subject profiled, not on the writer. Nevertheless, your voice matters, as it always does in writing. Sound like a well-informed insider with an intimate knowledge of your subject. That is how you project authority. Beyond that, voice depends largely on point of view, how you understand your subject.

For example, listen to these paragraphs from Achenbach's profile of John McPhee:

> McPhee's dedication to his students was, and is, remarkable, given the other demands on his time. One never got the sense that he wished he could be off writing a magazine story for *The New Yorker* rather than annotating, and discussing face-to-face, a clumsy, ill-conceived, syntactically mangled piece of writing by a 20-year-old.
>
> He met with each of his 16 students for half an hour every other week. Many of his students became professional writers, and he lined up their books on his office shelf, but McPhee never has suggested that the point of writing is to make money, or that the merit of your writing is determined by its market value. A great paragraph is a great paragraph wherever it resides, he'd say. It could be in your diary.
>
> I think he loves it when students run off and become field biologists in Africa or elementary school teachers," Jenny Price '85 tells me. She's now a writer, artist, and visiting Princeton professor.

Much of the profile depicts McPhee as a daunting, indeed, intimidating task master; in these paragraphs we see his dedication to his students and how he cared so much about them—the human touch, without which his methods of teaching writing might only have driven students away. Because of these paragraphs we can see why McPhee's students remained so attached to him long after the course they took with him was over. The admiring voice of the author seems entirely justified.

Developing and Organizing Your Profile

The following organizational principles apply to arranging your materials:

- Start with something memorable, an attention-getting opener that indicates what your profile is about and why it matters to you and your reader.

- Provide most of your background information next, after you have your reader's attention and interest.

- Structure the remaining material by looking for a sequence that makes sense. For instance, you may need to describe a situation before you cite what your subject said or did. Or perhaps one story or memory may provide a good lead-in to or context for another.

- Save something especially memorable for the conclusion. You want to end as strongly as you began.

Commonly writers set out to follow a plan and then depart from it as they draft. The plan they thought would work has to be modified or even abandoned as they write. If that is what happens to you, do not be concerned. As long as the final version of your profile has a structure that readers can understand and follow, you have solved whatever organizational problems you may encounter.

Revising Your Draft

Writing is revising. A first draft is a start, but most need significant rewriting—for instance, parts taken out, new parts added, and parts rearranged. The strongest revisions begin with your own assessment. It is a good idea to put your draft aside for a while, preferably a day or two. Then, when you have some distance from it, go back and read what you wrote.

Try to see it as your readers will see it. The questions in The Art of Questioning will help you find ways to improve the draft.

THE ART OF QUESTIONING | Revision Checklist for Writing a Profile

1. **Does the draft create a memorable impression?** What word or words best state your angle, or interpretation, of your subject?
2. **Is there anything in the profile that does not contribute to the impression?** If so, it should be background information. Cut anything else.
3. **Does your draft capture your subject's full humanity?** If yours seems "flat," one-dimensional, revise by adding anecdotes, descriptions, comments from other people, and so on to reveal more sides or aspects of your subject. Here is a major opportunity for improving your paper by developing it better.
4. **Does your profile have immediacy and intimacy?** Isolate the places in your paper where you have described your subject, so that the reader can see and hear what you experienced. Go back to the notes you took during exploration and research. **What details might be added?** Sight and sound usually dominate descriptions, but touch, smell, and taste can sometimes contribute as

well. Developing your descriptions is another way to make your profile more effective.

5. **Have you quoted your person and/or cited snippets of revealing conversation?** *Your reader needs to hear your subject talking.* What was said and in what way, with what gestures, facial expressions, tone of voice, and so on?

6. **Have you made your relationship with your subject clear?** Read through your paper again, concentrating entirely on voice and self-presentation. **What is your attitude toward your subject?** Where does it emerge most clearly and forcefully? **How do you sound to your reader?** Do you think how you sound is appropriate given your relationship to the person?

7. Does your profile at least imply questions like: **What matters in life? How should we live? How ought we to deal with other people?** Find the places in your essay where ethical questions like these are relevant. Can you develop them better without turning your profile into a sermon or moralistic lesson?

■■■ ACTIVITY 6.2 *Collaborative Activity*

Getting a Second Opinion

Either before you attempt a revision or at some point during the revising process, it always helps to have someone else, such as a classmate, a tutor, your instructor, a willing friend, look at your draft. Be sure that the person understands the assignment and what you are trying to do to create the memorable impression profiles make.

Share the questions listed in the previous section with the person reviewing your draft. Show the person what you have done or plan to do to improve the draft. Then ask for the person's honest and full assessment and any suggestions for improvement. ■

■■■ ACTIVITY 6.3 *In Your Own Work*

Revising Your Draft

After assessing the draft yourself and getting a second opinion, formulate a revision strategy—that is, an approach to carrying out the revision. Here are some suggestions:

■ First, decide what you think the useful criticism and suggestions are. Not all the feedback will be equally helpful, and some of it will not help at all. Reassess your own self-criticisms—do you still see the same problems?

■ Second, being as specific as you can, make a list of items you intend to work on. "The first anecdote on page 3 needs more descriptive detail" is an example of what we mean by specific.

- Third, divide your list into two categories: revisions that will change all or much of the paper—called global revisions—versus spot revisions that require only altering a paragraph or two in one place.

- Fourth, do the global revising first. Ponder the best order for doing them. For instance, if you decide to rearrange sections in your profile, do that first before working on transitions or other flow problems.

- Fifth, after completing the global revisions, deal with the spot revisions by beginning with those most likely to improve your draft the most.

Remember that revisions cannot be done all at once, in one step. Focus your attention on solving one problem at a time. *Remember also that carrying out your plan will often result in unplanned insights.* You might discover, for instance, that in developing one anecdote you now see connections with another. Adjust your plans to take full advantage of revision surprises. ■

Student Example: Excerpts from Molly Tilton's Draft

Molly Tilton's profile, "Mr. Santa Claus," appears on pages 108–11. Let's look at some excerpts from her first draft so you can see some of the significant improvements revision can make.

Excerpt 1: Opening Paragraph

In the back corner of an office in United Liquors' headquarters in Braintree, Massachusetts, the phone rang. Terri, the director of The Ray Tye Medical Aid Foundation, answered; she yelled, "Mr. Tye, Senator Ted Kennedy is on the phone, and has a prospective patient for the foundation." Mr. Tye took the call and then came into Terri's office to explain to her a young child's life-threatening situation.

In her revised opening, Tilton gets to the point faster:

In a back corner of United Liquors' headquarters in Braintree, Massachusetts, lives are being saved. Mr. A. Raymond Tye, a prominent businessman and philanthropist, strides into his place of work one morning with his cane and a mission. "Terri," he cries, "Come into my office to discuss some prospective patients for the foundation, twin boys conjoined at the head. They need our help." From that point the real work begins.

Excerpt 2: Paragraph 6 about Terri

Terri, the director of the foundation, is faced with tough decisions every day. She, along with Mr. Tye, decides on the patients the foundation will support. Doctors and politicians call The Ray Tye Medical Aid Foundation asking for financial help for someone they know. Patients and their family members fill out online applications asking for medical assistance. It is Terri's responsibility to contact hospitals to find out more about the patient's condition, as well as keeping in touch with ill patients. The majority of applications come from Haiti, Iraq, China, and Massachusetts; the foundation does not pay for travel costs but usually sets up patients with another foundation who can assist them. The foundation reviews all patient applications but only helps those who are facing life-threatening ailments and do not have health insurance.

In her revision of this paragraph, Tilton uses **specific details** to bring more life-like immediacy to Terri, allowing readers to see her as a real person:

> Terri Carlson, the director of the foundation, has worked for the foundation for two years. Prior to this, she worked for United Liquors as credit manager. In recent years, Terri, a devoted wife and mother of two, has worked long hours while juggling her responsibilities at home. She wears business attire every day to work, showing her serious attitude, but her bright red hair exemplifies her bubbly spirit. Even though Terri is in her 40s, she has the high-pitched voice of a child and gets excited over the littlest accomplishments. Her lovable personality makes it easier for people all over the world to connect with her, even over the phone. As the director, Terri has the responsibility to read through the applications, contact hospitals about patients' conditions and medical histories, find the hospitals with the most expert specialists, keep in touch with current patients, and establish lasting relationships with recovered ones. She is able to accomplish all of this with only the aid of a computer, a telephone, and a calculator.

▓▓■ ACTIVITY 6.4 *In Your Own Work*

Revising for Focus and Development

Exchange your draft with another student and help each other find ways to improve focus and development. Look especially for lack of sufficient detail in description. Also remember other options for development in profiles, such as quotations and reported conversations. ■

▓▓■ ACTIVITY 6.5 *In Your Own Work*

Using Visual Supplementation

A picture may not be worth a thousand words, but having some can help your reader visualize your subject and places associated with the information gathered through interviews and conversations. They can also confirm what you say about your subject. Consider using photos if you have not included them; if you have included them, consider how to acquire better ones if you are not entirely happy with them. Also consider order and placement. If there is more than one, which should come first, second, and so on? Where in the paper should you place a photograph? Usually placing it close to the paragraph it is most relevant to works best. ■

Editing Your Revised Draft

Excessive repetition is a common editing problem. When the same word is used too frequently, readers notice. Writers seldom detect unintentional repetitions by silent reading; read your draft aloud so you hear them.

Because Molly Tilton's angle on the founder and the foundation itself was so respectful, and because Mr. Tye was so much her elder, Molly chose to refer to him throughout the essay as Mr. Tye rather than by his full name on first mention and from then on by his last name only, as is customary. This decision created some passages where editing for repetition would have streamlined the writing, such as the excerpt below from paragraph 5.

Original Version

Mr. Tye has provided hope to thousands of people all over the world with his selfless acts and has constantly encouraged others to share what they can for those in dire need. The impact Mr. Tye has had on others shows tangibly in the hundreds of thank you notes and hugs he has received since 2002, the year of the foundation's establishment. Mr. Tye's office is decorated with wooden sculptures from Africa and steel plaques from organizations that have honored Mr. Tye for his remarkable work. In May 2009, Catholic Charities honored Mr. Tye for his philanthropic efforts throughout the city of Boston; making him the first Jewish man to receive a Catholic Charities award.

There are several options for ways to refer to people:

1. Use a pronoun
2. Use a synonym or substitute word
3. Use a different version of the person's name

Using these options, Molly created the edited version below:

Revised Version

A. Raymond Tye has provided hope to thousands of people all over the world with his selfless acts and has constantly encouraged others to share what they can for those in dire need. The impact his generosity has had on others shows tangibly in the hundreds of thank you notes and hugs he has received since 2002, the year of the foundation's establishment. Mr. Tye's office is decorated with wooden sculptures from Africa and steel plaques from organizations that have honored him for his remarkable work. In May 2009, Catholic Charities honored him for his philanthropic efforts throughout the city of Boston, making Mr. Tye the first Jewish man to receive a Catholic Charities award.

▓▓■ ACTIVITY 6.6 *In Your Own Work*

Editing for Other Repeated Words

When you notice the same word appearing in sentences in sequence, there are two ways to reduce the repetition:

1. Think of a different word but one that still sounds natural—not as if you found it in the thesaurus.
2. Combine two of the sentences into one.

In the sixth paragraph of Molly's essay, the word *work* appears several times, as a verb and as a noun. Practice reducing repetitions by editing the passage below. Compare your edited version with those of others in your class.

Terri Carlson, the director of the foundation, has worked for the foundation for two years. Prior to this, she worked for United Liquors as credit manager. In recent years, Terri, a devoted wife and mother of two, has worked long hours while juggling her responsibilities at home. She wears business attire every day to work, showing her serious attitude, but her bright red hair exemplifies her bubbly spirit. . . . ■

■■■ ACTIVITY 6.7 *In Your Own Work*

Detecting and Editing Repetitions

Read through your revised draft with special attention to the problem of repeated words. You might ask someone else to read the paper and circle or underline repetitions if you have trouble detecting them. Use the suggestions in the student examples above to add more variety or conciseness as you reduce the repetitions. ■

REVISED STUDENT EXAMPLE

Tilton 1

Molly Tilton

Professor Channell

Writing 205

April 4, 2011

Mr. Santa Claus

In a back corner of United Liquors' headquarters in Braintree, Massachusetts,   1
lives are being saved. Mr. A. Raymond Tye, a prominent businessman and philanthropist, strides into his place of work one morning with his cane and a mission.
"Terri," he cries, "Come into my office to discuss some prospective patients for the
foundation, twin boys conjoined at the head. They need our help." From that point
the real work begins.

> Short introductory paragraph gets to the point and the action quickly. Gains reader interest and attention.

Tilton 2

At the end of Campanelli Drive sits a gray warehouse. The mirrored glass walls on   2
the sides of this building contribute a faintly contemporary architectural style, but the
building is of little significance to the town of Braintree otherwise. The only cars that
travel down the road are large supply trucks and employee vehicles. When you walk
into the building's lobby, Sheila, the Braintree division's secretary, greets you with a
smile and asks how she might assist you. On the first floor, over sixty United Liquors
employees work diligently in cubicles. Up the stairs, in a recently renovated part of the
building, you reach a common meeting room and a door to the right with a sign reading, "The Ray Tye Medical Aid Foundation." Inside are three cubicles, and in the back
left corner is Mr. Tye's personal office. Terri Carlson is the only employee of the foundation. Her cubicle has one large desk, one computer, a chair, two file cabinets, a printer,
and three cabinets full of office supplies, all she needs to operate this foundation.

> This and following paragraphs supply needed background knowledge.

The Ray Tye Medical Aid Foundation was started to offer financial assistance   3
to people around the world who suffer life-threatening illness and need in-hospital
medical care to save their lives. In honor of Tye's 80th birthday, his wife, friends and
family collected two million dollars in order to establish The Ray Tye Medical Aid
Foundation. This small foundation has helped to save or prolong 183 lives. Patients
have been helped no matter what their location, race, sex, or religious affiliation. The
patients that the foundation has helped are from all over the world, including the U.S.
This past year, I had the privilege of being the first volunteer to work at this foundation; it was in this capacity that I became closely acquainted with Terri and Mr. Tye.

> Establishes writer's connection with her subject and, therefore, her authority.

Mr. Tye is a first-generation entrepreneur who started his own company,   4
United Liquors, which went on to become one of the largest liquor distributors in
Massachusetts. Living a colorful life, he attended Tufts University, fought in World
War II, and fathered five children. Now in his 80's, he has dedicated his life to helping others, and received countless accolades for his philanthropic efforts. He always
dresses in professional attire, making him a serious business man, which most find
intimidating, until he lets out his vibrant smile. His appearance speaks to his kind
spirit, from his white bushy eyebrows to his portly belly. In fact, Terri often tells the
story of one patient, a cancer survivor, who referred to Tye as "Mr. Santa Claus."

> Needed background material, but includes personal details about Tye that make him human, engaging.

Mr. Tye has provided hope to thousands of people all over the world with his   5
selfless acts and has constantly encouraged others to share what they can for
those in dire need. The impact Mr. Tye has had on others shows tangibly in the
hundreds of thank you notes and hugs he has received since 2002, the year of the
foundation's establishment. Mr. Tye's office is decorated with wooden sculptures
from Africa and steel plaques from organizations that have honored Mr. Tye for his
remarkable work. In May 2009, Catholic Charities honored Mr. Tye for his philanthropic efforts throughout the city of Boston, making him the first Jewish man to
receive a Catholic Charities award. Mr. Tye states on the foundation's website:

> It is a strong belief of my own that giving should really be called receiving
> because the elemental act of giving returns many pleasant rewards to the giver.
> In fact, it might be said that there is not a more self-serving act than a liberal
> manifestation of generosity. . . . Seeing the happiness generosity creates in the
> recipients is another positive reinforcement—a big return for a small investment.

Accordingly, the motto of The Ray Tye Medical Aid Foundation is simply "We will
never stop caring."

Terri Carlson, the director of the foundation, has worked for the foundation for   6
two years. Prior to this, she worked for United Liquors as credit manager. In recent
years, Terri, a devoted wife and mother of two, has worked long hours while juggling her responsibilities at home. She wears business attire every day to work,
showing her serious attitude, but her bright red hair exemplifies her bubbly spirit.
Even though Terri is in her 40s, she has the high-pitched voice of a child and gets
excited over the littlest accomplishments. Her lovable personality makes it easier
for people all over the world to connect with her, even over the phone. As the
director, Terri has the responsibility to read through the applications, contact hospitals about patients' conditions and medical histories, find the hospitals with the
most expert specialists, keep in touch with current patients, and establish lasting
relationships with recovered ones. She is able to accomplish all of this with only
the aid of a computer, a telephone, and a calculator.

Use of memorable detail to confirm Tye's achievements.

Good use of material gathered from her subject's own writing.

Tilton 4

Each week, the foundation receives four or more lengthy applications from   7
people around the world seeking help. All prospective patients must fill out an
online application. Terri and Mr. Tye review all patients' applications but help only
those who face life-threatening conditions and do not have health insurance.

Recently, media in the United States told the story of twin Egyptian boys   8
whose heads were conjoined. These boys, Mohamed and Ahmed Ibrahim, are
patients that Tye discovered himself. On a Sunday morning in August 2002, he
read an article about them in *The Boston Globe* and decided to help them. Their
operation was estimated to cost two million dollars; the Ray Tye Medical Aid
Foundation donated $100,000, making it one of the leading donors. The thirty-four
hour operation was successful in October 2003, and the boys have been making
steady progress since then. After their extensive surgery and therapy, the boys
learned how to walk on their own and learned how to speak English.

> Use of specific, extended example to illustrate the help Tye's foundation provides.

Mohamed and Ahmed live happy and healthy lives with their family, thanks   9
to Mr. Tye and Terri's tireless efforts to make a difference in their lives. They were
able to see for themselves the progress the twin boys had made when they visited
Braintree, Massachusetts, in September 2009. At the time of the twins' visit, Mr.
Tye stated to a Boston news reporter: "If you can do something to save a life there
is an inner feeling of satisfaction that you can derive from nothing else."

> Short, to-the-point concluding paragraph wraps up the profile in a memorable way.

Courtesy of Molly Tilton

CHAPTER 7
Presenting Information

WITH MORE THAN FIVE BILLION GIGABYTES OF DIGITAL CONTENT CRE-ATED EACH DAY, no one can doubt that we live in the information age. With all this information at hand, and browsers like Google to help us find it, we can answer one key question about information rather easily: What is known about "x"? with "x" representing almost any topic. However, two other questions matter more when we write to communicate information:

- **What do my readers need or want to know?**
- **How can I help them understand what the information means?**

These questions are so important that no other purpose for writing has so many genres devoted to answering them: maps, brochures, newspaper and maga-zine articles, dictionaries, encyclopedias, journals for people in specialized areas of study, documentary films, websites, and owner's manuals, among many others. The list is so long and includes every communication medium because modern, open societies depend on access to information. Every context for writing—college, business, community, government, even personal communication—generates enormous amounts of informative writing. Presenting information well, then, is an important skill.

Sixteenth-century philosopher Sir Francis Bacon said, "Knowledge is power." But knowledge only has power when it is communicated well.

© Universal Images Group/Getty Images

What Is Presenting Information?

Information is **data,** *what we commonly call "the facts," interpreted and organized to make it useful to others.* By interpreting and present-ing the information we are exposed to, we construct **knowledge,** *our understanding of any subject.* "Knowledge is power," as the philoso-pher Francis Bacon said: It enables us to do things we otherwise could not do. For most of history we had no idea that microscopic organ-isms existed, much less that some cause disease. The science we call microbiology put all the information together and interpreted it, so that now we know this virus or that bacterium causes a particular disease. Because of such knowledge we have gained the power to both prevent and cure many diseases.

The Concept Close-Up shows the relation of data to information and knowledge.

CONCEPT CLOSE-UP   Assessing Data

Data (the facts) are *statements about a topic that are not in dispute.* From all the facts gathered about a topic, writers select **information,** *data a particular reader-ship needs or wants to know.* **Knowledge** results from *the interpretation the writer gives the information*—what the writer takes it to mean. The following triangle depicts the relation between data, information, and knowledge:

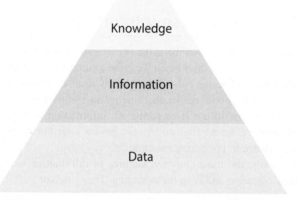

Because data are the base of the triangle, what we assume to be true beyond question, it is especially important to be critical of "the facts." Data must be all of the following:

Accurate	We can be misled by sources who thought they were telling the truth (misinformation); we can be misled by people who knew they were telling lies (disinformation).
Current	Data can be out of date: once true, but false now.
Sufficient for the need at hand	Data can be too little or too much: If too little, we do not have enough to go on; if too much, we are confused or overwhelmed.
Communicated in a way the intended readership can understand	Much technical data is accurate, current, and sufficient but useless to us because we do not understand the words and numbers that express it.

Why Present Information?

Knowledge is always power—the power to help others, to correct misinformation, to increase our understanding of ourselves and the world.

Communicating information is so important that it dominates writing in all areas of our society. In the academic world, textbooks, handouts, lectures, and course websites are all primarily informative. In the business world, e-mails, memos, reports, performance assessments, and quarterly earnings are primarily informative. In community life, local magazines, community newsletters, signs posted along streets announcing meetings, and most presentations done in schools and other civic gathering places are primarily informative. Indeed, our society moves by and through a sea of information that keeps everything afloat and at the same time threatens to drown us in too much of a good thing. For this reason we all have a high stake in managing information so that it does not overwhelm us. The next question, therefore, is especially important.

How Do Writers Present Information?

The key idea in informative writing is the *reader's need or desire to know something.* We lose sight of this sometimes when we go to a standard reference work, like a dictionary. What we find seems "just there," off by itself in a book without relation to anything else. Yet we would not be checking up on a word if we felt no need to know what it means or how to use it correctly. All information is motivated by need or desire, and therefore, for a writer, *sizing up a reader's need or desire and satisfying it* define the challenge of presenting information.

Consequently, the most common features of informative writing are meant to catch readers' attention and keep them reading. These include:

- **Anecdotes,** *short narratives* that help readers connect with the topic and relate it to their lives.

- **"Up-front" statements that indicate why the information matters,** or how readers can profit from knowing it.

- **Headings that indicate where the writer will answer the reader's key questions,** such as why something happens, how the reader can avoid bad consequences or act to make good ones more likely, and so on.

- **Statements that create a realistic context for readers,** such as how to buy or sell something wisely, solve practical problems, or understand a widely discussed issue better.

The simple truth is that we have abundant information and a shortage of reader attention. Informative writers, therefore, compete with each other to gain and hold readers. Remember this and you will understand how to compose effective informative writing.

Beyond reaching readers, what matters most is **genre,** *the specific kind of informative writing you are doing.* We are about to examine two of many informative genres: a magazine article and a newspaper story. As all genres do, each of these conforms to certain **conventional expectations**—that is, *what people expect to find in a specific genre.* As you read the following selections, consider how each meets your expectations for the kind of writing usually found in a magazine article and a news story.

READING **7.1**

Tomorrow, I Love Ya!

ERIC HOOVER

A senior writer for the Chronicle of Higher Education, *Eric Hoover specializes in college admission and enrollment issues. In this selection his subject is the extensive research done on procrastination, a problem for most people, including college students.*

Joseph R. Ferrari has a name for people who dillydally all the time. Sometimes, he spits out the term as if it were stale gum or a polysyllabic cuss word. When he dubs you a "chronic procrastinator," however, he does not mean to insult you. He is just using the psychological definition for someone who habitually puts things off until tomorrow, or next week, or whenever. The afflicted need not feel lonely: Research suggests that the planet is crawling with dawdlers.   1

Procrastinators vex Mr. Ferrari, a psychology professor at DePaul University, yet he owes much to the dilatorily inclined. Without them he could not have helped blaze a trail of inquiry into procrastination (the word comes from the Latin verb *procrastinare*—"to defer until morning"). The professor is as prompt as the sports car that shares his name, but he sees the symptoms of compulsive stalling everywhere.   2

Central point of piece: the complexity of procrastination.

Mr. Ferrari and other scholars from around the world are finding that procrastination is more complex—and pervasive—than armchair analysts might assume. And helping people climb out of their pits of postponement is not as simple as giving them a pill or a pep talk.   3

The task is particularly challenging in the hothouses of procrastination known as college campuses. Free time, long-term deadlines, and extracurricular diversions conspire against academic efficiency. Students are infamous for not tackling their assignments until the jaws of deadlines are closing.   4

Calls attention to the extent of the problem, especially among college students.

Professors may call such students slackers or sloths; psychologists define them as "academic procrastinators." According to recent studies, about 70 percent of college students say they typically procrastinate on starting or finishing their assignments (an estimated 20 percent of American adults are chronic procrastinators).   5

Choosing to do one task while temporarily putting another on hold is simply setting priorities, which allows people to cross things off their to-do lists one at a time. Procrastination is when one keeps reorganizing that list so that little or nothing on it gets done.   6

Emphasizes the seriousness of the problem by pointing to consequences.

For some students, that inertia has costs. Researchers say academic procrastination raises students' anxiety and sinks their self-esteem. The behavior also correlates with some of higher education's thorniest problems, including depression, cheating, and plagiarism among students.   7

Dozens of colleges have created counseling sessions or workshops for procrastinators. Yet Mr. Ferrari and other researchers say many institutions treat the problem superficially instead of helping students analyze their own thought processes and behavioral patterns in order to change them. Give a hard-core procrastinator nothing more than time-management tips, they warn, and you might as well hand him a page of hieroglyphics.   8

"Telling a chronic academic procrastinator to 'just do it' is not going to work," Mr. Ferrari says. "It's like telling a clinically depressed person to cheer up."   9

Learning about Loafers

Laggards have always been tough cases. Even God could not inspire St. Augustine of Hippo, the fourth-century philosopher and theologian, to act right away. As he slowly came to accept Christianity, Augustine wrote in *Confessions,* the future bishop wavered. Clinging to temporal pleasures, Augustine famously asked of God: "Give me chastity and continency—but not yet."   10

Late in his life, Leonardo da Vinci, the genius who missed deadlines, lamented his unfinished projects. Shakespeare's Hamlet pondered—and pondered—killing his uncle Claudius before sticking him in the final act. Grady Tripp, the English professor in Michael Chabon's novel *Wonder Boys,* couldn't finish his second book because he refused to stop writing it.   11

In a world of unmade beds and unwritten essays, the postponement of chores is commonplace. Now and again, humans put aside tasks with long-term rewards to savor immediate pleasures, like ice cream and movies, through a process called "discounting." For chronic procrastinators, however, discounting is a way of life.   12

> Introduces key term: Discounting.

The scientific study of procrastination was (appropriately enough) a late-blooming development relative to the examinations of other psychological problems. Only in the 1980s did researchers start unlocking the heads of inveterate loafers, who suffer from more than mere laziness.   13

Mr. Ferrari, a co-editor of *Procrastination and Task Avoidance: Theory, Research, and Treatment* (Plenum Publications, 1995), has helped clarify the distinction between delaying as an act and as a lifestyle. Not every student who ignores assignments until the last minute is an across-the-board offender, known to psychologists as a "trait procrastinator." Many students who drag their feet on term papers might never delay other tasks, such as meeting friends for dinner, showing up for work, or going to the dentist.   14

As Mr. Ferrari explains in *Counseling the Procrastinator in Academic Settings* (American Psychological Association, 2004), a book he edited with three other scholars, there is no typical profile of an academic procrastinator (though family dynamics may influence the behavior). Studies have found no significant relationship between procrastination and intelligence or particular Myers-Briggs personality types.   15

Research does show that academic procrastinators tend to lack self-confidence, measure low on psychologists' tests of "conscientiousness," get lost in wishful thoughts, and lie low during group assignments.   16

> Characteristics of academic procrastinators.

In one study, Mr. Ferrari found that students at highly selective colleges reported higher rates of academic procrastination than students from less selective institutions. In another, the motives for academic procrastination among students at an elite college differed from students' motives at a nonselective one (the former put off assignments because they found them unpleasant, while the latter did so because they feared failure or social disapproval).   17

Two types of procrastinators.

Mr. Ferrari identifies two kinds of habitual lollygaggers. "Arousal procrastinators" believe they work best under pressure and tend to delay tasks for the thrill. "Avoidant procrastinators" are self-doubters who tend to postpone tasks because they worry about performing inadequately, or because they fear their success may raise others' expectations of them.

18

Other findings complicate fear-of-failure theories. Some researchers say an inability to control impulses explains procrastinators best. And a recent study by Mr. Ferrari and Steven J. Scher, an associate professor of psychology at Eastern Illinois University, suggests that people who are typically negative avoid assignments that do not challenge them creatively or intellectually, whereas people who are typically positive more easily tackle less-stimulating tasks.

19

Science is not likely to resolve the mysteries of procrastination anytime soon. After all, among researchers a debate still rages over the very definition of procrastination. Mr. Scher suspects there are different types of the behavior, especially if one defines it as not doing what one thinks one should do.

20

"A common thing that many people put off is doing the dishes," Mr. Scher says. "But there are also times when those same people will all of a sudden find that doing the dishes is the most important thing they have to do—thereby putting off some other type of task."

21

Homework-Eating Dogs

Psychologists do agree on one thing: Procrastination is responsible for most of the world's homework-eating dogs. Where procrastinators go, excuses follow.

22

Links procrastination with lying to excuse it.

Students who engaged in academic procrastination said more than 70 percent of the excuses they gave instructors for not completing an assignment were fraudulent (the lies were most prevalent in large lecture classes taught by women who were "lenient"), Mr. Ferrari found in one study. In another, procrastinating students generally said they experienced a positive feeling when they fibbed; although they did feel bad when they recalled the lie, such remorse did not seem to prevent them from using phony excuses in the future.

23

Mr. Ferrari has also experimented with giving bonus points for early work. In a study published in the journal *Teaching of Psychology,* he found that such incentives prompted 80 percent of students to fulfill a course requirement to participate in six psychological experiments by a midpoint date. On average, only 50 percent had done so before he offered the inducement.

24

Major criticism of current approach of many professors to procrastination: students encouraged not to meet deadlines.

Mr. Ferrari believes that academe sends mixed messages about procrastination. Most professors talk about the importance of deadlines, but some are quick to bend them, particularly those who put a premium on being liked by their students. In one of Mr. Ferrari's studies, 90 percent of instructors said they did not require the substantiation of excuses for late work.

25

"We're not teaching responsibility anymore," Mr. Ferrari says. "I'm not saying we need to be stringent, strict, and inflexible, but we shouldn't be spineless. When we are overly flexible, it just teaches them that they can ignore the deadlines of life."

26

Ambivalence about deadlines pervades American culture. People demand high-speed results, whether they are at work or in restaurants. Yet this is also a land in which department stores encourage holiday shoppers to postpone their shopping until Christmas Eve, when they receive huge discounts. And each year on April 15, television news reporters from coast to coast descend upon post offices to interview (and celebrate) people who wait until the final hours to mail their tax returns.

27

"As a society," Mr. Ferrari says, "we tend to excuse the person who says 'I'm a procrastinator,' even though we don't like procrastinators."

28

But do all people who ignore assignments until the 11th hour necessarily suffer or do themselves harm?

29

One of Mr. Ferrari's former students, Mariya Zaturenskaya, a psychology major who graduated from DePaul last spring, says some last-minute workers are motivated, well organized, and happy to write a paper in one sitting. Although students who cram for tests tend to retain less knowledge than other students, research has yet to reveal a significant correlation between students' procrastination and grades.

30

A finding contrary to what many people think.

"Some students just need that deadline, that push," Ms. Zaturenskaya says. "Some people really are more efficient when they have less time."

31

Treating the Problem

Before Jill Gamble went to college, she had little time to waste. As a high-school student, she had earned a 3.75 grade-point average while playing three sports. Each night she went to practice, ate dinner, did her homework, and went to bed.

32

After matriculating at Ohio State University, however, her life lost its structure. At first, all she had to do was go to classes. Most days she napped, spent hours using Instant Messenger, and stayed up late talking to her suite mates.

33

As unread books piled up on her desk, she told herself her professors were too demanding. The night before her Sociology 101 final, she stayed up drinking Mountain Dew, frantically reading the seven chapters she had ignored for weeks. "My procrastination had created a lot of anxiety," Ms. Gamble recalls. "I was angry with myself that I let it get to that point."

34

Extended example of common college student procrastinator and efforts to remedy the problem.

She got a C-minus in the class and a 2.7 in her first quarter. When her grades improved only slightly in the second quarter, Ms. Gamble knew she needed help. So she enrolled in a course called "Strategies for College Success."

35

The five-year-old course uses psychological strategies, such as the taking of reasonable risks, to jolt students out of their bad study habits. Twice a week students spend class time in a computer lab, where they get short lectures on study skills. Students must then practice each skill on the computer by using a special software program.

36

Instructors use weekly quizzes to cut procrastination time from weeks to days and to limit last-minute cramming. The frequent tests mean one or two low scores will not doom a student's final grade, ideally reducing study-related stress.

37

Students complete assignments at their own pace, allowing faster ones to stay engaged and slower ones to keep up, yet there are immovable dates by which students must finish each set of exercises. Enrollees learn how to write and follow to-do lists that

38

reduce large tasks, such as writing an essay, into bite-size goals (like sitting down to outline a single chapter of a text instead of reading the whole book).

Each student must also examine his or her use of rationalizations for procrastinating. 39 The course's creator, Bruce W. Tuckman, a professor of education at Ohio State, says he also teaches students to recognize the underlying cause of procrastination, which he describes as self-handicapping.

> Another explanation for procrastination: provides ready excuse for not doing well.

"It's like running a full race with a knapsack full of bricks on your back," Mr. Tuckman 40 says. "When you don't win, you can say it's not that you're not a good runner, it's just that you had this sack of bricks on your back. When students realize that, it can be easier for them to change."

Many of the worst procrastinators end up earning the highest grades in the class, 41 Mr. Tuckman says. And among similar types of students with the same prior cumulative grade-point averages, those who took the class have consistently outperformed those who did not take it.

> Treatment for procrastination can work: The problem has solutions.

After completing the course, Ms. Gamble says, she stopped procrastinating and 42 went on to earn a 3.8 the next semester. Since then, she has made the dean's list regularly, and now helps counsel her procrastinating peers at Ohio State's learning center.

"In workshops, we'll say, 'How many of you identify yourselves as procrastinators?' 43 and they will throw their hands in the air and giggle, even though procrastination is a very negative thing," Ms. Gamble says. "Why do we do this so willingly? The answer is that we let ourselves procrastinate. If someone was doing it to us, we wouldn't be so willing to raise our hands."

A Universal Problem

Psychologists generally agree that the behavior is learned and that students choose 44 to procrastinate, even though they may feel helpless to stop. Mr. Ferrari, the DePaul professor, describes the behavior as a self-constructed mental trap that people can escape the same way smokers can kick the habit.

Mr. Tuckman qualifies his optimism by saying one cannot hope to cure procrastination 45 so much as reduce it.

"It's very hard to go from being a hard-core procrastinator to a nonprocrastinator," 46 says Mr. Tuckman, one of many researchers who has developed a scale that measures levels of procrastination. "You're just so used to doing it, there's something about it that reinforces it for you."

Scholars are learning that procrastination knows no borders. At a conference 47 of international procrastination researchers this summer at Roehampton University, in England, Mr. Ferrari and several other scholars presented a paper that compared the prevalence rates of chronic procrastination among adults in Australia, England, Peru, Spain, the United States, and Venezuela. They found that arousal and avoidant procrastinators were equally prevalent in all of the nations, with men and women reporting similar rates of each behavior.

Interesting cultural variation in attitudes toward procrastination.

That is not to say all cultures share the same view of procrastination. Karem Diaz, a professor of psychology at the Pontifical Catholic University of Peru, has studied the behavior among Peruvians, whose expectations of timeliness tend to differ from those of Americans.

48

"In Peru we talk about the 'Peruvian time,'" Ms. Diaz writes in an e-mail message. "If we are invited to a party at 7 p.m., it is rude to show on time. . . . It is even socially punished. Therefore, not presenting a paper on time is expected and forgiven."

49

Few Peruvians are familiar with the Spanish word "*procrastinacion*," which complicates discussions of the subject. "Some people think it is some sexual behavior when they hear the word," Ms. Diaz says. Yet the professor has been intrigued to find that some Peruvians identify themselves as procrastinators, and experience the negative consequences of the behavior even though social norms encourage it.

50

Strategies for helping people bridge the gap between their actions and intentions vary. A handful of colleges in Belgium, Canada, and the Netherlands have just begun to develop counseling programs that draw on cognitive and behavioral research. The early findings: Helping students understand why they dawdle and teaching them self-efficacy tends to lessen their procrastination—or at least make it more manageable.

51

Timothy A. Pychyl, an associate professor of psychology at Carleton University, in Ottawa, Ontario, says group meetings are a promising approach, particularly those in which students make highly specific goals and help each other resist temptations to slack off. "For many people, it's an issue of priming the pump . . . as simple as making a deal with oneself to spend 10 minutes on a task," Mr. Pychyl says. "At least the next day they can see themselves as having made an effort as opposed to doing nothing at all."

52

Clarry H. Lay, a retired psychology professor at York University, in Toronto, who continues to counsel student procrastinators, uses personality feedback to promote better "self-regulation" among students. In group sessions, he discusses the importance of studying even when one is not in the "right mood" and of setting aside a regular place to work. Some participants become more confident and efficient. Others see improvements, only to experience relapses.

53

Clever and memorable ending.

Each semester one in five students miss the first session. Some sign up early but never show, while others arrive late or attend sporadically. But Mr. Lay understands. The counselor is a chronic procrastinator himself.

54

Questions for Discussion

1. Hoover and the experts he cites do not mention the impact of technology on procrastination. How big a role does time spent on social networking or other online activities (watching videos, playing games) play in your

tendency to put off tasks? How big a role does it play in accomplishing such tasks?

2. Ferrari, one of the scholars Hoover cites, distinguishes "arousal procrastinators" from "avoidance procrastinators." State the difference in your own words. Do you think it is possible to sometimes be one, sometimes the other, depending on the task? Can arousal and avoidance be combined, working together to cause procrastination?

3. How did Hoover attempt to gain your attention at the beginning of the article? If you wanted to keep on reading, what did he say that piqued your interest?

■■■ *Thinking as a Writer*

What Is the Rhetorical Situation?

1. What is Hoover's *purpose* in writing this essay? What is his *angle* on the topic? How would you describe his *voice*?

2. Who is Hoover's intended *audience*? Is he writing for instructors, for college students who procrastinate, for all college students, for lawyers, or for some other more general readership? Is there anything in the article you can cite that implies his target readership?

3. Using the Concept Close-Up: Assessing Data (page 113) as a guide, answer the following questions: What data does Hoover draw on? How did the article inform you—that is, what does it say that is news to you? What do you know about procrastination as a result of the information he presented and how he led you to understand it? ■

■■■ *Collaborative Activity*

Organizing Headings

As a class or in small groups, analyze the structure of the four subheadings in Hoover's article. How does he divide each heading into parts, points, or kinds of information? Does his organization of the headings seem logical to you and easy to follow? Why or why not? ■

■■■ *Collaborative Activity*

Integrating Sources

> For more on using and documenting sources, see Chapters 19, 20, and 21.

Hoover handles source material well by integrating it into his prose; identifying the names and qualifications of his sources; and mixing summary, paraphrasing, and quoting. As a class, work through all or part of his article, studying what he does with each use of source material and listing the various techniques employed. ■

READING **7.2**

Major Survey Challenges Western Perceptions of Islam

AGENCE FRANCE-PRESSE (AFP)

The following news story comes from AFP, the French equivalent of our AP (Associated Press) or UPI (United Press International), whose purpose is to inform the public about what is happening in the world. As you read, consider how you might use the article if you were preparing to write a paper about Muslim popular opinion.

Feb 26, 2008

WASHINGTON (AFP)—A huge survey of the world's Muslims released Tuesday challenges Western notions that equate Islam with radicalism and violence. 1

The survey, conducted by the Gallup polling agency over six years and three continents, seeks to dispel the belief held by some in the West that Islam itself is the driving force of radicalism. 2

It shows that the overwhelming majority of Muslims condemned the attacks against the United States on September 11, 2001 and other subsequent terrorist attacks, the authors of the study said in Washington. 3

"Samuel Harris said in the *Washington Times* (in 2004): 'It is time we admitted that we are not at war with terrorism. We are at war with Islam,'" Dalia Mogahed, co-author of the book *Who Speaks for Islam,* which grew out of the study, told a news conference here. 4

"The argument Mr. Harris makes is that religion is the primary driver" of radicalism and violence, she said. 5

"Religion is an important part of life for the overwhelming majority of Muslims, and if it were indeed the driver for radicalisation, this would be a serious issue." 6

But the study, which Gallup says surveyed a sample equivalent to 90 percent of the world's Muslims, showed that widespread religiosity "does not translate into widespread support for terrorism," said Mogahed, director of the Gallup Center for Muslim Studies. 7

About 93 percent of the world's 1.3 billion Muslims are moderates and only seven percent are politically radical, according to the poll, based on more than 50,000 interviews. 8

In majority Muslim countries, overwhelming majorities said religion was a very important part of their lives—99 percent in Indonesia, 98 percent in Egypt, 95 percent in Pakistan. 9

But only seven percent of the billion Muslims surveyed—the radicals—condoned the attacks on the United States in 2001, the poll showed. 10

Moderate Muslims interviewed for the poll condemned the 9/11 attacks on New York and Washington because innocent lives were lost and civilians killed. 11

"Some actually cited religious justifications for why they were against 9/11, going as far as to quote from the Koran—for example, the verse that says taking one innocent life is like killing all humanity," she said. 12

Meanwhile, radical Muslims gave political, not religious, reasons for condoning the attacks, the poll showed.   13

The survey shows radicals to be neither more religious than their moderate counterparts, nor products of abject poverty or refugee camps.   14

"The radicals are better educated, have better jobs, and are more hopeful with regard to the future than mainstream Muslims," John Esposito, who co-authored *Who Speaks for Islam,* said.   15

"Ironically, they believe in democracy even more than many of the mainstream moderates do, but they're more cynical about whether they'll ever get it," said Esposito, a professor of Islamic studies at Georgetown University in Washington.   16

Gallup launched the study following 9/11, after which U.S. President George W. Bush asked in a speech, which is quoted in the book: "Why do they hate us?"   17

"They hate . . . a democratically elected government," Bush offered as a reason.   18

"They hate our freedoms—our freedom of religion, our freedom of speech, our freedom to vote and assemble and disagree with each other."   19

But the poll, which gives ordinary Muslims a voice in the global debate that they have been drawn into by 9/11, showed that most Muslims—including radicals—admire the West for its democracy, freedoms and technological prowess.   20

What they do not want is to have Western ways forced on them, it said.   21

"Muslims want self-determination, but not an American-imposed and defined democracy. They don't want secularism or theocracy. What the majority wants is democracy with religious values," said Esposito.   22

The poll has given voice to Islam's silent majority, said Mogahed.   23

"A billion Muslims should be the ones that we look to, to understand what they believe, rather than a vocal minority," she told AFP.   24

Muslims in 40 countries in Africa, Asia, Europe and the Middle East were interviewed for the survey, which is part of Gallup's World Poll that aims to interview 95 percent of the world's population.   25

Questions for Discussion

1. All informing is motivated by some need or desire to know something. What need or desire does this article satisfy? How does it attempt to catch and hold reader attention?
2. Information often corrects misinformation or disinformation, which in turn leads to misunderstanding. How might this article correct some misunderstanding?
3. Information varies in the degree of importance it has for individual people. How important is the information in this article for you? How could you use it for a paper in a college course?

■■■ *Thinking as a Writer*

What Is the Rhetorical Situation?

1. What is the writer's *purpose* in this article? What is the AFP's *angle* on the topic? How would you describe the piece's *voice*?

2. Who is this article's intended *audience*? Is it written for people who are experts about Muslim culture and beliefs, for people who are curious to learn more about Muslims, for people with some degree of bias against them, for Muslims themselves, for politicians, for the French or American reading public, or for some combination of these groups? Is there anything in the article you can cite that implies its target readership?

3. Using the Concept Close-Up: Assessing Data (page 113) as a guide, answer the following question: How does this AFP article turn information into knowledge? Specifically, how does it interpret the data from the survey so that readers understand what it means? ■

The Assignment

Compose an informative article that satisfies a readership's need or desire to know something. Depending on your instructor's requirements, your article can draw from personal experience (for example, a hobby, sport, or internship) and incorporate information gained from all forms of research (for example, print and online materials, interviews, and questionnaires).

What Can I Write About?

Promising informative topics can come from readings in any college class, from national and local news, from personal experience, or from online sources. Consider the following possibilities:

- **Personal experience.** Hobbies, sports, physical fitness, diets, gardening, cooking, and the like can be promising topics.

- **Work experience.** Businesses rely on the flow of information, so topics where you work are good possibilities. You may be an expert on something interesting to other people, such as how to get the best deal in purchasing a car.

- **Your community.** Community affairs are also a rich source of informative topics, such as the rules that govern home renovation in certain historical districts or the policies for coping with homeless people.

Consider writing in one of the common informative genres:

- **Book or movie review.** Provides guidance for what to read or see.

- **Technical description.** Explains how something works—for example, hydroponics, growing plants in liquid mediums rather than soil.

- **Cause-and-effect essay.** Explains why things happen, such as the increase in allergies when most other human health problems have declined in the United States.

- **Report.** Summarizes the findings of surveys, tests, or field observations—for example, how effective red-light cameras are or how well new software for class registration works.

How Do I Present Information? Questioning the Rhetorical Situation

Begin by picturing a **rhetorical situation** for your writing project, a real-world context for communicating. You should consider the *key variables in any act of communication:* a writer with something to say, a reader the writer wishes to reach, and a kind of text appropriate to the writing task. These three variables will affect many decisions in the composing process.

Writer: What Is My Purpose, and What Impression Should Readers Have of Me?

Your purpose is to provide accurate, current, and sufficient information to meet the needs and interests of your readers. "Accurate" and "current" simply mean that you should avoid, to the best of your ability, **misinformation,** *data that misrepresents reality or was once accurate but is not so now.* Because misinformation is common, both in print and Internet sources, check the information you find against other sources, especially if the content seems biased, is inconsistent with common sense or with what you know already, or is otherwise suspect. "Sufficient" is entirely relative to your reader: If you are an experienced stamp collector, for instance, you could easily overwhelm readers just taking up the hobby with too much information or assume that they know things beginners would not know.

See Chapter 17, pages 350–56, for guidance on how to evaluate sources.

Informative writing has a wide range of voices and styles, depending mainly on the topic and the readership. A light touch joined with humor might work well for informing amateur cooks about the amazing array of olive oils currently sold, but a piece for parents about the relative safety of car seats for young children must sound serious and concerned throughout.

An informative writer should be a helpful guide and therefore use **plain style:** *simple, direct sentence structure and ordinary, everyday vocabulary and illustrations.* Include technical information only as required, and be sure to explain what you include at the level your audience can comprehend.

Audience: Who Is My Reader?

The key question in selecting your readership is: **Who would profit most from knowing what I know?**

All good writing is reader aware, but informative writing is especially so because *what qualifies as information depends on who is reading it.* For example, an article describing ways to protect your computer from viruses might be informative for a new computer user but not informative to a technical expert or to someone who does not own a computer.

Select your readership with care, paying special attention to the background knowledge you assume readers have. If you assume too little, you will have to provide too much background; if you assume too much, you can have a readership you cannot reasonably expect to inform. An article about the latest computer game, for example, might be written for readers at an intermediate or advanced level of experience but not written for someone without experience or for people who create such games and thus know as much or more than you do.

Text: What Moves Can I Make?

The basic moves of informative writing are:

- Identify your topic.
- Define and illustrate key terms.
- Supply background information as needed, depending on the level of knowledge you assume your readers have.
- Provide a context for your topic, such as how common procrastination is, misinformation about Muslims, or the costs of some problem in the workplace.
- Indicate why your topic matters—for example, it will help people cope better with procrastination; it will show that the opinions of a minority of Muslims should not be confused with the opinions of most Muslims; it will help people vote as well-informed citizens.
- Limit your topic as necessary to meet space requirements (for instance, discuss the amount of time wasted as a result of some workplace problem).
- Divide your topic into parts, and divide those parts into parts, so that your reader can concentrate on one large point or issue at a time and so that each large point or issue has a set of paragraphs that deal *only* with that issue or point.
- Depending on the nature of your topic, describe *how* it works, *what* motivates it, *how* to use it appropriately or safely, and so on, *going into detail in those places where your reader most needs the information.*

For examples of these strategies at work, consult Readings 7.1 and 7.2 or the revised student example at the end of this chapter.

How Do I Present Information? Engaging the Writing Process

No two people compose in exactly the same way, and even the same person may go through the writing process in different ways with different assignments. Nevertheless, because no one can attend to everything at once, there are phases in handling any significant writing task. You begin by preparing to write, generating content and finding your angle.

The next phase is planning and drafting your paper, getting a version, however rough it may be, on paper or screen so that you have something to work with during the next two stages: (1) revising your draft, making changes to the content, arrangement, and style of your writing, and (2) editing your draft to correct problems at the paragraph and sentence level, such as lack of focus and coherence, awkward or unclear sentences, and errors of grammar, spelling, and punctuation.

Exploring Your Topic

In this phase you are *finding something to say,* generating ideas and content, which includes discovering your angle or point of view.

Let's assume the most challenging informative writing situation: a "cold" topic, one selected by someone else—a professor, a boss, the head of a committee you are on—and one that requires research because you know little or nothing about it. How do you begin? Organizing your efforts by answering the following questions will help.

What Does the Task Require?

Some informing situations call for only minimal interpretation. If your assignment is to trace sales patterns over the past ten years for a particular item your company makes, you can do that with charts and graphs combined with short commentary. In contrast, if your assignment is to write about potential power struggles among the various ethnic groups in Afghanistan, you will need to do more than tell your readers about the ethnic groups. You will need to analyze the potential for conflict, cooperation, and alliances, not only as they exist now but also as they are likely to exist in the future. Clearly, in this case, far more interpretation is necessary and appropriate.

However, make *a firm distinction between informing and arguing.* Informative writing typically avoids **open advocacy**—that is, *defending a position on a controversial issue with the intent to convince or persuade your readers.* Because many informative topics are controversial, you may need to describe the range of existing opinion. In interpreting existing opinion, you can say which point of view seems most acceptable to you and explain why. However, defending your opinion or someone else's at length would be inappropriate.

What Research Will I Need to Do?

We recommend brainstorming your topic first, writing down what you know and think about it in two or three fifteen-minute sessions separated by short breaks. Write whatever comes to mind without being concerned about how good it is. Step back and examine what you have; then ask, **"What do I need to know?"** Make a list in answer to this question, and you are prepared to get the most from research.

If you are assigned to write about a topic you know little about, organizing a "plan of attack" by answering some preparatory questions—such as, "What do I already know?" and "What do I still need to know?"—will help get the process rolling.

© Laurence Mouton/ PhotoAlto/PunchStock/ Getty Images, RF

THE ART OF QUESTIONING   Assessing News Stories

When you encounter a news story in doing research, use these questions to help you assess it.

1. **What is the writer's point of view?** Every news story is written by someone who has a point of view, a purpose for writing, and the potential for bias.
2. **Who would find this story worth reading?** Information is told to someone, some audience or readership.

3. **What makes this information newsworthy?** Information is published because it is newsworthy: that is, it is surprising, interesting.

4. All news stories include answers to the prime journalistic questions: **Who? What? When? Where? Why? How?** Answer these questions for the article you are assessing, being careful to distinguish what the writer says from sources cited.

5. **Who and what are mentioned and why?** News stories often mention people, books, organizations, conferences, and the like connected with the story. Use the references to pursue further research.

Information comes either from print and online sources or from **field research,** which involves *collecting your own information, such as conducting polls, interviewing experts, making firsthand observations, or carrying out simple experiments.* See Chapter 15, Planning a Research Project, and Chapter 16, Finding Sources, for guidance. Be sure to keep careful notes as you work your way through the source material (see pages 358–63) so you know which information came from what source and so you do not confuse your own comments about the source material with the material itself.

How Can I Evaluate the Research?

Answering the following questions will be especially useful when evaluating research.

1. **Is the data current?** Remember that a book or article published this year is likely to contain information that is at least two to three years old. Check it against more up-to-date sources of information, such as online data banks.

2. **How was the data generated?** In general we rely on a source's reputation for reliability, credentials, and qualifications. However, some information requires more. The newspaper article about Muslim popular opinion we examined earlier (pages 122–23) does not tell us what questions the 50,000 respondents were asked, what choices they were given in answering the questions, how they were selected, or the time period during which the poll was taken. All of these factors can strongly influence the results, so we cannot rely simply on the good reputation of the Gallup organization. We need to find out more to ensure that the results are reliable.

3. **What sources did your source use?** Most published articles cite multiple sources of information. For information you are relying on most, go to the primary source: for example, the reporter who was an eyewitness to the event, the scientist who conducted the experiment, or the expert who recorded the observations. In short, *consult the sources your source cites.*

4. **What interpretations are consistent with the data?** The first three questions focus attention on assessing your information; this question asks you to assess your own response to it. No one can do research without forming conclusions about what the information means. Forming conclusions helps you interpret the information that matters most in informing your reader. However, *let the best information you have drive your interpretation rather than imposing an interpretation you had before researching the information.* Put another way, adjust your thinking to the information rather than the information to your thinking.

■■■■ ACTIVITY 7.1 *Writer's Notebook*

Evaluating Sources

First, use the guidelines for evaluating sources (Chapter 17, pages 350–56) to assess your sources. Some might be too old, not directly relevant, or suspect because the writer may be biased by affiliation with a special interest group.

Second, sort the sources that are left into two groups by relevance and quality:

■ The two or three you will rely on the most.

■ The two or three you will probably use less, such as for only one section or paragraph in your paper.

As you assess your sources, be sure to preserve your thinking in notes to yourself. You may need to refresh your memory as you write and revise. ■

Preparing to Write

In evaluating your sources, you are already sorting out information you might use from all the information you have.

How Can I Decide Which Information to Include?

Consider the following questions:

1. **What do my readers know already?** You can either not mention such information or briefly refer to it to remind your readers.

2. **What do my readers need to know?** This is the key question. For most topics you can find much more general information than you can possibly include. However, what counts is only (1) what will be news to your readers, information they do not have, and (2) selecting from that news what is most relevant to how your readers will use the information. In a student essay about illegal immigration, for example, the writer selected information she considered most relevant to voters in the upcoming general election. That is, she asked herself, "Of everything I know about illegal immigration, what do well-informed voters need to know?" Ask yourself a similar question in deciding what information to include on any topic.

How Can I Find My Angle?

1. **What impact do you want your information to have?** In informative writing, what even qualifies as information depends on your readers. It makes sense, then, that your angle will also be reader-centered. The student example (pages 135–41) provides a good illustration of angle. The student wanted to impress upon her readers that not treating people kindly at work is not just a social or personnel problem but a big financial problem.

2. **In what framework is my information best understood?** In the case of illegal immigration, economics provided the best angle because supply-and-demand drives the entire process. There are usually jobs on our side of the border, well-paid jobs from a migrant worker's point of view, and grinding poverty and lack of opportunity on Mexico's side. Readers must understand the

economics of illegal immigration to understand the topic at all. Hence, the student's choice of economics as her framework was ideal for her topic.

Drafting Your Paper

Begin by recalling what informative writing does: *It makes information relevant or interesting for readers; turns facts into something that matters, has meaning, a point.* What this means in practice is that selection depends on giving your readers "news"—things they do not know—and getting them to understand why the new information matters.

Select from all your information *what counts or is significant:* the results of the latest research, data your readers will not know, information that is surprising and/or that runs counter to what most people believe or imagine. Also select information *based on the story you can tell about it*—that is, in how it comes together to make a point, illuminate a problem, or clarify a cause or effect.

What Stance and Voice Are Appropriate for Presenting Information?

It is important to inform your readers, to provide facts or data they do not know or may have forgotten. Even more important, however, is interpreting the information you provide. *What you have to say about the information should be center stage.*

Consequently, reconsider your **stance** and angle, your point of view on your topic. For example, which of the following are you doing?

- Challenging beliefs and attitudes based on misinformation or disinformation?
- Enabling your readers to do something they otherwise could not do or not do as well?
- Explaining a cause-and-effect relationship?
- Describing a problem and ways to solve it?
- Giving advice based on experience with your topic?

There are many other possibilities—*what matters is that you know what you are doing and why.* Perhaps you will change your angle as you write; perhaps in assessing your draft you will find another angle you like better and write the second draft around it. Nevertheless, being as clear as you can about what motivates the information you are providing helps to focus and sustain your first draft.

Also consider what **voice** is appropriate for this aim and genre. Information requires your take on what the information means and why it matters, and therefore your voice will emerge mainly in your commentary. Eric Hoover's voice (see pages 115–20) emerges best in *commenting on his information,* as, for example, in the following sentences:

> Mr. Ferrari and other scholars from around the world are finding that procrastination is more complex—and pervasive—than armchair analysts might assume. And helping people climb out of their pits of postponement is not as simple as giving them a pill or a pep talk.
>
> The task is particularly challenging in the hothouses of procrastination known as college campuses. Free time, long-term deadlines, and extracurricular diversions conspire against academic efficiency. Students are infamous for not tackling their assignments until the jaws of deadlines are closing.

The underlined words convey Hoover's attitude toward procrastination, the seriousness of the problem, the urgent need to understand and attend to it.

How Might I Use Images and Graphics to Present Information?

When appropriate, plan to use photographs, drawings, maps, tables, and graphics for presenting readers with new information. Use graphics when you can because they:

- Take less space than giving information in prose.

- Are easier for readers to understand, remember, and refer to.

- Separate data from your commentary on what the data mean.

Here's the basic principle in deciding whether to use graphics: *Use graphics to present information; use writing to tell your story about the information.*

Developing and Organizing Your Information

Develop an informative article effectively by doing the following:

- Pull together closely related material from several sources.

- Offer your own comments—explanations, illustrations, and ways of understanding the source material.

Consider this example from Hoover's article:

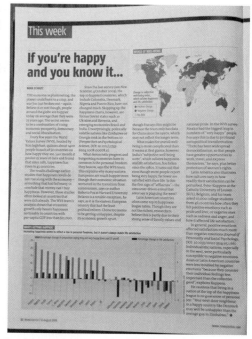

> Mr. Ferrari identifies two kinds of habitual lollygaggers. "Arousal procrastinators" believe they work best under pressure and tend to delay tasks for the thrill. "Avoidant procrastinators" are self-doubters who tend to postpone tasks because they worry about performing inadequately, or because they fear their success may raise others' expectations of them.
>
> Other findings complicate fear-of-failure theories. Some researchers say an inability to control impulses explains procrastinators best. And a recent study by Mr. Ferrari and Steven J. Scher, an associate professor of psychology at Eastern Illinois University, suggests that people who are typically negative avoid assignments that do not challenge them creatively or intellectually, whereas people who are typically positive more easily tackle less-stimulating tasks.
>
> Science is not likely to resolve the mysteries of procrastination anytime soon. After all, among researchers a debate still rages over the very definition of procrastination. Mr. Scher suspects there are different types of the behavior, especially if one defines it as not doing what one thinks one should do.

Organizing information boils down to *answering reader questions in a sequence that makes sense.* The answer to one question implies another question, the answer to which implies yet another question, until you run out of questions that need

Images and graphics are an effective way to present information because they are easy for readers to understand and they add visual interest.
© The McGraw-Hill Companies, Mark Dierker

See online Chapter 23 for detailed guidance on the design and use of visuals.

Passage pulls together information from two sources, defines two kinds of procrastinators, and indicates how complex the procrastination problem is.

answering to adequately inform your audience. In "Tomorrow, I Love Ya!" (pages 115–20), Hoover answers many questions, such as:

- What is procrastination? (paragraphs 1–6)
- What harm does it do? (paragraph 7)
- Why do people procrastinate? (paragraphs 18–21)
- What can be done about procrastination? (paragraphs 36–42)

▓▓▓ ■ ACTIVITY 7.2 *In Your Own Work*

Planning Your Draft

You have the information selected from the research you did for your topic. You know the readers you want to reach. Now imagine a conversation with your readers. Given your topic, what questions would they ask? List those questions as they occur to you. Look also at the information you have selected. What questions do they answer? List those as well.

Looking at your list of questions, ask, **"What question comes first?"** Often it will be the definitional question, **"What is it?"** Sometimes the first question is, **"Why does my topic matter?"** Or, **"What background knowledge does my reader need to understand or appreciate the importance of my topic?"**

Whatever you decide the first question must be, it will imply the next, which in turn will imply still another. Order your questions accordingly, and you have a plan for your draft. ■

Revising Your Draft

When you complete your draft, do a self-assessment. The revision questions that follow will help.

1. Early in the paper **have you indicated why your information is important?** How does it relate to your reader's life, crucial decisions, or topics she or he would find interesting?

2. Facts or data amount to misinformation if they are not reported accurately. **Are there any instances where the facts or data you report seem unlikely or contradictory?** Check what you say the facts are against your source.

3. Currency matters because information becomes misinformation if the data is seriously out of date. **Are there any instances where data cited might be too old?**

4. Information must be sufficient for the need at hand, which means there must be enough to satisfy your readers. **Are there places where you need more than you provide? Are there places where you offer too much,** which might confuse or bore your readers?

5. Information does no good if your readers cannot understand it. **Have you explained what the information means** *at the level appropriate to your readership?*

6. Informative writers need to be consistent in their assumptions about what their readers know and think about the topic. **Have you assumed too much or too little about what your readers know before reading your paper?** Have you

addressed misconceptions and unwarranted positive or negative attitudes they are likely to have?

7. **Have you adopted an angle, a single point of view, to help your readers follow your presentation?** Have you limited your discussion only to matters relevant to your angle?

8. **Have you organized your information into sections—major divisions of your topic—and structured each section to develop content relevant to that section only?** Would using headings, as Eric Hoover does (pages 115–20), help both you and your reader understand your paper's organization better?

9. **In reporting your data, have you mixed quotation, paraphrase, and summary? Have you identified the qualifications of your source?**

10. **Are there places where the information could be handled more efficiently by using visuals, such as photographs, drawings, and/or graphics?** If you have used graphics or plan to add them in revision, be sure to refer to each graphic and discuss what it means in your paper.

Excerpt from Student Amie Hazama's Draft

When writers use subheadings to identify the purpose of different sections of their papers, they still need to attend to the need for transitions as well, to show how each subdivision connects with the one before. This paper uses APA (American Psychological Association) style, so you will notice some differences from MLA style in the way sources are cited. Here is an example from the draft of the student paper printed in final form on pages 135–41.

Introduction

Hazama's first subheading.

A typical day at the office begins for Amanda. Walking to her cubicle, she passes Joe, who seems in a hurry and returns her "Good morning" with just a nod. Later, in a meeting, a phone goes off, distracting everyone. The owner shuts it off but does not offer an apology. On her lunch break, Amanda fills the empty coffee pot in the kitchen and throws out the empty sugar packages lying crumpled on the counter. After lunch, her boss asks her to make some copies, but first she has to spend extra time fixing the jammed photocopier. Back at her desk, she tries to concentrate on a project while two co-workers talk loudly in the next cubicle about a basketball game the night before. Finally, after a long day at work, Amanda is fatigued and stressed.

What Is Workplace Incivility?

Hazama's second subheading.

Workplace incivility is the subject of much research. Christine Pearson and Christine Porath (2005) define the problem as "low intensity deviant behavior that violates workplace norms for mutual respect and may or may not be intended to harm the target" (p. 8). It is called "low intensity" because it is subtle, often unconscious, and frequently not even recognized by managers and workers. Examples of uncivil behavior range from sending a nasty, demeaning note and publicly undermining an employee's credibility to not returning phone calls and failing to acknowledge others in the hall. More extreme examples include bullying by bosses (Hauser, 2011).

The problem with Hazama's draft is the writing's **flow,** its *movement from paragraph to paragraph.* In her revised version, she opened the second section with a short transitional paragraph to show the connection between the two subdivisions of the paper.

What Is Workplace Incivility?

Little acts of insensitivity like those described above are just part of the job for many employees. However, they are also part of a problem that is costing businesses in lost productivity and workers in lost job satisfaction.

Editing Your Revised Draft

A rule of thumb is that no more than 10 percent of the total words in your paper should be direct quotations. (See Chapter 18, pages 364–65 for more about when and when not to use direct quotations.) The solution is to use paraphrase, but when the source contains simple data, rewording it adequately takes some effort. In the original passage below, Hazama's wording is too close to that of the source.

Original Version of the Draft

In the book *Rude Awakenings,* Gonthier (2002), researchers found that as a result of workplace incivility 22% decreased work efforts, 10% decreased the amount of time spent at work, 37% reduced their commitment to the organization, and 12% quit companies to avoid rude instigators (p. 26).

The actual source wording was: "The researchers found that as a result of uncivil behavior at work:

- 22 percent of respondents intentionally decreased work efforts,
- 10 percent decreased the amount of time they spent at work (absenteeism),
- 28 percent lost time avoiding instigators, . . .
- 37 percent reduced their commitment to the organization, . . . and
- 12 percent actually quit companies to avoid rude instigators."

In the edited version Hazama made the wording more her own.

Edited Version

In her book *Rude Awakenings,* Gonthier (2002) reports that 22% of the victims of incivility decreased their work efforts, 10% increased their absenteeism, 37% felt less commitment to their employer, and 12% went so far as to quit their jobs to get away from the offenders (p. 26).

▣▣■ ACTIVITY 7.3 *In Your Own Work*

Editing for Adequate Paraphrasing

When editing, pay special attention to the passages of information you have taken from sources. You may need to do more rewording to avoid accidental plagiarism, which is just as serious as intentional plagiarism. You may want to recast some of the material into charts or other visuals, not only to avoid a poor paraphrase but also to present the information more vividly. ■

Running head: BEING NICE IS GOOD BUSINESS   1

Being Nice Is Good Business

Amie Hazama

Southern Methodist University

BEING NICE IS GOOD BUSINESS 2

Being Nice Is Good Business

A typical day at the office begins for Amanda. Walking to her cubicle, she 1
passes Joe, who seems in a hurry and returns her "Good morning" with just a nod.
Later, in a meeting, a phone goes off, distracting everyone. The owner shuts it off
but does not offer an apology. On her lunch break, Amanda fills the empty coffee
pot in the kitchen and throws out the empty sugar packages lying crumpled on
the counter. After lunch, her boss asks her to make some copies, but first she has
to spend extra time fixing the jammed photocopier. Back at her desk, she tries to
concentrate on a project while two co-workers talk loudly in the next cubicle about
a basketball game the night before. Finally, after a long day at work, Amanda is
fatigued and stressed.

What Is Workplace Incivility?

Little acts of insensitivity like those described above are just part of the job 2
for many employees. However, they are also part of a problem that is costing businesses in lost productivity and workers in lost job satisfaction.

Workplace incivility is the subject of much research. Christine Pearson and 3
Christine Porath (2005) define the problem as "low-intensity deviant behavior that
violates workplace norms for mutual respect and may or may not be intended to
harm the target" (p. 8). It is called "low-intensity" because it is subtle, often unconscious, and frequently not even recognized by managers and workers. Examples
of uncivil behavior range from sending a nasty, demeaning note and publicly
undermining an employee's credibility to not returning phone calls and failing
to acknowledge others in the hall. More extreme examples include bullying by
bosses (Hauser, 2011).

Incivility is the opposite of civility, which is being aware of and respecting 4
others. P.M. Forni is a civility expert and Professor of Italian Literature at Johns
Hopkins University. In his book *Choosing Civility,* Forni states, "Courtesy, politeness, manners, and civility are all, in essence, forms of awareness. Being civil
means being constantly aware of others and weaving restraint and consideration

---

Hazama decided to use an anecdotal introduction just as Eric Hoover did in his article on procrastination. After reading through this paper, consider what other options would have made an equally effective opening to draw in readers.

Hazama uses questions as subheadings to let the reader know what they will learn in each section of the paper.

Hazama uses the comparison mode of development to define the concept of incivility.

Hazama's angle is to show the wearing effects of incremental exposure to small acts of incivility. She wants to make readers care about the victims.

This paper is documented according to APA (American Psychological Association) style, which is commonly used in the social sciences. See pages 411–34 for a full treatment of APA style.

BEING NICE IS GOOD BUSINESS   3

into the very fabric of this awareness" (Forni, 2002, p. 9). Forni's "Three R's" of

civility are "respect, restraint, and responsibility" (as cited in Hauser, 2011). Saying

a simple "please" and "thank you," putting trash in the proper receptacles, and sig-

naling before making a right hand turn are examples of civility (Forni, 2002, p. 9).

Civility is everywhere in daily life. Unfortunately, so is incivility.

What Are the Causes of Workplace Incivility?

Incivility has become common in the workplace. Pearson and Porath (2005, p. 7)   5

surveyed close to 800 U.S. employees to find out about their personal observations

of incivility while at work. Ten percent said they witnessed it on a daily basis, and

twice that number, twenty percent, said they themselves were victims of it "at least

once per week." Experts give several reasons for the increase. Oddly, one cause

suggested by Giovinella Gonthier (2002), a civility consultant in Chicago, is the rise

of equality in the workplace, caused by the feminist and civil rights movements

of the 1960s. In the past, people who were superiors showed their high positions

through manners and other "rituals of behavior" (p. 8), but in a more democratic soci-

ety, we have dropped the manners that used to "prop up" unequal relationships (p.

9). In that same period, young people disillusioned by government and the Vietnam

War "lost respect for tradition," and this generation went on to raise their children

permissively. Everything just became more casual (Gonthier, 2002, pp. 4–5).

Pearson and Porath (2005) bring in a more recent cause: In our high-tech,   6

fast-paced workplaces, people believe being nice takes too much time and

"impersonal modes of contact do not require courtesies of interaction . . ." (p. 7).

Also, there is the "me first" attitude common in the competitive workplace (p. 7)

and the Gordon Gekko types, with the "impetuous, rude, 'everyone else be

damned' personality" that many people associate with success ever since the

movie *Wall Street* (Gonthier, 2002, p. 3).

What Are the Ramifications of Incivility at Work?

All of this incivility is costly to businesses. Porath estimates that "stress and   7

lost productivity" as a result of incivility costs the United States' total economy

---

As a transition into the causes of incivility, Hazama sets up a context for learning more about incivility—its prevalence in the workplace today.

Hazama now turns from the causes of the problem in business to the effects on business.

BEING NICE IS GOOD BUSINESS   4

multi-billion dollars each year (as cited in Hauser, 2011). Pearson and Porath (2005)

have found that "incivility corrodes organizational culture and that employees who

are on the receiving end will respond in ways that are costly to their organiza-

tions" (p. 8). For example, two thirds of the victims of incivility reported that they put

less effort into their work, four out of five said they lost time worrying about bad

experiences, and 63% said they went out of their way to avoid being around the

person who offended them (Hauser, 2011). In her book *Rude Awakenings,* Gonthier

(2002) reports that 22% of the victims of incivility decreased their work efforts, 10%

increased their absenteeism, 37% felt less commitment to their employer, and 12%

went so far as to quit their jobs to get away from the offenders (p. 26). Incivility and

disengagement go hand in hand, and they result in a very high level of people

who are not actively engaged with their jobs. A Gallup study (2006) found that only

27% of workers reported feeling "engaged" while at work, while 59% described

themselves as "not engaged." Still another 14% were "actively disengaged," which

means they purposefully undermined the efforts of their co-workers.

> Note that Hazama has done a good job of synthesizing sources. This paragraph blends information from her three major sources.

     There are additional costs to management. Resolving worker conflicts can   8

take up 13% of executives' time, almost seven weeks of the year for any one boss

(Pearson & Porath, 2005, p. 8). Replacing workers who leave can cost as much

as 2.5 times the annual salary of the job if it is a high-profile job and interviewees

have to be flown in and paid to move (Gonthier, 2002, p. 27). Replacing lost cus-

tomers is another concern because sales will decline if disgruntled workers are in

customer service positions and take out their frustrations on the customers, a com-

mon occurrence. Forni (2002) states, "A stressed, fatigued, or distressed person is

less inclined to be patient and tolerant, to think before acting, and to be aware of

the needs of others" (p. 139). Gonthier (2002) reports that 58 to 62% of customers

will change to a different company if employees treat them rudely (pp. 30–31).

> A logical question to end this discussion is, "What can be done to solve the problem?"

What Can Be Done to Reduce Workplace Incivility?

     In order to accomplish civility in the workplace, leaders must lead the way.   9

Robert D. Ramsey (2008), who works in personnel administration and writes for

BEING NICE IS GOOD BUSINESS   5

management publications, says supervisors have the ability to do the most to turn

around a bad working atmosphere (p. 4) and "create a culture of civility at work" (p. 5).

Ramsey has devised a six-step action plan. First, managers must act as role models;

they must represent civility in all their actions. Forni agrees, saying, "The attitude of

the leader . . . has an enormous impact on the overall climate" of the workplace (as

cited in Hauser, 2011). Programs like CREW (Civility, Respect, and Engagement in

the Workplace) have shown that when leaders set the example, civility has a way of

going viral, "infecting" other workers to act in equally courteous ways (Hauser, 2011).

Secondly, Ramsey (2008) says business relationships should become more   10

personal, encouraging considerate and respectful behavior. A worker is more likely

to act in a rude fashion through an impersonal encounter through the telephone or

e-mail. Some businesses will not allow e-mails between workers who have offices

on the same floor (p. 5). Next, issues between workers must be addressed. A leader

needs to actively mediate disputes and remind workers of expectations and bound-

aries for behavior. Pearson and Porath (2005) echo this advice. They tell leaders,

"When incivility occurs, hammer it" (p. 14). Ramsey's fourth step is about conse-

quences. An authority figure must make policies and rules that delineate the proper

conduct on the job, and carry through with the consequences when workers violate

them. Ramsey says it is amazing how quickly people become more civil when their

raise or promotion depends on it (p. 5). Fifth, business leaders can offer training pro-

grams, civility courses, and workshops on ethics, respect, responsibility, awareness,

and etiquette. An example is the CREW program mentioned earlier and created for

the Veterans Health Administration. Workers from all over the country fly to Cincinnati

for three-day training sessions (Hauser, 2011). Ramsey's last step addresses how to

develop trust among workers. Leaders should devise exercises that involve team-

work, even if they seem "childish," like "having an employee fall backwards into the

arms of co-worker, counting on the other party to catch him safely" (p. 6).

Through their individual actions, employees can also maintain civility in their   11

workplace. As Forni states, "Corporate responsibility does not erase individual

BEING NICE IS GOOD BUSINESS   6

responsibility" (Forni, 2002, p. 140). The little things add up to make either a bad

day, like Amanda's, or a good one. Gonthier (2002) says, "Always say hello or

good morning or good afternoon as you encounter co-workers on your rounds.

And, of course, respond in kind if they initiate the exchange" (p. 110). A simple

greeting shows a concern for their well-being. Also, compliments for a job well

done will influence others to continue to work hard.

    Listening properly will result in better teamwork and acceptance of each   12

other's ideas. Being a cooperative listener includes responding in the right man-

ner with questions and body language. A listener must show that he or she is lis-

tening by making eye contact, saying remarks to show engagement and repeating

the speaker's thoughts to show comprehension (Forni, 2002, p. 52).

    Other people's space must also be respected in a working environment. In   13

order to maintain privacy, workers should keep noise levels down and distractions

to a minimum (Forni, 2002, p. 102). Many tensions in the workplace arise from

common facilities and resources. Resources at work are shared with all of the

workers; therefore, if a worker creates a mess, he or she must clean it immediately

so others do not have to clean up after them. Anyone who uses an appliance must

make sure that he or she has left it in working condition (Gonthier, 2002, p. 125).

If each worker takes responsibility for his or her actions, everything runs more

smoothly and people are not tired and irritated by the end of the day.

Conclusion

    Everyone benefits from a civil workplace. Joan Wrangler, an executive coach   14

working at NASA's Goddard Space Flight Center, created a personal relations

program there. She has discovered the huge difference that civility makes in pro-

ductivity and creativity: "Civility is part of the foundation for bringing out people's

brilliance. If you want to touch people's smartness and bring out their brilliance, then

you need to be able to create a space where people feel safe enough to speak, to

listen to one another, to be heard, to offer support, to coach one another"(as cited

in Hauser, 2011). That sounds like the kind of place everyone would like to work.

> This quotation sums up the civil workplace and points to its outstanding quality from the standpoint of both the employer and the employee: Every boss wants brilliant workers and every worker wants a chance to shine.

BEING NICE IS GOOD BUSINESS   7

References

Forni, P. M. (2002). *Choosing civility: The twenty-five rules of considerate conduct.*
    New York, NY: St. Martin's Press.

Gallup study: Feeling good matters in the workplace. (2006, January 12). *Gallup
    Management Journal.* Retrieved from http://gmj.gallup.com/content/20770/
    Gallup-Study-Feeling-Good-Matters-in-the.aspx

Gonthier, G. (2002). *Rude awakenings: Overcoming the civility crisis in the
    workplace.* Chicago, IL: Dearborn Trade Publishing.

Hauser, S. (2011). The degeneration of decorum: Stress caused by rude behavior
    in the workplace might be costing the U. S. economy billions of dollars a year.
    Workforce Management, 90.1, 16. Retrieved from http://find.galegroup.com
    .proxy.libraries.smu.edu/gtx/start.do?prodId=AONE&userGroupName=txshr
    acd2548

Pearson, C., & Porath, C. (2005). On the nature, consequences and remedies of
    workplace incivility: No time for "nice"? Think again. *Academy of Management
    Executive,* 19.1, 7–18. Retrieved from http://www.realmarcom
    .com/documents/conflict/pearson_incivility.pdf

Ramsey, R. (2008). The case for civility in the workplace. *Supervision,* 69.12, 3–6.
    Retrieved from http://find.galegroup.com.proxy.libraries.smu.edu/gtx/start.do?
    prodId=AONE&userGroupName=txshracd2548

Courtesy of Amie Hazama

CHAPTER 8

Exploring a Concept

IN THE FIRST CHAPTER, WE INTRODUCED A KEY QUESTION FOR CRITICAL THINKING: What does that word mean? It is an especially valuable question because the meaning of many words is open to question. For example, when someone claims that the Internet is the most *democratic* communication technology ever developed, what does the person mean by "democratic"? Is the Internet any more democratic than, say, television? If so, in what ways? Question what the word *democratic* means and you begin thinking critically about a statement that usually passes as uncontroversial.

This chapter is about how to explore the meaning of words. We are most interested in exploring words that name concepts like "democracy"—words that we use in talking about ideas that are important to us. We use these words so often and in so many different contexts that we might wonder if they mean anything at all. Consequently, writers who use words responsibly often elaborate on their meaning, or they may write simply to explore the meaning of a concept.

■■■ ACTIVITY 8.1 *Collaborative Activity*

Thinking about the Core Meaning of Concepts

The **core meaning** of a concept refers to *what most people think of when the concept is mentioned.* It is therefore important in exploring concepts. The following chart depicts the results of two surveys of Americans, one in 1998 and one in 2013, who were asked what a middle-income household makes.[1]

A middle-income household is one making

September 2013		December 1998	
Less than $30,000	9%	Less than $30,000	5%
Between $30,000 and $40,000	13	$30,000–$39,999	22
Between $40,000 and $50,000	23	$40,000–$49,999	24
Between $50,000 and $75,000	29	$50,000–$74,999	35
Between $75,000 and $100,000	16	$75,000–$99,999	7
Between $100,000 and $150,000	5	$100,000 or more	2
More than $150,000	2		

Note: In each income category the pollsters supplied in 2013 up to $100,000, Americans were most likely to identify their own income bracket as middle-income.

Source: NBC News/*Wall Street Journal,* September 2013.

1. American Enterprise Institute. "What Does Middle Class Mean?" *Political Report,* 1 Mar. 2015. Copyright © 2015 American Enterprise Institute. Reprinted with permission of the American Enterprise Institute. All rights reserved.

In small group or class discussion, consider the following questions:

1. Compare the numbers from 1998 and 2013. What trend do you see?
2. How would you answer the question now?
3. "Working class" is another common category. What relation do you think it has to "middle class"?
4. In addition to income, what other characteristics do you associate with "middle class"?
5. What would you say the core concept of "middle class" is? ◼

What Is Concept Exploration?

A **concept** is *a category, a way of grouping objects, attitudes, beliefs, and behavior that we consider related.* Cars, trucks, SUVs, and golf carts are all grouped as "vehicles." **Concept exploration** *examines concepts in an effort to understand what they mean and how they are used,* often with some practical question in mind. Should flag-burning count as "free speech"? The Supreme Court has ruled that it does, but many Americans believe that burning a flag is not speech and amounts to an unpatriotic act that should not enjoy constitutional protection.

CONCEPT CLOSE-UP   The Nature of Concepts

- ◼ **Concepts can be concrete, like Barbie dolls, or abstract, like Barbie culture,** a set of values associated with the toys and studied by sociologists interested in gender roles.

- ◼ **Concepts are often value-laden, implying positive or negative judgments.** For instance, the concept of "empathy" designates something positive and good for people to have. The concepts of being "callous" or "uncaring" are the opposite of empathy and therefore negative.

- ◼ **Concepts vary across cultures.** What is "fashionable" in Paris can be "immoral" in certain Islamic societies and just "odd" in many places in the United States.

- ◼ **Concepts vary across time.** As a society's circumstances change, its concepts also change. "Exurb," for example, arose as a concept when people moved farther out from urban centers, beyond suburbs. We invent new concepts to characterize new realities and drop old ones as the realities they refer to cease to exist.

Concepts can vary across cultures. What may be considered "fashionable" in one country may be considered odd or immoral in others.

© Tristan Savatier/Getty Images, RF

Why Explore Concepts?

We *define* concepts like "quark" to explain what they mean for readers unfamiliar with the terms, but we seldom explore scientific or technical concepts because of their precise, limited meaning. We *explore* abstract concepts like "democracy" and "empathy" because their meanings are not so precise and limited. Understanding them better matters because such words belong to our value systems and influence our behavior. For example, Mike Rose, now a distinguished professor of English, explains in his book *Lives on the Boundary* that he almost flunked out of college his freshman year. Influenced by the concept "individualism," he refused to seek help when he could not understand the assigned books. Similarly, Jamie Cummins, who explores "gender" at the end of the chapter, does so to determine whether we might be "trapped . . . by our ideas of appropriate behavior for men and women."

Concept exploration appears in newspaper stories and editorials, in scientific and philosophical books and articles, in blogs online, and in many other **genres,** or kinds of writing. It also appears in every context for writing. In a workplace setting we might need to assess how "democratic" the Internet is; in personal writing, we might explore what being a "friend" to someone ought to mean; and in academic writing, defining the word "novel" might be crucial to an essay exam.

How Do Writers Explore a Concept?

What should we ask when we want to think seriously about the meanings of a concept and its applications to life? Following are some basic questions that stimulate thinking about exploring concepts.

1. **What are the dictionary definitions of the concept?** Have definitions changed over time? Have the word's emotional associations changed, especially in a negative or positive direction? Four centuries ago, for example, "innovation" was a negative word, implying the work of a troublemaker, whereas now the word glows with all that is good and desirable.

2. **What are the root meanings of the word?** "Democracy," for example, comes from two Greek words meaning "people rule." It is not surprising, then, that "democratic" now means for many Americans much the same thing as "popular."

3. **In what contexts do people use the concept?** In one situation, "fairness" means that everyone gets an equal share of something—as even young children know when a treat is being distributed. In another situation, "fairness" means *unequal*

distribution, as when one person or one group has contributed more than another to a successful enterprise and therefore deserves a greater share of the reward.

4. **Is conflict or disagreement at hand when the concept is used?** "Freedom" often runs headlong into "social responsibility." Smoking in enclosed public spaces was once common in the United States; now it is rarely permitted.

5. **What is the practical impact of the concept?** "Subprime mortgages" and financial contracts called "derivatives" so damaged the American and global economy that the investor Warren Buffett called them "weapons of mass destruction." Many people do not understand that file-sharing of copyrighted materials is "theft" in the same sense as, for example, stealing someone's car.

6. **What company does this concept keep, and what distinctions are there among related ideas?** "Marriage," for example, connects with many other concepts, such as "soul mate," "monogamy," the "union of a man and a woman," "reproduction," and so on. Increasingly the connected concepts are being separated from the institution as the institution itself changes.

7. **What have other writers said about the concept?** About "justice," for example, a Supreme Court justice famously said, "Justice too long delayed is justice denied." What is the relation of "justice" to "timeliness"?

8. **What confusions or uncertainties surround the use of the concept?** For example, the concept of "preemptive war" is used to justify a surprise attack on an enemy who is about to attack you. Can we distinguish between "preemptive war" as self-defense and the use of the concept to disguise a motive like expanding a country's territory by attacking a weak neighbor?

READING **8.1**

The Supreme Chutzpah

JACK ACHIEZER GUGGENHEIM

Last term something novel occurred at the nation's highest court. A decision of the U.S. Supreme Court used the word "chutzpah" for the first time. The decision was written by Justice Antonin Scalia in National Endowment for the Arts v. Finley, and addressed the interaction between government funding and free speech. Chutzpah is a Yiddish word connoting brazenness. A federal court in the Northern District of Illinois noted in a decision a couple of years ago that chutzpah means

1

The Yiddish word chutzpah *has become one of the many words in common use that English has borrowed from other languages. In this article, which was adapted from a longer piece published in the* Kentucky Law Journal, *a prominent Jewish legal scholar discusses the use of the "chutzpah" concept in federal court rulings, including a recent one by Supreme Court Associate Justice Antonin Scalia. As you read, note the shades of meaning the word has, especially in relation to the context in which it is being used.*

Antonin Scalia, Senior Associate Justice of the U.S. Supreme Court

© AP Images/Jessica Hill

shameless audacity; impudence; brass. Leo Rosten's *The Joys of Yiddish* defines chutzpah as a Yiddish idiom meaning "gall, brazen nerve, effrontery." But neither English translation can do the word justice; neither definition can fully capture the audacity simultaneously bordering on insult and humor which the word chutzpah connotes. As a federal district court in the District of D.C. noted in 1992, chutzpah is "presumption-plus-arrogance such as no other word, and no other language can do justice to."

> Common meanings of the word contrasted with the more specific implications it has in Yiddish.

Perhaps the classic "legal" definition of chutzpah is the closest; a person who kills his parents and pleads for the court's mercy on the ground of being an orphan. However, in defining chutzpah in the context of American jurisprudence it is also important to note, as a court in the federal district of New Jersey did in 1995, that "Legal chutzpah is not always undesirable, and without it our system of jurisprudence would suffer.

2

> Chutzpah's negative and positive connotations—that is, sometimes the word condemns, sometimes it praises.

Part of the uniqueness of Yiddish words like chutzpah is that their meaning varies depending on context and degree. In the right circumstances and to the right degree chutzpah may intimate spunk. But in the wrong situation or to an improper degree, chutzpah implies insolence. In fact chutzpah can have such negative connotation that the word itself has occasionally caused litigation. For example, Senator Charles Schumer was sued, unsuccessfully, on the basis that his statement, "In Brooklyn, we have a word for something like that—chutzpah" was false and defamatory.

3

The unique shades and subtleties that Yiddish allows have made it a language of choice in recent American jurisprudence when English fails to provide a word with the proper connotation. The Seventh Circuit noted in 1995, Yiddishisms such as chutzpah "have become absorbed into standard English and are now applied to members of all racial and ethnic groups." According to Judge Alex Kozinski of the Ninth Circuit, Yiddish is quickly supplanting Latin as the spice in American legal argot. The earliest reported case that uses a Yiddish word is believed to be a New York surrogate court's decision of 1929.

4

> Argot: language specific to a particular field or discipline.

As Judge Kozinski has noted, more recently the U.S. Court of Appeals for the Second Circuit incorrectly defined a bagel; the word "kibbitz" has appeared in at least 10 decisions; the word "maven" has appeared in at least four decisions; the word "klutz" has appeared in at least three decisions; and the word "schmooze" in at least one decision.

5

> Specific examples of other Yiddish words used in legal contexts.

> Points to the frequency with which Yiddish terms are used in law.

Provides short history of the word's use in judicial proceedings.

Chutzpah made its federal debut in a 1973 opinion. Since then the Court of Federal Claims has created a "Chutzpah Championship," the D.C. Circuit a "Chutzpah Award," and the Federal Circuit a "Chutzpah Doctrine." It was only a matter of time until the U.S. Supreme Court invoked its own chutzpah. National Endowment for the Arts v. Finley, a case that addressed the government's right to choose which expression to sponsor, provided the perfect forum for the Court to exercise its own right to express itself.

6

Points out why Scalia's use of the word may be especially significant.

It was especially apropos that Justice Scalia used the term. Justice Scalia has been admired even by his ideological dissenters for his appropriate sense of humor in discussing deeply important subjects such as religion and politics. Furthermore, Justice Scalia, a devout Catholic raised in Queens, has repeatedly called for more expressions of tradition and religion in American society. The use of the word chutzpah, with its historical roots and association with Judaism, may fulfill such a role. It also comports with his legal philosophy. He favors the "nonpreferentialist" view which posits that government may support religion in general but not in a way that prefers any particular religion. For Justice Scalia to use a term of a Jewish cultural language in a Supreme Court decision could be viewed as in keeping with the nonpreferentialist legal doctrine.

7

Cites Scalia's actual use of the term and explains the context in which it was used.

In National Endowment for the Arts, a number of performance artists and an artists' organization brought an action against the NEA, claiming that the denial of grant applications violated the artists' constitutional rights. Justice Scalia felt exasperation for both the artists' challenge to the statute and the NEA's interpretation of the statute, and even Justice Sandra Day O'Connor's majority decision. In his concurrence, he agreed with the majority that the statute was constitutional. However, he apparently found that the NEA's interpretation of the statute as merely instructional and not mandating viewpoint based discrimination was truly chutzpah, writing: "It takes a particularly high degree of chutzpah for the NEA to contradict this proposition, since the agency itself discriminates—in favor of artistic (as opposed to scientific, or political, or theological) expression."

8

It is interesting to note that although Justice Scalia felt the need to define the words "decency" and "respect" and called on the use of the *American Heritage Dictionary* to do so, he did not define "chutzpah," no doubt because the word is so obviously a part of the English lexicon.

9

Speculates on what the common use of the word implies about American society—that is, increasing pluralistic tolerance.

What does increasing use of the word chutzpah signify? Perhaps it reflects the developing mosaic of the United States. American Jewish lawyers initially faced discrimination in the United States. Large law firms were closed and bar associations turned a cold shoulder. But now a Yiddish term is used in a U.S. Supreme Court decision with hardly any notice. The salad bowl has replaced the mixing pot, and the cucumbers, tomatoes, and even the avocados are becoming accepted. And maybe this is the most fantastic chutzpah of all; while the world has an unfortunate history of prejudice, in America tolerance and pluralism are becoming traditional values.

10

Jack Achiezer, Guggenheim. "Jewish Law Commentary: Examining Halacha, Jewish Issues and Secular Law." Adapted from an article in the *Kentucky Law Journal*, Volume 87, Book 2. Copyright © 1999 University of Kentucky College of Law. Reprinted by permission.

Questions for Discussion

1. Recall instances in which you have used the word *chutzpah* and/or you have heard it used or read it in print. Which meaning or meanings of the word as defined above did your/others' use approximate? Were the uses positive or negative in connotation?
2. Guggenheim offers much information about the history of chutzpah in legal contexts. Why is this information important and interesting?
3. The author claims great cultural and social significance for the use of the term chutzpah by a Supreme Court justice and by Scalia in particular. Summarize what he says. Do you agree with his interpretation?

■■■ *Thinking as a Writer*

What Is the Rhetorical Situation?

1. What Is the author's *purpose* in writing this article? What is his *angle* on the topic? How would you describe his *voice*?
2. Who is the intended *audience*? The article appeared in the *Jewish Law Community,* which is not intended only for lawyers. Who would read this publication? Is there anything you can point to in the article that implies the target readership?
3. Using the eight questions for how to explore a concept (pages 144–45) and the marginal annotations to the article, evaluate how the author develops his view of chutzpah. That is, how does he define, illustrate, and explore the notion of chutzpah? ■

R E A D I N G **8.2**

What Is Civility?

P. M. FORNI

Maybe I was coming down with change-of-season influenza. If so, I should really consider buying a little white half mask for my subway ride home.

—Sujata Massey

For many years literature was my life. I spent most of my 1
time reading, teaching, and writing on Italian fiction and
poetry. One day, while lecturing on the *Divine Comedy,*

This reading comes from a best-selling book, Choosing Civility: The Twenty-Five Rules of Considerate Conduct. *The author is a professor of Italian literature and civility at Johns Hopkins University, where he directs The Civility Initiative at Johns Hopkins. Before offering readers his "rules" for showing consideration toward others, Forni lays the groundwork by exploring the concept of civility.*

I looked at my students and realized that I wanted them to be kind human beings more than I wanted them to know about Dante. I told them that if they knew everything about Dante and then they went out and treated an elderly lady on the bus unkindly, I'd feel that I had failed as a teacher. I have given dozens of lectures and workshops on civility in the last few years, and I have derived much satisfaction from addressing audiences I could not have reached speaking on literature. I know, however, that reading literature can develop the kind of imagination without which civility is impossible. To be fully human we must be able to imagine others' hurt and to relate it to the hurt we would experience if we were in their place. Consideration is imagination on a moral track.

Sometimes the participants in my workshops write on a sheet of paper what civility means to them. In no particular order, here are a number of key civility-related notions I have collected over the years from those sheets:

2

Respect for others	Decency	Trustworthiness
Care	Self-Control	Going out of one's way
Consideration	Concern	Friendship
Courtesy	Justice	Friendliness
Golden Rule	Tolerance	Table manners
Respect of others' feelings	Selflessness	Lending a hand
Niceness	Etiquette	Manners
Politeness	Community service	Morality
Respect of others' opinions	Tact	Moderation
Maturity	Equality	Propriety
Kindness	Sincerity	Listening
Being accommodating	Honesty	Abiding by the rules
Fairness	Awareness	Compassion
Good citizenship	Being agreeable	Peace

This list tells us that

- Civility is complex.
- Civility is good.
- Whatever civility might be, it has to do with courtesy, politeness, and good manners.
- Civility belongs in the realm of ethics.

These four points have guided me in writing this book. Like my workshop participants, I am inclusive rather than exclusive in defining civility. Courtesy, politeness, manners, and civility are all, in essence, forms of awareness. Being civil means being constantly aware of others and weaving restraint, respect, and consideration into the very fabric of this awareness. Civility is a form of goodness; it is gracious goodness. But

3

it is not just an attitude of benevolent and thoughtful relating to other individuals; it also entails an active interest in the well-being of our communities and even a concern for the health of the planet on which we live.

Saying "please" and "thank you"; lowering our voice whenever it may threaten or interfere with others' tranquility; raising funds for a neighborhood renovation program; acknowledging a newcomer to the conversation; welcoming a new neighbor; listening to understand and help; respecting those different from us; responding with restraint to a challenge; properly disposing of a piece of trash left by someone else; properly disposing of dangerous industrial pollutants; acknowledging our mistakes; refusing to participate in malicious gossip; making a new pot of coffee for the office machine after drinking the last cup; signaling our turns when driving; yielding our seat on a bus whenever it seems appropriate; alerting the person sitting behind us on a plane when we are about to lower the back of our seat; standing close to the right-side handrail on an escalator; stopping to give directions to someone who is lost; stopping at red lights; disagreeing with poise; yielding with grace when losing an argument, these diverse behaviors are all imbued with the spirit of civility.

Civility, c*ourtesy, politeness,* and *manners* are not perfect synonyms, as etymology clearly shows. . . . *Courtesy* is connected to *court* and evoked in the past the superior qualities of character and bearing expected in those close to royalty. Etymologically, when we are courteous we are courtierlike. Although today we seldom make this connection, courtesy still suggests excellence and elegance in bestowing respect and attention. It can also suggest deference and formality.

To understand *politeness,* we must think of *polish.* The polite are those who have polished their behavior. They have put some effort into bettering themselves, but they are sometimes looked upon with suspicion. Expressions such as "polite reply," "polite lie," and "polite applause" connect politeness to hypocrisy. It is true that the polite are inclined to veil their own feelings to spare someone else's. Self-serving lying, however, is always beyond the pale of politeness. If politeness is a quality of character (alongside courtesy, good manners, and civility), it cannot become a flaw. A suave manipulator may appear to be polite but is not.

When we think of good *manners* we often think of children being taught to say "please" and "thank you" and chew with their mouths closed. This may prevent us from looking at manners with the attention they deserve. *Manner* comes from *manus,* the Latin word for "hand." *Manner* and *manners* have to do with the use of our hands. A manner is the way something is done, a mode of handling. Thus *manners* came to refer to behavior in social interaction—the way we handle the encounter between Self and Other. We have good manners when we use our hands well—when we handle others with care. When we rediscover the connection of *manner* with *hand,* the hand that, depending on our will and sensitivity, can strike or lift, hurt or soothe, destroy or heal, we understand the importance—for children and adults alike—of having good manners.

*Civility'*s defining characteristic is its ties to *city* and *society.* The word derives from the Latin *civitas,* which means "city," especially in the sense of civic community. *Civitas* is the same word from which *civilization* comes. The age-old assumption behind civility is that life in the city has a civilizing effect. The city is where we enlighten our intellect and

4

5

6

7

8

refine our social skills. And as we are shaped by the city, we learn to give of ourselves for the sake of the city. Although we can describe the civil as courteous, polite, and well mannered, etymology reminds us that they are also supposed to be good citizens and good neighbors.

Questions for Discussion

1. Forni begins by arguing that learning to be kind to others is as important to a college education as learning about literature—or presumably any other area of academic study. Do you agree? If so, can kindness be taught? How?
2. A common way to explore concepts is to write about other closely related concepts. Forni offers a long list of other concepts associated with civility (paragraph 2). Does the list help you to understand civility better? Why or why not?
3. Much has been written in recent years about the loss of civility in American life. Writers point to people engrossed with their laptops and cell phones rather than talking with the people around them. They also point to lack of cooperation in our politics, saying that Democrats and Republicans view one another as enemies rather than people who have different views on policy issues. Do you see a loss of civility? If so, do you see the alleged decline in civility as a problem?

▮▮▮ *Thinking as a Writer*

What Is the Rhetorical Situation?

1. What is the author's *purpose* in writing this passage? What is his *angle* on the topic? How would you describe his *voice*?
2. Who is the intended *audience* for this passage (and for the larger book)? Is Forni writing for students in an academic setting or for a more general public? Is he writing for people who are already well informed about notions of civility or for people who might not have thought much about the concept? Is there anything in this excerpt you can cite that implies the author's target readership?
3. A common way to explore concepts is to consider their etymologies, their root meanings or origins. Forni does this in his discussions of *courtesy, politeness,* and *manners.* Do the root meanings of these words, including *civility* itself, help you to grasp these concepts better? Why or why not? ▪

P.M. Forni. "What Is Civility?" *Choosing Civility: The Twenty-Five Rules of Considerate Conduct,* St. Martin's Press, pp. 7–13. © 2002 by P. M. Forni. Used by permission of the author.

The Assignment

See Chapter 16, Finding Sources, pages 336–49, and Chapter 17, Evaluating Sources, pages 350–56, for kinds of sources you could consult.

Write an essay exploring a concept. Depending on your teacher's instructions, you may draw from personal experiences, interviews, and observations as well as from reference works, books, and articles. Be sure to use the key questions for exploring a concept (pages 144–45). Some or all of them will help you see how to think critically about your concept and discover options for writing about it.

What Can I Write About?

Your instructor may assign a concept to explore. When asked to choose your own, consider the following (see also Figure 8.1):

See Chapter 5, Interpreting Experiences, for guidance, and page 71 for more ideas.

- **Personal experience.** Draw on your personal experience to select a concept for exploration. For example, seeing mothers interacting with their children in line at the bank or grocery store may prompt you to consider the concept "child rearing." An experience from childhood or adolescence that made you consider concepts such as "innocence" or "naïveté" could also be explored.

- **Blog posts.** A student from Sweden described how the concept of "friendship" in his country differs from the concept in the United States. The post received many comments from other bloggers, opening up further exploration of a challenging concept.

- **Book reviews.** Nonfiction books especially can offer either new concepts or interesting analyses of familiar ones. You can respond to the author's exploration with comments of your own.

Here are some other sources for concepts to explore:

- **Class readings.** Concepts from the readings in this chapter—"chutzpah," "courtesy," "gender roles"—or in other texts you are reading for class could be concepts for exploration.

- **Personal reading.** An article in your campus newspaper or in a magazine like *Time* or *Sports Illustrated* could provide a concept ("fairness in the media," "cheating in sports").

- **Campus issues.** For example, "plagiarism" or "going green" are good concepts for exploration. Speakers at your college or university may also discuss intriguing concepts.

- **Concepts in your community.** For example, "third place" is used to designate where people spend time besides home and work.

- **Concepts in your workplace.** For example, in a summer or regular job you may have encountered a concept such as "malware," a name for computer viruses, Trojans, and worms.

- **Concepts from foreign languages or cultures.** If you have studied a foreign language, you have probably encountered concepts unique to that language, which have no precise English equivalents. Such concepts can make interesting

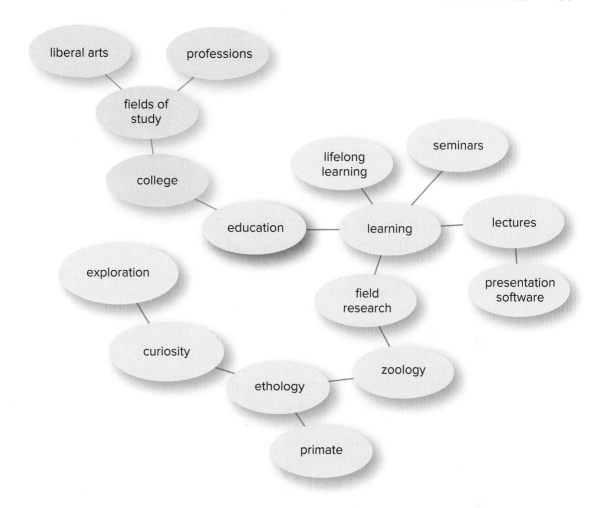

FIGURE **8.1**

What Should I Write About?

Think of one interesting broad concept and then come up with as many concept "offshoots" as you can. Sometimes brainstorming with a visual diagram can help you come up with the perfect topic to write about.

explorations, especially if you have lived in or visited countries where the language is spoken and can offer insight into how the concept is actually used.

- **Concepts from cultures in the United States.** Our country is in large part a collection of cultures, people of different races, ethnicities, nationalities, religions, languages, and so on. Perhaps you were raised in or have extensive experience with one of these cultures and can discuss a concept its people often use.

▩▩■■ ACTIVITY 8.2 *Writer's Notebook*

Will It Work? Testing Your Concept

If you are in doubt about a concept you have chosen, try writing about it as fast as you can for about 15 minutes. If you find the ideas are flowing, you probably have a concept suitable for you to write about. As an alternative, write an e-mail to a friend or classmate explaining why you have chosen the concept and what you foresee saying about it. Ask for feedback. Either or both methods should help you test the concept before you commit yourself to a draft. ■

How Do I Explore Concepts? Questioning the Rhetorical Situation

Begin by picturing a **rhetorical situation** for your writing project, a real-world context for communicating. You should consider the key variables in any act of communication: a writer with something to say, a reader the writer wishes to reach, and a kind of text appropriate to the writing task. These three variables will affect many decisions in the composing process.

Writer: What Is My Purpose, and What Impression Should Readers Have of Me?

Exploratory writing is "thinking aloud"—for this assignment, putting on screen or paper how you have gone about trying to understand a concept. You may explain the concept and concepts related to it, but your primary purpose is to explore, not to inform or explain. You may also argue *for* your understanding of the concept— usually near the end of your essay, after your exploration is over—but your primary purpose is to explore, not to argue for your interpretation. The key to exploration is to **postpone closure,** which means *letting your mind play with the concept* rather than informing or arguing.

Consequently, your readers should see you as a *thoughtful guide* to the concept, someone asking and pursuing interesting questions. They should see you as someone with an open mind, not as someone who has all the answers.

Reader: Who Is My Audience?

As with all writing projects, you should imagine a group of people who might read your paper. Your instructor will evaluate your work, and part of that evaluation is how well you communicate with your reader. Beyond that, you need to write for a reader because doing so will help you decide what to say and how to order what you say. Therefore, one of the key questions you need to ask yourself often as you write and revise a draft is, **"What does my reader need?"**

Remembering this will help you imagine your reader: *Your purpose for writing determines your role as a writer, which in turn implies a role for your reader.* In this case, your purpose is exploration and your role is an explorer, someone engaged with the meaning of a challenging concept. You are displaying your thought process as you ponder the concept's dictionary definition, its root meanings, what other writers have said about it, how the concept is used, and so on. Without having to say it, you are inviting your readers to "come and think about this concept with me." You are saying, "Here's what I am thinking," which implies that you want what you say to stimulate their thinking.

Note how different this role for the reader is from informing or arguing. When you inform, your reader becomes somebody who needs or wants to know what you know. When you argue, your reader becomes someone you are trying to convince or persuade. Exploration is different: You want your readers to think through a concept with you.

Text: What Moves Can I Make?

The genre represented in Readings 8.1 and 8.2 and in the student example at the end of this chapter (pages 163–67) is the exploratory essay. The basic moves are as follows:

- Introduce the concept you intend to explore.
- Indicate why the concept needs to be explored.
- Cite the views of experts on the concept and comment on what they say, and/or . . .
- Cite dictionary meanings, root meanings, examples of how the concept is used, and so on (see the key questions on pages 144–45 for other possibilities) and comment on them, and/or . . .
- Cite your own experiences or observations that contribute to your thinking about the concept.
- Propose a core or basic meaning for the concept.
- Offer your view of what the concept means, including, when relevant, your evaluation of how the concept is used or misused.

How Do I Explore Concepts? Engaging the Writing Process

No two people compose in exactly the same way, and even the same person may go through the writing process in different ways with different assignments. Nevertheless, because no one can attend to everything at once, there are phases in handling any significant writing task. You begin by preparing to write, which includes generating content and finding your angle.

The next phase is planning and drafting your paper, getting a version, however rough it may be, on screen or paper so that you have something to work with during the next two stages: revising your draft by making changes to the content, arrangement, and style of your writing; and editing your draft to take care of problems at the paragraph and sentence level, such as lack of focus and coherence, awkward or unclear sentences, and errors of grammar, spelling, and punctuation.

Exploring Your Topic

In this phase you are *finding something to say,* generating ideas and content, which includes discovering your angle or point of view.

Generating Ideas and Gathering Materials

See Chapter 15, pages 332–34, for guidance on keeping a working bibliography.

The following six questions will help you come up with ideas and more than enough content for your essay. Make handwritten notes as you work your way through these questions, or preserve your notes and comments on a computer file reserved for this assignment. Be sure to indicate the sources from which all your information comes.

1. **What is the definition and history of the concept?** Start with the meanings of the concept as listed in a college-level dictionary. Distinguish the *concept's meanings* (called **denotation**) from the *implications of the concept* (called **connotation**). For example, "empathy" means the ability to feel what someone else is feeling (denotation); its connotations are always positive, implying a sensitive, caring person. Many dictionaries also show the word's **etymology** *(its derivation or root meanings).* The *Oxford English Dictionary (OED)* is particularly good for illustrating etymology because it gives example sentences showing how the concept has been used in the past.

2. **What other concepts are related to the concept you are exploring, and how are they related?** Concepts can be discussed only by using other concepts. What words were used to define your concept? What **synonyms** *(words that mean approximately the same thing)* did your dictionary supply? What synonyms can you think of? What synonyms are listed in a thesaurus?

   Consider also concepts closely related to your concept that are not synonyms. Forni offered a list of forty-two concepts related to civility (page 149). You can find things to say about your concept by simply listing all the related concepts you can think of. Add to your list by writing down related concepts other writers have used to discuss your concept (see question 4).

3. **What metaphors are used to discuss your concept?** A metaphor is an implied comparison. People talk about "argument," for instance, using the concept of "war." Arguments are won and lost; we shoot down or demolish opposing views; evidence is ammunition. Consider how this metaphor influences how people think about argument and behave when they argue. It certainly works against listening thoughtfully to people we disagree with or empathizing with opponents in a dispute.

   Concepts are metaphorical more often than we realize. Expose and examine the metaphors in your concept. Remember also that language is full of **dead metaphors,** *comparisons used so habitually that people no longer recognize them as metaphors.* The language of war used to discuss argument is a good example. When you encounter dead metaphors, invent fresh ones that might restore life to your concept. For example, why not present argument as dialogue or negotiation?

See Chapter 16 for advice on finding suitable print and online sources.

4. **What has been written about my concept?** Using your library's online catalog and an all-purpose periodicals database, such as Academic Search Complete, InfoTrac, JSTOR, and ProQuest, find sources in which your concept

is discussed. Then conduct a Google search on your sources' authors to learn about their background, their areas of expertise, and their perspectives on your concept. Keep copies of your sources, make notes about what the authors say, and add your own reactions and comments.

See Chapter 18 for advice on taking notes and making comments on source material.

5. **Do different groups of people use the concept differently?** The most common sources of difference are race and ethnicity, gender, class, age, religion, and sex. "Equal opportunity," for example, may mean one thing to those born into privilege, something else to those born into poverty. "Community" may mean one thing to your grandparents and another thing to you. Consider how your concept may be understood by members of different groups. What conflicts or misunderstandings might result? How might your view of the concept help reduce conflict or misunderstanding?

6. **How do people actually use the concept?** Field research, such as surveys and interviews, can help you gain insight into your concept. One student exploring gender surveyed her fellow musicians' choices of instruments and found that instruments were "masculine" and "feminine"—that is, women tended to choose certain instruments (the flute, for example), while men tended to choose others (such as the drums). She was intrigued by how these gender concepts influenced musicians' choices. Consider conducting your own survey or interviewing a campus expert to learn more about your concept.

See Chapter 15 for guidance on conducting field research.

■▨■■ ACTIVITY 8.3 *Collaborative Activity*

Discussing Your Concept

If you keep a blog or if your class has an online discussion board, write a post about the concept you are exploring. Include any interesting results from answering the six questions above for generating ideas. Ask participants to post comments, contribute questions for exploration, and share their own experiences. ■

Drafting Your Paper

As you move toward writing your first draft, focus attention on angle, organization, and voice.

How Can I Find My Angle?

Angles are typically **contextual,** *derived from your life situation.* For example, the context for "The Supreme Chutzpah" was the author's experience as a law clerk for a judge on the U.S. Court of Federal Claims. He wanted Americans to understand a pervasive concept in Jewish culture. The context for a college student wrestling with the concept "indie music" might be her own role as a DJ at the college radio station and the kinds of music her definition of "indie" would allow her to play. Concept exploration is usually motivated by practical needs, problems, or questions that arise at work, at home, in the community, or in one of many other contexts provided by life.

Finding an angle often means writing about what you know. For example, if you work at an indie radio station and have an opinion about what indie music is, write about it.

© Ilene MacDonald/ Alamy, RF

To determine your angle, consider the following questions:

1. **What context do I bring to the concept?** A student who surveyed fellow musicians about gender and instrument choice brought the context of playing in an orchestra. Any way that your concept can be connected with school, work, sports, family, or social life can help you find an angle.

2. **What outcome do I want for my exploration?** Forni wanted his readers to appreciate how complex "civility" is and to understand why he considers civility so important. Cummins explored "gender" to call attention to how limiting rigid notions of "masculine" and "feminine" can be.

3. **How can I challenge existing notions of the concept?** Everything you read about a concept can be questioned in some way, and often your angle can come from finding a particularly fertile question. When we read Guggenheim's article, for example, we wondered whether the positive connotations of "chutzpah" have their origin in Yiddish at all. Perhaps we brash Americans admire "gall, brazen nerve, effrontery" much more than traditional Jewish culture did.

4. **What distinctions might I make?** By their nature, concepts lump things together. Perhaps your angle can come from making one or several distinctions. The Swedish student who explored "friendship" thought Americans confused friend with acquaintance. That was his angle, and it worked well.

Organizing Your Exploratory Essay

Consider arranging your material as described below.

Introduction A good technique for opening exploration papers is to say what most people think about a concept and why it needs rethinking. Other options include:

- A quotation showing a particularly good or particularly bad understanding of the concept.
- A personal narrative about how your exploration got started.

Body One way to organize the draft is chronologically, beginning with your initial view of the concept and explaining the stages in which your understanding grew. See the student essay at the end of this chapter for an example. A chronologically organized draft would emphasize breakthrough moments, when your major insights occurred.

You can also organize around sources. Arrange your sources around a sequence of points they make or a set of questions they help to answer, and be sure to comment on them as they relate to your angle.

Conclusion   Depending on your angle, conclude with the results of your exploration, whatever they are:

- How does your understanding of the concept work or fail to work in the context you brought to it? For example, the idea that band or orchestral instruments have a gender might end by considering boys who choose the flute and girls who choose the tuba. How do you explain choices that do not fit gender stereotypes?
- What outcome did you want from exploring the concept? Emphasize the results of your exploration, such as a clearer notion of friendship, a healthier view of romantic love, or an understanding of how much human society depends on civility.
- What challenge to the typical notion of your concept can you offer? For example, instead of the sharp contrasts that usually go with masculine and feminine gender categories, you could say that most people are a mix of the two genders, and therefore "masculine" and "feminine" tend only to distort reality.
- What distinctions seem important to you? For example, besides the usual distinction between friend and acquaintance, it might be interesting to discuss something relatively new—"friending," which can occur with people who are neither friends nor acquaintances.

Leave your readers with the feeling that your exploration made headway, but you need not resolve all issues or questions. Some explorations end by calling attention to problems, issues, and questions requiring further thought.

What Voice Is Appropriate for Exploring a Concept?

Saying what you mean involves voice, how you sound to your readers, so we need to consider voice in exploratory writing. Voice depends on function, on what a writer is doing. When we explore concepts, three functions are in play: informing, questioning, and asserting. All three functions and voices are present in "The Supreme Chutzpah" (pages 145–47), but listen especially to the author's voice in the following passage:

> Part of the uniqueness of Yiddish words like chutzpah is that their meaning varies depending on context and degree. In the right circumstances and to the right degree chutzpah may intimate spunk. But in the wrong situation or to an

improper degree, chutzpah implies insolence. In fact chutzpah can have such negative connotation that the word itself has occasionally caused litigation. For example, Senator Charles Schumer was sued, unsuccessfully, on the basis that his statement, "In Brooklyn, we have a word for something like that—chutzpah" was false and defamatory.

His voice sounds like the knowledgeable insider, who is sharing with us the subtle range and never-fully-explicit meanings of chutzpah in Yiddish.

Revising Your Draft

Because exploration depicts the thought process itself, laying it out for readers to follow, revision should not conceal or obscure the twists and turns of your thinking. Instead, *revise to highlight discoveries,* to expose how your thought unfolded. The Art of Questioning checklist below provides questions to guide assessment of your or another student's draft.

THE ART OF QUESTIONING — Revision Checklist for Explaining a Concept

1. Does the paper explore the concept, opening it up to questioning rather than only informing or presenting an argument? Isolate passages that clearly explore. How can they be improved?
2. Is the author's angle on the concept clear, and does the writer provide a reason for exploring the concept in the introduction? What is the angle? Where is the reason discussed?
3. Does the author explain the context within which she or he will be exploring the concept? Recall that "context" for this paper means the concept's place in the writer's life. Where specifically are the connections with context made? What possible questions might a reader have that go unanswered?
4. Is the paper organized around the stages marking the writer's unfolding insights into the concept, around sources and the insights into the concept they provide, or in some other way that makes sense? If not, what changes in organization would help the reader follow the exploration better?
5. Has the author made the exploration specific enough to show how the concept is used, by providing examples and illustrations that demonstrate how people use the concept? Where in the paper does this happen? Where might the author provide additional supporting evidence?
6. If the author has used sources, how well are the authors of these sources introduced as people whose opinions on the concept should matter? To see how to incorporate sources, look at one of the readings (pages 145–47 and 148–51) or the student example (pages 163–67).
7. Is there too much quotation, paraphrase, and summary of sources and not enough commentary on the sources? Find places where the author has said

For more help on incorporating sources into your text, see Chapter 18, pages 357–78.

See Chapter 18, pages 364–69, for guidance on using quotations, paraphrase, and summary.

something about sources cited. To what extent do the comments express his or her own point of view and voice?

8. Has the author brought the exploration to some degree of closure by drawing a conclusion about what he or she learned? Should more be concluded? Why? Remember that closure in exploratory writing can include mentioning problems, issues, and questions that need further thought.

Student Example: Excerpts from Jamie Cummins's Draft

Student Jamie Cummins explored the concept of gender. He encountered specific challenges with his opening and using sources.

Problems with the Opening   A paper's opening is important because it is the first thing your audience will read. In the rough draft of this chapter's featured student essay (see pages 163–67 for the revised draft), Cummins opened with a dictionary definition and then moved into a quotation from one of his sources, an expert on the topic of gender roles:

> Gender is defined in the dictionary as "kind, sort, class; also genus as opposed to species." And that's just it. Gender is a word meaning what *kind* of human are you. Most would say, "I am a male" or "I am a female." But the words "male" and "female" refer to their sex. Gender has nothing to do with one's biological make-up, but more of an element of one's identity—"'gender' is masculinity and femininity" (Kimmel 3).

Compare this opening with the opening of his second draft (page 163). Which do you like better? Why?

Problems with Using Sources   Because your readers have not read the sources you cite, you need to comment on what sources say and set up quotations and paraphrases with enough context so readers can understand them. Here is Cummins's first effort to integrate a source:

> The idea that our gender is influenced and developed in elementary, middle and high school is explored by C. J. Pascoe, a sociologist at the University of California at Berkeley. Among many things, Pascoe explores the idea that school is "an organizer of sexual practices, identities, and meanings" (26) in her book, *Dude, You're a Fag: Masculinity and Sexuality in High School.* She also notes that "the heterosexualizing process organized by educational institutions cannot be separated from, and in fact is central to, the development of masculine identities" (27). Specifically, C. J. Pascoe refers to the "Mr. Cougar" competition in the high school she did her field work in. Candidates for the "Mr. Cougar" title performed short skits, usually mocking boys who are less masculine than the stereotypical "manly man." These skits reinforce the idea that the stereotypical "manly man" is strong, big and powerful. The "manly man" must also have a girlfriend and

must frequently have sex. The skits made being a "manly man" seem essential, and "male femininity [. . .] is coded as humorous" (4). Referring to one of the "Mr. Cougar" skits, Pascoe writes that "the skit fostered and encouraged masculinity as heterosexual" (45). The "Mr. Cougar" skits make it seem like one has to prove his own masculinity to be considered heterosexual. She reinforces the concept that because of "heterosexualizing" schools, gender is shaped and developed in elementary, middle and high school.

Compare this version to paragraphs 6 and 7 in the revised version. Note how much better he handles context for and commentary on his source.

Editing Your Revised Draft

In working with sources, you often need to summarize what they say. A wordy summary can obscure the ideas rather than present them clearly. Compare the following two versions of a summary Jamie Cummins used for one of his sources. The original version reads like a list of disconnected points stated by author Michael Kimmel:

Original Version

> These sentences describe the original source by listing points Kimmel makes, but they do not show how the points relate to each other.

> Passive voice obscures the point: Inequality causes gender differences.

Kimmel explains that "virtually every society known to us is founded upon assumptions of gender difference and the politics of gender inequality" (2). He believes that "gender difference is the product of gender inequality" (4) rather than the other way around. Kimmel focuses more on gender inequality and the "differences *among* men and *among* women" (9) rather than just explaining how they are different. He also mentions that "gender difference is the product of gender inequality" (4). Because of the inequality between men and women, their resulting gender is affected. Kimmel notices that "the organizations of our society have evolved in ways that reproduce both the differences between women and men and the domination of men over women" (15). His words reinforce that it is society that determines and develops our gender.

The original passage is 132 words; in the revised version, Cummins cuts the word count down to 95. In the following passage, note how Cummins makes this summary both shorter and easier for readers to follow.

Edited Version

> The color coding in this revision shows the improved coherence in the revised summary, as each sentence picks up a point from the one before and carries it forward.

> Sums up argument's main point.

Kimmel explains that "virtually every society known to us is founded upon assumptions of gender difference and the politics of gender inequality" (2). While most people assume that inequality is caused by gender difference, Kimmel sees inequality as the cause, not the result, of gender difference. Gender inequality exists because "the organizations of our society have evolved in ways that reproduce both the differences between women and men and the domination of men over women" (15). In other words, societies dictate that the sexes have distinctly different roles in order to keep the sexes unequal.

REVISED STUDENT EXAMPLE

Cummins 1

Jamie Cummins

Professor Channell

Writing 205

24 August 2011

Exploring the Concept of Gender

In her book *Mindfulness,* Ellen J. Langer says that people can be "trapped by   1
categories" or concepts from the past. One example she gives is "masculine/femi-
nine" (11). I began to wonder how trapped we might be by our ideas of appropriate
behavior for men and women. Many will say that because of men and women's
biological makeup, our gender is simply something one is born with—an instinct,
of sorts. But is this true? I decided to explore the concept of gender and gender
roles to see how different the sexes really are.

> **Explains motivation for his exploration of "gender."**

First, I looked into definitions of the word *gender.* I found that it can be inter-   2
changed with the word *sex* in common use, but social scientists use gender to
refer to social roles and sex to refer to biological differences. According to the
Oxford English Dictionary, gender is a "euphemism for the sex of a human being,
often intended to emphasize the social and cultural, as opposed to the biological,
distinctions between the sexes." If it is just a euphemism for sex, do we need it at
all? Why should social distinctions need to be emphasized?

> **Results of dictionary information, including root meanings. Note his comments on the information.**

I read the introduction to a book by a leading writer on gender, Michael   3
Kimmel, titled *The Gendered Society.* He says, "'Sex' refers to the biological appa-
ratus, the male and the female—our chromosomal, chemical, anatomical organization. 'Gender' refers to the meanings that are attached to those differences within
a culture" (3). Kimmel believes that these meanings are socially constructed (9) in
order to keep the sexes unequal.

> **Use of another writer's view of gender.**

Cummins 2

Kimmel explains that "virtually every society known to us is founded upon   4
assumptions of gender difference and the politics of gender inequality" (2). While
most people assume that inequality is caused by gender difference, Kimmel sees
inequality as the cause, not the result, of gender difference. Gender inequality
exists because "the organizations of our society have evolved in ways that reproduce both the differences between women and men and the domination of men
over women" (15). In other words, societies dictate that the sexes have distinctly
different roles in order to keep the sexes unequal.

This is an interesting theory, but I wonder how different are men and women,   5
really? Kimmel acknowledges the biological differences but his social construc-
tionist approach explores "the differences *among* men and *among* women" and
has determined that "these are often more decisive than the differences between
women and men" (9). The diagram below, taken from his book, shows that there
is greater variation within the bell curve representing each sex than there is
between the sexes. The shaded area in the middle is the overlap showing how
similar men and women really are. Kimmel says the "interplanetary" view of men
as from Mars and women from Venus just reinforces the myth of gender difference, but really, we are all from planet Earth (11).

So if men and women are not so different, where do they get the idea that   6
they are? Kimmel says it is the social institutions of family, workplace, politics,
and schools "where the dominant definitions are reinforced and reproduced
and where 'deviants' are disciplined" (15). I saw gender roles at my high school,
but I never thought school itself played a role. A recent book shows how this
happens.

C. J. Pascoe, a sociologist, observed a typical public high school for an entire   7
year and found that the school reinforced ideas of masculinity as white, athletic,
and heterosexual. In her book, *Dude, You're a Fag: Masculinity and Sexuality in
High School,* she describes a popularity contest called the "Mr. Cougar" competition. Candidates for the "Mr. Cougar" title performed short skits, in which they
mocked boys who did not fit the stereotype of the "manly man."

Use of
another writer
as a concrete
example of
gender role
conditioning.

Cummins 3

In one skit, titled "The Revenge of the Nerds," the candidates for Mr. Cougar   8
appeared at first as weak and effeminate, dressed in nerdy clothes. Pascoe says
the audience thought this was hysterically funny because "male femininity . . . is
coded as humorous" (4). The nerds' girlfriends were then kidnapped by other boys
dressed as "gangstas." To get "their women" back, the nerdy boys had to bulk up
by lifting weights. The girls were depicted as trophies awarded to the nerds once
they had transformed themselves into manly men and proved their masculinity
by rescuing the girls from the gangstas (45). When our class discussed this reading, many students reported that their high schools had similar contests, but they
thought Pascoe was overanalyzing, and it was all just in fun. But I have seen all of
this first hand.

Many different organizations promote male masculinity. At all levels of educa-   9   Draws on his
tion, there is pressure to conform to the "normal" gender image. If one does not   experience in
                                                                                        this paragraph
act "girly" or "manly," they are shunned. Most will eventually find out that one does   to illustrate
not have to have sex, lift weights, or have a girlfriend to prove their masculinity.   gender role
                                                                                        conditioning.
Actually, no one should ever have to *prove* their gender, especially since exagger-
ated gender roles reinforce inequality of the sexes.

But women have made gains in equality, so it's logical to ask, since con-   10   Poses a
cepts of gender change with time, could our society's concept of masculinity be   significant
                                                                                        question
changing? Sharon Jayson, the author of the article "Guys Try to Read Society's   explored in the
Road Map for Behavior," says yes and no. Boys are getting mixed signals about   paragraph.
sexuality and how to develop their masculine identity. An American Psychological
Association study found 19% of the male high school students in the study
received conflicting messages; some told them they had to be tough and others
that they had to be nice. Andrew Smiler, an assistant professor of psychology
at the State University of New York–Oswego, says boys learn that women are
equals, but "we haven't changed masculinity" (qtd. in Jayson). Jayson quotes a
professor of counseling who says "a large proportion of young males [still] view
drinking and having sexual conquests as the appropriate way to begin to prove
they are an adult male." Girls send boys the message they should be sensitive

Cummins 4

and show their feelings, but boys are still sending each other the old "macho" message.

I was ready to accept that gender differences are totally social, but I still had 11 to ask, "Is it possible that male and female brains are different in a way that would affect their behavior?" Some researchers believe that the sexes have innately different ways of thinking. Simon Baron-Cohen, a psychologist at Cambridge University, believes that "there are interesting differences between the *average* male and female mind. Recognizing these could lead to a mutual respect of difference" (77). He says studies show that females have more empathizing brains, while men have more systemizing brains (78). Women are more likely to share, take turns, show sensitivity to facial expressions, talk about emotions, and make eye contact. In contrast, a male brain is more likely to pay attention to relevant details, pursue math, science and physics, read maps, and show interest in mechanical systems. Even one-day old baby boys will "look longer at a mechanical mobile, which is a system with predictable laws of motion, than at a person's face, an object that is next to impossible to systemize" (86). This may be evidence that difference is innate, not learned.

What disturbed me was that Baron-Cohen's article supports the idea that 12 men are the dominant sex. Baron-Cohen tries to avoid discussing the politics of power and inequality in his article. He insists that the differences are "on average." Researchers found individual men with empathizing brains and individual women with systemizing brains; thus, "there is no scientific justification for stereotyping . . ." (92). However, by claiming that men have more systemizing brains, he shows why they are the dominant sex. We all know that those who are talented mathematicians, scientists and physicists get paid more than people in caretaking roles. And in today's society, money *is* power. If men are biologically stronger in these fields, they will be the ones who are more apt to make the money.

I have begun to think that gender is not a helpful concept for the human race, 13 since as Kimmel argues, it is based in inequality. He says that if we could eliminate gender inequality, "we will remove the foundation upon which the entire edifice of

Poses another key question he explores in this paragraph.

Calls attention to a disturbing implication of the innate difference view.

Concludes with his tentative view of "gender" as the source of stereotypes.

Cummins 5

gender difference is built" (4). Eliminating the concept of gender would be impossible, but we need to be aware of how it creates inequality and causes both men and women to be trapped in stereotypes.

- -

Page break

Cummins 6

Works Cited

Baron-Cohen, Simon. "Does Biology Play Any Role in Sex Differences in the Mind?" *The Future of Gender.* Edited by Jude Browne. Cambridge UP, 2007, pp. 77–97.

Jayson, Sharon. "Guys Try to Read Society's Road Map for Behavior." *USA Today,* 26 Aug. 2008, p. 09D.

Kimmel, Michael S. *The Gendered Society.* 3rd ed. Oxford UP, 2008.

Langer, Ellen J. *Mindfulness.* Da Capo Press, Perseus Books, 1989.

Pascoe, C. J. *Dude, You're a Fag: Masculinity and Sexuality in High School.* U of California P, 2007.

CHAPTER 9

Comparing Perspectives

IN CHAPTER 1 WE DISCUSSED THE DIFFERENCE BETWEEN A QUESTION OF FACT AND A QUESTION OF OPINION. "Does playing video games improve visual response time?" is a question of fact. It can be answered by finding reliable current data. Questions of opinion, however, are open to debate. "Should sales of violent video games be restricted to people age eighteen or older?" is a question of opinion. On questions like this, we find a range of perspectives, all of which could be well informed.

Who is right? What should we think? When people encounter conflicting perspectives, two responses are common:

1. "It's just a matter of opinion." It *is* a matter of opinion, and to that extent the response is justified. However, this response usually implies that all opinions are equally sound.

2. "Since everyone is entitled to his or her opinion, I'll take whatever position appeals to me."

The problem with these responses is that they shut down further critical thought on the question.

A third response—one that opens up further thought—is to compare conflicting perspectives carefully, identifying the most intelligent perspective by asking questions like the following:

- Which opinion is backed by the best current information?

- Who offers the most convincing reasoning?

- How can I reconcile the best points in one opinion with the best points in another?

As we explore viewpoints, we accept some ideas and reject others. Eventually we draw our own informed conclusion about where the truth lies.

What Is Comparing Perspectives?

Comparing perspectives is the examination of the differences among **perspectives** (*opinions* or *points of view*). People have different perspectives because of different backgrounds and prior knowledge. For example, parents of young children are more likely to favor restricting the sale of violent video games, while people who work in the video game industry are more likely to favor open access.

Central to writing a comparison of perspectives is **synthesis,** a Greek word that means "putting together." An effective mash-up, for example, is a synthesis of different songs to create a new whole. In the academic world, most writing relies on synthesis, blending information and ideas from multiple sources to develop and support a single point of view.

Why Write to Compare Perspectives?

Your answer to any question depends on your perspective. For example, if someone asked you whether Facebook has been a positive social influence on young people, your answer would depend on your experience with Facebook. To get a broader perspective, you must move beyond your own knowledge and experience, deepening your understanding by comparing and evaluating the views of other people. On the Facebook question, for example, you might evaluate what psychologists and educators have had to say and compare their perspectives with those of your friends and classmates. The key questions for comparing perspectives, then, are the following:

- How do different people answer the question?
- Which perspectives seem most valid after careful examination?
- What can I use from these perspectives to answer the question more fully and thoughtfully for myself?

Finding what others think can complicate our thinking. But getting a mix of viewpoints stimulates thought. A good panel discussion can be more invigorating to an audience than a single person lecturing. Similarly, reading multiple perspectives opens your mind.

Why *write* to compare perspectives? Writing helps us do the following:

- Identify the specific points being discussed
- Analyze where opinions intersect and diverge
- Determine, point by point, the differences and similarities
- Reflect on the points under debate
- Formulate our own view

Writing a comparison of perspectives results in more precise and informed thinking about a question.

Comparisons of perspectives are common in business and community contexts, such as deciding which candidate to vote for, choosing a course of action after hearing a range of proposals, or soliciting the views of multiple consultants on some complicated issue or problem. In personal and academic contexts, people compare perspectives whenever they read reviews of colleges, books, and movies, and all researched writing involves exploring what experts have said.

Genres that compare perspectives include the introductions to books and scholarly articles in which the writer surveys previous scholarship on the topic, book reviews that compare how two or three books treat the same subject, and exploratory essays using multiple sources.

How Do Writers Compare Perspectives?

Like any kind of serious thinking, comparing perspectives works best if you have a method for your investigation:

1. Start by posing a question, not of fact but of opinion, a question on which reasonable people might disagree. It could be a question you wish to research, such as, "Do sports build character?" or "Do same-sex schools educate girls (or boys) better than coeducational ones?"

2. Next, ask how people have answered the question. This involves some kind of research.

3. Compare how people have answered the question.

THE ART OF QUESTIONING — Some Ways Writers Compare Perspectives

For more on concepts, see Chapter 8, Exploring a Concept, pages 142–67.

1. **What is the central question addressed in all the readings?** What is the key question implied in each viewpoint you have read?

2. **What are the key terms or concepts used in discussing this question, and how do the writers define these terms?** Is there disagreement about the meaning of key terms?

3. **How do the authors answer the question, and where do their answers agree or disagree?** Which authors provide the best evidence in support of their views?

4. **What conclusions or insights into the central question have you been able to reach as a result of comparing perspectives on it?** Which perspectives do you want to incorporate into your own answer to the question?

The following reading is an example of comparing perspectives. Note that the author answers all four of the questions listed above.

READING 9.1

An *abstract* is an article summary common in scientific journals and databases. An abstract helps researchers decide whether an article is relevant to their research without having to read it.

Which Character Should Sports Develop?

ANDY RUDD

The reading below is excerpted from an academic article in the social sciences by a psychologist at Florida State University. It is the introduction to a long article on the relationship between sports and character. In the social sciences, such as psychology, writers typically preface their articles with an abstract and a comparison of viewpoints uncovered through their research, a genre known as the "literature review."

Abstract

For years, strong claims have been made that sport builds character. Despite such claims, a "winning at all cost" mentality can frequently be seen within all of sport. The reason for this paradox may relate to confusion

Passive voice is customary in articles in the social sciences and natural sciences.

around what it means to demonstrate character. The purpose of this article is to show that there are indeed two distinct types of character that are espoused in the sport milieu. One type is related to social values (social character) the other related to moral values (moral character). Following an explication and comparison of these types of character, a recommendation is made for a needed emphasis towards the development of moral character.

Explains and compares the views before making his recommendation.

Introduction

Typically when an athlete or team at any level of sport is considered to have displayed character, the word "character" is associated with a host of values such as teamwork, loyalty, self-sacrifice, perseverance, work ethic, and mental toughness. As a specific example, a high school athletic director defined an athlete's character as "a willingness to try no matter what the situation. An attempt to continually improve; a willingness to give all up for the cause; and sacrificing without expectations." In another example, a high school coach asserted: "Character is the belief in self-worth and your own work ethic. . . ." (Rudd, 1999).

Article uses APA (American Psychological Association) documentation style, common in the social sciences.

In professional sport, character has been defined similarly. For instance, consider a newspaper article that headlined, "The Arizona Diamondbacks Attribute Their Success to Character." Specifically, the article highlighted the Diamondbacks as players who work hard and don't complain about salaries (Heyman, 2000). Consider also an issue of *Sports Illustrated* in which New England Patriots' Troy Brown commented on former teammate Drew Bledsoe's ability to play with a broken finger and lead his team to victory. Brown stated, "It showed a lot of character" (Zimmerman, 2001, p. 162).

Presents more examples of *character* as a social value to demonstrate that this understanding of character is widespread.

However, in contrast to the notion that an athlete of character is one who displays values such as teamwork, loyalty, self-sacrifice, perseverance, work ethic, and mental toughness, sport scholars in the area of character development have defined character with a different set of values. Sport scholars, including sport philosophers and sport psychologists, more commonly define an athlete of character as one who is honest, fair, responsible, respectful, and compassionate (Arnold, 1999; Beller & Stoll, 1995; Gough, 1998; Shields & Bredemeier, 1995). For example, Arnold (1999) states, "In terms of moral goodness, or what I refer to as moral character, it involves a life that complies with such virtues as justice, honesty, and compassion" (p. 42).

Offers the other perspective of *character* as a moral value and cites several writers who hold it.

It does indeed seem, therefore, that there are two distinct definitions of character maintained by two camps. The first camp consists of coaches, administrators, and players who may typically define character with social values such as teamwork, loyalty, self-sacrifice, and perseverance. This could be designated as "social character." The second camp consists of sport scholars, and people of earlier generations still alive, who typically define character with moral values such as honesty, fairness, responsibility, compassion, and respect. This is commonly referred to by many of them as "moral character." The existence of these two camps, each with their respective definitions of character, suggests that there is confusion and disagreement concerning the definition of character in sport. (Of course, there may be some "in the middle" who accept an overlapping, possibly conflicting set of values to describe the term "character.")

Identifies patterns in the viewpoints and sums up the differences between the two.

1

2

3

4

Offers an insight into what the comparison has revealed and why it matters. Concludes with view he favors.

As a result of the above, the differences in the way character is defined may provide strong evidence why many feel there is a lack of sportsmanship in competitive sport today. Similarly, these same people decry the "winning-at-all-cost" mentality that seems to prevail in athletics (see, for example, "A Purpose," 1999; Hawes, 1998; Spencer, 1996). Many coaches, athletic administrators, and parents may indeed place such a premium on social values such as teamwork, loyalty, self-sacrifice, and work ethic that they forget, or at least downplay, any emphasis on time-honored moral values such as honesty, fairness, responsibility, and respect.

5

References

Arnold, P. (1999). The virtues, moral education, and the practice of sport. *Quest, 51*(1), 39–54.

Beller, J. M., & Stoll, S. K. (1995). Moral reasoning of high school student athletes and general students: An empirical study versus personal testimony. *Pediatric Exercise Science, 7*(4), 352–363.

Gough, R. (1998). A practical strategy for emphasizing character development in sport and physical education. *Journal of Physical Education, Recreation, & Dance, 69*(2), 18–23.

Hawes, K. (1998). Sportsmanship: Why should anybody care? *NCAA News,* 1, 18.

Heyman, J. (2000, May 22). They're 'good guys, good players.' *Statesman Journal,* 3B. A purpose pitch. (1999, May 17). *Sports Illustrated,* 90, 24.

Rudd, A. (1999). [High school coaches' definitions of character]. Unpublished raw data.

Shields, D., & Bredemeier, B. (1995). *Character development and physical activity.* Champaign, IL: Human Kinetics.

Spencer, A. F. (1996). Ethics in physical and sport education. *Journal of Physical Education, Recreation & Dance, 67*(7), 37–39.

Zimmerman, P. (2001, September 3). New England Patriots. *Sports Illustrated, 95*(9), 162–163.

Questions for Discussion

1. In the first and second paragraphs, what similar ideas connect the examples Rudd provides?
2. One of the keys to responding to anything we read is to evaluate it according to our own experience. What have you learned about character from participating in sports or from observing sports events?
3. Which of the two groups does your perspective on character in sports conform to, or does it include some of both views? If so, do you see conflict in your definition?

■■■ *Thinking as a Writer*

What Is the Rhetorical Situation?

1. What is Rudd's *purpose* in writing this literature review? What is his *angle* on the topic? How would you describe his *stance* and *voice*?
2. Who is this essay's intended *audience*? Is Rudd writing for his psychologist peers, for students with an interest in the topic, for athletes, for a more general public, or for another specific group? Is there anything in this essay you can cite that implies his target readership?
3. Using The Art of Questioning on page 170 and marginal annotations to the article, explore how the author develops his comparison of perspectives. What are the key moves he makes and in what order does he make them? ■

Portfolio of Readings on the Ethics of Eating Meat

The following four readings offer a range of opinions about how meat production and consumption could be more ethical than it currently is. These essays are arguments intended to provide an opportunity for you to explore and compare a range of perspectives. We will use these readings to demonstrate how to compare perspectives, which is the writing assignment for this chapter. As you work through each reading in the portfolio, use the critical reading skills covered in Chapter 2: awareness of the author and his or her purpose and audience; the claim and reasons (since most "perspective" pieces are arguments); and the key terms and assumptions. When preparing to compare texts, you should begin annotating them the first time you read them, noting similarities and differences as you go.

READING **9.2**

The Human Cost of Animal Suffering

MARK BITTMAN

Until a couple of years ago I believed that the primary   1
reasons to eat less meat were environment- and health-related, and there's no question that those are valid reasons. But animal welfare has since become a large part of my thinking as well. And I say this as someone not known to his friends as an animal-lover.

The first perspective in our portfolio comes from Mark Bittman, who writes about food, cooking, eating, health, and the effects of our dietary choices upon the environment. His opinions and recipes appear in his six books and regular columns in the New York Times, *where this reading originally appeared. As the title indicates, Bittman is concerned here with the conditions in which animals are raised and slaughtered for consumption, and the possible consequences to the human psyche, or spirit, if their suffering does not matter to us.*

If we want a not-too-damaged planet to live on, and we want to live here in a way that's also not too damaged, we're better off eating less meat. But if we also want a not-too-damaged psyche, we have to look at how we treat animals and begin to change it.

2

We can start by owning up to the fact that our system is industrialized. And as horrible as that word—"industrialized"—seems when applied to what was once called animal husbandry, it is *precisely* the correct term. Those who haven't seen this, or believe it to be a myth perpetrated by PETA, might consider reading *Every Twelve Seconds: Industrialized Slaughter and the Politics of Sight,* recently published by Timothy Pachirat. (This isn't a review, but the book is superbly written, especially given the grimness of the subject.)

3

You might think that "every 12 seconds" refers to the frequency with which we kill animals, but in a moment you'll realize that that's impossible: we process more than nine billion animals each year—hundreds per second. No, 12 seconds is the frequency with which the Omaha slaughterhouse where Pachirat worked for five months killed cattle, a total of around 2,500 per day.

4

Pachirat, whom I interviewed by phone earlier this week, took the job not as an animal rights activist but as a doctoral candidate in political science seeking to understand the normalization of violence. Like others, he concluded that our isolation from killing allows us to tolerate unimaginably cruel practices simply because we don't see them. But Pachirat emphasizes that it's not only we—consumers—who are isolated from the killing, but workers: at his plant only seven people out of 800 were directly involved with live cattle, and only four with killing.

5

Not that the other workers have it easy: *Every Twelve Seconds* shatters any belief you might have about the system treating animals with a shred of decency. "The sheer volume, scale and rate of killing," Pachirat told me, "the way the animals form a continuous stream rather than individual creatures, makes it clear the animals are seen as raw material. The cattle are called 'beef' even while they're alive—and that not only protects people from acknowledging what they're doing and that they're doing it to sentient beings, it's also accurate, a reflection of the process itself."

6

Our assertion of our right to treat animals as we do iron or lumber or car doors—to treat them as widgets—is not cannibalism, but it's hardly consistent with our keeping of adored pets.

7

Meat-eaters may assert that this is somehow justifiable, because we "need" to eat meat—just not cats or dogs or goldfish—to live. And even though we don't (in fact, there's increasing evidence that too much of it is harmful . . .), we have more than two million years of tradition to point to, we have bodies that process meat well and even thrive on it in limited amounts and we have a love of eating animal flesh that for most of us may not go away any time soon.

8

None of which justifies egregious maltreatment. (Yes, vegan friends, I get that killing animals, period, is maltreatment. This ambivalence, or hypocrisy if you prefer, is for every ambivalent or hypocritical omnivore or flexitarian a puzzle, and scale is an issue.) That maltreatment must first be acknowledged in order for us to alleviate it.

9

And that acknowledgment is forthcoming. The allure—and habit!—of meat-eating may be too strong for most of us to give it up, but recognizing its consequences is a move toward a middle ground: a place where we continue to eat animals but exchange that privilege (that's what it is) for a system in which we eat less and treat them better,

10

one that allows our children to make more humane decisions. Because once we accept that farm animals are capable of suffering (80 percent of Americans believe this to be true), we might well wonder what they've done to deserve such punishment.

The most publicized stories about industrial agriculture represent the exceptions that prove the rule: the uncommon torture of animals by perverse individuals in rogue operations. But torture is inherent in the routine treatment of animals as widgets, and the system itself is perverse. What makes *Every Twelve Seconds* different from (for example) a Mercy for Animals exposé is, says Pachirat, "that the day-in and day-out experience produces invisibility. Industrialized agriculture perpetuates concealment at every level of the process, and rather than focusing on the shocking examples we should be focusing on the system itself."   11

At that point we might finally acknowledge that raising, killing and eating animals must be done differently. When omnivores recognize that our way of producing and eating meat reduces not only slaughterhouse workers but all of us to a warped state, we'll be able to bring about the kind of changes that will reduce both meat consumption and our collective guilt.   12

Pachirat says he has changed as a result of his experience, becoming increasingly interested in what he calls "distancing and concealment." He now intends to work on those issues as they relate to imprisonment, war, torture, deployment of drones and other sophisticated weaponry that allow impersonal killing. And it's because these connections make so much sense that we should look more carefully at how we raise and kill animals.   13

"I didn't get into this to focus on animal issues," he told me, "but my own relationship to eating meat has been transformed, and I now forgo it altogether. It's just not worth the pleasure when you know the system."   14

When we all know the system, we'll be even more eager to change it.   15

READING 9.3

Eating Well vs. Being Good

DAVID KATZ

n my prior post about "best" diets, I promised to address the ethics of eating animals. I turn now to that topic.   1

On the basis of both health and ethics, the case for eating a mostly plant-based diet is strong.   2

The health case is all but irrefutable. It is impractical to cite all of the relevant evidence here. If one goes to the National Library of Medicine website and types   3

The next perspective on the ethics of eating meat comes from David Katz, a medical doctor who is board-certified both in internal medicine and in preventive medicine and public health. He founded and directs the Yale-Griffin Prevention Research Center at Yale University. Katz is a frequent blogger on Huffington Post's "The Blog," where he posted this reading, in which he carefully lays out the most common arguments about the ethics of meat consumption and subjects them to logical critique and evaluation.

"vegetarianism AND health" into the search box, more than 730 peer-reviewed articles pop up. I cite some portion of that evidence in the chapter on vegetarianism (chapter 43 for those who have the book) in my textbook, *Nutrition in Clinical Practice, 2nd Edition* (2008). In this pop culture forum, however, we may reasonably limit ourselves to the view from altitude and noting that relevant citations include intervention studies, nutrient studies, epidemiologic studies, trans-cultural comparison studies and ethnographic studies of cultural transitions.

But before the more zealous carnivores start sharpening spears or pitchforks, and despite my prevailing support for the vegans, I must add that neither on the basis of health, nor ethics, do I find a decisive case for only eating *only* plants.   4

The surest sign you're on the middle path is that people on both sides of you are telling you why you're wrong (often in terms unsuitable for prime time). In this instance, I anticipate the wrath of staunch carnivores and devout herbivores alike. Oh well.   5

I addressed in my prior post the evidence against veganism as the ONLY health-promoting diet. Rather than revisit that argument here, I will simply reassert the takeaway message. Both entirely plant-based and mostly plant-based diets have been linked to powerful health benefits as compared to the typical American diet, the many glow-in-the-dark constituents of which might be hard to assign confidently to either the plant or animal kingdom. There have been no decisive, long-term comparison trials of optimal omnivorousness versus optimal vegetarianism, and perhaps never will be. The evidence available shows that eating only plants can reduce heart disease risk by 70 percent or more, and so can adopting a Mediterranean diet that includes animal foods. Impassioned arguments to the contrary notwithstanding, on the basis of evidence—it's a draw.   6

Eating only plants—whether vegetarianism or veganism—is generally a good idea, and when practiced well, an excellent idea—for health; for the kinder, gentler treatment of our fellow species; and for the preservation of our planet. That is a trifecta if ever there was one, so I lend my very strong support to well-practiced vegetarianism.   7

But the fact that there are variations on the theme of eating well—both health-related and ethics-related variations—allows for more of us to opt in, and fewer to renounce the whole enterprise.   8

The ethical case against eating animals generally originates with our place in the animal kingdom. We are, of course, animals. We are not vegetables, or minerals and, in a time-honored, if admittedly simplistic cataloging of the universe, there's nowhere else to hide. Ethical arguments ensue from one of two fundamental assertions: We are like other animals, or we are different from them.   9

Let's start with being like other animals. I embrace this as the stronger claim not only on the basis of richly detailed renderings of evolutionary biology and molecular genetics,   10 but on the basis of a far more intimate knowledge. Two animals—dogs, to be specific—are among the very best friends I have.

Living with these two animals and sharing friendship with them allows me to see just how much alike we are. I love them, they love me. I know joy, anxiety, fear, anticipation, delight and irritation—and so, very clearly, do they. I can be impatient, thankful, annoying, loyal, affectionate and contrite—and so can they. I can solve problems, and so can they—albeit less complex ones (of course, they also create less complex problems!). I like some people and dislike others—so do they. I remember what matters to me—and they remember what matters to them.   11

By any measure that counts—intelligence, resourcefulness, capacity to love, self-awareness, loyalty—I find that Bramble, Zouzou and I differ only by degree, not kind. We are much alike. And of course, this isn't only about my dogs, or dogs in general. All animals are related at one remove or another, and all life is a continuum.   12

The ethical case builds from there. It is inarguably wrong (at least in modern society) for humans to practice cannibalism and eat other humans. Other animals are members of the extended animal family. It is therefore wrong for, presumably, lesser versions of all the same reasons to eat other animals. Rationalizing the eating of some animals, but not others, is rank "speciesism."   13

But this argument quickly falls apart under scrutiny. If it is wrong for humans to eat animals because we are so alike, then what applies to us must apply to them. In other words, the logical extension of this thinking must be: It is wrong for *any* animal to kill and eat any other animal.   14

This is just silly. It is silly for many reasons, among them the fact that some animals are obligate carnivores and could not survive by any means other than killing and eating other animals (sometimes in drawn-out, painful and rather brutal ways). It is also the very height of presumption for creatures born into a natural world to declare that natural world in its normal workings "unethical." It would be as if carbon-based life forms decided it was unethical to use up carbon in making life forms. We could assert it, but it would be nonsense.   15

We should extend this reasoning a bit and note that it would be silly for modern humans to declare animal eating by pre-modern humans unethical. While there seem to be some differences of opinion among anthropologists about the extent to which our forebears were hunters vs. gatherers, there appears to be universal consensus that they were both. Hunting extends even beyond the timeline of our species, to populate earlier entries into the genus Homo. Was it unethical for Homo *erectus* to hunt and eat what it killed?   16

There would be no modern ethical vegans had there been no Stone Age hunters feeding their ancestors, because those ancestors would have starved before ever making babies. (As I have noted on prior occasion, people who don't survive to make babies make very poor ancestors.) In contrast, there could certainly be modern meat-eaters whose meat-eating ancestors were fed by hunters, with no help required from   17 ethicists. I am not sure it is reasonably in the purview of ethicists to declare as unethical something on which their existence depends.

It cannot be unethical for animals to kill and eat other animals. And it cannot be unethical for humans to have done so throughout their history. So can we make the ethical case based on how different we are from both other species, and our former selves?   18

In one sense, no. Biologically, we are the same as our former selves—at least the same as we have been for tens of thousands of years, if not far longer. And while we might argue we are fundamentally different from other animals, that might as readily destroy as make the argument against eating them. If animals are so different from us, why extend to them the same ethical considerations we apply to ourselves?   19

But in another sense, there is a case to be made based on how different we now are from other species, and our former selves. That sense is our impact on the planet.   20

In our voracious, resource-devouring multitudes, we are exerting a force no other species has ever approached, and which our Stone Age ancestors could not have imagined. In that sense, we are genuinely different.   21

The ethical issue has little to do with whether or not we eat animals. Instead, it has everything to do with how we turn them into food. Knowing, willful neglect or abuse of any creature by any other is unethical. It may be that only humans can be "knowing" about such things, which would give us a basis to limit ethical considerations to ourselves. It allows us to exonerate the occasional brutality of lions, or Komodo dragons. But if fully conscious, premeditated abuse of one creature by another is *not* unethical, it's hard to see how anything is.   22

A growing mass of humanity with a penchant for meat inexorably drives the supply side toward methods of mass production, involving cost-savings and corner-cutting. Animals are fed food unrelated to their native diets. They are crowded together. They are dosed with antibiotics and hormones. There are expedient means of turning creatures into chops and patties that, according to a litany of first-hand accounts, play out very cruelly.   23

In other words, the mass production of meat can obliterate the life of the animal whose meat it is. A steer is turned into something other than a creature—it's just a whole bunch of hamburgers on the hoof. By almost any defensible definition of ethics, the practices that ensue from depending on animals for food to the extent that we do—are over the line.   24

Let's wrap up. Staunch proponents of veganism tend to over-interpret the evidence for plant-based eating, strong as it is. While it is clear that eating mostly plants is far better than hardly eating plants prevails in the U.S., it does not follow that eating only plants is the only way to eat well. Advocates of meat-eating who base their arguments on our ancestral consumption of meat overlook how radically different modern, domestic, mass-produced animal flesh is from the variety our ancestors ate.   25

As for the ethics, there are too many of us Homo sapiens on the planet already, and every reason to believe there will be many more of us before we control our population growth. Most of us who can, eat too many animals and animal products. The combination of our multitudes and our appetites results in the mass production of animal foods, which in turn results in—or at least invites—terrible abuses.   26

Perpetrating abuse while knowing it is abuse is unethical, if anything is. Eating animals may not be intrinsically unethical, but the means in this case may un-justify the ends. If we must maltreat animals to produce the volumes of animal food we demand, then we should stop demanding such volumes of animal food.   27

There is, however, some latitude left in the solution.   28

It would be fine if all of us were to eat only plants. But if most of us were to eat mostly plants, we could raise many fewer animals for food, and could treat those we do . . . ethically. There is more than one way to eat well and do good. The prevailing norm at present, however, isn't one of them.   29

READING **9.4**

The Ethics of Eating Meat

PAUL SCHWENNESEN

Like David Katz's piece, this one also appeared originally on Huffington Post's "The Blog." The author, Paul Schwennesen, after graduating from the U.S. Air Force Academy, went on to earn a master's degree in government from Harvard University. Now living in rural Arizona, he is a rancher who raises grass-fed beef in environmentally and ethically conscious ways, as he explains in this reading.

I kill animals for a living.   1

I do it so others, as well as myself, can eat them. This accident of circumstance probably disqualifies me from any serious ethical discussion of meat eating. After all, I can hardly claim objectivity. Then again, who can? I live very close to the forces of nature that give (and take) life and therefore have an informed, if undoubtedly nearsighted, sense of what it is I do.   2

But is it ethical?   3

Asking whether eating meat is "ethical" is like asking whether having sex is ethical. Biological imperatives do not pander to such arbitrary distinctions.   4

My meat-eating is ethical, in the sense that it is not gratuitous; I understand intimately the implications and contradictions of my consumption. I know how it is that my beeves are born, the grasses they like and the ones they don't. I've saved the lives of calves and butchered their mothers in the same afternoon. I thank each for the age-old   5 sacrifice of prey to predator and I swear they understand. I neither rejoice in the blood nor shy from it. This is life. This is ethics.

For me, my proximate, deliberate understanding of what I do defines ethical behavior as a whole: the social moderation of otherwise unrestrained individual yearnings. In my mind, eating #906 (a red mottle-face cow with upturned horns currently braising in the slow cooker) is an ethically different activity than eating a Big Mac on the run.

6

The fact that I feel comfortable making such a distinction indicates something fundamental about ethics: they evolve. Our current handwringing over what we eat is clearly a privilege born of abundance. Room for such ruminations is only created after the belly hasn't room for anything else. We agonize over meat consumption because we can afford to. Lucky us.

7

"Ethics" exist as social shorthand; a distilled collective conscience that varies with the social reality it reflects. Ethics do not stand like clean-cut traffic cops in the path of natural urges; they are more like cautionary rumble-strips as we careen down lives strewn with choices. Ethical consumption of meat, therefore, is based upon timing, circumstance, and conscientious understanding of what society deems appropriate. In modern Western culture at least, you are "unethical" if you cannot moderate a biological sexual urge. It is likewise "unethical" to fulfill biological carnivorous urges upon, say, kittens.

8

We have evolved from a society in which nearly everyone knew the intimate realities and consequences of eating meat to one in which nearly no one does. We have commercially outsourced the twinge of guilt, the pang of discomfort, the heart-race of witnessing a death to just a handful among us. Is there an ethical distinction between the deaths caused by a yeoman farmer who grimly butchers a hog in the fall and a minimum-wage factory worker who mechanically butchers six thousand in a morning? Many of us now see an ethical nuance. Our physical capacities to produce and consume have altered dramatically in the last sixty years; our ethical capacity to accept these realities is altering as well.

9

My occupation, as a result, caters to omnivores and more than a few "recovering vegetarians" who prefer (apparently) the conscientious killing I practice. I therefore raise my cattle with sentiment but cannot stray into the realm of sentimentality. I recognize that life rests upon the consumption of the unwilling. I obey this ecological truth while simultaneously working within the artificial, changeable lines society delineates. This too, is natural.

10

Eating meat, particularly #906, is ethical because most people think it is. That is, perhaps, about all one can say.

11

READING **9.5**

Reciprocity: A Foundation for Balance

CLARA SUE KIDWELL, HOMER NOLEY, AND GEORGE E. "TINK" TINKER

The final reading in our portfolio comes from a book about Native American religious views, written by three influential Native American scholars and theologians. Clara Sue Kidwell founded and directed programs in Native American studies at the University of Minnesota, University of California at Berkeley, and University of Oklahoma. Homer Noley is director of the National United Methodist Native American Center at Claremont Graduate University, and George E. "Tink" Tinker has been a member of the faculty at Iliff School of Theology since 1985, teaching courses in Native American cultures, history, and religious traditions. This selection, taken from their book, A Native American Theology, *explains the Native Americans' view of humans' ethical relationship to the earth, including plants and animals.*

The American Indian notion of reciprocity is fundamental to all human participation in world-balancing and maintaining harmony. Reciprocity involves first of all an understanding of the cosmos as sacred and alive, and the place of humans in the processes of the cosmic whole. It begins with an understanding that anything and everything that humans do has an effect on the rest of the world around us. Even when we cannot clearly know what that effect is in any particular act, we know that there is an effect. Thus, Indian peoples, in different places and in different cultural configurations, have always struggled to know how to act appropriately in the world. Indeed, this knowledge seems to be the consistent purpose of all Indian creation stories. Knowing that every action has its unique effect has always meant that there had to be some sort of built-in compensation for human actions, some act of reciprocity. 1

The necessity for reciprocity becomes most apparent where violence is concerned, especially when such violence is an apparent necessity as in hunting or harvesting. Violence cannot be perpetrated, a life taken, in a Native American society, without some spiritual act of reciprocation. I am so much a part of the whole of creation and its balance, anything I do to perpetrate an act of violence, even when it is necessary for the survival of our families and our communities, must be accompanied by an act of spiritual reciprocation intended to restore the balance of existence. It must be remembered that violence as a technical category must extend to all one's "relatives." Thus, a ceremony of reciprocity must accompany the harvesting of vegetable foods such as corn or the harvesting of medicinals such as cedar, even when only part of a plant is taken. The ceremony may be relatively simple, involving a prayer or song and perhaps a reciprocal offering of tobacco. 2

Many tribes maintained very extensive and complex ceremonies of reciprocation to insure continuing balance and plentiful harvests. Likewise, there is a tradition of mythic stories that accompany such ceremonies and function to provide the theoretical foundation for the ceremonies. Ultimately, all of these stories function further to insure the continuing respect of the communities who tell the stories for all the parts of the created world, all the relatives, upon which the people depend for their own well-being. 3

Even gathering rocks for a purification ceremony (sweat lodge ceremony) calls for care and respect, prayers and reciprocation.

In the same manner, ceremonies involving self-sacrifice (typically called "self-torture" or "self-mutilation" by the missionaries and early ethnographers) also come under this general category of reciprocation. In the Rite of Vigil, (vision quest), which is very widespread among Indian peoples of North America, as well as the Sun Dance,* the suffering the supplicant takes upon himself or herself is usually thought of as vicarious and as some sort of reciprocation. Since all of one's so-called possessions are ultimately not possessions but relatives that live with someone, an individual is not giving away a possession when he or she gives a gift to someone else. In actuality the only thing a person really owns and can sacrifice is one's own flesh. Thus these ceremonies of self-sacrifice tend to be the most significant ceremonies of a people.

4

While missionaries typically thought of these ceremonies as vain human attempts to placate some angry deity, Indian communities know that these ceremonies were much more complex than that. Rather, they are much more often thought of as vicarious sacrifices engaged in for the sake of the whole community's well-being. Moreover, they are thought of as ceremonies that came to the community as a gift from the Sacred Mystery in order to help the community take care of itself and its world. Thus, the Sun Dance is considered a ceremony in which Two-Leggeds† participate with the Sacred in order to help maintain life, that is, to maintain the harmony and balance of the whole. All these ceremonies, then, especially those that anthropologists call "world renewal," function as part of the constantly on-going process of creation.

5

Hunting and war, for example, typically involved a complex ceremonial preparation before a contingent of warriors or hunters left their home. The Osage War Ceremony (nearly identical to the ceremony performed before a buffalo hunt) involved an eleven-day ritual, allowing enough time to affirm the sacredness of life, to consecrate the lives that would be lost in war, and to offer prayers in reciprocation for those potentially lost lives.[1] In the hunt, most Indian nations report specified prayers of reciprocation, involving apologies and words of thanksgiving to the animal itself and the animal's spirit nation. Usually, this ceremonial act is in compliance with the request of the animals themselves as the people remember the primordial negotiations in mythological stories.‡ Thus, formal and informal ceremonies of reciprocation are a day-to-day mythic activity which has its origin in mythological stories in which human beings were given permission by the animal nations to hunt themselves for food. The resulting covenant, however, calls on human beings to assume responsibilities over against the perpetuation of violence among four-legged relatives. Even after the hunt or battle,

6

Sun Dance: Many tribes practiced some form of ritual, sacrificial dance in which young men attached themselves with leather straps to a pole. In many versions of the dance, the ends of the straps pierced the men's chests. The dancers' suffering was a sacrifice for the good of the whole community.
†*Two-Leggeds:* The Native Americans traditionally categorized animal life as two-legged and four-legged, rather than as human and non-human. These traditional categories maintained the belief that all life forms are kin to each other.
‡*Primordial negotiations in mythical stories:* Many Native American creation stories include an explanation of how the two-leggeds and four-legged animals determined which would eat the other. The question was settled by a race. There are many versions of the story. Paul Goble wrote and illustrated an outstanding children's book titled *The Great Race of the Birds and Animals,* based on the Cheyenne and Sioux legends.

those who participated must invariably go through a ceremonial cleansing before re-entering their own village. Not to do this would bring the disruption of the sacred caused by the perpetration of violence right into the middle of national community life and put all people at risk.[2]

Animals, birds, crops, and medicines are all living relatives and must be treated with respect if they are to be genuinely efficacious for the people. The ideal of harmony and balance requires that all beings respect all other beings, that they respect life and avoid gratuitous or unthinking acts of violence. Maintaining harmony and balance requires that even necessary acts of violence be done "in a sacred way." Thus nothing is taken from the earth without prayer and offering. When the tree is cut down for the Sun Dance, for instance, something must be offered, returned to the spirit world, for the life of that tree. The people not only ceremonially and prayerfully ask its permission but also ask for its cooperation and help during the four days of the dance itself.

7

American technological and economic development cannot embody the Indian ethic of reciprocity. It is not enough to replant a few trees or to add nutrients to the soil. These are superficial acts to treat the negative symptoms of development. The value of reciprocity which is a hallmark of Indian ceremonies goes to the heart of issues of sustainability, which is maintaining a balance and tempering the negative effects of basic human survival techniques. There is no ceremony among any people for clear-cutting an entire forest.

8

End Notes

1. See Francis La Flesche, *The War and Peace Ceremony of the Osage Indians,* Bureau of American Ethnography, Bulletin 101 (1939).
2. Leslie Silko's famous novel, *Ceremony* (New York: Viking, 1977), is precisely about such a situation. The novel deals with the healing and cleansing of a World War II veteran for whom a new ceremony had to be devised. Social and spiritual complexities of disintegration and alienation had made it much more difficult for the Laguna people and for himself. Thus, his healing has to do with the healing of the whole community and not just himself.

The Assignment

Read at least two perspectives addressing a topic of current interest. In an essay, explore the perspectives by noting where authors address the same or similar questions, and compare their answers. Decide which views seem most valid. Conclude by discussing how your exploration contributed to your understanding of the topic.

What Can I Write About?

If your instructor does not provide you with a set of readings that provide different views on a single question, you have several options for finding them:

See Chapter 16, pages
343–44, for guidance on
using library databases.

See Chapter 16, pages
344–47, for guidance on
Internet searches.

- **Reviews of artistic works and performances.** You could compare reviews of a film, play, or musical performance.

- **Opinion columns assessing political candidates or proposed legislation.** If you are writing in an election year, you could compare candidates' positions on a single issue. Newspapers often run opinion columns where you can find at least two views on a current political issue.

- **Viewpoints on issues in current events or popular culture.** News articles often cite a few expert viewpoints on the topic, which you could use as a starting point. Use a library database to search for articles by these authors. You can also search using keywords for opinions and articles on an issue. Newspapers often run "debates," in which they publish several columnists' responses to a single question. For example, see the online feature "Room for Debate" in the *New York Times.* The reference librarians at your school can also help you locate a variety of views on a topic.

How Do I Compare Perspectives? Questioning the Rhetorical Situation

Begin by picturing a **rhetorical situation** for your writing project. Remember that rhetoric means *effective communication.* You are not just writing a paper; you are also communicating. You should consider the key variables in any act of communication: a writer with something to say, a reader the writer wishes to reach, and a kind of text appropriate to the writing task. These variables will affect many decisions you make during the composing process.

Writer: What Is My Purpose, and What Impression Should Readers Have of Me?

The assignment in this chapter specifies a purpose for comparing perspectives: to explore the range of opinions on a single question and to draw an original conclusion informed by your reading and critical thinking. In college writing, this is a common purpose, since most research papers begin with an exploration of the research.

This project, then, will help you develop a crucial college skill you will also use regularly in daily life as you analyze competing bids, for example, or assess the arguments of political candidates vying for your vote.

Audience: Who Is My Reader?

As with all writing projects, imagining your audience will help you decide how best to represent the viewpoints you are comparing. You will need to place perspectives in context for your readers by identifying each writer and providing information about his or her background. Readers expect writers to represent the

To get a broad perspective on a topic, compare and evaluate the views of other thinkers. Does everyone, for example, think that Facebook improves friendships? Which perspectives seem most valid after careful examination?

© mediaphotos/Getty Images, RF

competing viewpoints fairly by providing accurate summaries of the various positions. Because the assignment requires comparing and evaluating viewpoints, your readers will need you to go beyond summary to identify the strengths and weaknesses of each position.

Text: What Moves Can I Make?

The basic moves are illustrated in Andy Rudd's comparison of views on character in sports (pages 170–72). The student example (pages 196–200) also illustrates the moves. In sum they are as follows:

1. Introduce a question upon which people take different positions.
2. Define any key terms central to the question.
3. Present the main point of each perspective in brief summary statements.
4. Look for patterns of agreement and disagreement, and compare what different people have to say on the same point.
5. Use quotation and paraphrase to show what different people say in defense of their viewpoints.
6. As you present your sources' viewpoints, respond with your own comments evaluating them.
7. Conclude with an evaluation of the viewpoints and what you learned from comparing them.

How Do I Compare Perspectives? Engaging the Writing Process

No two people compose in exactly the same way, and even the same person may go through the writing process in different ways with different assignments. Nevertheless, because no one can attend to everything at once, there are phases in handling any significant writing task. You begin by preparing to write, generating content and planning your draft. The next phase is drafting your paper, getting a version, however rough it may be, on screen or paper so that you have something to work with during the next two stages: revising your draft by making changes to the content, arrangement, and style of your writing; and editing your draft to take care of problems at the paragraph and sentence level, such as lack of focus and coherence, awkward or unclear sentences, and errors of grammar, spelling, and punctuation.

We will illustrate this process for comparing perspectives using this chapter's portfolio of four readings (pages 173–83) on the ethics of eating meat. We will guide you through strategies for finding points for comparison and organizing an exploratory essay around them.

Exploring Your Topic

Plan to spend at least half of the time allotted for this project on the preparation stage: careful reading and considerable informal writing, both in the margins and in notes either online or in a notebook.

Choosing and Narrowing Your Topic

As you choose readings on your topic, be sure that the authors are addressing not just the same topic but *the same question or questions* about the topic. For example, although some of our portfolio readings mention the health benefits of reducing meat consumption, the key question addressed in each case has to do with ethics, not health.

Read your selections critically, as described in Chapter 2 on page 13, and illustrated in the strategies and activities throughout the chapter. These strategies include the following preparations before reading:

1. Find out about the author and his or her likely bias.

2. Skim the reading to see the main ideas as evident in the introduction, paragraph openings, and the conclusion. Look for keywords that appear in other readings you are considering for your comparison.

What Does That Word Mean?

On any topic, certain words are central to the discussion, as in our reading about the concept of character in sports.

The keyword in our example about the ethics of eating meat is *ethical.* Critical thinking, as we say in Chapter 1, begins with a basic question: What does that word mean? Ethical does not simply mean "right" as opposed to wrong; according to the definition in the *Oxford English Dictionary,* it means that which "conforms to moral principles or ethics; morally right; honorable; virtuous; [and] decent." However, the closer we look at the word and how it is used, the more we see that people might disagree on what exactly makes an action, like eating meat, moral or immoral.

Many people argue that raising cattle in crowded conditions, as pictured here, makes eating meat unethical.

© sponner/Getty Images, RF

■■■■ ACTIVITY 9.1 *Writer's Notebook*

Exploring Terms

List the key term or terms that are used in your question. Then look up the term(s) in a comprehensive dictionary like the *Oxford English Dictionary (OED)*. Write a paragraph or two explaining what you discovered about the origins and definitions of your key term or terms. ■

When humans depended on hunting and gathering for survival, there could be no question about the morality of killing a deer, for example. Today, as David Katz argues, dietary science has proven that meat, while nutritious in moderation, is not essential for survival. If we could get by on tofu but prefer the taste of meat, are we as ethical in consuming it as were our Paleolithic ancestors? As rancher Paul Schwennesen says, "'Ethics' exist as social shorthand; a distilled collective conscience that varies with the social reality it reflects." The meaning of this term, *ethical,* will be crucial to the different answers people have today to the question, "Is it ethical to eat meat?"

Preparing to Write

Beyond gathering your readings and assessing them critically, the key step in preparing to write is to look for ways to synthesize what the perspectives say.

Finding Ways to Synthesize

Writing a good comparison depends on synthesis, bringing together what different people have to say on similar points. A useful strategy for finding connections among sources is to identify the main points in any one source and turn them into questions. Questions are helpful in making connections across readings because once you have identified a question, you can look to see how different writers answer it. For example, in the first of our portfolio readings, we see Mark Bittman saying:

> If we want a not-too-damaged planet to live on, and we want to live here in a way that's not too damaged, we're better off eating less meat. But if we also want a not-too-damaged psyche, we have to look at how we treat animals and begin to change it.
>
> We can start by owning up to the fact that our system is industrialized. And as horrible as that word—"industrialized"—seems when applied to what was once called animal husbandry, it is precisely the correct term.

In this passage, Bittman makes two important points:

- The inhumane treatment of animals is bad for human mental health.
- Meat producing has changed from animal husbandry to an industrialized system.

By turning these statements into questions, we have a better tool for finding connections across the readings. Besides Bittman, who else has something to say on the following questions?

- Are there psychological consequences for us when meat producers are indifferent to animal suffering?

- How has large-scale production and slaughter changed the ethics of eating meat?

■■■ ACTIVITY 9.2 *Collaborative Activity*

Turning Main Points into Questions

In groups of two or three, review the four readings on the ethics of eating meat, identifying the main points in each. State the question that each main point answers. Then find passages in two or more of the readings that answer the same question. What similarities and differences do you find among the answers? ■

BEST PRACTICES   Advantages of Turning Key Points into Questions

1. Different sources will give different answers to the same question, but *stating the question* will help you bring the readings together.
2. Questions can help you *organize your essay point by point,* showing how each question is addressed by different sources; this approach is preferable to presenting entire perspectives, one after another. The latter organization results in summaries, whereas the former compares and comments on specific differences among the perspectives.

Mapping Ideas on a Comparative Grid

Another way to identify points of similarity and difference in multiple sources is to map the ideas on a grid, such as the one on page 189. Begin by identifying the questions answered by the main points in each selection. Then indicate where the answers can be found in the readings.

Additional Ways to Track Connections across Perspectives

As you read into a second or third person's perspective, try one or more of these suggestions to help keep control over your sources:

- Annotate each reading with references to page numbers in other sources that address the same questions.

- Use color-coded highlighters to mark passages addressing the same questions in different readings.

- Write informally to discuss where the authors agree or disagree and respond with your own opinion about who has the best viewpoint. See Chapter 2, pages 28–29, for a model. In the next section, we show an example of a student's informal writing in response to one question in common across the readings on ethical meat consumption.

Question	Bittman (pages 173–75)	Katz (pages 175–79)	Schwennesen (pages 179–80)	Kidwell, Noley, Tinker (pages 181–83)
What is unethical meat production?	par. 9: "egregious mistreatment"	par. 22: "knowing, willful neglect or abuse of any creature"	par. 9: "factory worker" who "mechanically butchers" thousands a day	par. 7: "gratuitous or unthinking acts of violence" with no respect for life
What is unethical consumption?	par. 5: Allowing ourselves to be unaware and isolated from maltreatment of the animals we eat.	par. 26: Consuming too many animals results in unethical production.	par. 6: "gratuitous" eating such as a "Big Mac on the run"; "Outsourcing" the killing and the guilt	par. 8: Failure to reciprocate with some prayer of thanks
Are there any psychological consequences when we don't care about the animals we are eating?	par. 2: "damaged psyche" par. 12: "warped state" par. 12: "collective guilt"		par. 6: People live without social restraints, give in to "unrestrained individual yearnings"	
How does Westerners' volume of meat consumption affect the ethics of eating meat?	par. 6: Animals seen as "raw material" even when alive	par. 23: Abuses of mass production to satisfy the desire of too many people for too much meat.	par. 9: In the past 60 years humans have increased their capacity "to produce and consume," and these realities should affect our attitudes toward ethical consumption	par. 8: "[T]echnological and economic development cannot embody the Indian ethic of reciprocity"

Using Informal Writing to Join the Discussion

One of the best ways to generate content is to write informally about how different people answer the same questions and to say what you think about their answers. You can do this as freewriting, a notebook entry, or a post on a discussion board to share with classmates who might be reading and comparing the same sources.

The advantage of this kind of informal writing is that you can later use it as part of the draft of your paper. It will need cleaning up, but it will have two essential qualities:

- A comparison with specific references to the sources you have read
- Commentary showing your own thinking in your own voice

You need to be part of the synthesis, too, so it is never too soon to begin to evaluate the viewpoints. Following is an example of a freewriting from student Conner Kline, whose comparison of perspectives on the ethics of eating meat concludes this chapter (see pages 196–200). As Kline reads the first three of his four sources, he uses freewriting to draw some connections across the readings.

Student Example: Freewriting Comparing and Commenting

Begins with the big question of whether humans should eat animals and shows that one author answers it.

Paraphrases Katz's answer to the question.

Comments on Katz's argument.

Raises the second question: What is the real ethical issue?

Draws a connection between two of the readings.

Makes a connection to a third source, which shows an alternative to the assembly-line style of slaughtering.

Draws some conclusions about the questions raised by these three readings.

While my friends and I eat meat, I know that many people avoid it for ethical reasons. Some people take a stand for animal rights and say that humans should not eat animals at all. Only one author really deals with this question. David Katz, the doctor, says it is illogical to say that we should not eat animals because they are so much like us, when they really are not like us, since they are eating each other. This makes sense to me. Eating them is totally different, ethically, from eating other humans. So if it's OK to eat them, what *is* the ethical issue? Katz says that the real ethical problem with eating meat is the way it's produced, with "conscious, premeditated abuse." This is one point where Katz and Bittman agree. Bittman is concerned about how the assembly line method of killing them treats them as just "widgets" rather than living creatures. In one slaughterhouse, a cow is killed every 12 seconds, so you see that wouldn't allow much time for the worker to think about what he is doing. Then, when I read the blog post by the rancher, Schwennesen, I saw that slaughtering can be more humane. Schwennesen takes pride in running an ethical ranching business. He says he butchers his own cows and takes the time to think about what he's doing. He says he thanks each one for "the age-old sacrifice of prey to predator and I swear they understand." You have to respect him for caring and being personally involved with the death of his cows. Why should these two different ways of killing cows matter to us as consumers? One kind of killing is not ethical, not done with any moral principles; it's just about making money. The other kind of killing, also for profit, at least acknowledges that the animal made a sacrifice, for which we should be thankful. We should not support the kind of meat production that objectifies a living creature as if its life didn't matter, but the factory meat is everywhere and so it's hard to avoid it and be an ethical eater.

▪▪▪ ACTIVITY 9.3 *In Your Own Work*

Respond to Ideas in Your Readings

As you read and reread each of the perspectives, record key points in a reading and respond to them with your own evaluations. Be sure to *refer to specific passages in the readings,* as in our freewriting example. ▪

Drafting Your Paper

Begin by considering your own point of view or angle:

What Is My Angle?

Even though some of the writers agree on major points, each of the authors comes to the topic from a unique professional, personal, or philosophical background.

- Mark Bittman is a food writer who has written cookbooks and food columns for the *New York Times*. He writes from the perspective of an expert concerned about diets that are healthy for us and for planet Earth. He is not a vegetarian but he has written a vegetarian cookbook. You can see his perspective in the title: "The Human Cost of Animal Suffering." He is interested in our mental health and the negative effects on our psyches of participating in animal cruelty.

- David Katz is a medical doctor with a special interest in nutrition and disease prevention. His perspective is more scientific and political than Bittman's. He founded Yale University's Yale-Griffin Prevention Research Center. Like Bittman, he is interested in sustainability and sustainable eating habits. He is a writer with several news and magazine blogs, where he expresses his opinions and attempts to influence public policy decisions in the best interests of global health.

- Paul Schwennesen writes from the perspective of an environmentally conscious rancher and independent entrepreneur. He owns the Double Check Natural Grass-Fed Beef ranch in southern Arizona, which sells meat to local markets in Arizona. He was educated at the U.S. Air Force Academy, University of Arizona, and Harvard University, where he received a Master of Liberal Arts in Government. He is politically active and interested in conservation and land management.

- Clara Sue Kidwell is the primary author of the book *A Native American Theology* (Orbis, 2001). Although she holds a Ph.D. in history of science, she turned to an interest in Native American studies, which she taught at the University of Oklahoma and University of California at Berkeley, among other schools. She was joined on this book by two Native American theologians: Homer Noley, who is a retired director of the National United Methodist Native American Center at Claremont School of Theology, and George E. "Tink" Tinker, a prominent scholar at Iliff School of Theology in Denver. These authors are writing from a Native American and Christian perspective, and their angle here is not so much on the ethics of eating meat as on the ethics of living in harmony and balance with all of creation.

These four readings, however, are arguments, not explorations. How does a writer find an angle while keeping an open mind? The answer is to think about why exploring the question matters to you personally. What perspectives are you inclined to hold? As you read to discover and compare other perspectives, put your own attitudes to the same test. Consider the following questions:

1. **What context do I bring to the question?** A person exploring perspectives on the relationship between wealth and happiness began by considering how her own upbringing in a military family fostered frugality and self-discipline.

2. **What outcome do I want for my exploration?** Having an angle means believing that your exploration matters. What do you hope to learn from reading multiple viewpoints? Someone planning to become a teacher chose to read about different perspectives on how young children learn. Her interest in education gave her an angle.

3. **Which perspectives are commonly held, and should they be challenged?** On any given question, we can usually name some popular perspectives. An angle can derive from challenging popular perspectives. For example, many Americans believe that everyone should go to college. We can look for selections supporting this perspective, as well as perspectives that challenge it.

What Voice Is Appropriate for Exploratory Writing?

You do not want your essay to read like a list of points: "Source A says _____. On this question, Source B says _____." Such a paper would be monotonous. *You need to be present in the paper, speaking as someone thinking through the questions and evaluating the various viewpoints.*

Use the informal writing you did as you read, evaluated, and responded to the readings to get your own voice into your project. Ask yourself what you would say to the author if he or she were present and you were doing an interview. Challenging perspectives is a good way to put voice into your paper, but make sure that your challenges are well reasoned, not attacks. You should sound fair, thoughtful, and receptive, willing to consider points of view that you do not find persuasive but that may contain valuable points or insights.

Developing and Organizing Your Synthesis

Drafting the essay for this project should not be difficult if you have highlighted your sources to identify passages that answer the same questions, annotated your sources to note points in common, and written informally to compare and respond to the perspectives you have gathered. Review your notes and then consider the following advice:

1. **Introduction:** How might I begin the paper? For your introduction, you could do the following:

   - Open with your own view before reading. In the body and conclusion, indicate how your thinking changed.

   - Open with the question that is the focus of your exploration. State it clearly and explain its importance.

   - Open with the main question you will address, such as, "Can eating meat be ethical? If so, under what conditions or in what circumstances?" You could move directly into your paper this way.

2. **Body:** How can I introduce and compare the perspectives? You could devote one or two paragraphs to setting up all of the perspectives, summarizing the

---

BEST PRACTICES Tips for Organizing Your Paper around Questions

- Check the lists of questions you have made for each perspective. Put these lists together now and identify questions that appear in multiple readings.

- Consider whether narrowing the focus of your exploration might help. An exploration of the ethics of eating meat could have had a much larger focus, such as the rights of animals not to be eaten, but that focus would have been too large for a short paper.

- Based on length requirements for the paper and how much you have to say about the questions, select the ones you intend to address.

- Order the questions logically. For example, a definition question makes more sense at the beginning of the paper. Discuss causes and then effects.

- Plan on multiple paragraphs for each question. You could, for instance, devote one paragraph to one source's answer and another to what the others say on the same question.

- Create transitions so that your reader will know when discussion of one question is over and another is beginning.

main position of each and introducing the key figures who hold that position, including full names and some background about their research. Or you could begin with the first question that cuts across at least two of the perspectives, introduce the perspectives, and present what each says in response to that question. Then move on to another question.

The essential point is that a paper that synthesizes ideas from multiple authors *needs to be organized around the questions that cut across the readings,* not around the readings themselves. If you devote the first part of your paper to just one author's views, the second to the second author's views, and so on, your paper will read like a summary rather than an exploration.

3. **Conclusion:** Your conclusion should review your evaluations of the different perspectives. Whose reasons were the most persuasive? What evidence was the most compelling? Construct a perspective of your own using what you have found convincing and compelling from all the sources. Use your conclusion to explain how you developed deeper insight based on comparing your sources.

Revising Your Draft

Revising this kind of paper usually involves improving the organization, looking more closely at the perspectives to make your exploration more specific, and including more of your own reactions to the authors' views. The Art of Questioning lists specific activities for helping you revise.

THE ART OF QUESTIONING | Revision Checklist for Comparing Perspectives

This checklist moves in descending order, from major challenges of this project to concerns to consider in every piece of formal writing.

1. **Did you explore?** Exploring means entertaining a question. To entertain a question means to hold it open and consider it thoughtfully. If you disputed a point before considering its merits, revise to show more open-mindedness before you declare that someone is wrong.

2. **How well did you represent the ideas of all the authors?** Did you draw on the sources to represent their views accurately and fully? Did you introduce the authors with full name on first mention and provide information about their credentials?

3. **How well did you organize the paper?** Check to see that you focus on one question at a time, not one source at a time. Did you bring in comparisons throughout your draft?

4. **How well did you work quotations into your paper?** Did you introduce quotations and follow up with explanation and commentary as needed?

5. **How well did you respond to the sources?** Did you provide enough commentary to show exactly what you agreed or disagreed with and why?

6. **How smoothly did the sentences flow?** Each sentence should prepare the reader for the one coming next. Read your draft aloud, listening for places where transitions are needed.

When you have limited time to revise a paper, you have to prioritize. Take care of the bigger problems first, the ones that alter your essay substantially. If smaller problems remain, solve as many as you can in the time you have. One common problem of drafts is inadequately developed paragraphs.

Student Example: Excerpt from Conner Kline's Draft

The following paragraph does not adequately introduce the authors of the source, and it jumps too quickly into the quotation about clear-cutting. In order to understand the point about forests and ceremonies, the readers need more background information about the Native American idea of ceremonies as reciprocation for taking anything from the Earth.

By opening the paragraph with the authors' names, Kline appears to be organizing his paper around his sources, not questions to explore. Also, he should include some information about the authors, who are experts on Native American religious beliefs.

The quotation about forests seems incoherent here because the analogy needs to be set up before the quote, not after it.

Draft Version

Clara Sue Kidwell, Homer Noley, and George E. Tinker would also agree that our industrialized system of mass-producing meat makes eating meat in our society unethical. In *A Native American Theology* they say, "There is no ceremony among any people for clear-cutting an entire forest" (44). This is because clear-cutting an entire forest is entirely wasteful, something that does not fall in line with the Native American belief of Reciprocity. Reciprocity is the idea that balance has to be maintained in the world. Therefore, only what is necessary can be taken, otherwise balance in the cosmos will be thrown off. Clear-cutting an entire forest, or factory farming, is entirely wasteful, which is why the theologians say that "American technological and economic development cannot embody the Indian ethic of reciprocity" (19).

Paragraph opens with an idea that is central to understanding the concept of reciprocity.

In the revised version, the source authors are introduced, which is more important than naming the title of their book, which will be found in the Works Cited list.

By mentioning tree-cutting here, the revised version sets the reader up for the quote about clear-cutting in the next paragraph.

The revised paragraph explains the concept of reciprocation more thoroughly and draws a comparison to another perspective.

Revised Version

According to Native American spiritual beliefs, humans have kinship with animals, plants, and the Earth itself. This is in line with their religious belief that everything has spirit, even things we think of as inanimate, like mountains. Clara Sue Kidwell, a professor of Native American studies, and theologians Homer Noley and George E. "Tink" Tinker explain that the traditional belief is that everything is sacred and alive, and that "anything and everything that humans do has an effect on the rest of the world around us" (41). Therefore, they have to use restraint and not just take as much as they want. When they take anything, such as killing an animal or cutting down a tree, they compensate through a ritual offering or prayer to restore the balance in the world. Like Schwennesen, Native Americans give thanks to the animal, but in their case more formally, through ceremonies, gifts, and sacrifices to honor the spirit of the animal. They make "apologies and words of thanksgiving to the animal itself and the animal's spirit nation" (Kidwell, Noley, and Tinker 43). They do these ceremonies not just for the animal, to show respect, but for the "sake of the whole community's well-being" (42).

Although many Native Americans today are poor and probably have to eat factory farmed meat, their traditional attitudes would make them object to our industrialized system of mass-producing meat. With their belief in reciprocity, they would oppose taking anything from the Earth in such a large scale that the balance cannot be restored. As Kidwell, Noley, and Tinker say, "There is no ceremony among any people for clear-cutting an entire forest" (44). Clear-cutting a forest, like factory farming, is unsustainable, wasteful, and disrespectful, which is why the theologians say that "American technological and economic development cannot embody the Indian ethic of reciprocity" (44).

Editing Your Final Draft

Nearly every draft can be improved by editing to reduce wordiness, vary sentence structure, and make word choices more specific. This is especially true in introductions. Once your writing project is complete, revisit the opening to see if it contains repetitions and other wordy sentence constructions, such as overuse of the verb *to be*.

Another common editing move is to trim direct quotations so that you do not include any of the quotation that is not relevant to your own point in using the quotation. For example, words that refer to material outside the quotation, such as words or phrases that worked as transitions in the original text, add clutter to your writing. Use ellipses to remove such expressions.

Original Version

David Katz, a medical doctor and Director of the Yale Prevention Center, agrees that the industrialized harvesting of animals is the real ethical problem. He says, "In other words, the mass production of meat can obliterate the life of the animal whose meat it is. A steer is turned into something other than a creature— it's just a whole bunch of hamburgers on the hoof" (23).

> This phrase provided a transition in Katz's essay that is not needed in Kline's paper.

Edited Version

David Katz, a medical doctor and Director of the Yale Prevention Center, agrees that the industrialized harvesting of animals is the real problem. Like Bittman, he shows that the process objectifies the animal. Katz says, "[t]he mass production of meat can obliterate the life of the animal whose meat it is. A steer is turned into something other than a creature—it's just a whole bunch of hamburgers on the hoof."

> Kline trimmed the quote to fit into his paragraph and added a comparison to one of his other sources to set up the quote better.

Another common problem is simply taking more of the original source than is necessary for you to make your point. This is a common problem because the words of the source are often so well-chosen that it is tempting to include them all. An alternative is to take just the words most relevant to your paragraph and embed them into a sentence of your own. This edit of a passage from Kline's draft shows that less can be more, in helping you make your own point more emphatically.

Draft Version

Bittman sees a problem, which he calls "the human cost of animal suffering." He says, "When omnivores recognize that our way of producing and eating meat reduces not only slaughterhouse workers but all of us to a warped state, we'll be able to bring about the kind of changes that will reduce both meat consumption and our collective guilt." Industrialized meat harvesting allows us to feel ethical about our massive demand for meat because we do not see the process in which animals are killed.

> The original passage went on to make a second point about what might solve the problem.

> The quote is more understandable placed near the end of the discussion of reciprocity. A common revision move is to make two paragraphs out of one, opening up complex ideas instead of expecting readers to infer the connections between statements.

Revised Version

The edited version uses less of the quotation, staying with the point of the paragraph, which is the cost in terms of mental health.

Bittman sees a problem, which he calls "the human cost of animal suffering." He believes that "our way of producing and eating meat reduces not only slaughterhouse workers but all of us to a warped state" because we deny the immorality of our actions. Industrialized meat harvesting allows us to feel ethical about our massive demand for meat because we do not see the process in which animals are killed.

REVISED STUDENT EXAMPLE

Kline 1

Conner Kline

Professor Channell

DISC 1312.014

4 December 2014

Making Meat-Eating Ethical

Opening makes a personal connection with the issue.

Almost everyone I know eats meat. To be honest I would have a tough time naming five people that I know personally who are vegetarians. Were my friends to know how their meat was obtained, however, I'm sure that I would know many more vegetarians.

Introduction clearly defines the scope of the exploration.

The issue I want to explore here is not whether humans should eat animals. That has been going on for a long time since humans first learned to hunt and raise domesticated animals for food. The problem is that meat-eating has become unethical because of the way animals are raised and killed today. Animals are abused, disrespected, and have their lives carelessly thrown away in the industrialized system known as factory farming.

This is the question that the various sources will be addressing.

Therefore, the question is how can we change our production and consumption of meat so that eating meat can be ethical?

The paper is organized around questions on the topic.

Why has meat production become so unethical? Mark Bittman, a food writer for *The New York Times,* says the problem is the industrialization of meat production. In factory farms and slaughterhouses, the animals are mistreated, and the workers

Brings in the first perspective, introducing the author and his main point.

1

2

ignore their suffering. Bittman uses Timothy Pachirat's book *Every Twelve Seconds: Industrialized Slaughter and the Politics of Sight,* to reveal what goes on. Pachirat, a political science professor who worked undercover in an Omaha slaughterhouse, describes how the distance established between the workers and the animals permits inhumane slaughtering: "The sheer volume, scale and rate of killing, . . . the way the animals form a continuous stream rather than individual creatures, makes it clear the animals are seen as raw material" (Pachirat qtd. in Bittman). The assembly line moves so fast that the workers don't see any one animal for more than a few seconds. In the United States alone, nine billion animals are killed each year, which equates to hundreds of animals being killed every second. Industrialization respects only the bottom line of corporations; its only concern is to harvest the most animals at the least expense with the least contact between the workers and the animals.

> The paragraph shows how Bittman supports his view.

> Brings in the second author's perspective on the first question. Kline is not organizing around his sources, but he does take more than one paragraph to compare two responses to the same question.

David Katz, a medical doctor and Director of the Yale Prevention Center, agrees that the industrialized harvesting of animals is the real problem. He says, "The ethical issue has little to do with whether or not we eat animals. Instead, it has everything to do with how we turn them into food." Like Bittman, he shows that the process objectifies the animal: "[t]he mass production of meat can obliterate the life of the animal whose meat it is. A steer is turned into something other than a creature—it's just a whole bunch of hamburgers on the hoof." Katz also discusses abuse on the feed lots, where cost-cutting practices include crowding the animals, feeding them grain (instead of their natural diet of grass), and giving them antibiotics and hormones to make them grow bigger, faster.

3

> Raises the second question.

Meat production is unethical, but does it have to be that way? What would have to change? Katz says we have to change. The corporations who employ factory farming are not the root cause of the problems; it's the fault of our society's massive demand for meat: "By almost any defensible definition of ethics, the practices that ensue from depending on animals for food to the extent that we do—are over the line." These factory farms only exist because we demand that they do. They are not forcing their factory-farmed meat on us; we are in fact demanding it. Katz points this problem out, saying, "A growing mass of humanity with a penchant

4

> This paragraph introduces Katz's main point: Meat production is done in unethical ways because the public demands it.

Kline 3

for meat inexorably drives the supply side toward methods of mass production, involving cost-savings and corner cutting." Similarly, Bittman says, "The allure—and habit!—of meat-eating may be too strong for most of us to give it up, but recognizing its consequences is a move toward a middle ground: a place where we continue to eat animals but exchange that privilege (that's what it is) for a system in which we eat less and treat them better. "Unless we can slow down our demand, animals will never be treated better.

Synthesizes two perspectives that agree on their answers to the second question.

If we did demand less meat, how would that change the way meat is produced? Would it be more humane? Paul Schwennesen, who writes a blog for *The Huffington Post,* is the owner of a family farm, the Double Check Ranch in Arizona. He argues that his meat production is ethical because it is humane. Schwennesen does not crowd his cattle into feed lots like most of the meat industry, but instead lets them graze on their favorite grasses and live the best life possible. Also, he slaughters them individually and attends to the slaughtering personally. He does not take this lightly. He says, "I thank each for the age-old sacrifice of prey to predator and I swear they understand. I neither rejoice in the blood nor shy from it. This is life. This is ethics." Schwennesen believes that his direct involvement with feeding and killing his cows makes his meat-eating ethical. He says, "For me, my proximate, deliberate understanding of what I do defines ethical behavior as a whole: the social moderation of otherwise unrestrained individual yearnings." Schwennesen is fully aware that eating meat is a privilege that requires restraint if it is going to be ethical.

Introduces the third question in the exploration.

Introduces a third source that shows how meat production can be more ethical.

5

Schwennesen's attitude toward raising and killing his cattle is surprisingly similar to traditional Native American attitudes of respect and responsibility for animals. According to Native American spiritual beliefs, humans have kinship with animals, plants, and the Earth itself. This is in line with their religious belief that everything has spirit, even things we think of as inanimate, like mountains. Clara Sue Kidwell, a professor of Native American studies, and theologians Homer Noley and George E. "Tink" Tinker explain that the traditional belief is that everything is sacred and alive, and that "anything and everything that humans do has an effect on the rest of the world around us" (41). Therefore, they have to

Introduces a fourth source that answers the question of how meat eating can be ethical.

6

Kline 4

use restraint and not just take as much as they want. When they take anything, such as killing an animal or cutting down a tree, they compensate through a ritual offering or prayer to restore the balance in the world. Like Schwennesen, Native Americans give thanks to the animal, but in their case more formally, through ceremonies, gifts, and sacrifices to honor the spirit of the animal. They make "apologies and words of thanksgiving to the animal itself and the animal's spirit nation" (Kidwell, Noley, and Tinker 43). They do these ceremonies not just for the animal, to show respect, but for the "sake of the whole community's well-being" (42).

This paragraph continues the explanation of the Native American idea of using Earth's resources ethically.

Although many Native Americans today are poor and probably have to eat factory farmed meat, their traditional attitudes would make them object to our industrialized system of mass-producing meat. With their belief in reciprocity, they would oppose taking anything from the Earth in such a large scale that the balance cannot be restored. As Kidwell, Noley, and Tinker say, "There is no ceremony among any people for clear-cutting an entire forest" (44). Clear-cutting a forest, like factory farming, is unsustainable, wasteful, and disrespectful, which is why the theologians say that "American technological and economic development cannot embody the Indian ethic of reciprocity" (44). The Native American idea of reciprocity agrees with the arguments of environmentalists like Mark Bittman, who says, "If we want a not-too-damaged planet to live on, and we want to live here in a way that's also not too damaged, we're better off eating less meat. But if we also want a not-too-damaged psyche, we have to look at how we treat animals and begin to change it."

7

Synthesis brings together two perspectives to show their similarity.

Introduces a fourth question for exploring the ethics of eating meat.

Bittman raises another important question: How does our consumption of unethically produced meat affect us psychologically? Does it matter if we don't know or care about where our meat comes from? Bittman sees a problem, which he calls "the human cost of animal suffering." He believes that "our way of producing and eating meat reduces not only slaughterhouse workers but all of us to a warped state" because we deny the immorality of our actions. Industrialized meat harvesting allows us to feel ethical about our massive demand for meat because we do not see the process in which animals are killed. We can refuse to recognize our role in animal suffering. This in itself is unethical. As Schwennesen says, "In my

8

Synthesis: Kline sees the connection between Bittman and Schwennesen on the problem of denying ethical responsibility.

Kline 5

mind, eating #906 (a red mottle-face cow with upturned horns currently braising in the slow cooker) is an ethically different activity than eating a Big Mac on the run." Schwennesen knows the exact cow he is cooking, but most people eat a Big Mac without even thinking that it ever was a cow.

Most informed people agree that the current way in which we obtain meat is unethical. These readings have shown that changes in people's habits and attitudes can lead to more ethical meat production and consumption. Stopping industrialized meat harvesting, as well as making the practices of Paul Schwennesen the norm in the meat industry, would all go a long way in making eating meat ethical. As these authors show, these changes will depend on the willingness of consumers to reduce their meat consumption and pay a little more for the privilege of eating meat. If we can afford to choose to eat meat ethically, we should do so.

9

> Draws a conclusion based on the reading about how meat eating can be ethical.

> Works Cited list begins on a new page.

Works Cited

Bittman, Mark. "The Human Cost of Animal Suffering." *Opinionator, The New York Times,* 13 March 2012, opinionator.blogs.nytimes.com/2012/03/13/the-human-cost-of-animal-suffering/?_r=0.

Katz, David. "Eating Well vs. Being Good: Can We Ethically Eat Animals?" *The Blog,* The Huffington Post, 20 Sept. 2011, www.huffingtonpost.com/david-katz-md/ethics-of-eating-animals_b_961242.html.

Kidwell, Clara Sue, Homer Noley, and George E. Tinker. *A Native American Theology.* Orbis, 2001.

Schwennesen, Paul. "The Ethics of Eating Meat." *The Blog,* The Huffington Post, 14 May 2012, www.huffingtonpost.com/paul-schwennesen/ethics-of-eating-meat_b_1510173.html.

CHAPTER 10

Critiquing an Argument

AN ARGUMENT IS A REASONED DEFENSE OF AN OPINION. When you hear or read an argument about a topic you find interesting, the first question you ask is, "What exactly did it say?" That is, you recall or reread the content. Then, depending on your reaction to the argument, you likely ask the following questions that respond to it: What do I agree with? What do I disagree with? Why?

When you answer these questions, you are engaging in **critique,** *offering a reasoned assessment of an argument.* We encounter critiques in letters to the editor in newspapers, in magazines that include reader responses to articles published in the previous issue, and in blogs devoted to some controversial issue or cause. The basic situation is always the same: First, someone writes an argument urging readers to believe or do something; next, a reader responds by agreeing or disagreeing (or doing some of both) and explaining why.

What Is a Critique?

A critique is a written assessment or review of the merits of someone's work. Reviews of concerts, for instance, are critiques; so are book reviews. When an instructor grades your work, he or she usually offers a brief critique of its strengths and weaknesses. In each case, the person evaluates the work according to a set of standards appropriate for the type of performance it is.

An argument offers reasons for believing or doing something. Therefore, a critique of an argument is a rational assessment of it, organized around one or more points of evaluation. It is not an attack or even necessarily negative. Critiques do not have to find fault; you can write to defend arguments, especially when you think others have wrongly criticized them.

Rational assessment includes understanding why people disagree. In large part, people disagree because they think about controversial issues or questions in different **contexts**—that is, *different frames of reference based on how they were raised; the life experiences they have had; what they know, believe, and value.*

CONCEPT CLOSE-UP Context and Critique

Arguments in newspaper opinion columns or magazines or websites are not actually the isolated pieces of writing they seem to be. They arise out of contexts, real-world situations as experienced and interpreted by their authors. People argue in response to things that happen in the news or in their lives. Real-world circumstances like economic class, political beliefs, or religious values influence people's arguments.

Context always matters for the following reasons:

- **Context is the key to understanding an argument as rhetorical communication.** Arguments are designed to move readers. We can understand an argument only by asking, "Who is the writer trying to convince or persuade?"

- **Context is the key to understanding why people disagree.** People look at issues from their own perspectives. An argument for making tuition loans easily available to college students might appeal to young people who cannot afford the cost of college. However, a student whose older sibling graduated from college and is now trying to repay a $20,000 debt might argue that easy loans are not the best solution to the problem.

- **Context is the key to understanding your response.** Arguments are also read within contexts—the background, knowledge, and experiences of the reader. Your initial reaction to an argument will depend on the point of view you bring to it. To judge an argument fairly, you will have to take this context into account.

ABC's long-running talk show *The View* is a great place to see arguments in action. The hosts and their guests discuss a variety of topics and engage in interesting, and often heated, discussions. An episode of *The View* may be a great place to start for practice with evaluating good, well-supported arguments versus bad ones.

© Steve Fenn/Disney ABC Television Group/Getty Images

Why Write to Critique an Argument?

Every day you hear or read the arguments of other people, in conversation, in books and magazines, on television, radio, and the Internet, in business meetings and community gatherings. There is no way to avoid arguments designed to influence what you think and do. Nor should we want to avoid them: Arguments and counter-arguments are democracy in action, one of the ways an open society works. However, good arguments must be distinguished from bad ones. This is the stake that you and all thoughtful people have in critique.

It is important to distinguish between a reaction and a critique. A reaction is just a "thumbs up" or "thumbs down" judgment, like responses to films we have seen. In responding to arguments, a reaction is simply agreement or disagreement without explaining why or offering any justification. In contrast, a critique offers reasons for agreeing or disagreeing. It attempts to defend an evaluation of an argument. Consequently, a critique can help us distinguish good arguments from bad ones.

How Do Writers Critique Arguments?

For more on the structure of argument, see Chapter 11, pages 227–28.

An argument advances a thesis or **claim,** *what the writer wants us to believe or do.* The claim is defended with reasons that explain and justify the claim, and the reasons are backed with evidence for accepting each reason. Critiques challenge the claim, the reasons, the evidence, or all three.

As you read the following arguments, focus on what the critiques challenge and why.

Why Sherry Turkle Is So Wrong

TOM STAFFORD

The book review is a common genre of argument critique. Tom Stafford, the author of this review of Sherry Turkle's Alone Together: Why We Expect More from Technology and Less from Each Other, *is a lecturer at the University of Sheffield in England. It appeared on his blog* idiolect *(http://idiolect.org.uk/notes/). The author of many influential books, Sherry Turkle is a distinguished professor at the Massachusetts Institute of Technology.*

(Attention conservation notice: a rambling 1800 word book review in which I am rude about Sherry Turkle and psychoanalysis, and I tell you how to think properly about the psychology of technology.)   1

> First person, informal style, appropriate for a blog. Thesis in last sentence: Turkle's evidence is weak.

This book annoyed me so much I wasn't sure at page 12 if I could manage the other 293. In the end I read the introduction and the conclusion, skimming the rest. Turkle's argument is interesting and important, I just couldn't face the supposed evidence she announced she was going to bring out in the body of the book.   2

> Anecdotes, short narratives about something experienced, are often not valued as much as evidence gathered from scientific studies.

Psychoanalysts are conspiracy theorists of the soul, and nowhere is that clearer than in Turkle's reasoning about technology. Page after page of anecdotes are used to introduce the idea that communications technologies such as email, Facebook and Twitter offer an illusion of intimacy, but in fact drive us into a new solitude. This might be true, it's an important idea to entertain, but pause for a moment to think how you would establish if it really was the case or not.   3

> Summarizes Turkle's position.

> An example of evidence Stafford considers unconvincing.

For Turkle, the evidence is all around, discerned by her keen psychoanalytically-trained psychologist's eye. A young woman chats to her grandmother on Skype for an hour a week— touching example of a relationship deepened and sustained? No! Unbeknownst to the grandmother the young woman uses that hour to catch up on her emails, leaving her unsatisfied with the Skype conversation, with vague feelings of guilt and a failure to connect. Turkle combines stories like these of people she's met with sweeping generalizations about how "we" feel—increasingly disconnected, overwhelmed and unable to tell where the boundary between work and home life is. Text messages, originally a substitute of the phone call you couldn't make, "very quickly . . . became the connection of choice" she announces. Really? For everyone?   4

> Questions assumptions not proven in the book.

Throughout Turkle seems to assume that this new age of communications technology has accelerated us into an age of dislocation and disconnection. This may be so, but a few anecdotes about people's unsatisfactory relationships and yearning for deeper intimacy and authenticity don't establish this. Here is the news: it was ever so. Now people wonder if their Facebook friends are true friends; previously we wondered if our friends on the team, or in the pub, were our true friends. Now we wish for romantic relationships without betrayal and inconvenience; previously this is what we wished for too. Ambiguity, failure and fear of disconnection are not a novel part of online relationships; they are part of   5 the human condition and it is mighty irksome that Turkle assumes the novelty of these things. She is seeing what she wants to see in the world around her. There is also an inherent conservatism in her assumption that things were better before this anarchy of technology was loosed upon the world, the assumption that not only were things better before, but that this was the way they were "supposed to be." The comic thing is that her historical benchmark is just as arbitrary—as if phone calls were a good and proper means of communication, a ceremony of innocence drowned by the destructive forces of text messaging and Skype. When the phone was invented there was a moral panic about what this technology would do for relationships, the same as there was a moral panic when printed books became widespread. There's no reason why we shouldn't invent a new form of communication, such as the text message, and have it fill a niche in the ecology of how we relate to each other. People haven't stopped making phone calls; they have augmented the way they communicate with text messages, not substituted texting for phoning.

Critique can challenge the emotional appeal of an argument as well as its logical appeal.

6 Reading the book it is hard to shake the impression that everything Turkle says is in slightly dismayed and hysterical tones: "Oh no! The kids are using text messaging!" "Oh no! People underestimate the distracting effect of checking their email!" "Oh no! The kids find face to face conversations threatening; the little dears can't live in the real world!"

7 Again: it was ever so. And of course, with anything new, you can always find some genuinely misled and bewildered people. Turkle has some striking examples of people who wish for relationships—both romantic and sexual—with robots. This shows, she says, that we are in the "robotic moment." It is not that robots are ready for our desires, but that our desires are now ready for the idea for intimacy with robots. A young woman yearns for a robot lover, wanting to trade her human boyfriend for a "no risk relationship"; an elderly woman saying that her robot dog "won't die suddenly and abandon you and make you very sad"; the genuinely astounding argument of David Levy's "Love and Sex with Robots" which proposes that soon we'll be fighting for the right to marry robots in the same way we fought for the right to marry people of the same sex. Are we only discussing these possibilities, asks Turkle, because we are failing each other in human relationships?

8 The impression I get is of a very earnest anthropologist, speaking to the young people of an alien tribe, ready to be shocked and titillated by their revelations. Do the people speaking to Turkle really believe what they say, or are they egged on by her credulity, just as the tribespeople compete to tell the anthropologist ever more outrageous things? Yes, yes I would prefer a robot lover. Yes, yes, real men are a disappointment—irritating, changeable—and the simulation of intimacy would be better than a risk of authentic intimacy.

9 My problem is not that people are seeking to escape human frailty and ambiguity with robots, but that Turkle seems to assume that there was ever a time when some people didn't try to escape human frailty and ambiguity. It isn't that we are newly dissatisfied with our relationships and newly struggling for authenticity. Rather it is that the old struggle has found a new form, that the eternal uncertainties we have about ourselves and each other are given a new light by technology.

Calls attention to the positive in Turkle's argument as well as the negative.

10 Turkle has an important point disguised by a boring pessimism. "Relationships with robots are ramping up; relationships with people are ramping down," she says—"Of

every technology, we must ask, Does it serve our human purposes?" This later point is vitally important. The idea that Turkle has proven that human relationships are "ramping down" due to the current communications technology is the distraction. This is just a generational cry of despair, common to every age, when one age group realizes they don't understand or don't like how their children behave.

True, we must ask how technology can be built to enhance our relationships, and true intimacy and authenticity are endangered, but it was always so and Turkle's speculations of doom help only to muddy the waters.

11

I find myself wondering why Turkle has this pervasive pessimism about our ability to sensibly navigate these new technologies. Perhaps it is related to the stance she seems to adopt to the characters that populate her anecdotes, which is of subjects under her microscope, an amorphous mass of "them" rather than unique individuals with stories and weaknesses just like all of us. This may just be my knee-jerk dislike of psychoanalysts but her stance towards these characters in her argument always felt condescending and arrogant, as if she alone possessed the objective stance, as if only she, with her psychoanalytic training, was expert enough to discern the loneliness and feel what they themselves didn't know they felt. Again, the tone reminded me of the naive anthropologist: Aren't they strange? Isn't their confusion fascinating?

12

Challenges the context Turkle brought to interpreting her evidence.

I would have had more faith in Turkle's reasoning if she talked more about her experience, rather than relating anecdotes from people she met at conferences and at Parisian dinner parties.

13

Turkle's underlying assumption is that technology is a thing separate from, or gets in between, authentic relationships. (There's a comparison to those who diagnose an addiction to the internet, as if the internet were a substance, when it is just a medium.) In fact, technology is part of relationships because it is part of our minds (see Andy Clark's book *Natural Born Cyborgs* for an exploration of this idea). Technology cannot get in the way of some kind of natural detection of reality because we never have direct contact with reality—it is always mediated by culture, history, language, expectations, and the whole architecture of our minds for understanding the world. As every psychologist should know, the idea of "virtual reality" is a misnomer because reality has always been virtual. A concrete example of this confusion is when Turkle assumes that she (alone) can tell the real (flesh and blood) encounters from the fake (technologically mediated) encounters. "The ties we form through the internet are not, in the end, the ties that bind" she says solemnly. This is a ridiculous generalization, and must be confusing to all those who met over the internet, or have had relationships deepened because of the internet. Can you imagine how ridiculous Turkle would sound if she'd made such a generalization about another medium. "The ties formed through writing are not the ties that bind," "The ties formed by those speaking French are not the ties that bind." Nonsense! Again Turkle has been distracted by her pessimism and her conservatism. The problem of human bonds is not a new one; we've always struggled to find rapprochement with each other. The internet doesn't change that. It does give the problem interesting new dimensions, and I've no doubt that we'll struggle collectively with these new dimensions for decades, but I don't see Turkle doing anything to make clear the outlines of the problem or advance any solutions.

14

An important counter-argument: Reality is always mediated in some way.

New technology is easy to think about, partly because the novel always stands out against the background of the old, and partly because it is easier to think about the material aspects of things, and the material aspects of technology can be ubiquitous (like text messages and email) or particularly entrancing (like robots). But let me give an alternative vision to Turkle's Cassandra wail. Rather than technology, a far more real threat to intimacy and authenticity in the modern world is the continuous parade of advertising which tries to hock material goods with the promise that they can give access to transcendent values. Cars which give freedom, cameras which give friendship, diamonds that give love and clothes that give confidence. Here is a cultural force, with a massive budget and the active intention to make us dissatisfied with our possessions, our lifestyles, our bodies and our relationships. How about we worry a bit more about that and less about the essentially democratic technologies of communication?

15

> A figure in Greek legend, Cassandra was a prophet or seer, someone who knew events before they occurred.

> Another important counter-argument: Not technology but rather consumerism is the problem.

Questions for Discussion

1. Any reader of this critique who has not read Turkle's book must depend on Stafford's summary of Turkle to judge his fairness. Do you think Stafford gives enough examples to show that her evidence is not sufficient or convincing? Do you have evidence from your own experience that technology is causing breakdowns in human interaction?
2. Do you believe that human relationships were better a generation or two ago? Why or why not?
3. What do you think about the impact of advertising on human relationships? Do you agree with Stafford (paragraph 15) that consumerism is the real threat to human relationships, not information technology?

▨▮ *Thinking as a Writer*

1. What is Stafford's *purpose* in writing this essay? What is his *angle* on the topic? How would you describe his *voice*?
2. Who is Stafford's *intended audience*? Is he writing only for people who share his prejudice against psychoanalysis and the use of anecdotes as evidence? Is he writing only for younger adults who grew up with information technology? Does he try to reach other readerships? Can you cite anything in the article that implies his target readership?
3. Using the Concept Close-Up box on page 201 and the marginal annotations to the article, show how Stafford uses *context* and the *conventions of critique* to raise doubts about Turkle's argument. If you were not convinced by his critique, what exactly did you resist in his arguments and why did you resist them? ▪

The Assignment

If your instructor does not assign one, locate any short (750–1,000 words) argument on a controversial topic and write a critique of it. Your instructor may specify a length for your paper. If not, write a critique of about 500 to 1,000 words. Later in this chapter, we offer some arguments for critique, including David Fryman on responding to opinionated professors (pages 210–11) and Shikha Dalmia (pages 224–26) on birthright citizenship.

What Can I Write About?

This assignment could be written in many genres, the most common of which is a letter to the editor of a newspaper or magazine. But it could also be an op-ed piece; a response to a post on a blog; a short article for a newspaper, magazine, or newsletter; or an assessment of a classroom discussion, debate, chat room exchange, public speech, or some other oral argument.

We suggest that you pick an argument you disagree with or an argument you partly agree with and partly disagree with in almost equal measure. It is harder to write a critique of an argument you find wholly convincing.

You can locate suitable arguments by recalling something you read in a newspaper or magazine or on a website; by doing subject searches in online library indexes like LexisNexis or Academic OneFile (see pages 343–44 for how to use these resources); and by using Google to search for information on a topic in the news. Consider also the following possibilities:

- **Class readings.** Class readings can provide arguments for critique, especially if the readings themselves are arguments.

- **Local news or observation.** Read your local and campus newspapers for arguments relating to your community. Sometimes these can be more interesting than overworked topics such as abortion or gun control.

- **Internet discussions.** Blogs are often good sources for arguments. Visit blogs on issues of public concern, such as National Public Radio's blog.

How Do I Write a Critique? Questioning the Rhetorical Situation

Begin by considering the **rhetorical situation,** *the key variables associated with you as writer; with your audience; and* © Asia Images Group/Getty Images, RF *with the genre, conventions, and expectations of your text.* Understanding the rhetorical situation will give you a stable sense of the whole, something definite to hold in mind as you work your way through the process.

Writer: What Is My Purpose, and What Impression Should Readers Have of Me?

Your purpose in writing a critique depends entirely on the argument you are responding to and how you feel about it. Sometimes you agree with the argument and wish to offer additional reasons and evidence for it; sometimes you partly agree and wish to indicate why you cannot accept the argument entirely; and sometimes you disagree completely and wish to refute the argument. Regardless of your exact purpose, your readers should see you as someone who has listened carefully to the argument, understood it, and taken the time to write a well-considered response. Above all, you should be concerned that your readers understand what you agree and disagree with and why.

Audience: Who Is My Reader?

Most critiques address the same readership that the argument hoped to reach. Therefore, one of the more important questions you can ask is, **"Who is the reader for the argument I am responding to?"** The answer to that question tells you who your reader is. However, some critiques deliberately respond to an argument from the point of view of another possible audience, usually one the argument overlooked or chose not to address. For instance, a young adult might critique Turkle's book from the viewpoint of someone immersed in the Internet and social media for an audience of other young adults likewise situated—clearly not the scientific audience Stafford (pages 203–6) had in mind. When most of what you have to say would appeal to a different readership or when you want to call attention to reader concerns the argument fails to consider, shifting audience can be an effective strategy.

Text: What Moves Can I Make?

A critique is *a coherent evaluation of somebody else's argument from your point of view.* The moves you will make, therefore, depend on the argument you are responding to and your particular "take" on it. The following are common moves in critique, just to give you a general idea of what can be done:

- **Expose an assumption the argument makes that you consider doubtful or unjustified.** For example, arguments about gender often assume a simple masculine-versus-feminine contrast. You can show that most people are a mix of the characteristics we associate with masculine and feminine. Challenging assumptions is especially important in argument critique because, if you accept the author's assumptions, you tend to accept the argument.

- **Single out the claim for attention and show that it is unclear, contradictory, or too broad or too narrow.** Even claims that seem powerfully persuasive can be called into question. "Justice too long delayed is justice denied," though often quoted, is unclear until "too long delayed" is specified. How long is too long? Furthermore, how broadly should we apply the claim? Are there good reasons, for example, that some criminal trials involving the death penalty should, including appeals, go on for months or even years?

- **Call attention to reasons you consider weak.** For example, people argue against mercy killing or euthanasia because Nazi Germany used it to justify murder of people it considered undesirable. Clearly what the Nazis did was not euthanasia. Just as clearly, the five states that currently permit euthanasia are not motivated as the Nazis were.

- **Challenge evidence the author advances to back up reasons.** The most common move is to cite **counter-evidence:** *data or facts that call data or facts cited by the author into question.* You can also, among many other moves, expose an author's source as biased or otherwise untrustworthy. An argument against gun control, for example, is vulnerable if the writer relies heavily or exclusively on the National Rifle Association (NRA) website. When evidence comes from any organization that advocates a cause and lobbies Congress, it is likely to be distorted.

- **Oppose the values in the argument with values of equal or greater importance the author did not recognize.** Our enormous investment in counterterrorism efforts after 9/11 is justified by the value of national security. But if national security is important, so also is our greatest national value, liberty. How much liberty have we lost by all the counterterrorism measures? How much more could we lose? Does the threat of terrorism really justify the liberty sacrificed?

- **Expose the implications of an argument when you can show that they are impractical, undesirable, or unacceptable.** For example, good arguments have been made for reinstating the draft and/or for requiring a certain period of mandatory service for young adults. You can point to how extremely unlikely it is that such a policy could pass Congress and become law. You could also show that such a policy would disrupt education and therefore result in fewer college graduates.

- **Question analogies the argument relies on.** In the years before World War II, Britain, France, and other European countries tried to appease Hitler and prevent war by making concessions to his demands. Ever since, any effort under any circumstances to negotiate with countries and leaders considered our enemies has been likened to appeasing Hitler. You can show why the analogy is weak. Perhaps the enemy leader is not out to conquer other countries or lacks the military strength to do so.

How Do I Write a Critique? Engaging the Writing Process

No two people compose in exactly the same way, and even the same person may go through the writing process in different ways with different assignments. Nevertheless, because no one can attend to everything at once, there are phases in handling any significant writing task. You explore the topic to get a sense of whether it will work for you and what you might be able to do with it; if the topic is working out for you, then you move into preparing to write, generating more content and planning your draft.

The next phase is drafting your paper, creating a version, however rough it may be, on screen or paper so that you can work toward the final draft. Getting there involves two further phases: (1) revising your draft, making major improvements in it, followed by (2) editing your draft, taking care of errors, sentences that do not read well, paragraphs lacking focus and flow, and so on.

Exploring Your Topic

To see how to explore the argument you are about to critique, we need an example argument to illustrate the process. Here is one on an issue of some concern on most college campuses. Read it once or twice, just to understand what it says and to form a first reaction to it.

READING **10.2**

Open Your Ears to Biased Professors

DAVID FRYMAN

David Fryman was a senior at Brandeis University when he wrote this opinion column for the school's newspaper, The Justice. *He is offering advice to younger college students who often encounter professors with political opinions different from those endorsed at home or in their local communities. Fryman's question is, How should they respond?*

One of the most important lessons I've learned in three years of higher education is the value of creativity and critical thinking, particularly when confronted with a professor whose ideology, political leanings or religious viewpoint fly in the face of what I believe. In fact, with a good professor, this should happen often. It is part of a professor's job to challenge you, force you to reconsider, encourage you to entertain new ideas and the like. My first year here, it bothered me. Some professors subtly endorsed certain ways of thinking over others without always justifying their biases. They offered opinions on issues beyond their academic expertise. Many showed partiality to the political left or right.

1

How should we react when a professor with a captive audience advances a perspective we find offensive, insulting or just ridiculous? Perhaps we would benefit from treating our professors, who often double as mentors and advisers, the same way that we're taught to approach great works of literature: with critical respect.

2

The truth is many faculty members are at the top of their fields. They read, write and teach for a living. We're generally talking about the most well-educated and well-read members of society. So when a professor has something to say about politics, religion,

3

war or which movie should win the Academy Award, I think it's a good idea to take him seriously.

It certainly doesn't follow, though, that there's a direct relationship between what a professor says and what's true. In fact, there may be no relationship at all. While our professors generally are leading scholars, some are also biased and fallible. I don't mean this as an insult. Professors are human beings and, as such, carry with them a wide array of hang-ups and prejudices.

4

Interestingly enough—if not ironically—our professors often teach us how to deal with biased and opinionated scholars like themselves. When we read novels, journal articles, essays and textbooks for class, we're taught—or at least this has been my experience—to be critical. We're expected to sift through material and distinguish between what holds water and what doesn't, what is based on reasoned analysis and what is mere speculation.

5

If we treat our professors similarly it should no longer bother us when they use the classroom as their soapbox. They have important things to say and we're here to learn from them. I've come to appreciate professors' opinions on a variety of issues not directly related to the subject at hand, and I think it helps us build relationships with them. While it's unfair for a professor to assign high grades only to students who echo their view or to make others feel uncomfortable to disagree, I prefer that professors be honest about what they think.

6

While it's a disservice to our own education to be intimidated or too easily persuaded by academic clout, it's just as problematic, and frankly silly, to categorically reject what a professor has to say because we take issue with his ideology, political leanings, religious views or cultural biases.

7

It's become popular, particularly among conservatives responding to what they perceive as a liberal bias in academia, to criticize professors for espousing personal views in the classroom. The ideal, they argue, is to leave students ignorant about their instructors' beliefs.

8

First of all, I think there's a practical problem with this strategy. It's more difficult to be critical if we're unsure where our professors stand. For the same reason that it's often helpful to have background information about an author before analyzing his work, it's useful to see our professors' ideological cards on the table. For instance, if I know my professor loves hunting and believes everybody should have firearms in his basement then when I hear his interpretation of the Second Amendment, I'm better equipped to evaluate his thoughts.

9

Secondly, if we proscribe what views may or may not be expressed in the classroom, we limit our own access to potentially useful information. Even if most of the extraneous digressions aren't worthy, every once in a while we might hear something that goes to the heart of an important issue. To limit this because we don't trust our own critical abilities is cowardly.

10

To return to the question I posed above: How should we respond to politically-charged, opinionated, biased professors? I think we should listen.

11

David Fryman. "On The Loose: Open Your Ears to Biased Professors." *The Justice: The Independent Student Newspaper of Brandeis University*, 31 Aug. 2004. Reprinted by permission of the author.

Forming a First Impression

It is impossible to read an argument without having some kind of response to it. Start by asking yourself, **"What is my first impression?"**

▪▪▪▪ ACTIVITY 10.1 *Writer's Notebook*

State Your First Impression

State your reaction simply and directly. Write it down in your notebook or a computer file reserved for this assignment. Read the selection again. Is your reaction changing? How? Why? ▪

Most of our students' first response to Fryman was favorable. He offered practical advice, and more appealing yet, *safe* advice. You may have had an entirely different reaction. First reactions cannot be right or wrong, good or bad. They just are what they are. The important thing is that *you* know what your reaction is.

Achieving Critical Distance through Analysis

Critiques require **critical distance** from first responses. "Critical distance" does not mean "forget your first response." On the contrary, first impressions often turn out to be sound. Critical distance does mean *setting your first response aside for a while so that you can think the argument through carefully.*

Use the questions for critiquing an argument in Best Practices to guide your analysis.

BEST PRACTICES Questions for Critiquing an Argument

1. **What is the context for this argument?** As we said earlier (pages 201–2), arguments take place in contexts—situations that prompt people to write. Ask, therefore, "Who wrote this? What prompted him or her to write? What might explain his or her perspective?"

2. **What is the author claiming?** Find the main point or thesis that the writer wants you to believe and/or be persuaded to do. Sometimes the claim will be stated, sometimes implied. Then ask: Is the claim clear and consistent? Is it absolute, no exceptions allowed? Is it reasonable, desirable, practical?

3. **What reasons does the author provide for accepting the claim?** Reasons answer the question: Why? Given the claim, what explains or justifies it? Like the claim, reasons will be stated or implied. Then ask: Does each reason actually explain or justify the thesis? How convincing is the reason? If the author reasons by means of an **analogy** (*comparison, reasoning that what is true in one case should be true in a similar case*), does the comparison really stand up to inspection?

4. **What evidence has the author given to support the reasons?** Reasons need support using examples, data, or expert opinion. Look at the evidence offered for each reason and ask: Does the evidence actually

support the reason? How convincing is each piece of evidence, and how convincing is the evidence for each reason taken together?

5. **What are the key terms, and what do they mean?** Writers use words, often without defining them, that should be carefully examined. When a claim is justified, for instance, as the right or moral thing to do, we need to ask what "right" or "moral" means in this case.

6. **What is the author assuming?** It is impossible to argue without assuming many things, and "assumed" means "not stated." Ask: What must I believe to accept that claim, or reason, or piece of evidence? Is the assumption "safe," something that any reasonable person would also assume?

7. **What are the implications of this argument?** The implications are what the argument suggests or implies. Like assumptions, implications are usually not stated. To uncover them, ask: If I accept this position, what logically follows from it? Are its implications acceptable or not?

8. **What values motivate the argument?** What priorities does the author have? What other priorities or values conflict with those of the author?

9. **What voice and character are projected in the argument?** We talk about voice and presence in writing, and these are important to an argument's effectiveness. How would you describe the speaker and on what evidence from the text?

10. **Who is the audience for the argument?** Who is likely to agree with this argument? Who might want to refute it? What might an opponent object to and why?

Example: Critiquing an Argument

Here is a model of how some of these questions could be applied to Fryman's argument (pages 210–11):

1. **Thesis: What is the author's main claim?**
   Fryman: College students should listen with critical respect to biased and opinionated professors.
   Comment: Be clear about the argument's main point. Note that with this argument you have to piece together the thesis from several statements Fryman makes.

2. **Context: What prompted the author to write the argument?**
   Fryman: In paragraph 8, Fryman explains the situation that prompted him to write this argument. Conservative students had been protesting what they saw as an abuse of academic freedom by liberal professors.
   Comment: Fryman is not arguing directly to conservative activists. Whom do you think he sees as his audience? How would his argument be different if he were to address the more politically active protestors?

3. **Reasons: What are some reasons, and how well do they hold up to examination?**
   Fryman: One reason given is: "Many faculty members are at the top of their fields."
   Comment: Clearly, this statement is a reason—it explains why the author thinks students should accord professors respect. We can respond by saying,

"Yes, some professors are quite accomplished *in their fields.* But when they venture outside them, do their opinions count for more than any other relatively well-informed person's?"

4. **Key terms: What words are important to the argument, and would there be any confusion about what they mean?**

   Fryman: "How should we react when a professor with a captive audience advances a perspective we find offensive, insulting or just ridiculous? . . . with critical respect."

   Comment: It is important to note that Fryman is not saying that students have to agree or even be neutral but rather that they should think critically as they listen.

5. **Assumptions: Does the author make any assumptions you might question?**

   Fryman: He is assuming that professors airing their views in class will not take away from class time devoted to material that must be covered.

   Comment: We might respond by suggesting that Fryman should have qualified his argument by putting a limit on how much class time might be devoted to professors airing their biases.

6. **Implications: What happens in reality if we accept the argument?**

   Fryman: He implies that students should tolerate whatever the professor dishes out.

   Comment: We can respond by saying, "How much student toleration is too much toleration? Suppose that a professor is openly sexist, for instance? Shouldn't we not only reject the opinions but also report the behavior to university authorities?"

7. **Analogies: How well do comparisons hold up?**

   Fryman: He compares the approach students should take to opinion-ated professors with the critical respect accorded great works of literature (paragraph 2).

   Comment: We can respond by saying, "Great works of literature have typically survived for years. We call them classics. Does it make sense to meet the casual opinions of professors the same way that we approach Shakespeare?"

■■ ■ ACTIVITY 10.2 *In Your Own Work*

Exploring Your Argument

If you are working alone on an argument, use the ten questions in Best Practices: Questions for Critiquing an Argument (pages 212–13) to find possible content for your critique. Record the results in your notebook, your computer file for this assignment, or online—for example, as a blog that presents the argument and your analysis of it.

If all members of your class are critiquing the same argument, divide into small groups of about three or four people and do an analysis. Share what your group found with the class as a whole in discussion. Summarize what each group came up with in your notebook, computer file, or online as a blog entry or e-mail addressed to the entire class. Indicate which analytical comments you consider strongest. ■

Personal Engagement in Critiques

Critique focuses on *what an argument says*. The challenge of critique is to discover what you can say back.

Part of a good critique is to test the argument against what you know about reality. Test what the argument says against your experience with life and the world, and against what you know about the topic. Add to your knowledge of reality by gathering information through research.

What Information Is Relevant to My Critique?

The following questions should help you add insights about an argument:

1. **What is my own experience with the topic or issue or problem the argument takes up?** In the case of Fryman's argument, when have the comments of "biased teachers" been illuminating or helpful to you? When have they been boring, irritating, or useless? What's the difference between the two?

2. **What relevant information do I have from reading or from some other source?** Perhaps you have heard other students complain about professors pushing their political convictions on their students. What did the students say? Did their complaints seem justified? Why or why not?

3. **What could I find out from research that might be relevant to assessing the argument?** Most arguments suggest opportunities for at least checking up on information relevant to the argument. For instance, you might investigate the idea of academic freedom. How does it apply to professors? How does it apply to students?

   See Chapter 16, pages 336–49, for detailed guidance on ways to research any topic.

4. **If the argument reasons from data, in what other ways might the data be interpreted? What other data might contradict the information given?** Research will often lead you to other arguments that interpret the same or similar data differently or that supply additional data the argument you are critiquing did not know or ignored. For example, arguments for stronger border patrol enforcement sometimes fail to mention that about 40 percent of undocumented immigrants came here legally and simply stayed. Enhanced border control obviously will have no effect on that group.

▓ ▓ ▓ ■ ACTIVITY 10.3 *In Your Own Work*

Assessing the Fit of Argument and Reality

In your notebook or computer file, sum up the results of applying the above questions. Freewrite about what you might add from your own experiences and observations or from research. Highlight the best insight you gained. It could be a major point in your critique, perhaps even the central point around which you structure it. ■

Preparing to Write

Thoughtful exploration of an argument—responding to what it says and pondering its fit with reality—results in much you could say. However, a critique is not a collection of comments or a list of criticisms. Rather it's *a coherent evaluation from a particular point of view*—your view. Consequently, formulating your position, your main point about the argument's validity, matters most.

Formulating Your Position

Your critique will need to focus on one main point: your position about the merits of the argument. You can reject an argument in general but see value in a part of it. You can accept an argument in general but with major reservations.

In response to Fryman's argument, a wide range of stances are possible. Someone in agreement could say:

> Fryman acknowledges that biased professors can be annoying, but he makes an effective argument that opinions have a role in the education process.

Someone disagreeing could say:

> Fryman would have a stronger argument if he did not imply that students should open their ears but not their mouths.

Or, among many other possible positions, someone could say:

> It is easy to agree with this argument in the abstract because Fryman avoids actually quoting any of the biased views he has heard.

■■■■ ACTIVITY 10.4 *In Your Own Work*

Formulating Your Position

Using the suggestions above, write a position statement. If you are having difficulty, consider the following possibilities:

- **Return to your first impression.** Perhaps a revised version can be your stance.

- **Review the statements in the argument that you found open to question.** Is there a pattern in your criticisms? Or perhaps one statement stands out from the rest and seems central? Your position may be implied in your most important criticism.

- **Do you detect one place where the reasoning breaks down?** You could focus your critique on the major weakness in the argument's case, that is, its claim, reasons, and evidence.

- **Look for places where the author's view of reality and/or what is needed or desirable part company with yours.** Your position might be that the argument sounds logical but is not realistic or practical.

- **Talk through possible positions with another student or your instructor.** Just talking helps, and sometimes a comment from someone else can help your stance emerge.

Sometimes you will discover the best statement of your position only through writing a first draft. For now, try out the stance that appeals to you most. You can always revise and rewrite. ■

Drafting Your Paper

In your first draft, focus on organizing and voicing your main points fully and clearly.

What Voice Is Appropriate for a Critique?

Voice   The voice of critique or analysis shares much in common with the voice of case-making: State your position clearly, directly, and forcefully, using a style more formal than conversation but less formal than a public speech. Remember that critique is not name-calling, insults, outrageous claims, or partisan bickering, but rather the calm voice of reason, opinions stated precisely and defended well.

See Chapter 11, page 248–49, for a discussion of voice in case-making.

Here is a good example of the voice for critique from Stafford:

> Psychoanalysts are conspiracy theorists of the soul, and nowhere is that clearer than in Turkle's reasoning about technology. Page after page of anecdotes are used to introduce the idea that communications technologies such as email, Facebook and Twitter offer an illusion of intimacy, but in fact drive us into a new solitude. This might be true, it's an important idea to entertain, but pause for a moment to think how you would establish if it really was the case or not.

This paragraph summarizes Turkle's position, something Stafford needs to do early in his critique so that readers know what he is talking about. But he also wants to convey his negative attitude toward psychoanalysis, so the paragraph begins with the memorable claim that "psychoanalysts are conspiracy theorists of the soul." That is, they claim to know, he thinks, what they have little evidence to support. It's all theory and guesswork. He combines this judgment with praise for the significance of Turkle's idea so that the reader can detect some balance and fairness in his criticism. At the same time, he is also preparing us for his extensive and confident attack on Turkle's evidence.

Your voice in critique, therefore, depends largely on how you assess the quality of the argument you are critiquing. Stafford boldly challenges Turkle's conclusions because he thinks her evidence would not convince a skeptical scientist. She needs real data, not anecdotes.

■■■■ ACTIVITY 10.5 *Writer's Notebook*

Reader, Purpose, and Voice

Add notes about the key variables to your position statement. Answer these questions: **Do you intend to address the same readers that the argument does? Why or why not? How *exactly* does your version of the truth differ from the author's, and how great is the difference? How friendly to the author do you want to sound?** ■

Developing and Organizing Your Critique

Organization   Whether you write first drafts in chunks and then fit them together or write from a plan more or less in sequence, have the following organizational principles in mind:

Introduction

- Begin by identifying the argument you are critiquing: who wrote it and for what group of readers, when and where it appeared, what it is about, and the position the author takes.

- Make your own stance clear and give it an emphatic position, near the end of your introduction.

Body

- From everything you found questionable in the argument, select *only* what is relevant to your stance. No one expects a critique to deal with everything an argument says or everything that can be said about it.

- *Don't let the order of the argument determine the order of your critique.* Organize around points that develop *your* position, and think about what order would have maximum impact on your readers.

- If you can say positive things, deal with these points first. Readers listen to the negative more willingly after hearing the positive.

Conclusion

Short critiques of short arguments do not need summarizing conclusions. Strive instead for a clincher, the memorable "parting shot" expressing the gist or main thrust of your response.

Development   For each part of your critique, you have many options for development. Here are some of them.

Introduction

Besides identifying the argument and taking your stance, you can also include material about context, background information, and a preview of your critique. A critique of Fryman's argument, for instance, might place it in the context of efforts to restrict academic freedom; research about the author might reveal relevant background information, such as what was happening at Brandeis University when he wrote the article. Previews summarize the points you are going to make in the order in which you are going to discuss them.

Body

Take up one point at a time. Each point will challenge either the reasoning of the argument or its fit with reality. If the former, be sure to explain inconsistencies or contradictions fully so that your reader understands exactly where and why the reasoning went wrong. If you want to show that it is unrealistic, provide counter-evidence from personal experience, general knowledge, or research.

Conclusion

To clinch your critique, consider the following possibilities: a memorable quotation with a comment on it from you; a return to a key statement or piece of information in your introduction that you can now develop more fully; a reminder to the reader of your strongest point with additional support or commentary.

Revising Your Draft

Write a brief assessment of your first draft. Exchange your draft and assessment with at least one other student, and use the critique revision questions in The Art of Questioning below to help each other decide what you each need to improve.

THE ART OF QUESTIONING — Revision Checklist for Critiquing an Argument

1. Look at all the places where you have summarized or paraphrased the argument. Compare them against the text. Are they accurate? Do they capture the author's apparent intent as well as what she or he says?
2. Locate the argument's context—the existing view or views the argument's author addressed. If the critique does not mention context, would it improve if it did? If so, where might a discussion of context work best?
3. Critiques seek the truth about some controversial issue or question. What is the issue or question the argument addresses? Is it stated in the critique? Does the difference between the argument's view of the truth and the view in the critique emerge clearly? If not, what could be done to make the difference sharper?
4. Underline the critique's main point or stance. Is it stated explicitly and early in the essay? Examine each critical point. How does it develop, explain, or defend the stance? Consider cutting anything not related to the stance.

Exchanging your draft with at least one other student and going over the Critique Revision Checklist together can help you decide what you each need to improve.
© Creatas/SuperStock, RF

5. Check the flow of the critical points. Does each connect to the one before it and the one after? If not, consider rearranging the sequence. How might one point set up or lead to another better?

6. What voice do you hear in the critique? The tone should be thoughtfully engaged, fair, balanced, and respectful, but also confident and forceful. Look for places where the tone might make the wrong impression. Consider ways to improve it.

Formulating a Plan to Guide Your Revision

The plan can be a single sentence or two: "I'll cut this, rearrange that, and add a section here." Or, if you work better from an outline, develop one now. The important thing is to have a definite, clear idea of what you want to do and what moves you will make to get the results you want.

Student Example: Excerpts from J. R. Solomon's Draft

The following passages are excerpted from student J. R. Solomon's draft critique of David Fryman's argument, "Open Your Ears to Biased Professors." These examples all illustrate common problems in first drafts of critiques.

Excerpt 1: Position statement not forceful enough

> Fryman believes that students should treat professors' personal opinions with critical respect. I agree, but think that his view is one-sided and therefore not fully persuasive.

All arguments present one position on an issue, so to say an argument is "one-sided" does not offer a valid critique. In fact, Solomon meant that the argument was unbalanced, tipping too far in favor of professors' powers. Here is the revised version:

> "Open Your Ears to Biased Professors," by David Fryman, a student writing for the Brandeis University paper, *The Justice,* deals with a common complaint among students: teachers who express their political or religious views in class. Fryman believes that students should listen to the personal opinions of professors with "critical respect." I agree, but the argument is not persuasive because Fryman describes an unbalanced situation where the professors have all the rights and the students have all the responsibilities.

Excerpt 2: Paraphrase or summary not accurate

> In my ethics class last year, my teacher . . . believed strongly in the right of homosexuals to marry. Some of the students, including myself, did not agree with her. Yet, when we tried to discuss our side of the issue, she cut us off. **Fryman neglects to discuss such instances when a teacher's opinions**

infringe on the students' right to open debate. I believe that if teachers can express their opinions openly in class, the students should be able to express theirs.

The bolded sentences do not accurately represent Fryman's argument. Fryman also believes that students should feel comfortable expressing disagreement with the professor and says so in his paragraph 6. Here is the revised version:

> Unfortunately, some professors do not want students to form their own opinions but rather convert to the professor's ideology. In my ethics class last year, the teacher told us she was a lesbian. In one of our discussions we spoke about gay rights, and whether or not gay marriage should be legal. She believed strongly in the right of gay people to marry. Some of the students, including myself, did not agree with her. Yet, when we tried to discuss our side of the issue, she cut us off. Although Fryman says "it is unfair for a professor to assign high grades only to students who echo their view or to make others feel uncomfortable to disagree," he does not go far enough to emphasize professors' responsibility in ensuring students have a voice.

Excerpt 3: Unfocused and underdeveloped paragraphs

> Because he is writing only to students, Fryman has very little to say about how professors should conduct themselves. He deals with the problem of bias as if only what students should do matters. Actually, professors have more responsibility. They're older, more knowledgeable, and more experienced. I think if professors are going to express their political and religious views in class, they should do so in certain ways or not do it at all.

These sentences move from professors to students and back to professors, ending with a vague point about what professors should do. In the revised essay, Solomon used the two main points to organize his entire critique. You can see parts of this draft paragraph in paragraphs 2 and 5 of the revised draft.

Editing Your Revised Draft

There is almost no revised draft that could not improve with proofreading for habitual errors and editing to tighten up the writing and make some points more clear. The highlighted words below indicate where the passage could be tightened up.

Original Version

> In my ethics class last year, the teacher told us she was a lesbian. In one of our discussions we spoke about gay rights, and whether or not gay marriage should be legal. She believed strongly in the right of gay people to marry. Some of the students, including myself, did not agree with her.

The edited version that follows reduces the repetition and tightens up the style by using the pronoun *it*.

Edited Version

In my ethics class last year, the teacher told us she was a lesbian. When the class discussed gay rights and gay marriage, she expressed her view that it should be made legal. Some of the students, including myself, did not agree with her.

One grammatical problem remains in the edited passage. The word *myself* is a reflexive pronoun; it should not be used unless the word *I* has already been used in a sentence ("I hurt myself"). However, the ethics class anecdote does not use the word *I;* the pronoun is treated as an object and should reflect this. This mistake—using *myself* instead of *me*—is common in casual talk; we tend to make it when we write too. Be alert to reflexives in your drafts.

Edited Version

Some of the students, including me, did not agree with her.

▧▩■ ACTIVITY 10.6 *In Your Own Work*

Editing Your Paper

Edit your own draft to eliminate errors, such as confusing plurals with possessives, using singular pronouns to refer to plural nouns, and misusing the reflexive pronoun *myself.* Exchange your edited paper with another student. Help each other find and correct any remaining errors. ■

REVISED STUDENT EXAMPLE

Solomon 1

J. R. Solomon

ENG 1301

Professor Crusius

12 October 2015

The introduction sets up the argument to be critiqued with information about its author and publication.

Indoctrination Is Not Education

"Open Your Ears to Biased Professors," by David Fryman, a student writing   1

for the Brandeis University paper, *The Justice*, deals with a common complaint

among students: teachers who express their political or religious views in class.

Fryman believes that students should listen to the personal opinions of professors

The introduction ends with a strong stance, or position, on the validity or merits of the argument.

Solomon 2

with "critical respect." I agree, but the argument is not persuasive because Fryman describes an unbalanced situation where the professors have all the rights and the students have all the responsibilities.

> **The first point in support of the stance that the argument is unbalanced.**

Because he is writing only to students, he has very little to say about how pro- 2 fessors should conduct themselves. Fryman deals with the problem of bias as if only what students should do matters. They should listen and evaluate the professor's views just as they would a book or journal article assigned in the class. This is what he means by "critical respect." It sounds good; however, class readings are likely to be on-topic and written by experts, while the professor's personal opinions may be off topic and not as well thought out as something published. The professor's views may not deserve so much critical attention.

> **Questions the validity of the comparison between professors' opinions and the views in readings.**

> **Questions an assumption about students at the heart of Fryman's argument.**

Furthermore, the students might not be ready to take on the responsibility for 3 evaluating the professor's opinions. Because professors know so much, they can appear very appealing to students who have not encountered an issue before. By leaving out other interpretations, the professor assures that students hear only the teacher's side, which does not allow students to form their own conclusions. I saw this happen in a government class which discussed the 2008 Presidential election. Most of the class did not know much about politics, and therefore accepted the professor's view completely. They didn't have the critical capacity Fryman assumes all college students have. Certainly professors should challenge students, but what my government professor did was convert.

> **The student connects the critique with his own experience of the issue.**

Unfortunately, some professors do not want students to form their own opinions 4 but rather convert to the professor's ideology. In my ethics class last year, the teacher told us she was a lesbian. In one of our discussions we spoke about gay rights, and whether or not gay marriage should be legal. She believed strongly in the right of gay people to marry. Some of the students, including me, did not agree with her. Yet, when we tried to discuss our side of the issue, she cut us off. Although Fryman says "it is unfair for a professor to assign high grades only to students who echo their view or to make others feel uncomfortable to disagree," he does not go far enough to emphasize professors' responsibility in ensuring students have a voice.

> **Challenges an assumption about professors.**

> **Personal experience showing the frustration when a professor does not allow disagreement.**

Solomon 3

<table>
<tr>
<td>

Explains an alternative to "critical respect" and shows why that alternative is more educational.

</td>
<td>

Professors are responsible for educating, not indoctrinating. They are older, more   5
knowledgeable, and more experienced. I think if professors are going to express their
political and religious views in class, they should do so in a way that invites critical dis-
cussion, not just "critical respect." Students should hear about other viewpoints so they
can think about all sides of the issue. The professor's views are one opinion, but not
the only right one. Professors should encourage students to form their own opinions.

</td>
</tr>
<tr>
<td>

Shows that Fryman's argument neglects another important responsibility of the professor.

</td>
<td>

Finally, Fryman fails to deal with the negative impact when teachers stray from   6
the subject matter of the course. In my ethics class, the teacher was always return-
ing to the issue of gay rights, even when the topic of discussion didn't relate to it.
Because she lacked restraint, the class spent too much class time on one issue. It
is the professor's responsibility to see that course material gets covered.

</td>
</tr>
</table>

I agree that professors should share their opinions with the class and students   7
should listen and learn from them. But the opinions should relate to the course content. Professors should not allow themselves to talk about just whatever happens
to be on their minds. Most of all, education should not be indoctrination. Opinions
should be discussed, not preached. A professor is a teacher, not a politician.

> Persuasive and memorable ending.

Sample Reading for Critique

READING **10.3**

The Bogus Case against Birthright Citizenship

SHIKHA DALMIA

> Shikha Dalmia is senior analyst at the Reason Foundation, a think tank advocating free markets and free thinking. She won the 2009 Bastiat Prize for Online Journalism.

Like gout, anti-immigration restrictionism[1] is a perennial affliction that comes and   1
goes with the seasons. And with Republicans gaining ground this political season,
get ready for a particularly painful bout of it.

Texas Rep. Lamar Smith, a committed restrictionist who now chairs the House Judiciary Committee, is already planning a big push to clamp down on undocumented aliens, especially by denying automatic or birthright citizenship to their children—a right enshrined in the 14th Amendment. Meanwhile, Republicans in five states—led by Arizona—are launching their own offensive to force Congress to repeal this right.

2

Such calls are not new. What is new is that they are gaining traction beyond a shrill nativist[2] minority. Some conservative libertarians are arguing that birthright citizenship is bad for the country—and some progressive libertarians are arguing that it is bad for immigrants. Not only are both wrong, they can't reconcile this position with their broader commitment to the constitution and limited government respectively. (In this column I will address only the conservatives, saving the progressives for the next.)

3

The most famous representative of the conservative view is George Will, whose recent column is an odd hagiographic[3] exercise lauding Smith—obviously calculated to pave the ground for Smith's birthright crusade that Will has openly embraced.

4

Smith is pushing a law in Congress to scrap this right, even though literally no one believes that it would pass constitutional muster. That's because the 14th Amendment is unusually clear about extending citizenship rights to everyone born on American soil except for children of foreign diplomats and American Indians (who belong to sovereign tribes). Eliminating these rights for anyone else will require three-quarters of the states to ratify another amendment.

5

Remarkably for someone who counsels deference to the original Constitution, Will has few qualms about this. Why? Because the authors of the 14th Amendment could not possibly have meant to extend birthright citizenship to illegal aliens given that no laws restricting immigration existed in 1868 when it was passed, he maintains. "Is it reasonable to presume they would have wanted to provide the reward of citizenship to the children of the violators of those laws? Surely not," he declares.

6

It's even more plausible, however, that if the authors failed to foresee something, it was not the law-breakers but the laws themselves. Hostility toward immigrants, especially the Irish who arrived in the wake of the potato famine, was certainly around in their time. But they still didn't pass such laws—perhaps because they thought that a country that had borne the sin of slavery to get cheap foreign labor should not erect barricades to keep out voluntary cheap foreign labor!

7

But if the failure to foresee events offered sufficient grounds for amending the Constitution, then we might as well throw out the whole document and begin anew. Would the Founders have written the First Amendment enshrining the freedom of press if they had known that the Internet would one day allow Wikileaks to release classified documents and jeopardize soldiers in the battlefield? Or the Second Amendment guaranteeing the right to bear arms in a world of cop-killing bullets? Or the Fourth Amendment's injunction against improper searches and seizures in an age of terrorism? Or the Fifth Amendment's prohibition against government takings of private property when rare species are allegedly facing extinction?

8

The 14th Amendment was written, among other things, to prevent Confederate states from denying citizenship to newly freed blacks. What comparable injustice would amending this amendment prevent? Restrictionists claim that birthright citizenship encourages pregnant women to illegally sneak into the U.S. for a just-in-time delivery so that their newborns can gain citizenship and later sponsor the parents for citizenship. They call these kids "anchor babies."

9

But *Time* magazine reported last year that of all the babies born in 2008 to at least one unauthorized parent, over 80 percent were to moms who had been in the United States for over one year. Actual instances of "birth tourism," where moms expressly came here to deliver babies on American soil, accounted for about two-tenths of 1 percent of all births in 2006. And most of these moms were not poor, illegal Hispanics—Smith's target group. They were rich Chinese moms on tourist visas.

10

Nor is it plausible that their intention was to use their kids to gain citizenship for themselves. Kids have to wait until 21 to seek legal status for illegal parents and the parents must typically then wait outside the U.S. for at least 10 years before they can obtain their green cards. About 4,000 unauthorized parents with kids who are citizens can avoid deportation every year. This, then, is the grand illicit citizenship racket that Will & Co. want a constitutional amendment to crack!

11

Conservatives argue that this amendment is necessary to enforce the rule of law. But the first principle of conservatism, constantly deployed against liberal reformers, is that it is not wise to make radical changes to long-standing laws and institutions for small gains. As Aristotle warned in the *Politics* two-and-half millennia ago: "[W]hen the improvement is small, and since it is a bad thing to habituate people to the reckless dissolution of laws, it is evident that some errors of both legislations and of the rulers should be let go; for the city will not be benefited as much from changing them as it will be harmed through being habituated to disobey the rulers . . . The easy alteration of existing laws in favor of new and different ones weakens the power of law itself."

12

Yet, here are conservatives now, disregarding their own wisdom and subverting the rule of law in the name of the rule of law to fight bogus causes.

13

Notes

[1] **Restrictionism**—This term refers to the belief that laws should put strict limits on immigration to the United States.

[2] **Nativism**—This more extreme term refers to the belief that the culture of a country's founding citizens should remain the dominant culture. Nativists thus oppose immigration by different racial and ethnic groups.

[3] **Hagiography**—While the word originally refers to the biography of a saint, it is now often used pejoratively to describe any writing in which the author heaps excessive and uncritical praise upon some person.

CHAPTER 11

Making a Case

YOU HEAR OR READ ABOUT SOME TOPIC THAT INTERESTS YOU (CALL IT "X"), and soon enough you form an opinion about it. Nothing much happens until someone asks you a key question, "What do you think about x?" This question starts many serious conversations, but it leads to stating opinions, not to **argument,** which means *a reasoned defense of an opinion.* To get to argument, you need a question with a sharper edge, a critical thinking question: *"Why* do you think this about x?" That is, "What reasons do you have to explain and justify what you think? What evidence do you have to back up your opinion?"

When you answer these questions, you are making a **case,** *arguing for a position by advancing reasons and evidence in defense of it.* Arguing a case occurs in many genres, including newspaper editorials, letters to the editor, blog posts, speeches, and personal letters.

What Is a Case?

A **case** develops an opinion about a controversial issue or question. It has three parts:

1. A **claim,** or thesis
    Example: College costs are unjustifiably high.
2. One or more **reasons** that explain or justify the claim
    Example: They have increased much more than inflation over the last thirty years.
3. Appropriate **evidence** to back up each reason
    Example: Data comparing the cost of living in general with increases in tuition and fees over the last thirty years.

The flow chart on the next page shows the structure of a case. A claim can be supported by one or more reasons.

CONCEPT CLOSE-UP	Visualizing the Structure of a Case

A case has the following structure:

> The claim answers the question, **What are you asserting?**
>
> Reasons answer the question, **Why do you make this claim?**
>
> Evidence answers the question, **What information confirms your reasoning?**

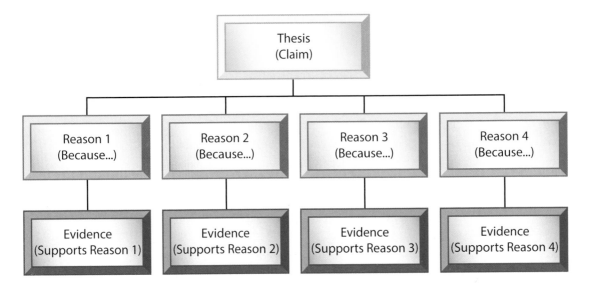

Why Make a Case?

An issue is controversial when reasonable people take different positions on it. One reason to make a case is to convince readers to accept one of those positions. For example, perhaps you feel that texting and talking on a handheld cell phone while driving should be banned. In an editorial or a blog you could make the case by pointing out how dangerous it is.

Proposing a ban on texting and driving is a good example of an issue you could make a case for.

© jinga80/Getty Images, RF

Convincing other people, however, is not the only motivation for making a case. We all have casual opinions we have never thought through. How valid is one of the unexamined opinions you have? The best way to answer that question is to attempt to make a case for it. If you cannot make a good one that other people find convincing, it may be time to change or modify your opinion. Making a case, then, is not only a challenge to convince others but also a testing of how sound your own opinions and reasoning are.

How Do Writers Make a Case?

Cases combine structure (claim, reasons, and evidence) with a strategy for engaging with the readers you most want to convince. For example, many people are in favor of lowering the drinking age from twenty-one to eighteen because they believe the higher drinking age is at least partly to blame for binge drinking. On the other hand, organizations such as Mothers Against Drunk Driving (MADD) support the legal age of twenty-one. They point to thousands of people who die each year in traffic accidents caused by drunk drivers and say that lowering the drinking age will only make a serious problem worse.

Suppose that you wanted to convince supporters of the current drinking age (twenty-one in most states) to alter their opinion. *You have to think as they think.* Everyone agrees that abusing alcohol is a big problem. You could argue that the issue is not age but rather moderation and responsibility whenever people drink. Moderation and responsibility are exactly what the current law cannot promote; prohibition cannot encourage moderation and responsibility. You could allay concerns about drunk driving by advocating stronger enforcement of the law. Without such a strategy, any case you make is likely only to strengthen the views of people who already share your position—not convince those whose view you want to change.

READING **11.1**

Building a Better Life through Greenways and Trails

TRAILS AND GREENWAYS CLEARINGHOUSE

An issue that matters to many people is the preservation of trails and greenways in cities and suburbs. Of course, economic incentives sometimes work against using space for these purposes because homes and businesses cannot be built where green spaces exist already or others are being created. Are the green spaces worth the land devoted to them? This article makes the case that they are.

To make a greenway is to make a community.
                              —Charles E. Little, *Greenways for America*

Necessary background information.

Greenways are corridors of protected open space   1
managed for conservation and recreation purposes.
Greenways often follow natural land or water

features, and link nature reserves, parks, cultural features and historic sites with each other and with populated areas. Greenways can be publicly or privately owned, and some are the result of public/private partnerships. Trails are paths used for walking, bicycling, horseback riding, or other forms of recreation or transportation.

2

Some greenways include trails, while others do not. Some appeal to people, while others attract wildlife. From the hills of inland America to the beaches and barrier islands of the coast, greenways provide a vast network linking America's special places.

> Stresses diversity and nationwide extent of green spaces.

Why Establish Trails and Greenways?

3

There are many reasons for preserving and improving the trails and greenways we have and for creating new ones. They improve the economy, promote good health, protect the environment, and preserve our rich and diverse American heritage.

> Summarizes reasons taken up in order in subsequent headings.

Economic Benefits

4

Trails and greenways provide countless opportunities for economic renewal and growth. Increased property values and tourism and recreation-related spending on items such as bicycles, in-line skates and lodging are just a few of the ways trails and greenways positively impact community economies.

> First reason.

In a 1992 study, the National Park Service estimated the average economic activity associated with three multi-purpose trails in Florida, California and Iowa was $1.5 million annually.[1]

5

According to a study conducted by the U.S. Fish and Wildlife Service, bird watchers spend over $5.2 billion annually.[2]

6

The impact on local economies can be significant. As Chris Wagner, Executive Director of the Greater Connellsville Chamber of Commerce, Pennsylvania, remarked,

7

> Evidence defending first reason. Note evidence includes data from two different sources and the testimony of a local official.

> Three new gift shops have recently opened, another bike shop, a jewelry store, an antique and used furniture store, a thrift shop, a Wendy's Restaurant and a pizza and sandwich shop. All this is happening, and only with the *prospect* of the trail opening in July. There is an air of excitement and anticipation now within this community, something Connellsville has not felt for many years.

Promoting Healthy Living

8

Many people realize exercise is important for maintaining good health in all stages of life; however, many do not regularly exercise. The U.S. Surgeon General estimates that 60% of American adults are not regularly active and another 25% are not active

> Second reason.

[1.] "The Impacts of Rail-Trails, A Study of Users and Nearby Property Owners from Three Trails." *National Park Service, Rivers, Trails and Conservation Assistance Program*, 1992.

[2.] "Economic Impacts of Protecting Rivers, Trails, and Greenway Corridors." *National Park Service, Rivers, Trails and Conservation Assistance Program*, 4th ed., 1995.

at all.[3] In communities across the country, people do not have access to trails, parks, or other recreation areas close to their homes. Trails and greenways provide a safe, inexpensive avenue for regular exercise for people living in rural, urban and suburban areas.

Environmental Benefits

| Third reason. |

Greenways protect important habitat and provide corridors for people and wildlife. The preserved Pinhook Swamp between Florida's Osceola National Forest and Georgia's Okefenokee National Wildlife Refuge protects a vital wildlife corridor. This important swampland ecosystem sustains numerous species, including the Florida black bear, timber rattlesnake, and the Florida sandhill crane. 9

| Evidence connects with news stories of almost annual floods, something readers know about and can easily appreciate. |

| Specific example used as evidence. |

Trails and greenways help improve air and water quality. For example, communities with trails provide enjoyable and safe options for walking and bicycling, which reduces air pollution. By protecting land along rivers and streams, greenways prevent soil erosion and filter pollution caused by agricultural and road runoff. 10

Greenways also serve as natural floodplains. According to the Federal Emergency Management Agency, flooding causes over $1 billion in property damages every year. By restoring developed floodplains to their natural state, many riverside communities are preventing potential flood damage. 11

| Appeals to feelings of alienation from nature in metropolitan America. |

Finally, trails and greenways are hands-on environmental classrooms. People of all ages can see for themselves the precious and intriguing natural world from which they often feel so far removed. 12

Preserving Our History and Culture

Trails and greenways have the power to connect us to our heritage by preserving 13

| Fourth reason. |

historic places and by providing access to them. They can give people a sense of place and an understanding of the enormity of past events, such as Native American trails and vast battlefields. Trails and greenways draw the public to historic sites. For example, the six-mile Bethabara Trail and Greenway in Winston-Salem, North Carolina draws people to the birthplace of the city, the original Moravian Christian village founded in the late 1700s.

Other trails preserve transportation corridors. Rail-trails along historic rail corridors provide a glance at the importance of this mode of transportation. Many canal paths, preserved for their historic importance as a transportation route before the advent of railroads, are now used by thousands of people each year for bicycling, running, hiking and strolling. Many historic structures along canal towpaths, such as taverns and locks, have been preserved. 14

[3.] "Physical Activity and Health: A Report of the Surgeon General." U.S. Department of Health and Human Services, 1996.

Building a Better Life

Strong conclusion appeals to quality-of-life issues and sentiments.

As new development and suburbs are built farther and farther from cities, open spaces have disappeared at an alarming rate. People spend far too much time in traffic, detracting from time that could be better spent with their families and friends.

15

Through their votes, thousands of Americans have said 'yes' to preserving open spaces, greenways, farmlands and other important habitat. During the 1998 election, voters in 44 states approved over 150 conservation-related ballot initiatives. Trails and greenways provide what many Americans seek: close-to-home recreational areas, community meeting places, historic preservation, educational experiences, natural landscapes and beautification. Both trails and greenways help communities build pride by ensuring that their neighborhoods are good places to live, so that children can safely walk or bike to a park, school, or to a neighbor's home. Trails and greenways help make communities more attractive and friendly places to live.

16

Questions for Discussion

1. This case appeared on a website where arguments are usually kept short to encourage online readers not to skip over them. Besides its brevity, what other features of this case should appeal to online readers?
2. Why does the case begin with the economic benefits of trails and greenways?
3. How does the case appeal to the values and feelings of readers? Were you moved by these appeals? Why or why not?

See Chapter 3, pages 32–38, for definitions of purpose, angle, and voice.

▪▪▪ *Thinking as a Writer*

What Is the Rhetorical Situation?

1. What is the *purpose* of the case? What is its *angle* on the topic? How would you describe its *voice*?
2. Who is the intended *audience*? Is there anything you can cite that implies the target readership? How do the four reasons appeal to various interest groups and points of view in the United States?
3. Using the chart on page 228 and the marginal annotations, discuss the organization of the case as a claim supported by reasons and backed by evidence. How is the case framed in the opening paragraphs? How does it close or conclude the argument in the last two paragraphs without just summarizing it? ▪

"Building a Better Life through Greenways and Trails." Trails and Greenways Clearinghouse. Courtesy of Rails-to-Trails Conservancy, www.railstotrails.org/.

The Case against Grades

ALFIE KOHN

I remember the first time that a grading rubric was attached
to a piece of my writing. . . . Suddenly all the joy was taken
away. I was writing for a grade—I was no longer exploring
for me. I want to get that back. Will I ever get that back?
                                    —Claire, a student (in Olson, 2006)

> Alfie Kohn is the author of thir-
> teen books and an influential
> speaker at universities and in
> business settings. Time *magazine*
> called him "perhaps the country's
> most outspoken critic of educa-
> tion's fixation on grades [and] test
> scores." As you read, pay special
> attention to Kohn's use of evi-
> dence from social science, cited
> in APA style, to support his claims.

By now enough has been written about academic assessment to fill a library, 1
but when you stop to think about it, the whole enterprise really amounts to
a straightforward two-step dance. We need to collect information about how
students are doing, and then we need to share that information (along with our
judgments, perhaps) with the students and their parents. Gather and report—that's
pretty much it.

You say the devil is in the details? Maybe so, but I'd argue that too much attention 2
to the particulars of implementation may be distracting us from the bigger picture—or at
least from a pair of remarkable conclusions that emerge from the best theory, practice,
and research on the subject: *Collecting information doesn't require tests, and sharing*
that information doesn't require grades. In fact, students would be a lot better off without
either of these relics from a less enlightened age.

Why tests are not a particularly useful way to assess student learning (at least the 3
kind that matters), and what thoughtful educators do instead, are questions that must
wait for another day. Here, our task is to take a hard look at the second practice, the
use of letters or numbers as evaluative summaries of how well students have done,
regardless of the method used to arrive at those judgments.

The Effects of Grading

Most of the criticisms of grading you'll hear today were laid out forcefully and 4
eloquently anywhere from four to eight decades ago (Crooks, 1933; De Zouche, 1945;
Kirschenbaum, Simon, & Napier, 1971; Linder, 1940; Marshall, 1968), and these early
essays make for eye-opening reading. They remind us just how long it's been clear
there's something wrong with what we're doing as well as just how little progress we've
made in acting on that realization.

In the 1980s and '90s, educational psychologists systematically studied the effects 5
of grades. As I've reported elsewhere (Kohn, 1999a, 1999b, 1999c), when students from
elementary school to college who are led to focus on grades are compared with those
who aren't, the results support three robust conclusions:

- *Grades tend to diminish students' interest in whatever they're learning.* A "grading orientation" and a "learning orientation" have been shown to be inversely related and, as far as I can tell, every study that has ever investigated the impact on intrinsic motivation of receiving grades (or instructions that emphasize the importance of getting good grades) has found a negative effect.

- *Grades create a preference for the easiest possible task.* Impress upon students that what they're doing will count toward their grade, and their response will likely be to avoid taking any unnecessary intellectual risks. They'll choose a shorter book, or a project on a familiar topic, in order to minimize the chance of doing poorly—not because they're "unmotivated" but because they're rational. They're responding to adults who, by telling them the goal is to get a good mark, have sent the message that success matters more than learning.

- *Grades tend to reduce the quality of students' thinking.* They may skim books for what they'll "need to know." They're less likely to wonder, say, "How can we be sure that's true?" than to ask "Is this going to be on the test?" In one experiment, students told they'd be graded on how well they learned a social studies lesson had more trouble understanding the main point of the text than did students who were told that no grades would be involved. Even on a measure of rote recall, the graded group remembered fewer facts a week later (Grolnick and Ryan, 1987).

Research on the effects of grading has slowed down in the last couple of decades, but the studies that are still being done reinforce the earlier findings. For example, a grade-oriented environment is associated with increased levels of cheating (Anderman and Murdock, 2007), grades (whether or not accompanied by comments) promote a fear of failure even in high-achieving students (Pulfrey et al., 2011), and the elimination of grades (in favor of a pass/fail system) produces substantial benefits with no apparent disadvantages in medical school (White and Fantone, 2010). More important, no recent research has contradicted the earlier "big three" findings, so those conclusions still stand. 6

Why Grading Is Inherently Problematic

A student asked his Zen master how long it would take to reach enlightenment. "Ten years," the master said. But, the student persisted, what if he studied very hard? "Then 20 years," the master responded. Surprised, the student asked how long it would take if he worked very, *very* hard and became the most dedicated student in the Ashram. "In that case, 30 years," the master replied. His explanation: "If you have one eye on how close you are to achieving your goal, that leaves only one eye for your task." 7

To understand why research finds what it does about grades, we need to shift our focus from educational measurement techniques to broader psychological and pedagogical questions. The latter serve to illuminate a series of misconceived assumptions that underlie the use of grading. 8

- *Motivation:* While it's true that many students, after a few years of traditional schooling, could be described as motivated by grades, what counts is the nature of their motivation. Extrinsic motivation, which includes a desire to get better grades, is not only different from, but often undermines, intrinsic motivation, a desire to learn for its own sake (Kohn 1999a). Many assessment specialists talk about motivation as though it were a single entity—and their recommended practices just put a finer gloss on a system of rewards and punishments that leads students to chase marks and become less interested in the learning itself. If nourishing their *desire* to learn is a primary goal for us, then grading is problematic by its very nature.

- *Achievement:* Two educational psychologists pointed out that "an overemphasis on assessment can actually undermine the pursuit of excellence" (Maehr and Midgley, 1996, p. 7). That unsettling conclusion—which holds regardless of the quality of the assessment but is particularly applicable to the use of grades—is based on these researchers' own empirical findings as well as those of many others, including Carol Dweck, Carole Ames, Ruth Butler, and John Nicholls (for a review, see Kohn 1999b, chapter 2). In brief: the more students are led to focus on *how well* they're doing, the less engaged they tend to be with *what* they're doing. It follows that all assessment must be done carefully and sparingly lest students become so concerned about their achievement (how good they are at doing something—or, worse, how their performance compares to others') that they're no longer thinking about the learning itself. Even a well-meaning teacher may produce a roomful of children who are so busy monitoring their own reading skills that they're no longer excited by the stories they're reading. Assessment consultants worry that grades may not accurately reflect student performance; educational psychologists worry because grades fix students' attention *on* their performance.

- *Quantification:* When people ask me, a bit defensively, if it isn't important to measure how well students are learning (or teachers are teaching), I invite them to rethink their choice of verb. There is certainly value in *assessing* the quality of learning and teaching, but that doesn't mean it's always necessary, or even possible, to *measure* those things—that is, to turn them into numbers. Indeed, "measurable outcomes may be the least significant results of learning" (McNeil, 1986, p. xviii)—a realization that offers a refreshing counterpoint to today's corporate-style "school reform" and its preoccupation with data. [. . .]

- *Curriculum:* "One can have the best assessment imaginable," Howard Gardner (1991, p. 254) observed, "but unless the accompanying curriculum is of quality, the assessment has no use." Some people in the field are candid about their relativism, offering to help align your assessment to whatever your goals or curriculum may be. The result is that teachers may become more adept at measuring how well students have mastered a collection of facts and skills whose value is questionable—and never questioned. "If it's not worth teaching, it's not worth teaching well," as Eliot Eisner (2001, p. 370) likes to say. Nor, we might add, is it worth assessing accurately.

Portfolios, for example, can be constructive if they replace grades rather than being used to *yield* them. They offer a way to thoughtfully gather a variety of meaningful examples of learning for the students to review. But what's the point, "if instruction is dominated by worksheets so that every portfolio looks the same"? (Neill et al., 1995, p. 4). Conversely, one sometimes finds a mismatch between more thoughtful forms of pedagogy—say, a workshop approach to teaching writing—and a depressingly standardized assessment tool like rubrics (Wilson, 2006).

[. . .]

9

Deleting—or at Least Diluting—Grades

"Like it or not, grading is here to stay" is a statement no responsible educator would ever offer as an excuse for inaction. What matters is whether a given practice is in the best interest of students. If it isn't, then our obligation is to work for its elimination and, in the meantime, do what we can to minimize its impact.

10

Replacing letter and number grades with narrative assessments or conferences— qualitative summaries of student progress offered in writing or as part of a conversation—is not a utopian fantasy. It has already been done successfully in many elementary and middle schools and even in some high schools, both public and private (Kohn, 1999c). It's important not only to realize that such schools exist but to investigate *why* they've eliminated grades, how they've managed to do so (hint: the process can be gradual), and what benefits they have realized.

11

Naturally objections will be raised to this—or any—significant policy change, but once students and their parents have been shown the relevant research, reassured about their concerns, and invited to participate in constructing alternative forms of assessment, the abolition of grades proves to be not only realistic but an enormous improvement over the status quo. Sometimes it's only after grading has ended that we realize just how harmful it's been.

12

To address one common fear, the graduates of grade-free high schools are indeed accepted by selective private colleges and large public universities—on the basis of narrative reports and detailed descriptions of the curriculum (as well as recommendations, essays, and interviews), which collectively offer a fuller picture of the applicant than does a grade-point average. Moreover, these schools point out that their students are often more motivated and proficient learners, thus better prepared for college, than their counterparts at traditional schools who have been preoccupied with grades.

13

In any case, college admission is surely no bar to eliminating grades in elementary and middle schools because colleges are largely indifferent to what students have done before high school. That leaves proponents of grades for younger children to fall back on some version of an argument I call "BGUTI": Better Get Used To It (Kohn, 2005). The claim here is that we should do unpleasant and unnecessary things to children now in order to prepare them for the fact that just such things will be done to

14

them later. This justification is exactly as absurd as it sounds, yet it continues to drive education policy.

[. . .]

Grades don't prepare children for the "real world"—unless one has in mind a world where interest in learning and quality of thinking are unimportant. Nor are grades a necessary part of schooling, any more than paddling or taking extended dictation could be described that way. Still, it takes courage to do right by kids in an era when the quantitative matters more than the qualitative, when meeting (someone else's) standards counts for more than exploring ideas, and when anything "rigorous" is automatically assumed to be valuable. We have to be willing to challenge the conventional wisdom, which in this case means asking not how to improve grades but how to jettison them once and for all.

15

References

Anderman, E.M., & Murdock, T.B., eds. (2007). *Psychology of academic cheating.* Burlington, MA: Elsevier Academic Press.

Bedell, J. (2010, July). Blog post.

Bower, J. (2010, March 28). Blog post.

Bower, J. (n.d.). Blog post. [Grading moratorium list]

Butler, R. (1988). Enhancing and undermining intrinsic motivation: The effects of task-involving and ego-involving evaluation on interest and performance. *British Journal of Educational Psychology, 58,* 1–14.

Crooks, A.D. (1933). Marks and marking systems: A digest. *Journal of Educational Research, 27*(4), 259–72.

De Zouche, D. (1945). "The wound *is* mortal": Marks, honors, unsound activities. *The Clearing House, 19*(6), 339–44.

Eisner, E.W. (2001, Jan.). What does it mean to say a school is doing well? *Phi Delta Kappan,* pp. 367–72.

Gardner, H. (1991). *The unschooled mind: How children think and how schools should teach.* New York: Basic Books.

Grolnick, W.S., & Ryan, R.M. (1987). Autonomy in children's learning: An experimental and individual difference investigation. *Journal of Personality and Social Psychology, 52,* 890–98.

Kirschenbaum, H., Simon, S.B., & Napier, R.W. (1971). *Wad-ja-get?: The grading game in American education.* New York: Hart.

Kohn, A. (1999a). *Punished by rewards: The trouble with gold stars, incentive plans, A's, praise, and other bribes.* Rev. ed. Boston: Houghton Mifflin.

Kohn, A. (1999b). *The schools our children deserve: Moving beyond traditional classrooms and "tougher standards."* Boston: Houghton Mifflin.

Kohn, A. (1999c, March). From degrading to de-grading. *High School Magazine,* pp. 38–43.

Kohn, A. (2001, Sept. 26). Beware of the standards, not just the tests. *Education Week,* pp. 52, 38.

Kohn, A. (2005, Sept. 7). Getting hit on the head lessons. *Education Week,* pp. 52, 46–47.

Kohn, A. (2006, March). The trouble with rubrics. *Language Arts,* pp. 12–15.

Linder, I.H. (1940, July). Is there a substitute for teachers' grades? *School Board Journal,* pp. 25, 26, 79.

Maehr, M.L., & Midgley, C. (1996). *Transforming school cultures.* Boulder, CO: Westview.

Marshall, M.S. (1968). *Teaching without grades.* Corvallis, OR: Oregon State University Press.

Matthews, J. (2006, Nov. 14). Just whose idea was all this testing? *Washington Post.*

McNeil, L. M. (1986). *Contradictions of control: School structure and school knowledge.* New York: Routledge & Kegan Paul.

Milton, O., Pollio, H.R., & Eison, J.A. (1986). *Making sense of college grades.* San Francisco: Jossey-Bass.

Neill, M., Bursh, P., Schaeffer, B., Thall, C., Yohe, M., & Zappardino, P. (1995). *Implementing performance assessments: A guide to classroom, school, and system reform.* Cambridge, MA: FairTest.

Nicholls, J.G., & Hazzard, S.P. (1993). *Education as adventure: Lessons from the second grade.* New York: Teachers College Press.

Olson, K. (2006, Nov. 8). The wounds of schooling. *Education Week,* pp. 28–29.

Pulfrey, C., Buch, C., & Butera, F. (2011). Why grades engender performance-avoidance goals: The mediating role of autonomous motivation. *Journal of Educational Psychology,* 103, 683–700.

Spencer, J. (2010, July). Blog post.

White, C.B., & Fantone, J.C. (2010). Pass-fail grading: Laying the foundation for self-regulated learning. *Advances in Health Science Education, 15,* 469–77.

Wilson, M. (2006). *Rethinking rubrics in writing assessment.* Portsmouth, NH: Heinemann.

Wilson, M. (2009, Nov.). Responsive writing assessment. *Educational Leadership,* pp. 58–62.

Questions for Discussion

1. According to Kohn, research on the impact of grading supports "three robust conclusions." State each conclusion in your own words. Based on your own experience with the educational system, would you say these conclusions make sense, seem sound and convincing? Why or why not?
2. Kohn mentions "today's corporate-style 'school reform' and its preoccupation with data." What does he have in mind? What have you read or heard about it? In your view, what motivates so-called school reform more, politics or the desire to help students learn more?
3. What does Kohn advance as an alternative to grading? Is it clear to you what he has in mind and how it would work? Do you think that you would have learned as much in school had you not been motivated by grades? Do you favor a pass/fail approach to college courses? Why or why not?

▰▰▰ *Thinking as a Writer*

What Is the Rhetorical Situation?

1. What is Kohn's *purpose* in writing this essay? What is his *angle* on the topic? How would you describe his *voice*?
2. Who is Kohn's intended *audience*? What strategies does he use to counter and disarm objections some in his audience might have to his claim?
3. The Kohn article illustrates cause-and-effect reasoning in case-making, a common strategy in arguments that examine a problem and propose a solution. How does Kohn understand the grading problem? What does he say causes the problem? How does he link his solution to the cause? ■

▰▰▰ *Collaborative Activity*

Examining Cause-and-Effect Reasoning

Working in groups of two or three, use the chart on page 228 to create a diagram that shows how Kohn uses the *conventions* for organizing an argument to structure his claim, reasons, and supporting evidence. How does Kohn frame his case? In what situation did Kohn present his case? How might it affect his ability to reach his audience? ■

The Assignment

Make a case for or against a position on a controversial topic, problem, issue, or question. You may propose a solution or criticize someone else's proposed solution. Be sure to analyze your audience, to build common ground, and to offer reasons and evidence that not only support your claim but also respond to readers' concerns.

Topics for case-making must be controversial, such as how to reduce suicide among veterans of the wars in Afghanistan and Iraq.

© JEWEL SAMAD/AFP/ Getty Images

What Can I Write About

Your topic must be controversial, something about which reasonable people could disagree. Matters of fact are not controversial. For instance, it is a tragic fact that many veterans of the wars in Iraq and Afghanistan have committed suicide. People do not disagree about this fact but rather about whether enough is being done to help prevent more suicides.

Besides selecting a controversial issue, pick one you know something about from personal experience. Civic activities, internships, and jobs can be rich sources of topics. Here are some other places to find topics:

- **Class readings.** Class readings may suggest possibilities. For instance, reading Kohn's article may lead you to other issues and questions involved with grading.

- **Local news.** Read your local and campus newspapers (especially the editorial page) or examine online news sources for controversial topics.

- **Internet discussions.** Visit blogs on topics that interest you. Many newspapers, magazines, and radio shows sponsor blogs that address controversial issues.

As you settle on a topic and begin to organize your thoughts, keep in mind the conventions of the argument described earlier in this chapter.

How Do I Make a Case?
Questioning the Rhetorical Situation

Begin by considering the **rhetorical situation,** *the key variables associated with you as writer, with your audience, and with the genre, conventions, and expectations of your text.* Understanding the rhetorical situation will give you a stable sense of the whole, something definite to hold in mind as you work your way through the process of writing your essay.

Writer: What Is My Purpose, and What Impression Should Readers Have of Me?

The *purpose* of a case is to seek assent through logic in the form of a carefully worded claim supported by compelling reasons and accurate, convincing evidence. Your readers need to feel that you have thought your opinion through and that you are knowledgeable about your topic. You may feel passionate about your position, but your stance should be dispassionate, calm, and fair. Treat other opinions and arguments with respect, even as you show that your evidence and reasons are stronger.

Audience: Who Is My Reader?

Cases aim to convince two groups: people weakly inclined to agree with your thesis and those inclined toward another position but willing to consider alternatives. Your case should strengthen the adherence of those favorably disposed to your thesis by giving them good reasons and strong evidence they may have lacked before. Your reasons and evidence should also appeal to readers entertaining other positions, but reaching them requires strategy. (See pages 248–49.)

You cannot expect to convince readers unalterably opposed to your opinion. For example, there is nothing you could say in favor of people living together before marriage that would convince readers who believe it is a sin prohibited by their faith.

Text: What Moves Can I Make?

A case requires a central contention, also called a thesis or a claim. It requires that the claim be explained and defended with reasons. It also requires that the reasons be backed by evidence of one kind or another. These moves are required because readers expect them when they are reading a case.

Other moves, however, are more a matter of choice, and include some or all of the following:

- **Define the key terms in your thesis.** If you use a word or phrase your readers may not understand or may understand in a way you do not intend, define the word or phrase. For example, *sustainable farming,* though now often used, has a range of meanings and is not well understood by people not involved in agriculture. Define it as you want it understood in your thesis.

- **Provide background information as needed for readers to have an adequate grasp of the context of your case.** Most people do not know, for instance, that the vast majority of criminal cases do not come to trial but are handled by a process called plea bargaining. Among other bad results of plea bargaining is pressure on the person accused of a crime to plead guilty even if he or she is innocent. In a case that targets plea bargaining for reform, this context of abuse of the procedure needs to be presented and explained.

- **Anticipate obvious objections to your case and respond to them.** For example, if your case requires an increase in taxes to finance the measures you support, you should recognize that many readers will not be convinced on this count alone. You can say that the tax increase will be small and the benefits great as compared to the cost.

- **Show awareness of and toleration of those who would argue against your case.** The tendency in too much argumentation now is to see the opposition as the enemy. This is bad strategy if you want to convince people who do not already agree with you. Whenever you can, then, show solidarity with the other side. Except for criminals who want to steal information, we all have a stake, for example, in online security. People differ not about the value of security but rather about how to achieve it.

- **Pay special attention to opening and closing your case.** Openers should create interest and motivate the reader to keep reading, as well as connect strongly to the case you are about to make. Endings should leave the reader with something memorable. Remember: Readers tend to recall best what they read first and last.

- **Maintain a voice throughout that is calm and reasonable.** Just as too many people demonize their opponents, too many arguers seem to think that sounding hysterical wins assent. It doesn't.

How Do I Make a Case? Engaging the Writing Process

No two people compose in exactly the same way, and even the same person may go through the writing process in different ways with different assignments. Nevertheless, because no one can attend to everything at once, there are phases in handling any significant writing task. You **explore the topic** to get a sense of whether it will work for you and what you might be able to do with it; if the topic is working out for you, then you move into **preparing to write,** generating more content and planning your draft.

The next phase is **drafting your paper,** getting a version on screen, however rough it may be, so that you can work toward the final draft. Getting there involves two further phases: **revising your draft,** where you make major improvements in it, followed by **editing your draft,** taking care of errors, sentences that do not read well, paragraphs lacking focus and flow, and so on.

Exploring Your Topic

For case-making, exploring your topic means examining the issues involved in it. If your assignment calls for research, do some general reading about your topic to discover what the issues are. See Chapter 15, pages 330–35, for how to find and take notes on source material. If your assignment does not call for research, rely on your general knowledge about the topic to formulate the issues.

Find the Issues

An **issue** is *a point of controversy always or frequently raised in connection with a particular topic.* For your topic, begin by asking, **"What are the questions that people disagree about when discussing this topic?"** For instance, the primary purpose of prisons is always an issue when prison reform is discussed. Some see prisons as primarily punishment for crime; others see them as primarily institutions that should rehabilitate criminals. "What should prisons do?" is the question. Other questions include the following: What should be done about prison overcrowding? How can we reduce assaults on inmates by other, violent inmates? Is prison a breeding ground for more criminal behavior after inmates are released? If so, what can be done to prevent this from happening?

■■■■ ACTIVITY 11.1 *Collaborative Activity*

Isolating the Issues

List the issues connected with your topic. The key question is, **"What do people argue about whenever this topic is discussed?"**

If your class is working with a common topic or you share your topic with at least one other student, you could collaborate to answer the following exploratory questions:

- What issues were you unaware of before you formulated them?
- What positions do people take on these issues?
- What is your view of these issues?

Consider your view of the topic now. If you had no opinion before examining the issues, are you beginning to form one now? If you had an opinion, is it changing significantly? Which issue interests you most? Consider focusing your essay on that issue. ■

Order the Issues (Stasis)

Discussing the issues is an important step in exploring a controversial topic. Ordering them can help as well. Here is an example that illustrates one way of ordering the issues involved in committing American troops to combat in a foreign country:

- Are vital American interests at stake?
  - If you say no, make a case against committing the troops.
  - If you say yes, move on to the next question.

- Have nonmilitary alternatives been exploited fully?
  - If you say no, make a case for increased diplomatic effort or some other measure not requiring American troops on the ground.
  - If you say yes, move on to the next question.

- Do the announced objectives make sense?
  - If you say no, make a case for changing the objectives.
  - If you say yes, move on to the next question.

- Can we realize our objectives in a reasonable amount of time with minimal loss of lives?
  - If you say yes, make a case for military intervention.
  - If you say no, make a case against it based on impracticality.

Ordering the issues in this way is sometimes called **stasis,** a Latin word that means "stop" or "stay." That is: If you think a proposed military intervention would not secure vital national interests, you stop with the first question and make a case against it. If you think nonmilitary options have not been pursued enough, you argue for more diplomacy, economic sanctions, or some other alternative. You "stay" with the second question—and so on, through the whole list.

You can order the issues connected with any controversial topic this way. Doing so can clarify your own thinking as you work toward an opinion or assess the one you have.

■■■■ ACTIVITY 11.2 *Writer's Notebook*

Committing to an Opinion

Cases require a considered opinion—that is, an opinion thought through carefully. Consequently, after finding and ordering the issues, you need to decide what your opinion is on the issue or issues you choose to address. Your opinion may change as you write and assess your first draft, but you cannot write a draft at all without one.

In a blog post or notebook entry, state your opinion about the issue you have settled on and the reasons you have for holding that opinion. ■

BEST PRACTICES   Working with Sources
in Making a Case

If your assignment involves research, consult Chapter 18, 357–78 on how to engage with sources and 364–70 pages for how to assess and incorporate source material in your paper. Keep the following points in mind as you work with your sources:

- Distinguish evidence from interpretation, or "spin." For example, in 2008 about 6,200 people died in Mexico as a result of the traffic in narcotics. Citing this figure, your source might argue that American tourists should avoid Mexico. There is no reason to doubt the 6,200 figure, but the interpretation is disputable: Drug-related violence seldom involves American tourists, and many destinations in Mexico are no more risky than some cities in the United States.

- Distinguish information from speculation. **Facts** are *uncontested, established data.* How the stock market performed over the last month is a matter of fact, as measured, for example, by the Dow Jones Industrial Average. Speculations are at most probabilities. How the stock market will perform over the next year is anyone's guess. You cannot ignore the facts, but you can use or not use speculation, depending on whether it helps you to make your case.

- Strive to maintain intellectual independence from the view your source has of the subject. Avoid distorting or misrepresenting the information in a source to fit what you want to believe, but feel free to interpret the information your own way, as you see the subject. For instance, you may support the screening of passengers before boarding commercial airliners as a necessary counterterrorism measure. If so, you cannot ignore considerable evidence that screening often fails to detect prohibited items that could be used for a terrorist act. Instead of ignoring or denying the evidence, you might argue that screening technology must improve.

Preparing to Write

Some writers prefer to go straight to drafting, working out their cases in several drafts. We recommend going through the following steps first, which most writers find helpful:

1. State your opinion as a claim or thesis.

2. Analyze the thesis to determine what you must argue to defend it adequately.

3. State the reasons you will use to explain or justify your thesis.

4. Select and order the evidence you will use to back up each reason.

These steps, described in more detail below, yield a **brief,** *an outline of your case.* Add ideas for an introduction and a conclusion, and you have all you need to guide your first draft.

State Your Opinion as a Claim or Thesis

You are still testing your opinion when you write a first draft of your case, because the value of any opinion depends on how strong a case you can make for it. Writers often change or modify their opinion as they compose or when they evaluate their first draft.

However, your first draft will be stronger if you attempt to state your opinion as a claim in a thesis statement before you begin drafting. An opinion is a general stance or point of view. For instance, in the second reading in this chapter (pages 233–38), Alfie Kohn argues that the grading system actually works against learning. More specifically, he points to "three robust conclusions" that develop his thesis that grading is counter-productive.

In preparing to write a case, the advantage of a thesis over an opinion is a *sharper focus, with carefully selected key terms.* It is therefore worth your time and effort to work toward a thesis before you draft.

To write a defensible claim or thesis, keep the following in mind:

- Your claim is a statement you will defend, not just a description of something that is factual.

  Not a claim: Student debt for government loans has grown to more than $20,000 for the average graduate, a heavy burden for young people just entering the workplace.

  Claim: The economy as a whole would benefit if the federal government would forgive student debts for higher education, which now average more than $20,000 per graduate.

  The first in this pair describes a problem. The second makes an assertion for doing something about the problem.

- The claim should be focused, specific, and directed at a particular audience, or readership.

  Too general: Many professors do not know how to make effective use of technology in teaching.

  Better: Professors who use presentation technology such as PowerPoint too often stifle creativity and student involvement in the class.

The second example in this pair is more refined, indicating specific directions that the argument will take. It is also clearly directed at educators. The more specific your claim, the easier it will be to decide what your paper will include.

■ Some claims may need to be qualified.

Too absolute: Professors should openly state their opinions on political issues in classes where such opinions are relevant to course content.	**Qualified:** Provided that they encourage students to discuss their own opinions freely, professors should be able to state openly their opinions on political issues so long as the issue is relevant to course content.

■ Think of objections your readers might have to your claim, and modify it to eliminate the possible objection.

Analyzing Your Thesis

To analyze a thesis means to detect the key terms that make the assertion. For example, consider this thesis: "*Huckleberry Finn* should be required reading in all American high schools." To defend the thesis adequately requires addressing all the key terms: why this *particular book* should be a *required* title on American literature lists and why *high school* is the best place to teach it.

Thinking about Reasons

The reasoning that led you to your claim will supply the reasons you will offer to explain and justify it to your readers. In listing your reasons, however, you can avoid potential problems by thinking carefully about the following questions:

■ **Does the statement of each reason say *exactly* what I mean to say?** The wording of your reason or reasons matters as much as the wording of your thesis.

■ **Do I need all the reasons I am thinking of using?** As a general rule, two or three reasons are better than four or five because they are easier for the reader to remember. *Concentrate on developing your best reasons well rather than offering all the reasons you can think of.*

■ **Does each reason clearly connect to the thesis by either explaining or justifying it?** Imagine your reader asking, "Why do you believe your thesis?" Each reason should answer this question.

■ **Are there advantages in taking up my reasons in a particular order?** In general, begin and end your argument with your strongest reasons. But also consider the possibility that one reason will lead naturally to another and therefore should come before it.

■ **If I have more than one reason, are they consistent with each other?** Make sure, for instance, that your first reason does not contradict your third reason.

Thinking about Evidence

Just as the reasoning that led you to your thesis supplies the reasons you will develop to convince your readers, so any information that led you to or confirmed your reasons will supply the evidence. Arrange the evidence you have under each reason.

Select and order your evidence in response to the following questions:

- **What kind of evidence does each reason require?** For example, if you are arguing for making cell phone use by drivers illegal, one of your main reasons will be the link of cell phone use with accidents. You'll need data—facts and figures—to back up your reason. If you also argue that such a law would not restrict personal freedom unduly, you will need other kinds of evidence—for example, laws banning the use of cell phones while driving are no more restrictive than laws against driving while intoxicated.

- **How much evidence do I need?** The answer is: *enough to overcome the degree of resistance your reader is likely to have.* Many Americans, for instance, assume that the federal government is already too big, too intrusive, and too expensive. Defending any proposal that would increase its role requires significant evidence for both need and positive results.

- **Have I mixed evidence types?** For example, when a reason requires hard data, you must supply it. But if you also have a statement from a respected expert confirming your reason, consider using it as well. Some readers are convinced more by authoritative statements than by hard data. You could also offer anecdotes, stories from people involved in an event, to confirm a reason. Stories from wounded soldiers who have served in Afghanistan or Iraq, for example, offer strong evidence for improvements in Veterans Health Administration hospitals. Many people find testimony more convincing than any other kind of evidence.

- **Have I selected the best pieces of evidence from all that I could use?** Just as it is better to develop two or three reasons well than four or five poorly, so it is better to offer two or three strong pieces of evidence than four or five that vary in quality. More is not necessarily better, and too much evidence can confuse and overburden your reader.

Student Example: Noelle Alberto's Brief

A brief, like the argument it summarizes, has a three-level structure: a statement of the thesis you intend to defend; a statement of each reason that explains why you hold your thesis; and a statement of the evidence that supports each reason.

In the following student example, Noelle Alberto develops a case that urges her fellow students to stop multitasking when they study.

> Claim: **Multitasking between recreational technology and studying impairs students' learning and does not prepare them for the real world of work.**
>
> Reason: *Multitasking increases the amount of time spent studying.*
>
> Evidence: Homework takes twice as long to complete with multitasking. (Source: Tugend)

Evidence: Switching tasks makes you have to relearn information to get back on track. (Source: Hamilton)

Reason: *Switching tasks requires relearning.*

Evidence: It prevents students from being able to store information learned through studying. (Sources: Rosen, Jarmon)

Reason: *Multitasking is poor preparation for the workplace.*

Evidence: Businesses don't want people who multi-task, they want people who prioritize. (Source: LPA)

Evidence: Multitasking decreases production ability of workers. (Source: Rosen)

Reason: *Multitasking decreases worker productivity.*

Evidence: Ability to pay attention to one thing at a time is a mark of mature thinking. (Source: Rosen)

Drafting Your Paper

Using your brief as a guide, write your first draft. Focus on the following concerns as you write.

What Stance and Voice Are Appropriate for a Case?

The conventional stance and voice for arguing a case has been the **middle style,** in contrast to the plain style common in informative texts and the passionate style of some public speaking. What does middle style sound like? Here it is in a passage from the Kohn reading (pages 233–38):

> By now enough has been written about academic assessment to fill a library, but when you stop to think about it, the whole enterprise really amounts to a straightforward two-step dance. We need to collect information about how students are doing, and then we need to share that information (along with our judgments, perhaps) with the students and their parents. Gather and report— that's pretty much it.

Read these sentences aloud and you can hear the voice of middle style: *It states its position clearly, directly, and forcefully.* It is more formal than chatting but not as formal as most public speaking.

Avoid the phony, overheated sensationalism of much talk radio and TV. Case-making has nothing to do with name-calling, insults, outrageous claims, and partisan bickering. Rather, argument is the calm voice of reason, one of the voices most admired and respected wherever productive interaction among people occurs: at universities, in business meetings, in community gatherings.

Finding Common Ground

To convince people who do not already agree with you requires not only that you supply good reasons and strong evidence—your case—but also that you find common ground with them and acknowledge their reasonable concerns and counterarguments. In short, strategy always matters in convincing, and strategy always means engaging with your reader. What can you do as you compose your draft to connect with your reader?

- **Make a concession.** For example, if you are writing against multitasking as a study habit, you can concede that multitasking may be fine—or even an advantage—with other, less demanding tasks than studying.

- **Offer a refutation or a counterargument.** For example, if you are writing in favor of lowering the legal drinking age to eighteen, you can provide evidence that doing so would not increase the number of drunk-driving accidents—a central belief of those who support the legal drinking age of twenty-one.

- **Show understanding of and sympathy for other positions.** For example, if you advocate maintaining a U.S. military presence in Afghanistan for an extended period, you can acknowledge the consequent cost in lives and treasure. If you can show that the results justify the costs, your argument is strengthened by confronting the facts directly.

See the Art of Questioning box for other strategies for reducing resistance and creating the common ground that case-making requires.

THE ART OF QUESTIONING   Finding Common Ground

To convince your readers, first ask these two questions:

1. **What are the opinions of people who differ from me?**
2. **Why do they hold these opinions?**

Then, based on your answers to these questions, ask three more:

1. **Do we share any goals, values, attitudes, or beliefs?**
2. **Can I agree with at least some of what they say?**
3. **What reasons and evidence can I present to change their viewpoint?**

Your answers to these questions can reduce the "us versus them" mentality that can make reasoning with those who hold alternative viewpoints frustrating and pointless. Furthermore, connecting with your readers does not mean weakening the case you are making; on the contrary, connecting strengthens your case by taking away objections and reducing resistance to the thesis you are defending.

Developing and Organizing Your Case

Start off by orienting your reader, providing what she or he needs to know to understand your topic and why it is significant. Establish the point of view toward the topic you want your readers to share with you. Make your own position clear. Divide the body of your paper into subheadings. The Best Practices box offers more suggestions to help you as you write.

BEST PRACTICES Drafting Your Case

1. Openers are important. Start your essay by putting your case in context. For example, the trails and greenways case (pages 229–32) opens by telling us what green spaces are and how they function—important because we can easily take their existence for granted.
2. Your reader may need background information to understand your case. Part of this will come from establishing the context in the opening, but sometimes additional information your reader lacks or may not remember will be necessary or desirable. Kohn (page 233, paragraph 4) points out that the case against grading goes back as much as eighty years ago.
3. Avoid summarizing, "in conclusion" conclusions. Strive instead for a memorable "parting shot," something with impact. Kohn's last sentence is a good example: "We have to be willing to challenge the conventional wisdom, which in this case means asking not how to improve grades but how to jettison them once and for all" (page 237).
4. Strive to maintain the dispassionate, calm, and fair voice of the middle style throughout your essay. Simple, forceful statements allow the thesis and its supporting reasons and evidence to stand out for your reader.

Revising Your Draft

Write a brief assessment of your first draft. Exchange your draft and assessment with at least one other student, and use the revision questions in the Art of Questioning box to help each other decide what you each need to improve.

THE ART OF QUESTIONING Revision Checklist for Arguing a Case

1. **Who is the target audience?** How is the case framed—introduced—to reach that audience? **Does the writer keep this audience in mind throughout the essay?**
2. Locate the claim as stated or implied. **Is the claim held consistently throughout the essay?**
3. Locate the line or lines of argument and the reasons that explain and justify the claim. Does the writer focus on one reason at a time, staying with it until it is completely developed? How effectively does each reason appeal to the audience? **Is each reason clearly connected to the line of argument it defends?**
4. **Do you detect a logical progression in the ordering of the reasons, so that the first reason leads to the second, the second to the third, and so on?** Is there a better way to order the reasons? Can you find weak reasons that should be cut? Can you suggest reasons not included that would make the case stronger?
5. **How much will the audience resist each reason?** Is there sufficient evidence to overcome the resistance? Is the evidence for each reason clear and relevant to the reason it supports?

6. **Do you see a better way to order the evidence for any of the reasons?**
7. Look at the conclusion. **How does the conclusion clinch the case, leaving the reader with something memorable?** Can you see a way to make the conclusion more forceful?

Formulate a Plan to Guide Your Revision

The plan can be a single sentence or two: "I will cut this, rearrange that, and add a section here." Or, if you work better from an outline, develop one now. The important thing is to have a definite, clear idea of what you want to do and what moves you will make to get the results you want.

Student Example: Excerpts from Noelle Alberto's Draft

The introduction from Noelle Alberto's first draft illustrates a common problem with arguments. It opens with generalizations that do not grab the reader's attention and show how the topic of the paper will matter to them.

> Long before the computer, people have always needed to multitask. Mothers dressed their children while getting ready for work and making breakfast. Men drank their morning coffee and ate breakfast on their drive to work. Multitasking has long been a part of our society, and now, technology has granted us new means of multitasking. This multitasking is now crucial to the younger generation's way of life, but it may be hurting them academically.

Alberto did a good job of creating a context for her case against multitasking, and her thesis is clearly stated in the last sentence. However, she could have used a specific example to connect with her intended audience: college and high school students. By using a source, she was able to revise her introduction to more effectively engage her readers' attention.

> A recent National Public Radio program described the study habits of a modern teenager, Zach Weinberg of Chevy Chase, Maryland. On a typical evening, he worked on French homework while visiting his e-mail and Facebook, listening to iTunes, messaging a friend, and playing an online word puzzle (Hamilton). According to the story, Zach is a successful student, but many studies of multitasking suggest that he could be better if he focused on one thing at a time. While human beings are capable of doing two things at once if one of those things does not require much attention, like driving and drinking your morning coffee, there are some things that require a single focus, like school work. Multitasking between studies and recreational technology is not an effective way to study.

Another common problem in arguments is using sources to support and develop points but not using enough from the source to make the evidence clear and convincing. Here is an example:

> David Meyer, a professor at University of Michigan, found that when you switch to a new task, the parts of the brain that are no longer being used "start shutting

things down—like neural connections to important information" (Hamilton). The work you were focusing on isn't as understandable, and when you finally get back to it you "will have to repeat much of the process that created [the information] in the first place" (Hamilton).

The source actually provides additional detail that could help Alberto more clearly explain the issue she is addressing. (Alberto's revised version of this passage appears in paragraph 3 of her final paper on page 254).

To catch this kind of revision problem, ask a friend to read your draft and to be completely honest about evidence from sources that you have not explained clearly.

Editing Your Revised Draft

Alberto's revised draft was well written. Most of her paragraphs were effective; each had an appropriate length and made a single point. In one case, however, a paragraph needed editing for wordiness and unnecessary repetition.

Original Version

This sentence repeats the idea in the first two sentences.

This sentence repeats the point of the third sentence.

The connection between sentences 5 and 6 is not tight.

Before concluding that multitasking is not functional in the business world, the writer should present the evidence for saying so.

The concluding sentence also repeats a point made earlier.

Another misconception is that multitasking prepares you for the business world. "Able to multitask" used to be considered a positive on employee résumés. Now, according to the U.S. Departments of Labor and Education, businesses want an employee who "selects goal-relevant activities, ranks them, allocates time, and prepares and follows schedules" ("Skills and Competencies"). Businesses are no longer looking for people who can multitask. They want people who can separate their tasks for the most efficient use of time. School is about preparation for the real world, and if multitasking is not functional there, it is also not functional in school. Furthermore, multitasking in the business world has been found to be completely inefficient. Christine Rosen of *The New Atlantis* writes how multitasking is "a serious threat to workplace productivity" and actually "costs the U.S. economy $650 billion a year in lost productivity" (Rosen 106). A study conducted at the University of London found that "workers distracted by e-mail and phone calls suffer a fall in IQ more than twice that found in marijuana smokers" (qtd. in Rosen 106). Multitasking has no business being in the workplace, and if multitasking is difficult and harmful in the business world, it has no place in a university either.

The edited version is more tightly organized and concise.

Edited Version

Another misconception is that multitasking prepares you for the business world. "Able to multitask" used to be considered a positive on employee résumés. However, multitasking has been found to be completely inefficient. Researchers found that "extreme multitasking—information overload—costs the U.S. economy $650 billion a year in lost productivity" (Rosen 106). A study conducted at the University of London found that "workers distracted by e-mail and phone calls suffer a fall in IQ more than twice that found in marijuana smokers" (qtd. in Rosen 106). Future employers do not value multitasking. Now, according to the U.S.

Departments of Labor and Education, businesses want an employee who "selects goal-relevant activities, ranks them, allocates time, and prepares and follows schedules" ("Skills and Competencies"). If multitasking is difficult and harmful in the business world, it has no place in a university either.

▨▨▧ ■ ACTIVITY 11.3 *In Your Own Work*

Editing Your Revised Draft

We called attention to one problem in Alberto's draft: paragraph structure and flow. Look for long paragraphs in your own draft and edit in ways similar to those demonstrated here. Go on to look for other problems, especially ones you know about from previous papers. ■

Every writer has editing problems. Keep a checklist of yours. For instance, list words that you misspelled. If you did not punctuate a sentence correctly, write down the sentence and circle or underline the correct punctuation mark. If you need examples to remember other types of problems—like editing for flow—take one from your paper. Check your revised draft for your most common problems.

Study your instructor's marks and comments on every paper. Add new editing problems to your list as needed. *Always check your next paper for the problems you have listed.* In this way you can reduce your characteristic editing problems.

REVISED STUDENT EXAMPLE

Alberto 1

Noelle Alberto

Professor Channell

English 120

29 April 2011

Multitasking: A Poor Study Habit

A recent National Public Radio program described the study habits of a mod-   1
ern teenager, Zach Weinberg of Chevy Chase, Maryland. On a typical evening, he worked on French homework while visiting his e-mail and Facebook, listening to iTunes, messaging a friend, and playing an online word puzzle (Hamilton).

Alberto 2

According to the story, Zach is a successful student, but many studies of multitasking suggest that he could be better if he focused on one thing at a time. While
human beings are capable of doing two things at once if one of those things
does not require much attention, like driving and drinking your morning coffee,
there are some things that require a single focus, like school work. Multitasking
between studies and recreational technology is not an effective way to study.

Claim.

One misconception that students may have about their multitasking is that they
are saving time. Some say that they feel they get more done in a shorter amount
of time, but they are actually not doing two things at once. They are switching from
one task to another, and constant task switching takes more time. Gloria Mark of the
University of California Irvine conducted a study in which business workers were
interrupted approximately every 11 minutes while working on a project. Each time, it
took them about 25 minutes to return their attentions to the original project (Tugend).
In study terms, if you interrupt yourself to check e-mail every ten minutes, a chapter
that would take thirty minutes straight through takes over an hour to complete.

2

First reason.

What happens when people shift from one demanding task to another? David
Meyer, a professor at University of Michigan, found that when you switch to a new
task, the parts of the brain that are no longer being used "start shutting things
down—like neural connections to important information." If a student is studying
French and interrupts to click open a message, the neural connections to the
French homework start to shut down. To restore his level of understanding, Meyer
says the student, "will have to repeat much of the process that created [the con-
nections] in the first place" (qtd. in Hamilton).

3

Paragraph 3
gives more
evidence
for the first
reason.

This frequent reconnecting to prior levels of focus and understanding is a
waste of time. It is time lost that could be used more efficiently. If students eliminated technological distractions during study time, they would be able to complete more work in a shorter amount of time with greater understanding. There is
always time to socialize after homework and studying have been completed.

4

Paragraph 4 is
a transitional
paragraph that
wraps up the
first reason.

Another misconception is that multitasking prepares you for the business
world. "Able to multitask" used to be considered a positive on employee résumés.

5

Alberto 3

Second reason.

However, multitasking has been found to be completely inefficient. Researchers found that "extreme multitasking—information overload—costs the U.S. economy $650 billion a year in lost productivity" (Rosen 106). A study conducted at the University of London found that "workers distracted by e-mail and phone calls suffer a fall in IQ more than twice that found in marijuana smokers" (qtd. in Rosen 106). Future employers do not value multitasking. Now, according to the U.S. Departments of Labor and Education, businesses want an employee who "selects goal-relevant activities, ranks them, allocates time, and prepares and follows schedules" ("Skills and Competencies"). If multitasking is difficult and harmful in the business world, it has no place in a university either.

Third reason.

Besides wasted time and money, another unfortunate effect of multitasking is the serious damage to students' ability to learn. Studies by psychology professor Russell Poldrack show if you multitask while learning, "that learning is less flexible and more specialized, so you cannot retrieve the information as easily" (qtd. in Rosen 107). Studies of blood flow in the brain show why. When people are task-switching, they use the "striatum, a region of the brain involved in learning new skills" (Rosen 107). In contrast people who are not multitasking "show activity in the hippocampus, a region involved in storing and recalling information" (Rosen 108). Amy Jarmon, dean at Texas Tech's School of Law, recalls a study comparing two groups of students in a large lecture class. One group of students was allowed to use laptops in class; they performed much more poorly on a memory quiz of lecture content than students not permitted to use laptops. The students who were able to check their e-mail and update their web pages during class were less capable of recalling because they were not using the hippocampus section of their brains.

6

This is the last reason because it has weight in showing how multitasking undermines intellectual potential.

Finally, if students get into the habit of multitasking, they could miss out on developing a personality trait prized by the most highly successful people. As Christine Rosen writes in *The New Atlantis,* that trait is "a finely honed skill for paying attention" (109). The great British scientist Sir Isaac Newton said his discoveries owed "more to patient attention than to any other talent" (qtd. in Rosen 109). The American psychologist William James wrote that the ability to pay attention

7

Alberto 4

marked the difference between a mature and an immature person: "The faculty of voluntarily bringing back a wandering attention, over and over again . . . is the very root of judgment, character, and will" (qtd. in Rosen). Maturity means recognizing that there is a time and place for everything. In meeting the challenges of college, I have realized the truth of this saying. When I go to the library to study, I leave my computer behind so that I will not be tempted to multitask. After an hour of focused school work, I have accomplished a great deal. It is also a good feeling to know that I have practiced self-discipline by not allowing my mind to wander.

> Brings author's personal experience into the paper to confirm a reason.

Multitasking is now part of every student's life. The facts indicate that we need to resist it more. Multitasking is not as helpful as many people think, and its very appeal is part of the problem. It is inefficient, reduces intelligence, and impairs recall. Zach Weinberg's mother worries that Zach's multitasking study habits will cause him to "[lose] out on other skills" like the ability to concentrate (Hamilton). To think deeply rather than shallowly, we need to be able to concentrate. Therefore, the best approach is to divide study time from social time. Focusing on one thing at a time will produce better outcomes now and in the future.

8

> Brings the paper back around to the student introduced in the opening, as a way to frame the argument.

Works Cited

Hamilton, Jon. "Multitasking Teens May Be Muddling Their Brains." *National Public Radio,* 9 Oct. 2008, www.npr.org/templates/story/.php?storyId=95524385.

Jarmon, Amy L. "Multitasking: Helpful or Harmful? Multitasking Has Been Shown to Slow Learning and Reduce Efficiency." *Student Lawyer,* vol. 36, no. 8, 2008, pp. 33–35.

Rosen, Christine. "The Myth of Multitasking." *New Atlantis*, Spring 2008: pp. 105–110.

"Skills and Competencies Needed to Succeed in Today's Workplace." North Central Regional Education Laboratory, Learning Point Associates, n.d. Accessed 7 Apr. 2009.

Tugend, Alina. "Multitasking Can Make You Lose. . .Um. . .Focus." *The New York Times,* 25 Oct. 2008, www.nytimes.com/2008/10/25/business/yourmoney/25shortcuts.html.

CHAPTER 12

Appealing for Action

APPEALING FOR ACTION, ALSO CALLED PERSUASION, BELONGS TO THE ANCIENT DISCIPLINE OF RHETORIC established by the Greek philosopher Aristotle about 2,500 years ago. The purpose of rhetoric, he said, was "to discover the available means of persuasion in any given case." Its driving question is, "How can I move this person (or those people) to do what I believe is good, right, or desirable?"

We began to practice rhetoric as children, when we persuaded our friends to play one game rather than another, or when we worked on our parents to persuade them to buy something we wanted. Persuasion has worked on us all our lives, through advertisements; sermons; editorials; and speeches, books, articles, and videos, as well as other genres that address controversial topics. Entire careers, such as those in communications or marketing, are devoted to persuasion. Persuasion plays a major role in personal and family life, in business, and in the community. It is important to examine more closely what persuasion is and how it works.

What Is Persuasion?

Advertising is one of the most common examples of moving people to action. We can learn a great deal about persuasion by studying advertisers' creative use of persuasive appeals, both verbal and visual, to market their products to targeted audiences.

Persuasion asks us to do something: spend money, give money, join a demonstration, recycle, vote, enlist, convict, or acquit. Like convincing people to change their perspective on an issue (see Chapter 11, pages 227–29, for an explanation of convincing), persuading them to take action for a cause also involves providing reasons and evidence for doing something, but it also appeals in other ways, especially by gaining our trust and confidence and by arousing emotions favorable to the action advocated.

CONCEPT CLOSE-UP   When Should You Persuade?

Pay close attention to what your course assignments call for, because the full range of persuasive appeal is not always appropriate. The more purely intellectual your topic and the more academic your audience, the more you should emphasize logical appeal, or making a good case. A clear thesis, supported by good reasons and backed by solid evidence, is usually what professors want.

When the issue is public, for example, matters of policy or right and wrong, persuasion's fuller range of appeal is typically appropriate. Making an argument for the creation

See pages 258–59 for a discussion of the full range of appeals.

Edward P. J. Corbett. *The Rhetoric and Poetics of Aristotle.* Modern Library, 1984.

of a homeless shelter in your community requires establishing your good character and personal involvement with the project as well as appealing to the emotions of your readers. *Persuasion appeals to the whole person:* mind, emotion, the capacity for trust and cooperation, even the appreciation for things said well.

College assignments calling for persuasion will often ask you to take knowledge gained from a course and use it to persuade others who lack it. For example, using what you learned from a course in environmental science, you might write an article urging Americans to buy smaller, fuel-efficient automobiles to reduce carbon dioxide emissions and oil consumption.

Why Write to Persuade?

Persuasion brings about change in the world, whether in national or local politics, in neighborhoods, on campus, in the workplace, or in personal relationships. For example, persuasion

- Sways elected officials to favor one policy over another.
- Induces people and nations to resolve conflicts peacefully rather than by violent means.
- Affects business decisions of all kinds, including how to promote a product or service.
- Influences college officials who set tuition rates and housing costs on campus.

No other kind of writing has more practical impact. If you want to make a difference in the larger world or your own community and feel it needs to change in specific ways, learning how to persuade other people is the key.

How Do Writers Persuade?

Getting people to take action requires more than good reasoning. Aristotle identified three kinds of appeal (Figure 12.1):

- *Logos,* or appealing to reason
- *Ethos,* or appealing to the character of the speaker
- *Pathos,* or appealing to the emotions of the listeners

In all three, you adapt your argument to the interests, beliefs, and values of a target audience.

For example, to save money and for other reasons, Americans are looking for alternatives to cars. One of these alternatives is the motorcycle or scooter. Suppose you were writing an essay entitled, "Getting around on Two Wheels."

First, what might you say to appeal to your readers' sense of reason, or logos? You could argue that

- Motorcycles cost far less than cars to buy and maintain.
- They use on average about one-third as much gas.

Writer
(Ethos)

Audience
(Pathos)

Message
(Logos)

FIGURE **12.1**

The Rhetorical Triangle

Aristotle identified three types of appeals used to persuade.

- They take up only about half as much parking space.
- With proper training and equipment, they are not as dangerous to operate as many people think.

Motorcycles could help solve many problems, including reduction in traffic, greenhouse gas emissions, and American dependence on oil.

Next, how could you use pathos, or emotional appeals? The main value here is the fun of motorcycling. Motorcycles are the mechanical horse—you do not drive them, you ride them—and it should be fairly easy to appeal to the American love for freedom and adventure.

Finally, how could you appeal to ethos, or character? If you are a motorcyclist yourself, you could draw on your own experience. If not, interview friends who ride and cite what they say: You can borrow *ethos* from others, particularly if they are subject experts.

THE ART OF QUESTIONING   What Really Persuades Us?

Many people say they are persuaded only by reasons and evidence. That is, *logos* matters most. Aristotle thought that *ethos* might be more powerful: If we think that a writer is intelligent, well informed, and trustworthy and has genuine concern for our needs, we will tend to believe most of what that person says. Look at advertising and you will probably conclude that *pathos* is the prime persuader. Nearly all ads appeal to emotions and attitudes most of all.

What do you think? Consider the last important decision you made. How did you persuade yourself to do one thing rather than another? If someone tried to persuade you, what kinds of appeal did the person use? Which of these appeals had the most impact on the decision you made?

READING 12.1

Where Sweatshops Are a Dream

NICHOLAS D. KRISTOF

Nicholas D. Kristof is a two-time Pulitzer Prize–winning columnist for the New York Times. A graduate of Harvard and Oxford, Kristof has lived all over the world and visited 140 countries. As you read the following editorial, ponder the complex issues it raises about opportunities in the developing world.

Before Barack Obama and his team act on their talk about "labor standards," I'd like to offer them a tour of the vast garbage dump here in Phnom Penh. 1

This is a Dante-like vision of hell. It's a mountain of festering refuse, a half-hour hike across, emitting clouds of smoke from subterranean fires. 2

The miasma of toxic stink leaves you gasping, breezes batter you with filth, and even the rats look forlorn. Then the smoke parts and you come across a child ambling barefoot, searching for old plastic cups that recyclers will buy for five cents a pound. Many families actually live in shacks on this smoking garbage.

Phnom Penh, Cambodia
© Jens Grossmann/laif/Redux

Mr. Obama and the Democrats who favor labor standards in trade agreements mean well, for they intend to fight back at oppressive sweatshops abroad. But while it shocks Americans to hear it, the central challenge in the poorest countries is not that sweatshops exploit too many people, but that they don't exploit enough.

Talk to these families in the dump, and a job in a sweatshop is a cherished dream, an escalator out of poverty, the kind of gauzy if probably unrealistic ambition that parents everywhere often have for their children.

"I'd love to get a job in a factory," said Pim Srey Rath, a 19-year-old woman scavenging for plastic. "At least that work is in the shade. Here is where it's hot."

Another woman, Vath Sam Oeun, hopes her 10-year-old boy, scavenging beside her, grows up to get a factory job, partly because she has seen other children run over by garbage trucks. Her boy has never been to a doctor or a dentist, and last bathed when he was 2, so a sweatshop job by comparison would be far more pleasant and less dangerous.

I'm glad that many Americans are repulsed by the idea of importing products made by barely paid, barely legal workers in dangerous factories. Yet sweatshops are only a symptom of poverty, not a cause, and banning them closes off one route out of poverty. At a time of tremendous economic distress and protectionist pressures, there's a special danger that tighter labor standards will be used as an excuse to curb trade.

When I defend sweatshops, people always ask me: But would you want to work in a sweatshop? No, of course not. But I would want even less to pull a rickshaw. In the hierarchy of jobs in poor countries, sweltering at a sewing machine isn't the bottom.

My views on sweatshops are shaped by years living in East Asia, watching as living standards soared—including those in my wife's ancestral village in southern China—because of sweatshop jobs.

Manufacturing is one sector that can provide millions of jobs. Yet sweatshops usually go not to the poorest nations but to better-off countries with more reliable electricity and ports.

I often hear the argument: Labor standards can improve wages and working conditions, without greatly affecting the eventual retail cost of goods. That's true.

Paragraph numbers: 3, 4, 5, 6, 7, 8, 9, 10, 11, 12

Margin annotations (left):

Establishes character by depicting what the writer knows firsthand. Also appeals to emotion, sympathy for the plight of the poor in places like Cambodia.

Author opposes Obama's policy. Gains additional character appeal by depicting his opponents as "meaning well."

Testimonials in support of the writer's thesis: factory jobs a step up for many desperately poor Cambodians.

Author shows appreciation for opponent's position, which he sees as moral but not realistic or well-informed.

More appeal to *ethos* or character: Believe me, he says, because I know from deep experience what is going on in East Asia.

Margin annotations (right):

The claim or thesis. In this case, it is disturbing to many readers who see sweatshops in wholly negative ways.

Appeal to reason: You cannot judge Cambodia and similar countries by American norms.

Shows awareness of argument counter to his and responds to it reasonably.

But labor standards and "living wages" have a larger impact on production costs that companies are always trying to pare. The result is to push companies to operate more capital-intensive factories in better-off nations like Malaysia, rather than labor-intensive factories in poorer countries like Ghana or Cambodia.

The practical problems of labor reform in a globalized economy: more appeal to reason.

Cambodia has, in fact, pursued an interesting experiment by working with factories to establish decent labor standards and wages. It's a worthwhile idea, but one result of paying above-market wages is that those in charge of hiring often demand bribes—sometimes a month's salary—in exchange for a job. In addition, these standards add to production costs, so some factories have closed because of the global economic crisis and the difficulty of competing internationally.

13

Author's proposed action: promote manufacturing in poor countries.

The best way to help people in the poorest countries isn't to campaign against sweatshops but to promote manufacturing there. One of the best things America could do for Africa would be to strengthen our program to encourage African imports, called AGOA, and nudge Europe to match it.

14

Among people who work in development, many strongly believe (but few dare say very loudly) that one of the best hopes for the poorest countries would be to build their manufacturing industries. But global campaigns against sweatshops make that less likely.

15

Concludes with powerful emotional appeal to actual people and concrete conditions.

Look, I know that Americans have a hard time accepting that sweatshops can help people. But take it from 13-year-old Neuo Chanthou, who earns a bit less than $1 a day scavenging in the dump. She's wearing a "Playboy" shirt and hat that she found amid the filth, and she worries about her sister, who lost part of her hand when a garbage truck ran over her.

16

"It's dirty, hot and smelly here," she said wistfully. "A factory is better."

17

Questions for Discussion

1. As you can easily imagine, this editorial has been very controversial, resulting in passionate responses, for and against the role of sweatshops. If you are persuaded by Kristof, what does he say that most moved you to agree? If you resist his argument, why did you not find it persuasive?

2. Photographs can be powerfully persuasive. How does the image that accompanies this editorial reinforce what the writer says? Is its appeal logical, ethical, emotional, or some combination of these?

3. Kristof's position is often criticized as a justification for exploiting foreign workers, who are typically paid far less than American workers and endure difficult and sometimes dangerous working conditions. Did he handle this criticism well? Where and how does he confront it? Are you persuaded? Why or why not?

■■■ *Thinking as a Writer*

What Is the Rhetorical Situation?

See Chapter 3, pages 32–38, for definitions of purpose, angle, and voice.

1. What is Kristof's *purpose* in his editorial? What is his *angle* on the topic? How would you describe his *voice*?
2. Who is the intended *audience*? Is there anything you can cite that implies the target readership? How do the rational, emotional, and ethical appeals work separately and together to persuade his readers?
3. Using the marginal annotations to the reading, discuss the organization of the editorial. How is it framed in the opening paragraphs? How does it close or conclude the argument in the last two paragraphs without just summarizing it? ■

READING **12.2**

The Factories of Lost Children

KATHARINE WEBER

Katharine Weber's subject matter in the following article (originally published in the New York Times*) is similar to Kristof's, but she bases her argument on tragic incidents involving child labor. How does Weber's use of persuasion differ from Kristof's? As you read, consider which argument is more appealing to you and why.*

Ninety-five years ago, March 25 also fell on a Saturday. At 4:40 p.m. on that sunny afternoon in 1911, only minutes before the end of the workday, a fire broke out on the eighth floor of the Asch Building, a block east of Washington Square in Manhattan.   1

The Triangle Waist Company occupied the top three floors of the 10-story building. There, some 600 workers were employed in the manufacture of ladies' shirtwaists, most of them teenage girls who spoke little English and were fresh off the boat from Russia, the Austro-Hungarian Empire and Italy. The fire, probably caused by a carelessly tossed match or cigarette butt (there were perhaps 100 men working at the Triangle), engulfed the premises in minutes.   2

The factory owners and the office staff on the 10th floor, all but one, escaped onto the roof and climbed to an adjacent building on Waverly Place. But on the eighth and ninth floors, the workers were trapped by a deadly combination of highly combustible materials,   3 workrooms crowded by dense rows of table-mounted sewing machines, doors that were locked or opened inward, inadequate fire escapes, and the lack of any plan or instruction.

Before the first horse-drawn fire engines arrived at the scene, girls—some holding hands, in twos and threes—had already begun to jump from the windows. The hundred-foot drop to the cobbled street was not survivable. The firemen deployed their nets, but the force of gravity drove the bodies of the girls straight through to the pavement, and they died on impact. 4

The ladders on the fire trucks were raised quickly, but the New York City Fire Department of 1911 was not equipped to combat fires above six stories—the limit of those ladders. The top floors of the Asch Building, a neo-Renaissance "fireproof" warehouse completed in 1901 in full compliance with building codes, burned relentlessly. 5

The workers trapped near the windows on the eighth and ninth floors made the fast and probably instinctive choice to jump instead of burning or suffocating in the smoke. The corpses of the jumpers, by some estimates as many as 70, could at least be identified. But the bodies of most of those who died inside the Triangle Waist Company—trapped by the machinery, piled up on the wrong side of doors, heaped in the stairwells and elevator shafts—were hideously charred, many beyond recognition. 6

Before 15 minutes had elapsed, some 140 workers had burned, fallen from the collapsing fire escapes, or jumped to their deaths. Several more, critically injured, died in the days that followed, putting the official death toll at 146. 7

But what happened to the children who were working at the Triangle Waist Company that afternoon? 8

By most contemporary accounts, it was common knowledge that children were usually on the premises. They were hidden from the occasional inspectors, but underage girls, as young as 9 or 10, worked in most New York garment factories, sewing buttons and trimming threads. Where were they on this particular Saturday afternoon? 9

There are no descriptions of children surviving the fire. Various lists of those who died 95 years ago today—140 named victims plus six who were never identified (were some of those charred remains children?)—include one 11-year-old, two 14-year-olds, three 15-year-olds, 16 16-year-olds, and 14 17-year-olds. Were the ages of workers, living and dead, modified to finesse the habitual violation of child labor laws in 1911? How many children actually died that day? We will never know. And now 1911 is almost beyond living memory. 10

But we will also never know how many children were among the dead on May 10, 1993, in Thailand when the factory of the Kader Industrial Toy Company (a supplier to Hasbro and Fisher-Price) went up in flames. Most of the 188 workers who died were described as teenage girls. 11

We will never know with any certainty how many children died on Nov. 25, 2000, in a fire at the Chowdhury Knitwear and Garment factory near Dhaka, Bangladesh (most of the garments made in Bangladesh are contracted by American retailers, including Wal-Mart and the Gap), where at least 10 of the 52 trapped in the flames by locked doors and windows were 10 to 14 years old. 12

And we will never know how many children died just last month, on Feb. 23, in the KTS Composite Textile factory fire in Chittagong, Bangladesh. The official death 13 toll has climbed into the 50's, but other sources report that at least 84 workers lost their lives. It's a familiar story: crowded and unsafe conditions, locked exits, hundreds of undocumented female workers as young as 12, a deadly fire. There may never be another tragic factory fire in America that takes the lives of children. We don't lock them into sweatshops any more. There are child labor laws, fire codes.

But as long as we don't question the source of the inexpensive clothing we wear, as long as we don't wonder about the children in those third world factories who make the inexpensive toys we buy for our own children, those fires will occur and young girls and boys will continue to die. They won't die because of natural catastrophes like monsoons and earthquakes; they will die because it has become our national habit to outsource, and these days we outsource our tragedies, too.

14

Questions for Discussion

1. Stories—in this case, an account of a tragic fire—can be as persuasive as an argument. How does the story establish Weber's **ethos,** *the appeal of character*? How does it appeal to her readers' sense of ethics, of right and wrong? How do the details of the story create a powerful appeal to **pathos,** or *emotion*?

2. Weber does argue—in the last paragraph. State her argument in your own words. Does it follow from her story? When we arrive at her argument, what does the story become for us? Is it a source of reasons or evidence or both?

3. As all persuasion does, Weber's article wants us to do something. What exactly does she want us to do? Read Kristof's editorial (pages 259–61). If we did what Weber wants, what impact would it have on Kristof's desired action?

■ ■ ■ *Thinking as a Writer*

What Is the Rhetorical Situation?

1. What is Weber's *purpose*? What is her *angle* on the topic? How would you describe her *voice*?

2. Who is the intended *audience*? What can you cite that implies the target readership? How does her story and argument appeal to her readers?

3. Discuss the organization of the editorial. How is the story about the Triangle Waist Company told? That is, in what order does the author tell us what we need to know? What does she emphasize and why? How does the argument close without just summarizing what she has said? ■

■■■ *Collaborative Activity*

Using Implied Judgments

Persuasion often depends on *implied judgments,* on *statements of fact that imply the writer's judgments without stating them.* For instance, many of the workers "were fresh off the boat from Russia, the Austro-Hungarian Empire and Italy." This language implies the factory bosses' attitude: The workers were expendable. There was a ready supply of labor on the next boat.

In class discussion or small group work, locate other instances of implied judgments in Weber's narrative. Spell out in each case what the statements of fact imply. Weber makes a clear argument against sweatshops. How would the argument change if Weber spelled out some of her judgments instead of leaving the reader to infer them? When should we say in so many words what the facts imply? When should we let our readers draw inferences themselves? ■

The Assignment

Write an essay on any disputed topic that asks your readers to take action. Your topic must be something about which reasonable people could disagree. In some cases, you might advocate doing nothing when other people want to take action or stop doing something that causes more harm than benefit.

What Can I Write About?

Remember that your topic must be controversial: Various courses of action are possible, and genuine choice exists. Matters of fact are not controversial. For instance, it is a tragic fact that many veterans of the wars in Iraq and Afghanistan have committed suicide. People disagree not about this fact but rather about whether enough is being done to help prevent more suicides.

Besides selecting a controversial issue, pick one you know something about from personal experience. Civic activities, internships, and jobs can be rich sources of topics. Here are some other places to find topics:

- **Class readings.** Class readings can suggest topics for persuasion, especially if the readings themselves are persuasive, like the examples in this chapter. For instance, if the sweatshop problem interests you, begin by finding out about the labor practices of the companies that make the clothing you and your friends wear.

- **Readings in other classes.** In a political science class, for example, you might study how presidential candidates are selected by the Democratic and Republican parties. The process is highly controversial, and many proposals for reform have been advanced. Perhaps one of the reforms struck you as especially desirable. Do some more reading about it; perhaps you have found your topic.

- **Local news or personal observations.** Read your local and campus newspapers for issues and problems of concern to your community. Take a walk around your neighborhood or campus, looking for problems that need solutions, such as wasted energy in offices, dorms, and classrooms.

- **Internet discussions.** If you keep a blog, you probably have a store of observations about issues that concern you, things you would like to see changed. Or visit blogs on issues of public concern, such as the "Opinionator" at the *New York Times,* which gathers opinions from a variety of contributors.

How Do I Appeal for Action?
Questioning the Rhetorical Situation

Begin by picturing a rhetorical situation for your writing project, a real-world context for communicating. You should consider the key variables in any act of communication: a writer with something to say, a reader the writer wishes to reach, and a kind of text appropriate to the writing task. These three variables will affect many decisions in the composing process.

Writer: What Is My Purpose, and What Impression Should Readers Have of Me?

The general purpose of persuasion is to move your readers to take action. Given your topic, consider exactly what action your readers can reasonably take. Weber's readers, for instance, cannot do much directly to stop unsafe working conditions, especially in foreign countries, but they can find out about how companies that make their clothes and other consumer products treat their labor force. Her readers can "vote with their pocketbook" by not buying goods produced by careless or grossly exploitive labor practices. Just as Weber does, ask your readers to do something realistic and concrete, something within their power.

Audience: Who Is My Reader?

In many cases, what you want done implies your audience so strongly that virtually no choice exists. For instance, Kristof's article (pages 259–61) addresses the Obama administration because only the president and his officials can influence policy toward sweatshops in foreign countries. In some cases, however, you could reasonably choose between two groups of readers or among or across several. For instance, if your topic is charter schools (privately owned and operated alternatives to public schools), your readers could be students, their parents, local political leaders, state legislators, officials directly involved with educational policy in your state, or some combination of these. In such a case, *choose the readership you know best* because it is difficult to appeal to an audience you know only as an abstract entity, such as state legislators. Once you make your choice, be sure to advocate action your readers can actually take. Parents cannot pass laws, but they can influence educational policy by voting for a candidate in your local district who favors the action you favor toward charter schools.

Text: What Moves Can I Make?

Persuasion joins the appeal of reasoning well to the appeal of the writer's character and to your reader's emotions. The moves of reasoning are discussed in Chapter 11, on pages 241–42. Possible moves for appealing to character and to emotion include the following:

Character

- If you have personal experience with your topic, share your experience with your reader. For example, an article encouraging your readers to become involved with Habitat for Humanity will be more persuasive if you have helped build a house for a poor family and can talk about how satisfying your participation was.

- Provide background and explanatory information as needed. For example, the Habitat for Humanity article could include information about the organization itself and how people can get involved. Readers respond positively to writers who are well informed.

- Show that you are thinking about your reader's concerns and interests. Advocating the purchase of a car powered by an electric motor obviously benefits the environment. But it also has benefits for an owner, which you can specify in detail. Readers tend to trust writers whose self-interest is either absent or subordinate to doing something that benefits them.

Emotion

- Share your emotional reactions through simple, direct statements of how you feel or felt. If you are writing about date rape, for example, and you are a victim, readers will sympathize with feelings of anger and helplessness. They will also expect to read about your emotional responses.

- Arouse appropriate emotional responses in your readers by depicting a situation that made you happy, sad, grateful, resentful, and so on—whatever emotion or emotions you felt and want your readers to feel. If you are writing about police profiling and you were stopped and interrogated, describing that experience can help readers who have never been "shaken down" to understand the damage profiling does.

- As a rule, it is not a good idea to say that people should not feel what they feel. However, sometimes common emotional responses to your topic can be inappropriate and an obstacle to persuasion. For example, influenced by the "Welfare Queen" stereotype, too many people see all people on welfare as lazy and dishonest. Counter these negative judgments by describing the actual circumstances of most recipients and/or by citing data that indicate that welfare fraud is the exception rather than the norm.

How Do I Write Persuasively?
Engaging the Writing Process

No two people compose an appeal for action in exactly the same way, and even the same person may go through the writing process in different ways for different projects. Nevertheless, because no one can attend to everything at once, there are phases in handling any significant writing task. You **explore the topic** to get a sense of whether it will work for you and what you might be able to do with it; if the topic is working out for you, then you move into **preparing to write,** generating more content and planning your draft.

The next phase is **drafting your paper,** getting a version, however rough it may be, on screen or paper so that you can work toward the final draft. Getting there involves two further phases: **revising your draft,** where you make major improvements in it, followed by **editing your draft,** taking care of errors, sentences that do not read well, paragraphs lacking focus and flow, and so on.

Exploring Your Topic

The following questions will help you delve into your topic and begin writing about it.

1. What do you want your readers to do?

2. Who are your readers? Describe them as specifically as you can. What about them will be relevant to your argument? Consider age, religion, income bracket, occupation, political orientation, education, and gender.

3. Reader awareness is important: How much will readers know about the problem, question, or issue you intend to address? What is their likely attitude?

4. Why do you care about this topic? What makes you a credible writer on behalf of your position?

5. What is the best reason you can give your readers for doing what you want them to do? State it as a sentence. Do you have a second reason in mind?

6. What additional ideas do you have for appealing to your readers? What values and beliefs can you appeal to?

7. If your topic requires more than general knowledge and personal experience, what sources have you found to support your argument? What additional material might you need?

See Chapter 11, page 229 for more information on case structure and strategy.

███ ▪▪ ACTIVITY 12.1 *Thinking as a Writer*

Responding to the Exploration Questions

Write answers to the seven questions above. Consider whether your topic may be too large for the space you have; limiting your topic can save time later, when you have to rewrite a draft that takes on too much. If you have good reasons in mind, write them down. If you have ideas for appealing to reader emotions, values, and beliefs, write these down too. Include whatever insights you have gained from personal experience. Exchange them with a partner via e-mail and/or in small group sessions in or out of class to help each other refine and develop ideas for and approaches to the first draft. ▪

Preparing to Write

Some writers prefer to go straight to drafting, working out their appeals in several drafts. We recommend going through the following steps first, which most writers find helpful.

Strategies for Appeals

As the readings above (Readings 12.1 and 12.2) and the student example at the end of the chapter (pages 278–82) show, you have many options in persuasive writing. Ask yourself the following questions as you begin to develop your essay:

- Is there an opportunity to tell a personal or a historical story? Weber provides a good model for storytelling as persuasion.

- How can I make a **case,** *an argument with reasons and evidence,* to support the action I advocate?

- How can I join the case to ethical and emotional appeals, persuading my audience through self-presentation and appropriate feelings?

- When I encounter good reasons for another course of action, how can I refute or use those reasons to favor my own? Kristof's opinion column is a good model for how to make this move.

- How can I defend my course of action as the best alternative in an imperfect world? Kristof does not defend sweatshops as ideally desirable but only as a step in the right direction for desperately poor people around the world. Student Natsumi Hazama (see pages 278–82) does not offer a perfect solution to the problem of too much pressure from Asian parents, only an approach that reduces the harm it does.

- How might I use photos and other visual means of persuasion effectively? For examples, see the photo that opens Kristof's editorial.

Doing Research

If the assignment calls for research, use the techniques for finding and evaluating sources (see Chapter 16, pages 336–49) to find articles, books, and online materials about or related to your topic.

Thinking More about Persuasive Appeals

Thinking through the appeals to reason, character, and emotion helps many writers build up confidence, energy for drafting, and a more detailed plan to guide the first draft.

The Appeal through Logic: Articulating a Claim

You know what you want your readers to do; try formulating it as a claim. These suggestions will help. Your claim is a statement you will defend, not just a description of something factual.

Original Version (not a claim)

Students are choosing majors based on future income instead of interests and abilities.

Revised Version (claim)

Students should find a major that excites their desire to learn rather than one that promises only financial rewards.

The claim should be focused and specific and directed at a readership.

Original Version (too general)

Parents need to be stricter.

Revised Version (better focused)

Parents need to teach children to be sensitive to other people in restaurants, stores, and other public places.

The claim uses concrete nouns and verbs, rather than vague and indirect wording, to make its point.

Original Version (vague)

One's natural abilities cannot grow into an established intelligence unless a person learns how to control their attention and concentration.

Revised Version (more concise)

Even highly talented people need to learn to control attention and concentration to develop their full potential.

Some claims may need to be qualified.

Original Version (too absolute)

High schools need a vocational track.

Revised Version (qualified)

Unless they send all their students to college, high schools should offer a high-quality vocational track.

■■■■ ACTIVITY 12.2 *In Your Own Work*

Refining Your Claim

Share several versions of your claim in class or by an e-mail exchange with one or several other students. Ask for feedback based on which version best states your thesis and creates least resistance in your audience. ■

Developing Reasons for Your Claim

Once you have a working version of the claim, begin to formulate reasons for it—why your readers should take the action you are arguing for. Focus on the fit between your reasons and the values and beliefs of your readers.

See the Best Practices box that follows for some places to find reader-oriented reasons.

BEST PRACTICES   Places to Find Audience-Based Reasons

- In the audience's *beliefs and values.* Think about their politics and the values of their culture or subculture.

- In *traditions and traditional texts.* What books, ceremonies, ideas, places, and people do they revere?

- In *expert opinion and/or data.* Draw on the reasoning of qualified experts your audience will respect—mention them by name and cite their credentials. Construct reasons from information and statistics taken from sources your readers will know and trust.

- In *comparisons or analogies* your audience would accept. Analogies work because they liken the less familiar and known to the more familiar and known. Those who oppose genetic engineering, for example, often reason that altering human genes is like altering nature—it has bad side effects.

- In establishing *cause and effect.* If you can show the action you would like the audience to take will lead to positive consequences, you have a good reason. Of course, you will need evidence to show that the cause-and-effect relationship exists.

Making a Brief of Your Case

The brief is a concise version of a logical argument. It has three levels:

1. The claim, what you want your readers to do
2. A reason or reasons explaining why
3. Evidence to support each reason

Briefs can help in preparing to write, but keep in mind that new ideas will come to you as you draft. Also bear in mind that a brief is not a plan for the whole paper, only its logical appeal.

Student Example: Natsumi Hazama's Brief

Student Natsumi Hazama wrote a persuasive paper urging Asian parents not to push their children so hard in school. Here is the brief she developed for her argument:

Claim: Asian-American parents need to moderate their demands for high career goals and obedience to parents, allowing their children to find goals and challenges that are right for them.

　　Reason: Too much pressure can lead to depression and even suicide.
　　　　　　Evidence: CNN.com article on college student suicides; *Chronicle of Higher Education* online article about depression and suicide at Cornell

　　Reason: Overprotective parenting does not prepare children for the independence of college life.
　　　　　　Evidence: Asian Outlook website quotes

Reason: Students will be more successful at careers they prefer, not the limited choices of engineering and medicine preferred by their parents.
Evidence: My personal experience

Reason: Constant pressure to do better rather than praise for what has been accomplished leads to low self-esteem.
Evidence: Class reading by Csikszentmihalyi

■■■■ ACTIVITY 12.3 *In Your Own Work*

Formulate Your Brief

Outline the logical case you will make. If possible, include supporting evidence for each reason. ■

The Appeal through Ethos: Presenting Good Character

Ethos is self-presentation. In general, you should

- Sound informed and engaged with your topic.
- Show awareness of your readers' views.
- Treat competing courses of action with respect but show that your solution is better.
- Refer to your values and beliefs, your own ethical choices.
- When appropriate, reinforce your ethos by citing information and expert testimony from sources your readers respect and trust.

See the Art of Questioning box below for a more specific list of ideas for establishing good ethos.

| THE ART OF QUESTIONING | Establishing Ethos with Your Readers |

1. Do you have a shared local identity—as members of the same organization, the same institution, the same town or community, the same set of beliefs?
2. Can you get your audience to see that you and they have a common cause or perspective?
3. Are there experiences you might share? These might include dealing with siblings, helping friends in distress, caring for ailing family members, struggling to pay debts, or working hard for something.
4. Can you connect through a well-known event or cultural happening, perhaps a movie, a book, a political rally, or something in the news?

■■■■ ACTIVITY 12.4 *Writer's Notebook*

Establishing a Persuasive Ethos

Write about what attitudes you could convey in your paper that will show your good character and values. What can you talk about that will get these appeals across to your readers? ■

The Appeal through Pathos: Using Emotional Appeals

Sharing your own emotions is the most honest way to appeal to your audience's feelings. However, simply saying what your feelings are will not arouse emotion in others. How can you arouse emotions?

Show the audience the *concrete images and facts* that aroused the feelings in you. Kristof used a photo and **testimonials, comments from people supporting his viewpoint,** to appeal to his readers' sympathies. Weber described the bodies of the burned workers in the Triangle fire, "trapped by the machinery, piled up on the wrong side of doors, heaped in the stairwells and elevator shafts . . . hideously charred, many beyond recognition."

In short, *give your readers a picture,* in words or otherwise.

▩▩▩ ACTIVITY 12.5 *Writer's Notebook*

Resources for Emotional Appeal

Freewrite to identify specific details and images related to your topic that move you. If you can, make lists of what you recall. Visit or revisit places relevant to your topic and take notes or pictures. ▪

Drafting Your Paper

By now you have generated many ideas for appealing to your readers. As you move toward drafting, first focus attention on two main concerns:

- **Your angle and your voice,** how you want to sound to your reader
- Your draft's **development and organization**

What Stance and Voice Are Appropriate for Persuasion?

Appealing for action is in part the calm voice of reason described in Chapter 11 (see the section, Writer: What Is My Purpose and What Impression Should Readers Have of Me? on pages 240–41): your opinion stated clearly, directly, forcefully, and with confidence. To this, persuasion adds the *controlled passion* of emotional appeal, designed to arouse appropriate feelings in your readers.

Look at paragraphs 10–14 in Katharine Weber's "The Factories of Lost Children" (pages 263–64). Here is the voice of controlled passion:

> We will never know with any certainty how many children died on Nov. 25, 2000, in a fire at the Chowdhury Knitwear and Garment factory near Dhaka, Bangladesh (most of the garments made in Bangladesh are contracted by American retailers, including Wal-Mart and the Gap), where at least 10 of the 52 trapped in the flames by locked doors and windows were 10 to 14 years old.

She gives the reader the facts, including the role of American companies in allowing the conditions that result in tragic loss of children's lives. She does not have to say, "This is outrageous, intolerable"; the facts say it for her. Along the same lines, when she cites several tragic instances in paragraphs 10–14, she links them together with the repeated statement, "We will never know how many children died." This is an excellent example of the voice of controlled passion.

Developing and Organizing Your Appeal

Here are some answers to common questions that will help with both development and organization.

1. **How might I open the paper?** Here are some possibilities:
   - An anecdote (short narrative) based on your own experience or something you found in a source.
   - A surprising fact or opinion relevant to your topic.
   - A question that will stimulate reader interest.
   - A description of a person or place relevant to your claim.
   - A memorable quotation, with commentary from you.

   Introductions are often more than one paragraph, and your claim can appear anywhere in the paper.

2. **What background material should I provide?** Here are two principles:
   - Offer *only* what your readers need.
   - Place it just before the section or sections of your essay where the background is relevant.

3. **Where will I show my connection to the topic?** The introduction is often a good place. Note, however, that Kristof waits until paragraph 10 to mention his Chinese wife, which increases his personal investment in his topic, established throughout the essay by details only firsthand experience with Cambodia could supply.

4. **Will I present opposing views and, if so, where?** How you handle opposing views depends on your reader's relationship to them. If you think your readers will have an opposing view, the best strategy is to engage it first in several paragraphs. Otherwise handle opposing views after your case and with less space devoted to them.

5. **How will I order my reasons?** If your case has three or more reasons, starting and ending with your stronger ones is good strategy. In developing your reasons, *remember that multiple paragraphs are often necessary to develop a reason.*

See Chapter 23 for more on using visuals.

6. **What visuals might I use and where should they go?** For example, a student who wrote against wearing fur added much to the *pathos* of her argument by including photographs of animals injured by trappers.

7. **How will I conclude my paper?** Try one of these ending strategies:
   - Look back at your introduction. Perhaps some idea you used there to attract your reader's attention could come into play again—a question you posed has an answer, a problem you raised has a solution.
   - End with a well-worded quotation, and follow it up with comments of your own.
   - Repeat an idea you used earlier in the essay, but with a twist. Weber took the word *outsource* and used it in a new way: Children "will die because it has become our national habit to outsource, and these days we outsource our tragedies, too."

Revising Your Draft

The strongest revisions begin with assessing the draft yourself. Put it aside for a day or two. *Take the point of view of someone reading your paper.* Ask the questions in the Art of Questioning box to assess it.

| THE ART OF QUESTIONING | Revision Checklist for Appealing for Action |

1. Is it clear what the author wants the readers to do? Where is it stated most clearly? Is this the best place to state it?
2. Does the paper have a shape and sense of direction? Does it have parts that clearly play their individual roles in making the argument? Could you make any suggestions for rearranging the parts to make it easier to follow?
3. Do the reasons for taking this action stand out as such? Are they good reasons for the intended audience? Is there a better way to order the reasons?
4. Has the author given enough evidence to support each reason?
5. Has the author shown awareness of and sympathy for the audience's perspective?
6. Are the individual paragraphs unified, and is their contribution to the section in which they appear clear?
7. Can you hear the author's voice in this paper? Do you think readers would find this voice appealing? Does the author exhibit a personal connection with the topic?
8. Where do you see the author using emotional appeals? Are they appropriate? Do they move you?
9. Do you have suggestions to improve the introduction and the conclusion?
10. Has the author smoothly integrated the sources used or just dropped them in?

■■■ ACTIVITY 12.6 *In Your Own Work*

Revising Your Draft

After getting a second opinion, formulate a revision strategy:

1. Decide what you think are the useful criticisms and comments. Reassess your self-criticisms—do you still see the same problems? Make a list of specific items you intend to work on. "The first point on page 3 needs more development" is an example of what we mean by specific.
2. Divide your list into two categories: big revisions that will change all or much of the paper and smaller revisions requiring only adding, deleting, or rewriting a paragraph or two.
3. Ponder the best order for doing big revisions. For example, suppose that you need to rearrange the order of your reasons and improve your tone throughout. Rearrange first because attending to tone will require changing many sentences, and each sentence revision can have an impact on the flow of ideas from sentence to sentence.
4. Finalize your plan with a step-by-step list. Usually the spot revisions can be done in any order, but tackle the ones requiring the most work first, leaving the easier ones for last. ■

Student Example: Excerpts from Natsumi Hazama's Draft

Common revision problems include improving opening paragraphs and making points more persuasive.

Revising Opening Paragraphs

A revised draft of Natsumi Hazama's paper appears on pages 278–82. To see how revision improved it, read the following excerpts from her first draft.

Original Version

One night in 1990, Eliza Noh got off the phone with her sister in college. Eliza knew her sister was depressed and something bad might happen. She sat down to write a letter to support and encourage her. But it was too late. By the time the letter arrived, her sister was dead. She had taken her own life. Eliza believed that too much pressure to succeed contributed to her sister's death. This tragedy led Noh to pursue a career in studying the effects of pressure on Asian-American students.

Revised Version

Growing up in an Asian-American family I was raised to stay close to my family and always to strive to be number one in my classroom. My parents were both born in Japan and came to America for my father's work. My father was a very intelligent man who wanted me to go into either medicine or engineering. My parents also made me go to Japanese School every Saturday to learn to read and write my native tongue. Going to school six days a week left no time for a social life. The girls at my English school would always have sleep over parties on Friday nights, but I was studying for my next Japanese test. I excelled in school, but that wasn't good enough. Even if I scored a 98 on my math test, my parents would say, "Why didn't you get a 100?"

Do you agree that opening with Hazama's own story is more effective? The original opening moved to paragraph 15; do you think this arrangement is better?

▓▓▒■ ACTIVITY 12.7 *In Your Own Work*

Revising the Introduction

Look at the opening of your own draft. Why did you choose to open the paper as you did? If you are not happy with the opening, do you see material elsewhere in the draft that might work better? If not, review opening strategies discussed above (page 274) and try one of those instead. ■

Revising to Bring Out the Structure of the Argument

Here is a body paragraph from Hazama's first draft, offering a reason and evidence in support of her claim.

Original Version

Dr. Henry Chung, assistant vice president for student health at New York University and executive director of the NYU student Health Center, says

"Asian-American/Asian students, especially males, are under unique pressures to meet high expectations of parents by succeeding in such traditional predetermined careers as medicine and engineering" (qtd. in Ramanujan). Asian students feel that even though they aren't interested in these fields they must major in them and they end up stressing themselves out. Because students major in fields that they aren't interested in they end up not doing as well in school as they could. If you don't have a passion for your job you feel like you are working twice as hard with loads of work on your shoulders.

Revised Version

Along with bringing home straight "A's," parents also urge their children to major in a subject that they see as respectable. Dr. Henry Chung, assistant vice president for student health at New York University and executive director of the Health Center, points out that "Asian-American/Asian students, especially males, are under unique pressures to meet high expectations of parents by succeeding in such traditional predetermined careers as medicine and engineering" (qtd. in Ramanujan). Even if these fields are not areas of strength or interest, Asian-American students feel that they must major in them. Their grades may start to slip, but as Nguyen at Berkeley says, "Some stay in these majors because they think that they need to. They're reluctant to leave because their parents don't understand: 'If you're not a doctor or engineer, then what are you?'" (qtd. in "Mental").

In the revised version, how has the argument emerged better in the opening sentence? How has it been supported better?

▪▪▪ ACTIVITY 12.8 *In Your Own Work*

Evaluating the Structure of Your Case

Look over the body paragraphs of your draft. Open with a point of your own; use your sources to support and develop it. Look over your entire draft. How could revising make your reasons stand out more? ▪

Editing Your Revised Draft

A common editing problem is integrating source material into your own writing.

Integrating Sources

Using sources responsibly means not only citing the source but also identifying the source by name. Hazama noticed that she was not always clear about whose words were in quotation marks. Here is an example of the problem:

See Chapter 18, page 364, for more on this important research skill.

Original Version

When kids come to college they receive conflicting messages. "The message at home is that their priority should be to look after their parents and take care of their families" ("Mental"). But the message you get at college and from your friends is that you need to learn to think for yourself and be who you are and do what is best for you. This is a different value than the Asian culture so Asian students feel guilty for not doing what they are supposed to be doing ("Mental").

As the underlined phrases in the edited version show, identifying your sources by name and qualifications not only helps your reader understand who is saying what, but also increases the authority of the quoted statements.

Edited Version

According to Diem Nguyen, a UC Davis student affairs officer, when Asian American students come to college, they sometimes end up partying too much because they are not used to this freedom (qtd. in "Mental"). Also, when kids come to college they receive conflicting messages. Nadine Tang, a psychotherapist who has counseled students at UC Berkeley, says they get the message at home that family is their top priority, but the message at college is "to be who you are, learn to be yourself and do what is best for you. . . . You feel guilty for not doing what you're supposed to and not fulfilling your obligations" (qtd. in "Mental").

■■■■ ACTIVITY 12.9 *In Your Own Work*

Citing Sources

If you are using the words of someone quoted in your source, are you *identifying the actual speaker of the words* as well as citing the source? If not, identify this person as Hazama did in the revised version above. ■

REVISED STUDENT EXAMPLE

Hazama uses paragraphs 1, 2, and 3, to tell her personal story, allowing non-Asian readers to understand the issue more concretely and the author to build her authority *(ethos)*.	Hazama 1 Natsumi Hazama English 1301 Professor Channell 25 August 2011 Is Too Much Pressure Healthy? Growing up in an Asian-American family I was raised to stay close to my family and always to strive to be number one in my classroom. My parents were both born in

Hazama 2

Japan and came to America for my father's work. My father was a very intelligent man who wanted me to go into either medicine or engineering. My parents also made me go to Japanese School every Saturday to learn to read and write my native tongue. Going to school six days a week left no time for a social life. The girls at my English school would always have sleep over parties on Friday nights, but I was studying for my next Japanese test. I excelled in school, but that wasn't good enough. Even if I scored a 98 on my math test, my parents would say, "Why didn't you get a 100?"

> Creates sympathy *(pathos)* for children treated this way.

When I was in 8th grade my father was diagnosed with colon cancer. He grew   2
very ill, and my parents actually knew that he was dying but didn't tell my sister and me. One week, all my relatives from Japan flew in; at the end of that week he passed away. It was a horrible experience, but my mother, sister, and I helped each other, and with the support of all of our family and friends we got through it.

Starting high school was completely different. Because my mother knew grow-   3
ing up without a father was hard enough, she just wanted me to be happy. Coming home with a few B's on my report card was okay now. My mother didn't pressure me to get good grades; she basically let me do whatever I wanted. I wasn't in the top 10% of my class, didn't get straight A's or take all AP courses. However, I was completely satisfied with my high school experience. I was part of the nationally ranked cheerleading team. I had higher self-esteem. I would give anything to have my father still alive, but I have learned to think for myself and to set my own goals.

> Strong emotional appeal to American belief in the value of a balanced approach to school and extracurricular activities.

> Shows good reader awareness: author not rejecting her culture—especially important for her Asian-American parent audience.

My situation before the death of my father is common among Asian-   4
American families. I understand it is part of my culture, which I value. However, Asian-American parents need to moderate their demands and allow their children to find goals and challenges that are right for them.

> Thesis: Note that it asks for a course of action Asian–American parents can take.

Wenju Shen and Weimin Mo, experts on educating Asian-Americans, describe   5
our ways as rooted in Confucianism: "The Confucian ethical code. . .holds that the first loyalty is to the family, even above their allegiance to their country and religion."

> Important section for explaining cultural norms to non-Asian audience—shows reader awareness again.

This closeness to family can bring pressures. In an Asian family the most   6
important thing is to always keep your "face." "Face" means family pride. "Family"

Hazama 3

means not only immediate relatives, extended relatives, dead ancestors, but also anyone with my last name. To fail in any obligation to the family is to "lose face" and bring shame to myself, my parents, my relatives, and all my ancestors.

First reason to reduce excessive pressure: escape stereotypes.	While family should be important, this cultural pressure to succeed helps to create harmful stereotypes. As Shen and Mo point out, the "whiz kid" stereotype of Asian-American students encourages their parents to maintain practices "not compatible with the values and beliefs of American society." Asian-American parents need to learn how to balance obligations to the family with the more individual values of Americans.

7

Second reason to reduce excessive pressure: greater personal fulfillment.	A more balanced approach to parenting will lead children to more fulfilling lives. Mihaly Csikszentmihalyi, a psychologist at University of Chicago, is noted for his work on happiness, creativity, and subjective well-being. His book, *Finding Flow,* describes the kind of family that leads children to develop their full potential: "they combine discipline with spontaneity, rules with freedom, high expectations with unstinting love. An optimal family system is complex in that it encourages the unique individual development of its members while uniting them in a web of affective ties" (88). Asian-American parents should raise their children more like this. Too much parental pressure hinders what Csikszentmihalyi calls "flow," a state of mind where the person is fully engaged in what he or she is doing for its own sake (29–32).

8

Third reason to reduce excessive pressure: not good preparation for independence of college.	For most Asian students, college is the first time they have spent a significant amount of time away from home. Because they aren't used to this responsibility and freedom that they have at college, these students don't know what to do with themselves. They are exposed to new experiences and as a result, they sometimes end up partying too much because they are not used to this freedom that they have.

9

They also receive conflicting messages. Nadine Tang, a psychotherapist who has counseled students at UC Berkeley, says the message at home is that family matters most, but the message at college is "be who you are, learn to be yourself and do what is best for you. . . . You feel guilty for not doing what you're supposed to and not fulfilling your obligations" (qtd. in "Mental").

10

	Fourth reason for reducing excessive pressure: puts young people in a bind.

That is what life is all about, fulfilling your own potential, as Csikszentmihalyi says. Unfortunately, even if Asian American students receive excellent grades in

11

Hazama 4

school, they tend to have a lower self-esteem than other students (Csikszentmihalyi 24). I think this is because their parents never praise them. Asian-American parents see success as a duty, so children should not receive praise; instead they are told to do even better and aim still higher (Shen).

Along with bringing home straight "A's," parents also urge their children to major in a subject that they see as respectable. Dr. Henry Chung, assistant vice president for student health at New York University and executive director of the Health Center, points out that "Asian-American/Asian students, especially males, are under unique pressures to meet high expectations of parents by succeeding in such traditional predetermined careers as medicine and engineering" (qtd. in Ramanujan). Even if these fields are not areas of strength or interest, Asian-American students feel that they must major in them. Their grades may start to slip, but as Nguyen at Berkeley says, "Some stay in these majors because they think that they need to. They're reluctant to leave because their parents don't understand: 'If you're not a doctor or engineer, then what are you?'" (qtd. in "Mental").

12

> Evidence for fourth reason: Asian-American expert opinion.

The result can be destructive to a student's mental health, often leading to anxiety and depression. These problems are more common in Asian-American students than in the general population ("Mental"). When Asian-American students are unhappy, they usually don't seek help, even though the best way to recover is to get counseling. Chung at NYU explains that in Asian culture "suffering and working hard are accepted as part of life, a cultural paradigm" (Ramanujan). Asian-American students don't get counseling because discussing emotional problems is a sign of weakness ("Mental"). They also do not tell their parents about their problems. As a psychologist at Baylor University, Dr. Dung Ngo, says, "The line of communication in an Asian culture goes one way. It's communicated from the parents downward" (qtd. in Cohen). If students can't express their anger and frustration, it turns into helplessness; they feel like there is no way out.

13

> Fifth reason to reduce excessive pressure: better mental health.

> Use of Asian-American authorities to back up fifth reason, sources her audience must respect.

Suicide is therefore common among Asian-American students. According to CNN, Asian-American women age 15–24 have the highest suicide of any ethnic group. Suicide is the second-leading cause of death (Cohen). At Cornell University,

14

Hazama 5

between 1996 and 2006 there were 21 suicides; 13 of these were Asian or
Asian-American students (Ramanujan).

CNN tells the story of how Eliza Noh, a professor of Asian-American studies at   15
California State University at Fullerton, decided to devote her studies to depression and suicide among Asian-American women. One night in 1990, she had been
talking to her sister, a college student, on the telephone. She knew her sister was
depressed. She sat down to write a letter to encourage her. It was too late. By the
time the letter arrived, she had taken her life. Noh believes that the pressure to
succeed contributed to her sister's death (Cohen).

I have lived both sides, living with pressure and without. Living without pres-   16
sure has enabled me to think for myself and be happier. Parents need to give their
children support and encouragement, allow them to make their own decisions
about goals, and most of all, stop pressuring them so much.

> Strong evidence for the harm of excessive pressure, both data and an actual instance of suicide.

Works Cited

Cohen, Elizabeth. "Push to Achieve Tied to Suicide in Asian-American Women." *CNN.
com/Health*, 16 May 2007, www.cnn.com/2007/HEALTH/05/16/asian.suicides/.

Csikszentimihalyi, Mihaly. *Finding Flow: The Psychology of Engagement with
Everyday Life*. Basic Books, 1997.

"Mental Health of Asian Youth a Growing Concern." *Asian Outlook—Challenges
for Today's Asian American Students*. Asian Pacific Fund, Fall/Winter 2007.

Ramanujan, Krishna. "Health Expert Explains Asian and Asian-American
Students' Unique Pressures to Succeed." *Chronicle Online,* Chronicle of
Higher Education, 19 Mar. 2006, www.news.cornell.edu/stories/2006/04/
health-expert-explains-asian-students-unique-pressures-succeed.

Shen, Wenju, and Weimin Mo. "Reaching Out to Their Cultures: Building
Communication with Asian American Families." *ERIC*, n.p., 1990. Accessed
15 Apr. 2008, archive.org/stream/ERIC_ED351435/ERIC_ED351435_djvu.txt.

CHAPTER 13

Writing an Evaluation

TO SURVIVE, HUMAN BEINGS HAVE ALWAYS ASSESSED THE WORLD AROUND THEM, asking, "How good is x?" and posing answers to that question, such as, "This plant was good to eat, this place good for hunting." In today's consumer-driven culture, anything can be evaluated and almost everything is; "x" could be a movie, a car, a company, or a health care plan.

Evaluation is so common that every genre of writing evaluates in some way or another: Editorials evaluate politicians and policies; consumer reports (including online reviews on sites like Yelp and Hotels.com) evaluate virtually every good and service; and reviews and journal articles evaluate literary works, scientific research, engineering designs, public opinion, and how well people behaved in the past—in short, anything people can study. In business, we assess how well a corporation did in the last quarter; in public life, we debate the value of a speech; in personal writing, we exchange e-mails or texts that judge yesterday's social event; and in academic writing, we compare solutions to a particular problem, such as how best to feed an overpopulated world projected to exceed nine billion people by 2050.

What Is an Evaluation?

An evaluation is always *someone's* judgment about the quality, utility, value, or beauty of something, so personal or subjective experience comes into play. We can acknowledge the subjective aspect of our judgments in many ways. For example, when warning a friend that a restaurant we recommend serves highly spiced food, we say something like, "You know me—I like hot food," which implies, "Don't go there if you don't."

Open societies like ours—in which people are free to offer opinions about anything—provide and encourage methods for making evaluations less subjective. For example, we are careful to compare "apples and apples" rather than "apples and oranges." We can usefully compare Miami Beach with other beach vacation destinations but not with the mountains of Colorado, where people go to ski, hike, or breathe mountain air.

Magazines like *Consumer Reports* offer evaluations of everything from small electronics to cars, providing reliable information for us to make the best choices possible.

Why Write to Evaluate?

Evaluations are *guides to conduct, ways to make informed choices about something.* Sometimes nothing less is at stake than survival, as when evaluations we consult lead us to drive a safe car, seek medical treatment from a highly rated hospital, or buy nutritious food that promotes health. More often evaluations enhance the quality of life, making it more pleasurable, or more efficient, as when we consult *Consumer Reports* or online user reviews before purchasing a refrigerator or laptop. Because some manufactured items are made better than others of the same type, reliable information matters in our selection.

Indeed, when we stop to consider all the evaluations we encounter every day and in every dimension of our lives, little else we can write or read is likely to have more practical impact. Our choices largely determine our present and shape our possibilities for the future, so making good choices matters deeply.

How Do Writers Evaluate?

People are inclined to ignore or dismiss evaluations that seem merely subjective. "It's just his or her opinion," we say. Some judgments, however, just *are* subjective by nature, such as questions of fashion or aesthetic taste. The fashion blogger Scott Schuman of "The Sartorialist" photographs people on the street that he deems fashionable, including the woman in Milan shown on this page.

Subjective judgments can have value. Someone's verdict about a style may be a reliable indicator of what is fashionable to people who care about fashion. Most of the blog's readers agreed that this woman has style.

In any case, we cannot exclude subjective judgments from evaluation, nor should we wish to, because they express an individual's **sensibility,** a *mostly nonconscious "feel" for what matters most or has high or low interest or value in his or her experience.* We all have sensibilities, and they matter to us. Tact and civility require us to respect them.

At the same time, we need evaluations that go beyond subjective impressions. The writer needs them for judgments to carry weight so that readers will listen and take an evaluation seriously. Readers need them to guide their conduct—to decide, for instance, if a book is worth reading. How can we offer an evaluation that is more than subjective?

Some evaluations are subjective but still valuable to those who care about the subject, such as opinions on fashion or taste. The fashion blog "The Sartorialist" features photographs of people on the street whom the blogger deems fashionable, such as this woman.

© Eugenio Marongiu/Getty Images, RF

CONCEPT CLOSE-UP Using Criteria for Evaluating

Criteria, a concept that originated in the Greek word for "judge," refers to *standards for evaluating something.* The singular form of the word is *criterion,* but the plural is more common because people usually have more than one standard in mind when making an evaluation.

Often we do not think consciously of the criteria we use when passing judgment. But when we rank some products or performances, such as Olympic diving, criteria assume great importance. Setting up criteria when writing an evaluation shows your engagement with whatever you are evaluating, implying that your judgment is not casual, hasty, or superficial. It shows that you have asked this important question: **What qualities define excellence in this and similar items?**

An evaluation is a form of argument because the writer makes a claim about the quality of something and supports the claim by showing how it meets or fails to meet the criteria. Evaluators may disagree about which criteria should be used when judging some things, such as a film or a travel destination. Considering the audience for a written evaluation will help the writer choose criteria that readers would find acceptable.

R E A D I N G **13.1**

2011 Motor Trend Car of the Year: Chevrolet Volt, a Car of the Future You Can Drive Today

ANGUS MACKENZIE

Motor Trend, one of the more influential car magazines, has a group of automotive experts select its "Car of the Year." Eagerly awaited and widely publicized and discussed, the annual evaluation receives careful scrutiny and much commentary. The award went to the Chevrolet Volt in 2011, and the task of justifying the choice fell on Angus MacKenzie, a staff writer for the magazine. As you read, consider how MacKenzie explains and defends the choice.

> Starts with summary evaluation.

" | expected a science fair experiment. But this is a moonshot."   1

Chris Theodore is a wily veteran of the auto   2
business, a seasoned development engineer whose impressive resume includes vehicles as thoughtfully executed as the Chrysler minivan and as tightly focused as the Ford GT.

> Invokes expert opinion to back up high positive assessment.

As one of the consultant judges on this year's COTY [Car of the Year] panel, Chris   3
brought the deep insight and professional skepticism you'd expect of someone who's spent his entire working life making cars. But our 2011 Car of the Year, Chevrolet's ground-breaking Volt, has blown him away.

Summary assessment of an expert, supporting *Motor Trend*'s choice.	"This is a fully developed vehicle with seamlessly integrated systems and software, a real car that provides a unique driving experience. And commuters may never need to buy gas!"

4

"This is a fully developed vehicle with seamlessly integrated systems and software, a real car that provides a unique driving experience. And commuters may never need to buy gas!"

Summary assessment of an expert, supporting *Motor Trend*'s choice.

5

Like all of us on the staff at *Motor Trend,* Chris is an enthusiast, a man who'll keep a thundering high-performance V-8 in his garage no matter how high gas prices go. But he nailed the Volt's place in automotive history: "If this is the brave new world, then it's an acceptable definition."

Concedes that Volt will not replace high-performance cars, but it is excellent for the kind of car it is.

6

In the 61-year history of the Car of the Year award, there have been few contenders as hyped—or as controversial—as the Chevrolet Volt. The Volt started life an Old GM [General Motors] project, then arrived fully formed as a symbol of New GM, carrying all the emotional and political baggage of that profound and painful transition. As a result, a lot of the sound and fury that has surrounded the Volt's launch has tended to obscure a simple truth: This automobile is a game-changer.

Background of the car.

© Zuppa Chris/Corbis Wire/Corbis

Engineering Excellence

7

The Volt boasts some of the most advanced engineering ever seen in a mainstream American automobile. The powertrain allows the car to run as an EV [electric vehicle], a series hybrid [electric or gas], or a parallel hybrid [electric plus gas], depending on how far you drive and how you drive. The secret sauce is how GM controls the powerflow between the 149-horse electric motor, the generator, and the 84-horse, 1.4-liter naturally aspirated internal-combustion engine. It's fundamentally different from the way Toyota handles things in the Prius.

Begins series of headings, criteria for assessing a car.

Contrast with chief competitor.

8

Attention to detail is impressive. The Volt's wheels, for example, are forged aluminum to reduce weight, shod with specially developed low-rolling-resistance tires. While some consumers may never need to regularly put gas in the car, the internal combustion engine will fire automatically from time to time to ensure the integrity of the fueling system, and to prevent the vehicle being stuck with a tank full of stale gas. And finally, the Volt is built on GM's highly flexible Global Compact Vehicle Architecture (other GCVA vehicles include the Chevy Cruze, the Opel Astra, and the forthcoming Opel Zafira minivan), which means its advanced powertrain can be easily adapted to other vehicle formats.

Flexibility, a chief virtue of the design.

Advancement in Design

9

As Toyota discovered with the Camry Hybrid, people who want to buy a vehicle with a highly efficient powertrain want everyone else to know they're driving a car with a highly efficient powertrain. Chevy clearly has watched and learned. The Volt's exterior design brings a unique look to the Chevy lineup. It's a compact that's clearly different from other small Chevys, yet clearly still one of the family. The front end graphic [appearance] is outstanding—strong, confident, and tastefully upscale.

Comments on appeal of body design.

10

Much of the exterior design obviously has been driven by the pursuit of aerodynamic efficiency. The sharp rear corners and high decklid with integrated spoiler are all about managing the airflow at the rear of the car. But the black graphic under the side windows and the heat-soaking black roof—both artifacts designed to link the car with the fundamentally different Volt Concept—seem somewhat gratuitous.

Minor criticism indicates objectivity, making the praise more believable.

11

The interior is relatively conventional, save for the impressive high-resolution—and highly interactive—instrument and center stack LCD [liquid crystal display] screens, and the center stack [instrument panel] itself, whose shiny, white surfacing and slightly hard-to-see, touch-sensitive switch gear seems like an obvious homage to Apple's iPod. (If you can't stand Steve Jobs, the center stack can also be finished in dark gray.) Plastic panels in the front doors allow an effective, low-cost means of changing the Volt's interior colorway [color scheme].

Stresses car's high-tech appeal.

Efficiency

12

The Volt's unique powertrain not only defies established labels; it also defies established methods of determining fuel economy. After all, this is a vehicle that will complete the standard EPA fuel economy test in full EV mode, making conventional mileage calculations impossible.

13

While it is entirely possible that a consumer able to use the Volt in pure EV mode most of the time could use no more than a tank of gas—9.3 gallons—a year (because as noted earlier the car will automatically start the internal-combustion engine at regular intervals to keep the fuel system functional and the gas fresh), it is not a perpetual-motion machine. It requires energy to move. Our testing showed that, in EV mode, the Volt uses energy at the rate 32.0 kW-hr/100 miles or a notional 105 mpg (based on the EPA calculation that a gallon of gas contains 33.7 kW-hr of energy). The internal-combustion engine sips gas at the rate of about 40 mpg.

Detailed technical evaluation-analysis of energy use to arrive at an overall equivalent of 72.9 mpg.

14

In a multiday, 299-mile test that involved a mixture of normal freeway and stop/start city driving (no hypermiling [special ways to drive that increase mileage])—and recharging the car overnight, as most consumers would—we used a total of 58.6 kW-hr of electrical energy, and 2.36 gallons of gas. Just counting the gas, the Volt returned 126.7 mpg. Converting the gas used to energy used (79.5 kW-hr) and adding that figure to the electrical energy used gave us a notional 72.9 mpg. That's impressive.

Safety

15

The Volt's standard passive safety equipment starts with a complement of eight airbags, including dual-stage front bags, kneebags, and side-impact bags for the driver and front passenger and roof-rail mounted head curtain bags that protect all four passengers. Active safety features include anti-lock brakes, traction control, and stability control.

Treatment of safety divides into two paragraphs: passive (seat belts, air bags) and active (handling, acceleration to avoid accidents).

16

The Volt chassis is nimble and responsive, and the low-rolling-resistance tires deliver better than average grip for this type of rubber. The Volt is not a sports car, but the acceleration (0–60 mph in 8.8 seconds in pure EV mode, and 8.7 in combined gas/electric mode) is competitive with conventional compacts, and more than adequate for safely merging onto a fast-moving freeway.

Value

All of that technology is expensive, which accounts for the Volt's $41,000 price tag. 17
Engineering the Volt required considerable investment by GM in vehicle systems integration that would normally be handed off to outside suppliers and contractors. But the cost of the Volt's powertrain and associated systems will come down as GM perfects lower cost components and is able to amortize [distribute cost of] the development across a larger number of vehicles. Meanwhile, consumers can apply for a $7500 federal tax grant, plus state grants, where available, to offset the Volt's relatively high purchase price. And our testing suggests that even if drivers regularly went 80 miles between charges, the Volt is significantly cheaper to run than regular hybrids.

> Indicates that GM put unusual amounts of money into developing the Volt.

> Emphasizes cost but sees this criterion in a larger picture where the price tag is not a special concern.

Using EPA average figures of 12¢ per kW-hr for electricity, and $2.80 for a gallon of 18
gas, the Volt costs just 3.8¢ a mile to run in EV mode, and 7¢ a mile with the gas engine running.

Performance of Intended Function

The Volt absolutely delivers on the promise of the vehicle concept as originally outlined 19
by GM, combining the smooth, silent, efficient, low-emissions capability of an electric motor with the range and flexibility of an internal combustion engine.

It is a fully functional, no-compromise compact automobile that offers consumers 20
real benefits in terms of lower running costs.

> Summary evaluation: Delivers for the type of car it is: "an intelligent hybrid."

The more we think about the Volt, the more convinced we are this vehicle represents 21
a real breakthrough. The genius of the Volt's powertrain is that it is actually capable of operating as a pure EV, a series hybrid, or as a parallel hybrid to deliver the best possible efficiency, depending on your duty cycle. For want of a better technical descriptor, this is the world's first intelligent hybrid. And the investment in the technology that drives this car is also an investment in the long-term future of automaking in America.

Moonshot. Game-changer. A car of the future that you can drive today, and every 22
day. So what should we call Chevrolet's astonishing Volt? How about, simply, Motor Trend's "2011 Car of the Year."

Questions for Discussion

1. The author admits that the Volt has been hyped and that the car itself is controversial. How does the article attempt to keep the reader from seeing the evaluation as just more hype? How does it imply that the car is solid and therefore should not be controversial?

2. Some Americans resented the federal bailout of GM, but many are also pleased that GM has apparently recovered from bankruptcy. How does *Motor Trend* appeal to patriotic pride in evaluating the Volt?

3. Note the use of **subheadings,** *the division of an article or essay into titled sections.* How did this technique help the author organize what he had to say? How does it help readers follow what he has to say?

■■■ *Thinking as a Writer*

What Is the Rhetorical Situation?

1. What is MacKenzie's *purpose* in writing this essay? Look at GM's website for the Volt. How is his purpose different from GM's? What is his *angle* or point of view? How would you describe his *voice*—that is, how does he sound to you?

2. Who is MacKenzie's intended *audience*? That is, who would read *Motor Trend*? What in the article's content best reveals the interests and values of the magazine's readers?

3. MacKenzie makes a strong claim: the Volt is a "game-changer." Such a strong claim requires strong support. How does he attempt to justify his claim? What different kinds of evidence does he use? ■

READING 13.2

'Precious' Mettle

ANN HORNADAY

© Lions Gate/Courtesy Everett Collection

The 2009 film Precious, *based on the 1996 novel* Push *by Sapphire, won numerous awards: at the Sundance Film Festival, the Audience Award and the Grand Jury Prize for best drama; at the Toronto International Film Festival, the People's Choice Award. Yet the film did not at first have financial backing for distribution and seemed unlikely to be a box office success when it was finally shown in theaters. Its popular success was a surprise— it earned almost five times what it cost to make. The following review by Ann Hornaday (The Washington Post) helps to explain the appeal of the film and shows us how to evaluate any work of art that does not fit neatly into existing categories.*

I n this drama, based on the novel *Push* by Sapphire, a pregnant Harlem teen (Gabourey 'Gabby' Sidibe) attempts to escape from her abusive mother and build a new life. Movies come, movies go. But a rare few arrive like gifts, sent by some cosmic messenger to stir the senses, awaken compassion and send viewers into a world made radically new by invigorated alertness and empathy. Such is the movie *Precious: Based on the Novel Push by Sapphire,* which surely qualifies as the most painful, poetic and improbably beautiful film of the year.

It's hard to believe that a movie that traffics so operatically in images of brutality and squalor can be so fleet, assured and lyrical. But such breathtaking contradictions abound in *Precious,* which in the course of introducing the viewers to unspeakable despair, manages to imbue them with an exhilarating sense of hope—if not in a bright and cheery future for the film's beleaguered protagonist, then at least in the possibilities of cinema as a bold, fluent and adamantly expressive art form.

That beleaguered protagonist is Claireece "Precious" Jones (played in an astonishing debut by Gabourey Sidibe), a 16-year-old girl who, as the movie opens, is still attending junior high school in 1980s Harlem. Morbidly obese, functionally illiterate, pregnant with her second child after being raped by her father, Precious lives with her mother, Mary (Mo'Nique), in a squalid apartment where she endures the latter's near-constant verbal, physical and sexual abuse. Precious's only escape from this lurid tableau is rich, glittery fantasy life, in which she has a "light-skinned boyfriend" and "good hair," dresses in ball gowns and carries a little terrier.

Precious is numb, shut down, locked behind protective layers of fat and clothing, her hooded eyes nearly sightless slits. She's invisible, even to herself: When she looks in the mirror, a blond, blue-eyed teenager gazes back. But when an attentive principal enrolls her in an alternative education program, Precious's mountainlike passivity and self-abnegation [self-denial] begin to give way to tiny, seismic temblors of transformation.

Adapted from a 1996 novel by the poet Sapphire, *Precious* has been a hit on the film festival circuit, earning a clutch of audience awards—and, at Sundance earlier this year, the support of Oprah Winfrey and Tyler Perry, who signed on as executive producers.

Director Lee Daniels *(Shadowboxer),* working from a script by Geoffrey Fletcher, doesn't flinch from confronting viewers with the most squalid, violent depredations Precious suffers at her mother's hands. But he instinctively knows when to offer viewers and his heroine much-needed relief, by way of brightly lit, sumptuously staged magical realist sequences portraying Precious's glitzy daydreams. He pulls off this audacious balancing act throughout *Precious,* which toes a vertiginous [dizzying] line between the grim and highly stylized.

But as adroitly as Daniels handles the multilayered details, textures and tones of *Precious*'s rich visual design, his most crucial task is giving his cast the space needed to deliver revelatory, searingly honest performances. Sidibe's nuanced, deeply sympathetic portrayal of a character who is almost completely inert for most of the movie recalls Billy Bob Thornton's highly praised breakout turn in *Sling Blade.*

Technically, hers is a far more difficult role than the toxic, rage-fueled monster brought to life by Mo'Nique, who delivers a performance that constantly teeters on the edge of going over the top, but somehow manages to stay on the side of credibility. Mo'Nique, best known and loved for her persona as a stand-up comedienne and comic actress, is rightly being praised for a brave performance untouched by vanity.

Together, she and Sidibe form a formidable dyad that gives *Precious* its dysfunctional centrifugal force. But the entire enterprise is best appreciated as a bracing ensemble piece, in which even the smallest roles harmonize flawlessly within the whole. The gorgeous Paula Patton breathes radiant but bone-weary life into what could have been a stock character of the tireless English teacher. Rather than the reassuring reversals of a miracle worker or "I can *reach* these kids!" speeches, her character, Ms. Rain, wrings incremental victories from a world proscribed by Rolodex contacts and bureaucratic red tape. And not one but two pop stars prove their dramatic bona fides in *Precious:* Lenny Kravitz as a cute, compassionate hospital nurse, and Mariah Carey, in a mousy wig and devoid of makeup, delivering a frank, utterly winning performance as a seen-it-all social worker.   9

"What does it mean when the author describes the protagonist's circumstances as unrelenting?" Ms. Rain asks at one point. That's precisely the question posed by *Precious,* in which the title character withstands such a constant plague of social ills that she's in danger of becoming little more than a simplistically drawn, even grotesque, poster child. (The same can be said for Mo'Nique's Mary, who in many ways embodies all-too-familiar stereotypes of welfare queens and the pathology of poverty.)   10

That *Precious* dodges these toxic assumptions, even while coming perilously close to perpetuating them, is a testament not only to the sensitivity and artistry of Daniels's filmmaking, but also to the fierce performances of actors who, rather than skimming the surface of their characters, invariably dive ever deeper inside, taking viewers with them.   11

That journey winds up being excruciating, exhausting, and, against all odds, deeply rewarding. Just how rewarding probably will become clear to viewers when they emerge from *Precious* to find that life outside the theater has come into a different kind of focus. *Precious* performs the same miracle as every great work of art: It gives its viewers new eyes, and the sense that they'll never see the world—or the people in it—in quite the same way.   12

Questions for Discussion

1. Whether from popular or high culture, evaluating artistic efforts is challenging. We must get beyond "I love it" or "I hate it." How does Ann Hornaday justify her high rating of *Precious*? What specifics does she offer to back up the positive evaluation?
2. One of the keys to evaluating anything made by human hands is to understand the intent of its maker. What does Hornaday think the director was doing to get

the film's material to work? How did understanding the director's contribution contribute to her evaluation?

3. Evaluation often uses comparison as a mode of development. What comparisons does Hornaday make? Did they help you better understand points she made?

▬▬■ *Thinking as a Writer*

What Is the Rhetorical Situation?

1. What is Hornaday's *purpose* in writing this review? In recommending this film, what does she focus on most to establish its artistic merit and appeal?
2. Who is Hornaday's intended *audience*? What does she assume her readers are familiar with? What does she assume they might need to know more about?
3. What relationship does she have with her readers? How would you describe the voice in this review? ■

The Assignment

Write a review evaluating a product, service, cultural event, institution, or anything else your instructor considers appropriate. You should be familiar with the subject of your evaluation and with other, similar products, services, events, and so on, so that you can knowledgeably set up criteria for assessment. If your instructor wants you to support your judgment of the subject with sources such as surveys and expert opinion, you should consider whether such sources are easily available.

What Can I Write About?

Your instructor may assign your topic. If you are asked to choose your own topic for this assignment, select something you know well from personal experience. Consider the following categories and examples:

- **A manufactured item:** a car, electronic device, item of clothing, office machine, sports equipment, home, apartment, or condo.

- **A service:** a restaurant, travel agency, tax preparation service, online dating service, university or college dining hall or exercise center.

- **A cultural item or place:** a television show, film, stage play, museum, musical performance, or sports event.

- **A print or online publication:** a novel, business report, textbook, advertisement, magazine, newspaper, website, blog, or social networking site.

- **Software:** a video game or computer program.

- **Travel destination or other place of interest:** a foreign city, attraction in your home town or near your campus, historical memorial, national park, or model community.

- **Proposed legislation or policy changes:** proposals to remedy on-campus problems such as parking, off-campus problems such as inadequate public transportation, ecological problems such as clean diesel engines in cars to reduce pollution, or national problems such as the dropout rate in education.

To explore additional topic ideas and see additional models for evaluation, read articles from *Consumer Reports,* book and movie reviews in magazines and newspapers, and online evaluations in blogs and on consumer sites.

How Do I Write an Evaluation? Questioning the Rhetorical Situation

Begin by picturing a rhetorical situation for your writing project, a real-world context for communicating. You should consider the key variables in any act of communication: a writer with something to say, a reader the writer wishes to reach, and a kind of text appropriate to the writing task. These three variables will affect many decisions in the composing process.

Writer: What Is My Purpose, and What Impression Should My Readers Have of Me?

Your purpose is to make a convincing case for your judgment of something. Beyond that, your judgment may serve a variety of purposes, such as helping readers appreciate a movie or a new album, or recommending—or warning against—a restaurant or hotel. You want to sound knowledgeable and be able to justify your opinion since readers may encounter other opinions the opposite of yours. Your readers should see you as someone who has arrived at an assessment thoughtfully. They will need to have confidence in the good reasons you offer for evaluating your topic as you have.

Audience: Who Is My Reader?

As with all writing projects, you should imagine a group of people who might read your paper. Having a readership in mind for your evaluation will help you decide what to say and how to order it. **"What does my reader need to know?"** is therefore one of the key questions you need to ask yourself often as you write and revise a draft.

Readers come to evaluations wanting to know about whatever you are assessing. You can assume interest; what readers want is information, including your assessment and what led you to it, which they will use to help them decide whether to buy the product, use the service, visit the local attraction, and so on. Clearly, readers of *Motor Trend* want and expect technical details such as how miles-per-gallon equivalents work for an electric car. Select the information you think will be most relevant to your readers.

Text: What Moves Can I Make?

The genre represented in the readings above (pages 285–91) and in the student example at the end of this chapter (pages 301–04) is the review or consumer report. Basic moves include the following:

- Indicate what you are evaluating immediately. Catch the readers' attention with an interesting move in the introduction. For example, the Volt evaluation opened with a catchy quotation. The movie review opened with a memorable claim: "the most painful, poetic and improbably beautiful film of the year."

- Provide background information the reader needs to put your topic in an appropriate context—the reviewer of *Precious,* for instance, tells us about the origin of the film in a novel and about the awards it has received.

- Explicitly lay out the criteria for your judgment and explain any criterion whose relevance may not be obvious.

- Use the criteria to structure your essay, as the writer of the Volt review did in a set of headings.

- State your overall assessment, usually early in your review, remembering that it can be positive, negative, or some mix of the two.

- Offer supporting details or specifics to justify and support your assessment, which may be observations from experience, research data, expert opinion—indeed, anything appropriate to your topic that meets your reader's need to know why you have assessed your topic as you have.

- Especially if you offer a negative review of something most people like or a positive review of something most people dislike, offer a defense of your evaluation—acknowledge that you are going against the popular judgment and explain why.

When selecting your evaluation topic, choose something familiar and interesting to you, such as a dining experience at a favorite restaurant.

© andresr/Getty Images, RF

How Do I Write an Evaluation?
Engaging the Writing Process

No two people compose in exactly the same way, and even the same person may go through the writing process in different ways with different assignments. Nevertheless, because no one can attend to everything at once, there are phases in handling any significant writing task. You **explore the topic** to get a sense of whether it will work for you and what you might be able to do with it; if the topic is working out for you, then you move into **preparing to write,** generating more content and planning your draft.

The next phase is **drafting your paper,** getting a version, however rough it may be, on screen or paper so that you can work toward the final draft. Getting there involves two further phases: **revising your draft,** where you make major improvements in your draft, followed by **editing your draft,** taking care of errors, sentences that do not read well, paragraphs lacking focus and flow, and so on.

Exploring Your Topic

Readers read evaluations to know more about a topic, not just how you rate it. Consequently, your task is partly informative, providing facts about your topic. Where will you find this information?

Many evaluations are based entirely on the author's experience with the product, service, vacation destination, and so on—with whatever you are evaluating. Begin, then, by brainstorming what you know from personal experience and observation. Write a list or a notebook entry with facts about your topic. How much do you actually know that is factual? If you cannot generate much by listing or freewriting, you may need to choose a different topic or dig further into the one you plan to write about.

Go back to your topic. If it is a film, watch it again. If it is a product, examine it more thoroughly. You may need to gather some information from sources, such as product information, film credits, and other basic facts appropriate to your topic. You may want to read what other experts have said, but bear in mind that you should make your own judgment aimed at your own audience, based on your experiences and opinions. However, another reviewer might remind you of points or criteria for evaluation.

Finding Criteria for Evaluating

Which comes first: making a subjective judgment about the quality of something or making a list of criteria and then deciding how well something meets the criteria? Human nature being what it is, most likely we form our opinions and then think of ways to justify them.

Whether you start with a set of criteria or a gut opinion, your evaluation should show that you have thought about reasonable standards of excellence for items similar to your topic, or your readers will not find your opinion credible. Asking questions will help you generate a list of criteria for judging your topic.

When your evaluation of something is solicited, such as when your college asks you to evaluate a course, you usually receive a list of questions: How well was the class organized? Was the professor prepared? How available was the professor for help? For this project, you will have to generate a list of questions appropriate to evaluating your topic.

■■■■ ACTIVITY 13.1 *Collaborative Activity*

What Makes Something Good?

Begin by listing the questions that people usually ask when evaluating items similar to your topic. If members of your class are writing about similar topics, get together to compare your lists of questions. Even if you are not writing on shared topics, a classmate or two can help you think of good points upon which to rate your topic. ■

■■■■ ACTIVITY 13.2 *Writer's Notebook*

Evaluating Your Criteria and Main Points

After you have generated a list of criteria for evaluating your topic, write informally in your writer's notebook to rehearse the main points you want to make in an evaluation of your topic. If you want to be able to see other classmates' ideas, everyone might post their ideas on an online discussion board. On your list of criteria, are there points upon which you would give your topic the highest rating? Are there other points where your topic falls short? How would you sum up your rating of your topic? ■

Preparing to Write

Some writers prefer to go straight to drafting after having explored a topic thoroughly. Others prefer to lay out a plan for the organization of the paper. Either way, it is good to take stock of the notes you have made and write a tentative thesis for your evaluation.

Stating Your Evaluation as a Thesis

The thesis of an evaluation is simply the main point about the quality of the topic. It does not have to go into all of the criteria used in the evaluation itself, but it should sum up the writer's opinion. For example, consider these sentences from examples earlier in the chapter.

- **From the evaluation of the Chevrolet Volt:** "This automobile is a game-changer." The review's angle is to show how truly revolutionary the car is.

- **From the evaluation of *Precious*:** "A rare few [movies] arrive like gifts, sent by some cosmic messenger to stir the senses, awaken compassion and send viewers into a world made radically new by invigorated alertness and empathy." The review focuses on the acting and directing that contributed to the movie's power.

■■■■ ACTIVITY 13.3 *Collaborative Activity*

Trying Out Thesis Sentences

Look over your prewriting notes and lists. What criteria do you think most contributed to your overall estimate of the quality of your topic? Try out some thesis sentences that express your opinion and point to a specific direction that your evaluation might emphasize. In groups of two or three, go over each other's ideas for the thesis and discuss what specific reasons each writer could use to defend that opinion. ■

Drafting Your Paper

Focus on angle, voice, and organization in drafting your paper.

What Angle and Voice Are Appropriate for an Evaluation?

As you begin drafting your evaluation, you should be conscious of your angle on the topic. A writer's angle is his or her point of view; it is the context in which the writer places the topic. Angle makes writing original and interesting and gives the writing personality, or what we have called voice. Two writers could give the same item equally excellent reviews based on the same criteria, but their written evaluations will likely have different angles and voice, depending on each writer's attitude toward his or her topic and relationship with his or her readers.

Ann Hornaday, the author of the review of *Precious,* pages 289–91, has a voice appropriate to her evaluation of the movie as art. For example,

> Director Lee Daniels *(Shadowboxer),* working from a script by Geoffrey Fletcher, doesn't flinch from confronting viewers with the most squalid, violent depredations Precious suffers at her mother's hands. But he instinctively knows when to offer viewers and his heroine much-needed relief, by way of brightly lit, sumptuously staged magical realist sequences portraying Precious's glitzy daydreams.

Hornaday's angle is the movie as an integration of opposites, balanced between realism and fantasy. As readers, we feel we are being introduced to a work of art as understood by an insider.

Knowing your topic well enough to have an angle on it and picturing readers who would find your angle interesting—these are the keys to writing with voice.

Thinking as a Writer: Developing and Organizing Your Evaluation

Write a first draft of your evaluation. In planning your draft, consider the suggestions in the Text: What Moves Can I Make? section on page 294, which will help you generate material to develop your thesis and organize the evaluation.

Revising Your Draft

Think of the first draft as raw material that could be rearranged for a better flow of ideas or improved emphasis. Have you put your points in the best order to make your evaluation forceful and easy for readers to follow? First drafts often need more development—specific details that readers cannot be assumed to know. Sometimes you will need to take out material that readers would find either too general or common knowledge or too specific and not relevant to their interest and level of knowledge on the topic. Consider who your readers are and what you might need to explain more or say less about, given their interest in your topic.

THE ART OF QUESTIONING   Revision Checklist for Evaluation

Use the following questions to review your own draft or to help classmates find ways to improve theirs.

1. Does the evaluation have an interesting opening that would engage readers' interest? What is the opening move, and what other options are possible?

2. Does the writer have an angle on the topic? What is the angle? Does the opening show enough personal engagement with the topic? How could the writer show more connection with the topic?

3. Is the main point about the topic clearly stated as an opinion about the quality of the topic? Does the thesis suggest the author's angle on the topic?

4. Who is the audience for this evaluation? Where might this essay appear if it were to be published online or in print? How much would this audience already know about the topic? Can you think of anything not covered in the draft that these readers might want to know?

5. How well-developed is this evaluation? Does it contain enough specific evidence to support the judgments made about the topic? Where might the draft need more specific development?

6. What other options are there for arranging the main points? Would any other arrangements offer an advantage, such as a more logical progression from minor to major criteria for evaluation?

7. How smoothly do the sentences flow? One common problem in first drafts is organization, including organization within paragraphs. It is especially hard for writers to find gaps in the train of thought because the writer knows how the ideas connect in his or her mind, even if the connections are not tight or clearly signaled on the page. Read through the draft again, paying attention to connections between sentences and the flow of ideas. (Read the section that follows, Student Example: Excerpts from Collin Dobmeyer's Draft, for more help with checking for coherence.)

Student Example: Excerpts from Collin Dobmeyer's Draft

One of the most common problems in first drafts is poor *organization of ideas,* or **coherence.** The writer thinks of several ideas, all worth developing, and wants to get them down in writing. Realizing that there is more to say on some point, the writer comes back to it later in the paragraph—or even in a later paragraph. The reader feels a gap in the train of thought when this happens.

Many drafts can be improved by simple rearrangement of ideas, with clear transitions to signal the reader about turns in the train of thought. The following example of revising for coherence comes from student Collin Dobmeyer's review of the video game *Halo: Reach*. The full revised paper appears on pages 301–4.

Excerpt from First Draft

Bungie really went out on a limb with *Halo: Reach*. They abandoned their previous faceless, emotionless, super soldier hero Master Chief in favor of a squad of Spartan super soldiers with faces and personalities. Among your teammates there is the able commander Carter, the emotional George, the introverted Emile, the snide engineer Kat, and the talkative sniper Jun. However, Bungie had better make us care about these characters if they want the player to care about their deaths. The extent to which they can make these characters relatable is a major deciding factor in the success of the game, which makes it a letdown that it doesn't quite work out. The problem stems from the gameplay. *Halo: Reach* is a game that centers on "run and gun" fighting. It is downright difficult to create sympathetic characters when all we see them doing is murdering every alien life form within 500 yards. It is also a problem because these characters lack depth. Every one of them is an unstoppable, immortal superman that doesn't even flinch when it comes time for their own deaths. The only character with human vulnerability is George, who ironically dies first.

> Dobmeyer assumes his readers know who produced the game.

> In the draft, Dobmeyer repeats the point about needing to care about the characters.

> In the draft, Dobmeyer turns to the problem of the game play style before completing the point about the lack of human characteristics.

Note how much better the flow of thought is after Dobmeyer revised for coherence.

Excerpt from Revised Draft

Bungie really went out on a limb with *Halo: Reach*. They abandoned their previous faceless, emotionless, super soldier hero Master Chief in favor of a squad of Spartan super soldiers with faces and personalities. Among your teammates there is the able commander Carter, the emotional George, the introverted Emile, the snide engineer Kat, and the talkative sniper Jun. However, Bungie had better make us care about these characters if they want the player to care about their deaths. The game fails to do so because nearly all the characters lack depth. Every one of them is an unstoppable, immortal superman that doesn't even flinch when it comes time for their own deaths. The only character with human vulnerability is George, who ironically dies first. From then on it becomes difficult to generate any strong emotional attachment to the characters.

This isn't to say that the characters are complete mindless robots; in fact many of them have developing personalities, but the game just doesn't spend enough time developing them beyond the super soldier demeanor. For this, I blame the game play. *Halo: Reach* is a shooter that centers on "run and gun" fighting. It is downright difficult to create sympathetic characters when all we see them doing is murdering every alien life form within 500 yards.

> Sets up the team.

> After setting up the team, Dobmeyer moves to the need for deeper character development.

> Dobmeyer's revision adds a transition into the role of the game style in failing to allow for the characters' development.

Editing Your Revised Draft

Editing for style can help you emphasize main points and bring out your voice and attitude. The coordinating conjunction *and* often causes a main point to almost disappear or seem like an afterthought. In his earlier drafts, Dobmeyer found a few places where he overused "and," as in the following passage:

Original Version

Will the game successfully build the story to a satisfying climax through a coherent series of events, or will it fall prey to a mindless open season on aliens? These are the factors that will determine *Halo: Reach*'s quality, and sadly Bungie missed the mark.

In the edited version, separating the verdict from the setup makes it a more forceful statement.

Edited Version

Will the game successfully build the story to a satisfying climax through a coherent series of events, or will it fall prey to a mindless open season on aliens? These are the factors that will determine *Halo: Reach*'s quality. Sadly Bungie missed the mark.

Consider the value of short sentences when you want to stress a point.

Another stylistic mistake is to put a main point into a dependent clause, especially one beginning with a pronoun like *that* or *which.*

Original Version

Instead of a coherent story, it's more like a series of isolated cut scenes strung together with violence. This problem ties in with a more general issue with *Reach,* which is the general lack of polish.

In the edited version, an appositive set off with a strong punctuation mark gives the second sentence a more forceful ending.

Edited Version

Instead of a coherent story, it's more like a series of isolated cut scenes strung together with violence. This problem ties in with a more general issue with *Reach:* the general lack of polish.

In the final example below, the point about Alex is first made with a dependent "that" clause.

Original Version

It's because she seems like a human with real emotions that Alex becomes an integral, and welcome, part of the story.

In this revision, the point about Alex is promoted to the main clause—and main point—of the sentence.

Edited Version

Because she seems like a human with real emotions, Alex becomes an integral, and welcome, part of the story.

REVISED STUDENT EXAMPLE

Dobmeyer 1

Collin Dobmeyer

Professor Channell

English 1301-010

27 October 2014

Is Classic Status Out of Reach?

Halo: Reach represents the culmination of the Bungie *Halo* franchise, which has run for nine years. Sales of *Reach* hit $200 million on the first day of its release in September 2010. Its popularity suggests it will be a classic, but will it? The series consists of four games: *Halo: Combat Evolved,* which was released back in 2001; *Halo 2; Halo 3;* and *Halo: Reach. Reach* brings the Bungie series to a close with a prequel whose events tie closely with the beginning of the first game. The player joins a group of elite soldiers known as Noble Team as they fight a losing battle to save the planet Reach from aliens. Normally this is where a reviewer should have written "SPOILER ALERT," but the outcome of the battle is quite clear from the outset with your character's helmet sitting in a smoldering crater with a bullet hole through the visor. Because the ending is known, the only chance this game has to make a huge impression on the player is how well Bungie can deliver the story line and personify the human characters.

The evaluation opens with the topic clearly stated and an interesting specific fact about it.

This question suggests the writer's angle on the topic: Will it be a classic?

Gives an overview of the game's plot.

Shows the two main criteria that the writer will use as the basis of the evaluation.

Dobmeyer 2

The question is: did Bungie manage to pull this game off well enough that 2
Halo: Reach deserves the title of "classic"? If the characters are not able to
engage the players' emotions, then *Reach* will fail to reach classic status because
the story is built around their deaths. The other indicator is how well the story
unfolds. Will the game successfully build the story to a satisfying climax through a
coherent series of events, or will it fall prey to a mindless open season on aliens?
These are the factors that will determine *Halo: Reach*'s quality. Sadly Bungie
missed the mark. *Halo: Reach* fails to deliver both characters and plot; as a result
it will never be remembered for anything but its sales figures.

> The thesis or main point that the evaluation will prove. Memorable summary judgment.

Bungie really went out on a limb with *Halo: Reach.* They abandoned their 3
previous faceless, emotionless, super soldier hero Master Chief in favor of a squad
of Spartan super soldiers with faces and personalities. Among your teammates
there is the able commander Carter, the emotional George, the introverted Emile,
the snide engineer Kat, and the talkative sniper Jun. However, Bungie had better
make us care about these characters if they want the player to care about their
deaths. The game fails to do so because nearly all the characters lack depth.

> Major criticism.

Every one of them is an unstoppable, an immortal superman that doesn't even
flinch when it comes time for their own deaths. The only character with human vulnerability is George, who ironically dies first. From then on it becomes difficult to
generate any strong emotional attachment to the characters.

© Bloomberg/Getty Images

This isn't to say that the characters are 4
completely mindless robots; in fact many of
them have developing personalities, but the
game just doesn't spend enough time developing them beyond the super soldier demeanor.
For this, I blame the game play. *Halo: Reach*
is a shooter that centers on "run and gun"
fighting. It is downright difficult to create sympathetic characters when all we see them
doing is murdering every alien life form within
500 yards.

> Further develops the reason for the lack of character development in the game.

Dobmeyer 3

Compares the game to other games with better character development that have reached classic status.

Looking at other classics like *Half-Life* brings the necessity of good characterization into sharp relief. For those of you who have played the game, think for a moment about how tedious the experience would have been in *Half-Life 2* if your supporting character Alex was just one step up from a help screen. Because she seems like a human with real emotions, Alex becomes an integral, and welcome, part of the story. The supporting characters in *Reach* just don't work in this position because the player does not see them as anything more than ordinance support. *Halo: Reach* will be remembered for trying to develop good characters, but they fall short of really making those characters human.

The writer knows that his audience is other game players. He speaks to them as a fellow gamer in a voice that includes appropriate sarcasm.

Finally we come to the most important part of *Reach:* the story. Too bad that there really isn't much to it. *Reach* is built around the simple premise of super soldiers fighting an alien invasion, a story that in the game world is only slightly less common than trees. *Halo: Reach* pretty much boils down to killing whoever is in front of you and progressing by finding more to kill. Nothing else actually happens during the game itself; all of the important dialogue and characterization occur during animated cut scenes, which gives the game a detached feeling. Instead of a coherent story, it's more like a series of isolated cut scenes strung together with violence.

Shows how the game fails to meet the second criterion.

This problem ties in with a more general issue with *Reach:* the general lack of polish. Polish in game creation is like editing and revising for a book, and just as essential. Having a polished game means that levels flow smoothly from one set to another, the Artificial Intelligence works without feeling artificial, and the scenes impart a feeling of wonder.

Gives more development about why the game fails to meet the second criterion.

Qualifies the review by stating ways in which the game excels. This move adds credibility to the writer, showing his knowledge and fairness.

I do have to give credit to Bungie for delivering the set. The scenery in *Reach* is unlike any other shooter to date. With vast backdrops of war raging in the distance, they almost manage to give the player the feeling of being part of something greater. I also give credit to Bungie for the A.I. Enemies in *Reach* react almost like real people and the Elites are downright cunning in their strategies. Too bad that after you have killed a few thousand of them as part of the campaign they cease to be scary or menacing in any way, shape or form.

5

6

7

8

Dobmeyer 4

What it amounts to is that Bungie liked the run and gun tactics a little too much. They allowed the game to become nothing more than a straight road between the same boring fight. The gameplay requires the player to keep his eyes glued to the action. As a result there is very little time to dwell on that wondrous feeling of being an integral part of a global mission. Polish could have taken care of that. If Bungie had taken the time to balance, or better yet, incorporate the scenery into the flow of the game *Halo: Reach* could possibly reach that elusive classic status. As it stands, it feels like Bungie made a set for *Lord of the Rings* just to perform a puppet show. The general lack of polish damages *Reach*'s case for classic status to the point where slamming out patches isn't going to fix the problem. Bungie really dropped the ball on this one.

9   Explains why the game did not succeed as a story.

Despite my despairing tone, *Halo: Reach* is not the worst game on the market today, but it isn't deserving of such massive hype either. The game is mediocre. It is another generic shooter with some pretty backgrounds and won't be remembered in a different light in a decade. Games like *Half-life* and *Deus Ex* with their wonderfully complex stories and in-depth character development will always trump *Halo: Reach* when it comes to classic status. For all of the people who are considering buying *Halo: Reach,* I advise putting it on the rent list for now and saving your money for *Half-life: Episode 3* if Valve ever gets around to making it.

10   Sums up the reviewer's judgment.

Stays with the angle of classic versus mediocre games.

Courtesy of Collin Dobmeyer

CHAPTER 14

Editing Fundamentals

IF YOU HAVE EVER GOTTEN A PAPER BACK COVERED WITH CORRECTION MARKS—for example, with comments in the margins like "What does this mean?" or "Don't follow you here"—and marked with a grade lower than you anticipated, then you know what happens when you do not edit well. Instead of responding to what you have said, your instructor is responding to problems with how you have said it.

Look and listen for problems in the following sentence from a student's paper:

One route that companies have already taken, and been successful, is to have meditation when something like sexual harassment occurs.

If your ear heard how awkward the sentence sounds, you know it needs editing. If your eye saw that the writer meant "mediation" not "meditation"—one little "t" makes a big difference—you can eliminate a significant mistake.

Looking and *listening* are two essential editing skills. A third skill is *rewriting* to solve problems. Consider this edited version of the sentence:

One successful route companies have already taken is to mediate sexual harassment disputes.

No one will be irritated or distracted by this sentence. It says what the writer meant, and the reader will understand its meaning immediately. In short, *nothing interferes with the meaning coming through*. That is what editing is all about.

You can learn to edit. A little knowledge about grammar can help, but you will need practice above all. Editing is a skill, learned as you do it. This chapter provides the fundamentals:

- Understanding the process of editing and how it fits into the writing process

- Knowing common problems to look and listen for

- Applying strategies for solving problems you find

Once you get into the habit of editing, with each paper you will find it easier to make your writing more clear, concise, and coherent. You will not need instructors' comments to find and correct the rough spots.

What Is Editing?

Editing is an intense effort to find and solve whatever problems remain in a piece of writing after revision. It amounts to paying attention to small details you may have missed earlier in the process. Editing includes

- Checking for **flow and focus within individual paragraphs**
- Checking for **flow and focus from one paragraph to the next**

- Reworking **awkward, wordy, or unclear sentences**
- Correcting **errors of grammar, spelling, and punctuation**
- Attending to **formalities,** such as parenthetical notation and works cited pages

Why Edit?

Perhaps you feel that editing should not matter very much. After all, it is content that counts. Saying something worth reading is the whole point of writing. However, *content cannot be separated from the way it is expressed.* Have you ever been irritated or distracted because background noise or a bad connection interfered with a cell phone conversation? A poorly edited paper is like a bad connection: It irritates and distracts readers. More seriously, if your sentences do not say what you mean, if readers struggle to understand your sentences, if your paragraphs wander, your thoughts and your message get lost.

Edit, then, *to communicate better with your readers.* Edit also because the impression other people have of you matters. An unedited or poorly edited paper says that the writer lacks either the skill or the discipline to attend to details. Judgments like "incompetent" or "careless" or even "illiterate" are common. Such judgments may seem unfair, but the consequences are real: poor grades, lukewarm recommendations, being stuck in low-level jobs.

BEST PRACTICES | Where Does Editing Belong in the Composing Process?

Focus on editing only when you have a draft you consider "final," the best you can do. Why?

First, editing requires undivided attention. Some writers edit as they compose, even while writing first drafts. We do not recommend it. Editing as you write slows down composing and takes attention away from where it ought to be, on saying what you have to say. In subsequent drafts, you can attend to **revision,** which deals with *large-scale changes in a draft* to achieve your purpose or meet the requirements of an assignment, develop your points more adequately, connect with your readers more consistently, improve your organization, and so on. **Revise first; then edit.**

Second, editing too soon is not efficient. If you edit a sentence or a paragraph in the first draft and then delete it during revision, you have wasted time and effort. Still worse, you might resist throwing out a sentence you have edited so carefully when it should be cut. Editing too soon can actually get in the way of something more important—revising and rewriting to solve major problems.

Finally, compulsive editing can easily lead to **writer's paralysis,** *being so critical of everything you write that you can hardly write at all.* When you are composing, let go, let thoughts and words flow. Save editing for later.

How Do Writers Edit?

Every semester students come to us with papers covered with correction marks and marginal commentary. They are shocked, puzzled. "But I read it over several times," they say, sometimes adding, "I even had a _____ [tutor, parent, or friend] look it over."

To this we say, "But editing is not 'reading' or 'looking over.' You cannot edit a paper by scanning through it."

When we read something, we *look through* the sentences to what is being said. To edit, you have to *look at* the sentences and paragraphs to see *how* things are said.

If you are working on paragraphs, take it one paragraph at a time; if sentences, one sentence at a time. Linger over each one, looking and listening for signs of problems. A good method for slowing down and listening is to read your draft out loud. Your ear will catch things that your eye might miss. Mark anything that bothers you. Then go back and rework the sentence or the paragraph until it does not bother you anymore. In short, **slow down.**

You may be thinking, "Won't this take a long time?" The answer is "Yes, much longer than reading over a paper." If you are working on a five-page, double-spaced paper, expect to spend at least forty-five minutes to an hour editing it. You will get faster with experience, but "fast" and "editing" never go together.

The most important thing to remember when editing your work is to *slow down.* Linger over paragraphs and words, and rework anything that bothers you.

© scibak/Getty Images, RF

- ■ Budget downtime. Try to get away from a paper for a day or two before editing it. You will be fresher and more detached from your writing.

- ■ Avoid trying to do all the editing at one time. Try fifteen- to twenty-minute sessions, with breaks in between. Otherwise it is hard to maintain the high level of concentration required.

- ■ After editing on your own, find a classmate who is also committed to editing. Exchange papers and help each other find the problems self-editing missed.

What Is the Spiraling Down Method?

We strongly advocate a **spiraling down method** of editing. That is, first address the flow from paragraph to paragraph; then the flow within paragraphs; and finish with attention to individual sentences, word choice, and errors. You will need to make several passes through your paper, once or twice at the paragraph level, once or twice at the sentence level. Spiraling down offers several benefits:

- ■ It keeps you from being overwhelmed by all the details; you can "divide and conquer."

- ■ A key principle of editing is: *The more you look for at one time, the less you find.* If you are examining paragraphs or sequences of paragraphs for coherence and flow, you are not likely to detect individual sentences that need work and vice versa.

- ■ It allows some problems to solve themselves. If you work on paragraphs first, any changes you make may fix or eliminate bad sentences, so you will not have to bother editing them. When you are working at the sentence level, some typos and grammatical errors may simply disappear during rewriting. Why hunt for errors before you give them a chance to go away on their own?

Working on Paragraph Sequences

The first focus of editing is working on paragraph sequences. Paragraphs are the building blocks of any piece of writing. Paragraphs, either singly or in groups, make up the sequence of moves that an author makes while composing. The sequence of paragraphs should create a smooth train of thought and a logical development of points.

Paragraphs may look like independent units, but actually *they mark off a move within a set of connected moves* that make up a section in a paper. A **move** is *an answer to an implied question,* something the reader needs to know. It is common in long essays and book chapters for multiple paragraphs to work together in making any one move. When two or more paragraphs work in unison to make a single move, we refer to them as paragraph groups.

Consider the following passage from P. M. Forni's "What Is Civility," a longer excerpt of which appears in Chapter 8. We have indicated the implied question each move answers.

Move 1: If *civility, courtesy, politeness,* and *manners* are near synonyms, what exactly does courtesy imply?

Civility, courtesy, politeness, and manners are not perfect synonyms, as etymology clearly shows. . . . Courtesy is connected to court and evoked in the past the superior qualities of character and bearing expected in those close to royalty. Etymologically, when we are courteous we are courtier like. Although today we seldom make this connection, courtesy still suggests excellence and elegance in bestowing respect and attention. It can also suggest deference and formality.

Move 2: What does politeness imply?

To understand politeness, we must think of polish. The polite are those who have polished their behavior. They have put some effort into bettering themselves, but they are sometimes looked upon with suspicion. Expressions such as "polite reply," "polite lie," and "polite applause" connect politeness to hypocrisy. It is true that the polite are inclined to veil their own feelings to spare someone else's. Self-serving lying, however, is always beyond the pale of politeness. If politeness is a quality of character (alongside courtesy, good manners, and civility), it cannot become a flaw. A suave manipulator may appear to be polite but is not.

Move 3: What do good manners imply?

When we think of good manners we often think of children being taught to say "please" and "thank you" and chew with their mouths closed. This may prevent us from looking at manners with the attention they deserve. Manner comes from manus, the Latin word for "hand." Manner and manners have to do with the use of our hands. A manner is the way something is done, a mode of handling. Thus manners came to refer to behavior in social interaction—the way we handle the encounter between Self and Other. We have good manners when we use our hands well—when we handle others with care. When we rediscover the connection of manner with hand, the hand that, depending on our will and sensitivity, can strike or lift, hurt or soothe, destroy or heal, we understand the importance—for children and adults alike—of having good manners.

P. M. Forni. "What Is Civility?" *Choosing Civility: The Twenty-Five Rules of Considerate Conduct,* St. Martin's Press, pp. 7–13. © 2002 by P. M. Forni. Used by permission of the author.

Here is the principle at work: *Every paragraph, or paragraph group, implies and answers a key question.* The purpose of each paragraph is to move the line of thought forward, in order, 1, 2, 3. . . . Once you see the logic, it is hard to imagine any other paragraph sequence for presenting the information.

Successful paragraph sequences work this way. Consequently, here is how to edit your own paragraph sequences:

1. Isolate each major section of your paper. If the paper is short, treat the whole paper as one section.

2. Check to see if each paragraph, or paragraph group, makes a *single* move in a sequence of connected moves. Use the implied-question-and-answer test demonstrated above.

3. If this is not happening, ask, **"What are the 1, 2, 3 (and so on) moves you need to say what you want to say?"**

4. Rewrite the section, making paragraphs that correspond to each move.

BEST PRACTICES | Editing Paragraph Sequences

Moving section by section through your paper, concentrate first on the *sequence* of paragraphs. Ask these questions:

1. **Does each paragraph or paragraph group have a definite function or purpose?** If you cannot say what function some paragraph performs, you may need to delete it or reconsider what moves you want to make in your paper.

2. **Do my paragraphs follow a logical sequence in building a train of thought for my reader to follow? Do I need to add more to the sequence or rearrange parts of it?** Add what is needed to existing paragraphs or add a new paragraph.

3. **Are there smooth transitions from one move to the next?** How could you signal the reader where a paragraph or paragraph group makes a new move or takes on a new function in the sequence of your paper?

▨▨■■ ACTIVITY 14.1 *Collaborative Activity*

Paragraph Sequencing Practice

The following passage looks like one paragraph but should actually be two. The sentences in both paragraphs have been scrambled and intermixed. Working with one or two other students, sort out the sentences and make them into two separate paragraphs. Be able to say what question each of the two paragraphs answers on the topic of underage drinking.

The laws in Europe do not limit alcohol consumption to people twenty-one or older. People experience alcohol in their earliest years, and therefore

Europe does not experience the same problem that the U.S. has. According to Elizabeth Whelan, alcohol-abuse researcher at Harvard, "prohibiting the sale of liquor to reasonable young adults creates an atmosphere where binge drinking and alcohol abuse becomes a problem." Enforcing a younger drinking age is not a way of extending the party to people of all ages, but an attempt to fix our present situation. Those that oppose the age eighteen legal drinking age have two major arguments to support their position. The first is that lowering the drinking age will only increase alcoholism. However, studies indicate that alcoholism is mostly a genetic disease. Furthermore, children imitate their parents. If children grow up in families where alcohol is abused, the chances are high they will misuse it too. The second argument is that drunk driving will increase. Drunk driving is certainly a major problem, but the vast majority of those arrested for it and who get into accidents are not illegal drinkers. The twenty-one drinking age is not the cure; young adults who drink responsibly is. ∎

▨▨▦ ACTIVITY 14.2 *In Your Own Work*

Editing Paragraph Sequences

Select any recent paper you have revised. Next to each paragraph, write down the question it implies and answers. Edit the order of the paragraphs to achieve a 1, 2, 3, and so on sequence. When you are done, print out your edited version and read through it carefully. Does it read better than before? What did you change, and why did you make the changes? ∎

Working on Individual Paragraphs

Editing paragraphs is the second focus of editing. At the paragraph level, editing focuses on coherence, meaning how well the sentences cohere, or stick together. When sentences cohere, we say the writing flows well, with no gaps in the train of thought.

BEST PRACTICES   Editing Paragraphs

Moving paragraph by paragraph through your paper, ask these questions:

1. **Does the first sentence indicate what the entire paragraph will be about?**
2. **Did you provide explanations, comments, and examples that *develop* the first sentence?**
3. **Is there flow, a smooth movement from sentence to sentence?**
4. **Does the paragraph connect to the previous one and to the following one?**

Elizabeth Whelan. "Perils of Prohibition: Why We Should Lower the Drinking Age to 18." *Newsweek,* 25 May 1995, p. 14.

Individual paragraphs function much like paragraph sequences: They are a sequence of connected moves. The difference is that a paragraph is a sequence of connected sentences. Consider the following example, a paragraph from student Lauren Knazze's blog:

> An interesting concept came up in Wellness class today. My instructor used the example of circus elephants to explain the idea. From their youth, circus elephants are trained to be helpless and hopeless. When they are little, they are chained to large boulders so that they cannot escape. Although they try, their efforts prove to be futile. When they grow larger, the elephants believe that they cannot escape, so they don't try. Even though they could pull the rocks and move away, the failures from before are enough to keep them stuck in place, with no resistance. My instructor's point was that people too become so stuck in their ways or so fearful because of past failures that they don't realize that they could change their lives for the better.

Notice how each sentence picks up the idea of the sentence before it and answers the question most likely posed in the reader's mind. In coherent paragraphs, the writer anticipates what the reader is likely to ask—and provides the answer in the very next sentence.

> An interesting concept came up in Wellness class today. (Introduces the topic.)

> My instructor used the example of circus elephants to explain the idea. (Answers the question: **What happened in Wellness class?**)

> From their youth, circus elephants are trained to be helpless and hopeless. (Answers the question: **What was the example?**)

> When they are little, they are chained to large boulders so that they cannot escape. (Answers the question: **What happens to the elephants?**)

> Although they try, their efforts prove to be futile. (Answers the question: **Then what happens?**)

> When they grow larger, the elephants believe that they cannot escape, so they don't try. (Answers the question: **What happens next?**)

> Even though they could pull the rocks and move away, the failures from before are enough to keep them stuck in place, with no resistance. (Answers the question: **What is the point of the example?**)

> My instructor's point was that people too become so stuck in their ways or so fearful because of past failures that they don't realize that they could change their lives for the better. (Answers the question: **Why was this idea important in a Wellness class?**)

Of course, neither writer nor reader is normally aware of the questions that each sentence answers. But when you find a paragraph that is not working, try making the

Courtesy of Lauren Knazze's blog

reader's questions explicit and test the next sentence to see if it answers the question. Sometimes the answer comes in a later sentence, and rearranging the sentences solves the problem.

A good paragraph coheres and flows. It **coheres,** *holds together,* because it is about *a single focus or theme*—for example, explaining an idea about personal empowerment. It **flows** because *each sentence answers a question the reader is likely to have asked in response to the previous sentence.*

How Transitions Connect Paragraphs

In addition to editing for the focus of each paragraph, we have to ensure that the beginning and end of each paragraph connect to previous and subsequent ones. These links, called "transitions," function much like turn signals on a car. Imagine that, as a writer, you are taking readers somewhere they have not been, and they are following you. Transitions, like turn signals, tell the reader you are about to turn down another road.

Look back at the three paragraphs from the Forni example (page 308). The first sentence claims that there are shades of difference in meaning among three words related to civility. As a reader you expect the author to explain the differences in the order of the words given. The rest of the first paragraph explains what "courtesy" implies, the second, "politeness," and the third, "manners"—just as we anticipate from the promise or commitment the first sentence makes. One, two, three (or more) sequences like this one are common ways of structuring paragraphs. The transitions are implicit in the sequence of items, ideas, or points themselves.

Transitions are not all alike. Sometimes the last sentence of the preceding paragraph does the linking, while the first sentence of the next one announces the new focus. How transitions happen matters less than making sure that they do. Look at all endings and beginnings of your paragraphs to make sure the transitions work as smoothly as possible.

▨■■ ACTIVITY 14.3 *Collaborative Activity*

Paragraph Editing Practice

In groups of two or three, edit the following paragraph to make a sequence of sentences with both a single theme or focus and development or movement. Use the implied question-and-answer method we have discussed to help discover a good sentence order. Feel free to cut, add, rearrange, and rewrite sentences. If you think a single paragraph should become two or more, do that as well. Create any needed transitions.

My day at the Boys and Girls Club of Greater Houston consisted of running around, playing, and laughing a lot. I graduated from St. Agnes Academy, where one hundred hours of volunteer work were required for graduation. The Boys and Girls Summer Day Camp is a day-care facility where families pay two dollars for an entire summer of supervision of their children while they are at work. From my experiences as a camp counselor I realize that some people you meet leave a strong impression. The children I worked with in the summer of 1997 were underprivileged minorities. I will never forget any of the children, but one little boy was special to me. ■

▨▨▨■ ACTIVITY 14.4 *In Your Own Work*

Editing Paragraphs

Select any recent paper you have written and edit the paragraphs for focus and movement. Look at each indentation. Is there a sentence near the opening of each paragraph that contains the main idea and keyword(s) that unites the paragraph? Look at the flow or connection between each sentence and the next. Does each sentence pick up an idea or key word from the sentence before it? ■

Working on Sentences

Working on sentences is the third focus of editing.

Sentences are the basic unit of expression. We speak mostly in sentences. With few exceptions, we write in sentences. Therefore, *reworking sentences is the heart of editing itself.*

BEST PRACTICES   Editing Sentences

1. Moving sentence by sentence through your paper, read each one aloud or subvocalize, "hearing" it in your head. Your ear is the key to detecting sentences that need editing. Mark sentences that sound bad to you.
2. Rework your sentence so the doer of the action comes first, followed by the action itself, the verb.
3. Look for sentence-level errors—for example, fragments, using a comma when you need a semicolon or vice versa, putting a comma after "although," incorrectly punctuating clauses beginning with the word *which.*

What a Sentence Must Do

It is no mystery. A sentence must

■ Say precisely what we mean

■ Make it easy for our readers to grasp what we mean

A sentence must do these two things; otherwise we have not *communicated.* Anything else takes a back seat. Writing correctly, for example, does not matter if communication has failed.

Why Do Sentences Go Wrong?

Sometimes we are not sure what we mean; we are confused or conflicted. Sometimes we know what we mean but lack confidence in what we want to say. Sometimes we have a general idea of what we want to say but cannot find the words. And sometimes we think we have said what we mean until somebody interprets our sentence in a way we did not intend or points out that our meaning is unclear.

Sentences go wrong because we do not have the point we want to make clearly in mind. Sentences also go wrong because it is difficult to see our own sentences as readers will see them. A sentence that seems perfectly clear to us puzzles or confuses our readers.

Editing is the time to detect uncertainties about what you want to say. You know the sentences you struggled with in writing your drafts and the feeling "this is still not quite right" even after you have revised. Step back and ask, "Why am I confused or conflicted here? What is keeping me from having confidence in what I want to say? What is wrong with that idea that keeps eluding the words to express it?" If you can diagnose the problem, you can get "in here" to line up with "out there." You will not always succeed, but give it your best effort.

Editing is also the right time to seek input from others. When we write a sentence, we get no immediate feedback—nobody is there to look puzzled or ask for clarification as there is in conversation. Instead, we have to *imagine* a reader's response, *anticipate* problems a reader might have, and rework sentences so that he or she will understand. We try, but even the most talented writers cannot always see their sentences "from the outside," as a reader will in responding to them. Therefore, all writers need an actual reader's response, and that is especially true for those sentences that are still bothering us after self-editing.

Edit your own writing first, but then seek out another set of eyes and ears to help you detect more of what you missed.

What Matters Most in Editing Sentences?

In a word: clarity. The first step is to make your writing sound more like something you would say. For example, read this sentence:

> The cessation of the employment of extraordinary means to prolong the life of the body when there is irrefutable evidence that biological death is imminent is the decision of the patient and/or the immediate family.

What does this thirty-five-word sentence mean? It sounds impressive and authoritative, but no one would say it. More likely, you would say something like this:

> Only the patient or the patient's family can decide to stop life support.

This thirteen-word sentence says what the writer means without making readers struggle to understand it. How did we arrive at this much better sentence? First, *simplify*. The two most important moves you can make in editing are to simplify and find an active verb.

- The "cessation of the employment of extraordinary means to prolong life" equals "stopping life support." What else could it be?
- If we are talking about life support, we must be talking about a patient who would otherwise be dead or likely to die, so why say anything about death at all?
- We found the subject performing the action—"the patient or the patient's family."
- We found the verb, the action the subject was performing, in the noun "decision," so we used the verb "decide."

BEST PRACTICES   Editing for Wordy Phrases

One way to write more plainly, simply, and directly is to look for the following common phrases, each of which has a more concise equivalent.

For these phrases . . .	Use . . .
at all times	always
biography of the life	biography
close proximity	near
due to the fact that	because
final result	final
first and foremost	first
for the purposes of	to
for the reason that	because
green in color	green
in order to	to
in spite of the fact that	although
in the event that	if
in the not-too-distant future	soon
in this day and age	today
is able to	can
is necessary that	must
mix together	mix
refer back	refer
repeat again	repeat
until such time as	until

We pick up these and many other phrases from conversation and use them without thinking about them. In editing we should weed them out of our sentences.

■■■ ACTIVITY 14.5 *Collaborative Activity*

Sentence Editing Practice

Working in groups of two or three, cut the excess verbiage from the following sentences. First, step back and ask: What is the writer trying to say? Find a plain, simple, direct way to say what the writer really means. Delete what you do not need to say it. Find the subject and combine it with an action, a verb.

1. Willy is so frustrated in his futile quest for riches and failure to achieve social approval due to the dreadful reality of his limitations that he consequently turns to a dream world.
2. The lessons I have learned and continue to learn of hard work and entrepreneurship are a great value and truth that shall be passed from me to my kids and to their kids and so on.
3. Americans are starting to worry again, because certain aspects of immigration, such as overpopulation and lack of education, which results in poverty, are beginning to affect America as a whole.

4. On many campuses, gays and lesbians have formed their own fraternities and sororities, not only coming out of the closet, but also benefiting from the social as well as the academic education a school offers.

5. I can only hope by the time my children grow up in this country that affirmative action will no longer be an issue so that they will be looked at as a student for academic ability, character, and personal attributes to do the best they can. ■

■■■ ACTIVITY 14.6 *In Your Own Work*

Eliminating "Deadwood"

Select any recent paper you have written and revised. Edit the sentences as you did in the previous exercise.

Tip: Read your sentences aloud to find the ones that need work. They'll sound like something nobody would say. Get rid of "deadwood" and your prose will immediately improve. ■

How Do We Detect Sentence-Level Errors?

Use your ear in editing: Listen to what you have written either in your head or by reading it aloud.

However, certain norms in speech are considered errors in writing, and you cannot rely on your ear to pick them up. In fact, the most common sentence-level errors relate to speech patterns we cannot carry over into writing. For instance:

As we've moved toward greater equality, a new struggle has emerged in America. New in that it focuses on sexual preference rather than race or gender.

The second sentence is a fragment, common in conversation, but usually considered an error in writing. Fragments are easy to fix. Many fragments can be eliminated simply by adding a comma and attaching them to the preceding sentence.

As we've moved toward greater equality, a new struggle has emerged in America, new in that it focuses on sexual preference rather than race or gender.

Proofreading

Proofreading is the fourth focus of editing. In publications, editors read the final page "proofs" or set type, looking for little errors. In writing a paper, proofreading similarly means looking very closely at the final manuscript to find the small, but nevertheless still important, errors.

By errors we mean, for example, the following:

■ Typing "minorities" (plural) when you mean "minority's" (possessive), or vice versa

■ Confusing "there" with "their" and "they're"

■ Confusing "to" with "too" and "two"

- Typing "it's" (contraction for "it is") when you mean "its" (possessive form of "it"), or vice versa
- Misspelled words
- Typos
- Omitting a word you meant to include, or typing a word or phrase twice
- Not putting titles in quotation marks or italics

These are the kinds of mistakes that proofreading must catch. You will find some of them as you "spiral down," working first with paragraphs and then with sentences. But if you do not proofread, you will miss too many. Furthermore, in reworking paragraphs and sentences, you will probably make a few more errors. Therefore, *proofreading is an essential, last focus of editing.*

BEST PRACTICES   Proofreading

Move sentence by sentence through your paper, *looking* for errors like misspelled words, typos, and word choice problems. *Look because most errors have to be seen, not heard, detected by the eye and not the ear.* Mark the errors. Go back and correct each one.

Proofreading cannot be omitted or done hastily because errors like these are easily and routinely detected by people assessing your writing. Nor can you rely on spell checks and grammar checks to find all such errors for you. Use the programs, but remember that they will miss many mistakes and sometimes tag something as an error that is not wrong.

Our general advice is to approach errors systematically. You will make mistakes. Some of these you will miss even with diligent proofreading. The ones you miss professors marking your papers will usually detect. *It is what you do with the marks on your papers that can make all the difference.*

What matters most are errors that occur regularly. They indicate that you do not recognize the error as an error or do not understand how to correct it in all cases. Talk to your instructor. Or look for the relevant section in the Connect Composition handbook available online. Then, having grasped the nature of the error, *make a note about it in an editing checklist you keep for yourself.* Write down a description of the error, what you typically do wrong and how to correct it. You might include an example or two, with corrections. Save this list in a notebook or in a computer file. Keep this editing checklist to consult the next time you have to proofread.

■■■ ACTIVITY 14.7 *Collaborative Activity*

Error Editing Practice

Working with two or three students, correct the errors in the following sentences. If you detect other editing problems, attend to them as well.

1. The administration has done everything they can to improve race relations, now we students must do our part.

2. Looking back at the foundling fathers of our country, they had very similar views about the federal government.

3. Parents install morals in there children; hoping they will make the right decisions as adults.

4. Once she escaped her strict upbringing at college, she lost all restraints, the perfect example of a girl who goes crazy her first year of freedom.

5. The book *The Beauty Myth,* by Naomi Wolf dedicates itself to the fact that women are controlled by their looks.

6. I was perfectly content living in a closed knit community, where everyone felt they were at home.

7. The worst part of the advertisement was their was a girl next to the man, messaging him. ■

▨▨ ■ ACTIVITY 14.8 *In Your Own Work*

Proofreading

Select any recent paper you have revised. Edit the sentences to eliminate errors like the ones discussed and illustrated above. Listening to your sentences can help, especially with some punctuation errors, but concentrate on *looking* for errors. What writing errors have you made in the past? Be sure to check for those in a separate step.

Tip: A good way to proof is by working backward, starting with the last sentence. Reading backward slows the process down and disrupts the flow from sentence to sentence so that you can *look at* the sentences for the errors you need to detect. ■

What Matters Most in Editing? Three Key Points

- **Editing is not just "cleaning up."** Cleaning up is proofreading, and that is important but is only the last step in editing. The purpose of editing is to detect and eliminate *everything* that gets in the way of communicating with your reader—and that means attending to much more than error. You need to work on your paragraphs and sentences even when they have no mistakes.

- **Editing requires time and concentration.** It is not "reading over" your final draft. It is working through your final draft methodically, first focusing on paragraph sequences and paragraphs, then on sentences, and finally on errors.

- **Keep an editing checklist** that helps you pay special attention to your particular editing problems. Study the marks and comments on every graded paper. When they relate to editing, add them to your list. If you do not understand an error or problem, ask your instructor to explain or consult our handbook. Add any notes you need to help remember the error or problem and how to fix it. Use the checklist as you edit your next paper.

Do these things, and your editing problems will diminish and you will gain fuller control over the ones that remain. You will be amazed at how much your writing will improve.

PART III

Researching
Writing

Recommended Genres for Further Practice connect

CHAPTER 15
Planning a Research Project

RESEARCH BEGINS WITH QUESTIONS, NOT JUST WITH A TOPIC. Without questions, research would be a haphazard and aimless task. One question is always relevant: "Given what I already know about my topic, what more do I need to know?" Asking it exposes the gaps in your existing knowledge and tells you what you need to focus on when doing research.

Research, however, is more interesting and creative than just gathering facts. For example, research can help us ask and answer a more important question: "What do the facts mean?" This question calls for critical thinking, which requires more questions and answers. For example, history textbooks are filled with facts, but they might have different facts or different interpretations of the same facts. A researcher might ask *why* textbooks' explanations of an event might differ. Could the differences have to do with the political climate of the time in which each was published? The writer could attempt to answer this question by finding textbooks published at different times, comparing their depictions of an event, and then relating them to what was going on politically when the books were written.

As a researcher what you are seeking most is *a question that you and your readers will find engaging, worth writing about, and worth reading.* We know, for instance, that wolves thrive in some environments and struggle in others. Why? One question we could ask is, "How does hunting by humans affect the behavior of species that are hunted?" Animal behaviorists are researching how wolf packs behave depending on whether they live in protected areas or in areas where hunting is permitted. What they have learned is worth writing about and sharing with readers—and if we have the opportunity, can even get us out into the field ourselves to do our own firsthand research.

If we think of research as just finding facts and quotations to add to a draft, we have missed what research is all about. *Research is about finding a question worth pursuing. Then it is about finding information and interpreting it in order to answer the question.* Put simply, research builds the foundation for writing.

When Is Research Necessary?

Research is needed whenever general knowledge and common sense are not enough. Most college writing requires research because instructors want students to go beyond assigned readings to increase the depth of their knowledge, analyze conflicting interpretations, and develop their own understanding of the course subject matter. After college, people conduct research on the job (for example, to analyze markets or prepare proposals for clients) and in community life (for example, to support their claim that a neighborhood should be rezoned or that school funding should be increased).

Research goes on throughout the writing process. In a college writing class, depending on the assignment, you may

- Conduct *preliminary research* to get basic information on a topic and stimulate your curiosity about it.

- Pursue *in-depth research* to satisfy that curiosity, answering your questions and acquiring the solid evidence you need to convince others.

- Continue your research as needed in revision to add support when a point is underdeveloped, your focus shifts, or new questions arise.

What Kinds of Sources Do College Researchers Use?

Most assignments encourage students to consult a variety of sources featuring different opinions on and approaches to a topic. The following discussion offers an overview of the kinds of sources available.

Primary Sources versus Secondary Sources

Primary sources are *data or artifacts, works of art or literature, before they have been interpreted by another researcher.* In the natural sciences and social sciences, primary sources may include data from observational studies, surveys,

To learn how to conduct observational studies, surveys, and interviews, see Chapter 16, pages 348–49.

Primary sources, such as the *Declaration of Independence*, are documents or works of art or literature that have not been interpreted by another researcher. They are uninterpreted works in their original form.

© Comstock/ PunchStock, RF

Secondary sources, like *National Geographic* magazine, demonstrate other people's ideas and conclusions about a topic, to which you can compare your own thoughts and conclusions.
© FRANCISCO GARCÍA VELASCO/NOTIMEX/Newscom

and laboratory experiments. In the humanities, they may include historical documents (the *Mayflower Compact,* the *Declaration of Independence*), works of art and film, novels and poetry, or letters, diaries, and manuscripts. In all disciplines, researchers may interview experts to learn about their research or their experiences firsthand. Primary sources provide raw materials for your own analysis and specific evidence for developing your points and supporting your reasoning.

Secondary sources, in contrast, *result from someone else's research.* For example, in a British literature course, your primary source might be Samuel Taylor Coleridge's poem "The Rime of the Ancient Mariner." Secondary sources would be interpretations of the poem by literary critics. Secondary sources also include general and specialized encyclopedias, most books, and articles in magazines and scholarly journals. They provide useful background or historical information; they communicate other people's ideas and conclusions about a topic, to which you can compare your own thoughts and conclusions. Also, in secondary sources you will find expert opinions that you can use to help formulate your own opinions and to support and develop your opinions. You may also use secondary sources to provide opposing views and opinions you would like to refute. Comparing the perspectives of secondary sources can help you construct a position of your own.

For more on how to compare sources, see Chapter 9, especially pages 187–90.

Popular versus Scholarly Sources

Secondary sources have a wide range of audiences; they may be magazine articles directed to the general public or highly specialized texts written by scholars for other professionals in their field.

Popular works offer accessible introductions to a topic and include the following:

- **Textbooks** Textbooks offer surveys of a field, such as this guide to writing. They can be a good place to begin research.

- **General Encyclopedias** Like textbooks, general encyclopedias (such as *Britannica Online* and *Wikipedia*) offer an overview of the basic information on a topic and therefore can serve as starting points for research. However, keep in mind that most assignments will require that you move on to more specialized sources. Footnotes and links in general encyclopedia entries can take you deeper into scholarship on the topic.

- **Magazines and Newspapers** Magazines and newspapers offer a wide range of information, from celebrity gossip to scientific discoveries. For most college research, instructors prefer that students avoid light reading titles such as *Cosmopolitan* and *USA TODAY* in favor of publications that offer more in-depth articles such as *Women's Health Weekly* and *The New York Times.*

- **Trade Books** Trade books are published by commercial presses (like HarperCollins, Knopf, and Simon & Schuster) and aimed at an educated segment of the general public, including students and professors. Trade books are typically more accessible than books published by scholarly presses, but the authors are often experts in their field who also publish more academic works.

Scholarly works include the following:

- **Specialized Encyclopedias and Dictionaries** Specialized encyclopedias and dictionaries are works devoted to specific topics and written by experts. You will find many in the reference section of your library; others, like *The New Palgrave Dictionary of Economics* and *The Blackwell Encyclopedia of Sociology,* can be accessed through your library's database offerings. Entries are written by experts and peer reviewed, which means that other scholars have had to approve the credentials of the writer and the accuracy of the material. Entries in specialized encyclopedias and dictionaries provide background information, define terms, and include suggestions for further reading.

- **Scholarly Journals** Articles in scholarly journals are written by experts and reviewed by other subject specialists before publication. Scholarly journals are specialized sources, so undergraduates might find reading their articles challenging. Such articles are highly reliable sources of in-depth information, however, so perseverance will pay dividends.

Magazines such as *The Atlantic* are popular sources intended for an intelligent and well-informed readership.

© The McGraw-Hill Companies. Mark Dierker, photographer

You can distinguish scholarly journals from popular magazines in several ways. First, scholarly journals do not include glossy advertisements. Second, the titles of scholarly journals, and the articles they publish, usually indicate specifically what they cover. For example, in the *American Journal of Family Therapy,* you will find articles such as "Understanding Online Gaming Addiction and Treatment Issues for Adolescents," whereas an article in a popular magazine such as *Psychology Today* will have a catchier title like "Why Johnny Can't Stop Playing Video Games." The examples in Figure 15.1 reveal the typical design features, vocabulary, and reading level of academic journal articles and articles in popular magazines.

The American Journal of Family Therapy, 37:355–372, 2009
Copyright © Taylor & Francis Group, LLC
ISSN: 0192-6187 print / 1521-0383 online
DOI: 10.1080/01926180902942191

**Understanding Online Gaming Addiction
and Treatment Issues for Adolescents**

KIMBERLY YOUNG

The Center for Internet Addiction Recovery, Bradford, Pennsylvania, USA

*Massive Muti-user Online Role-Playing Games or MMORPGs as
they are often called are one of the fastest growing forms of Internet addiction, especially among children and teenagers. Like an
addiction to alcohol or drugs, gamers show several classic signs
of addiction (Grusser, Thalemann, and Griffiths, 2007). They become preoccupied with gaming, lie about their gaming use, lose
interest in other activities just to game, withdrawal from family
and friends to game, and use gaming as a means of psychological*

- **Scholarly Books** Scholarly books are written by experts in the field and published by university presses. They are rigorously reviewed by other experts in the
  field (a process known as peer review) before publication, and they are intended
  for an audience of other scholars in the same field. You can depend on authors of
  scholarly books to cite their sources and to include a bibliography at the end of
  the book. The style of the writing can range from accessible at the undergraduate
  level to highly technical.

We will talk later about how to find these and other sources (see Chapter 16, pages 338–47) and how to evaluate such sources (Chapter 17, pages 350–56), but this overview should give you an idea of the main kinds of sources available to you.

Print Sources versus Digital Sources

The distinction between online and print sources is not as relevant as it used to be since most print sources are becoming available digitally. Libraries subscribe to databases that provide online the full text of many magazine and journal articles. Increasingly, e-books are available through libraries' book catalogs.

How Do I Plan a Research Project?

Writing a research project can be a big undertaking. To minimize anxiety and keep your progress on track, first break the project down into stages.

Stages of a Research Project

The stages of research include preliminary thinking and research; focused research; informal writing, drafting, and revising; and, finally, editing and proofreading (Figure 15.2).

1. Preliminary Thinking and Research

- If you are writing in response to an assignment prompt, reread it to make sure you understand your instructor's guidelines for the project.

- Brainstorm appropriate topics for questions or problems that interest you personally; confer with your instructor for advice if needed.

- Begin a research log, which is a record of your progress (see Best Practices: Habits of Successful Researchers, page 327).

- Brainstorm possible research questions, and then browse a variety of sources, bibliographies, and indexes to test the availability of resources for answering these questions.

- Decide on a research question, or determine if you need to do more preliminary research before forming a research question.

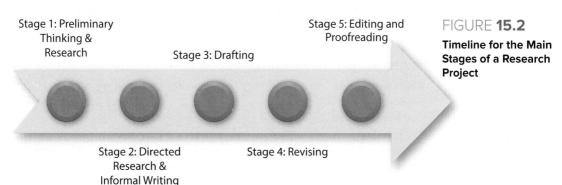

Stage 1: Preliminary Thinking & Research

Stage 3: Drafting

Stage 5: Editing and Proofreading

Stage 2: Directed Research & Informal Writing

Stage 4: Revising

FIGURE **15.2**

Timeline for the Main Stages of a Research Project

2. Focused Research and Preliminary Writing

- Identify keywords to use as search terms.
- Find and evaluate sources and begin your working bibliography.
- Consult a librarian if you need help.
- Write notes about all relevant materials; make printouts and photocopies of the sources you will rely on the most.
- Refine your research question.
- Write a preliminary version of your thesis.

3. Planning and Drafting

See Chapter 23, online, for guidance on using photographs, drawings, tables, and graphs.

- Work out a plan for developing your thesis, such as an outline or flowchart.
- Decide which sources you will draw on to develop each part of the plan.
- Consider what information you could best present visually.
- Begin drafting; *incorporate and cite your sources as you draft.*
- Decide what additional information you need, and do more research.

4. Revising Your Draft

See Chapter 14, pages 305–18, for a systematic approach to editing.

- Refine your thesis if necessary. Rewrite as required to improve your first draft.
- Confer with peers or your instructor to discuss organization and development.
- Do additional research to make underdeveloped sections more specific.

5. Editing and Proofreading Your Draft

For keeping a list of your common errors, see Chapter 14, page 318.

- Read your draft aloud for style, flow within and across paragraphs, and conciseness.
- Review suggestions in Chapter 18 for help with smoothly integrating paraphrases and quotations; edit as needed.
- Run spelling and grammar checks.
- Proofread again, paying special attention to your list of common errors.
- Check the correct MLA or APA formats for in-text and end citations.

Scheduling Your Research Project

With your calendar or planner in hand, assign dates for completing each task in the stages described above. You may want to start at your project's due date and work your way backward.

How much time should you allot to each stage? That depends on the length and complexity of the assignment and the amount of time you have. We offer a schedule below for a four-week project. Adjust the schedule accordingly.

- **Week 1:** Choose a topic, develop a research question, and begin to find and evaluate potential sources.

- **Week 2:** Continue preliminary research, reading and analyzing sources; finalize your research question, and draft a preliminary thesis.

- **Week 3:** Outline and write your first draft. Be sure to incorporate and cite your sources as you draft. Decide what further research you will need to develop this draft, and conduct additional research.

- **Week 4:** Reread and (if possible) get feedback on your draft from a writing tutor, your instructor, or peers; revise your thesis (if necessary), rewrite as needed, edit for style and integration of quotations; proofread and prepare your paper according to your instructor's submission guidelines.

BEST PRACTICES   Habits of Successful Researchers

Following the suggestions below, you can remain in control of any research project.

1. **Plan your work and work your plan.** If you stay on schedule and do some work every day, you will greatly reduce the stress of doing a major research assignment. *Consistent work is the key.*

2. **Take initiative.** The difference between an outstanding research project and a poor one often comes down to motivation. *Get engaged and stay engaged* from the time you get an assignment until it is ready to turn in.

3. **Keep a research log.** Doing research is like making your own path through a forest; if you do not keep track of where you have gone and what you have found, you can waste too much time retracing the same territory. *Keep a log or daily record of your research* as described later in this chapter on page 330.

   See Chapter 2, pages 12–31, for guidance on critical reading.

4. **Employ a range of reading skills.** Researchers change reading styles to suit their purposes. They browse indexes, bibliographies, and the Internet to scout out possible sources. They skim articles and books to get the gist and determine the writer's angle. But when they find a suitable source, they slow down and dive deeper, reading critically and annotating and taking notes.

5. **Avoid premature closure on research and thinking.** The best resources are not necessarily the first ones you find. If your instructor suggests a minimum number of sources, you will need to gather more so you can pick the best ones. Keep an open mind. Do not decide you know the answer to your research question and seek out only the information that supports your answer.

6. **Ask for help.** Librarians want to help, but you have to initiate contact. If you look for information for more than thirty minutes without success, ask a librarian.

How Do I Choose and Narrow a Topic?

An effective research project must focus on a topic that you can do justice to in the allotted space. A typical research project cannot meaningfully examine topics as broad as animal rights, bank regulation, global warming, health care reform, or terrorism. Many complete books have been published on narrower topics than these. To narrow a topic to one that you can usefully explore in a brief assignment, look in some of the places listed below.

- **Course Readings** Many topics for research papers come from course readings. Look at chapter headings and subheadings for ideas about subtopics, and take note of narrower topics while reading. If your text has an index, look at entries and subentries. For example, students researching the dangers faced by illegal immigrants in the Southwest wanted to find out more about the people engaged in human smuggling. To narrow the topic, they looked at the entry for the smugglers, called *coyotes,* and found subentries on coyotes as gangsters, the macho image of coyotes, and the operations of coyotes.

- **Catalogs and Databases** In Chapter 16, Finding Sources, we show how to find resources using library databases and Internet search tools such as Advanced Search in Google. (See pages 343–47 for help with searching databases and using Web search engines.) Reading the titles of articles and other sources on your general topic is a good brainstorming technique, as the titles alone can suggest interesting ways to focus a research question. For example, some titles that came up in a search about college student debt suggest possible questions for further research:

Article Titles Found in a Database	Questions for Research Inspired by the Article Titles in a Database
"A Lifetime of Student Debt? Not Likely"	Should colleges offer courses in budgeting and managing personal finances?
"College Students' Knowledge and Use of Credit"	
"Credit Card Debt, Stress and Key Health Risk Behaviors among College Students"	Is there a relationship between excessive credit card debt and other high-risk behaviors?
"When Life Gets in the Way of Paying for College"	How are high college costs affecting the life choices of young adults?

- **Specialized Reference Sources and Research Guides** You can also find inspiration and background material on your topic in reference works such as specialized dictionaries and encyclopedias (in print and online) and in research guides on college library websites. For more on specialized encyclopedias and reference guides, see pages 339–42 in Chapter 16, Finding Sources.

- **Your Own Interests** Topics for research can be found in your own backyard. For example, a student needing to write a paper on small businesses noticed that a restaurant he frequented had closed recently. He found his topic: the difficulties of running a restaurant. Another student had to write on a class-assigned paper having to do with the environment. Looking around her neighborhood, she noticed many smaller, older homes being torn down, only to be replaced by much larger, new homes that removed existing trees and grass and required more energy to heat and cool. She had found her topic: the teardown epidemic.

How Do I Turn a Topic into a Research Question?

No matter how narrow your topic, you will not write an interesting paper without *a meaningful question that you and your readers will want answered.* Your research question will give you an angle on your topic, something that matters to you.

To turn your topic into a research question, try the following:

- **Use the reporter's questions.** Ask yourself *who, what, where, when, why,* and *how.* On this list, the words most likely to produce a good question are *why* and *how* because these lead to analysis and evaluation. "How did the national debt become so enormous?" is a good example. But do not rule out the other question words because they can also lead to thought-provoking questions like "What personality types are most attracted to social networking sites?"

- **Use critical thinking questions.** Critical thinking is analytical. With "x" being your topic, you might ask

  - What are the causes of "x"? (For example, why are rural areas in the United States losing population?)

  - What are the implications or effects of "x"? (For example, what happens to children's learning when letter grades are abolished?)

  - What larger context or contexts does "x" belong to? (For example, is graffiti in public places art or vandalism?)

  - What issues are people debating about "x"? (For example, on the topic of drug wars in Mexico, people are debating the possible entry of United States contract employees to assist the Mexican government. Is this a good idea?)

  - What do most people think about "x"? How could you question the conventional thinking? (For example, conventional thinking about curing traffic congestion on freeways is to widen them. Is there any evidence that this thinking is wrong?)

- **Look at your topic from different perspectives.** Consider how different groups of people might look at your topic from different angles. On the topic of tearing down houses to build bigger ones: How do developers look at an older neighborhood with small homes, many in disrepair, sitting on valuable land? How is this perspective different from that of a young couple with children who want a large home in a close-in neighborhood? What about members of the neighborhood who want to see their property values go up? Any of these perspectives can furnish an angle on the topic.

Student Example: Turning a Topic into Research Questions

In the case of the student who wanted to write on the topic of teardowns, she could approach research by asking:

■ What are the causes of the teardown epidemic?

■ Why do people want to replace traditional small homes with giant new ones?

■ Why do Americans think they need such large houses?

■ How does this change impact the neighborhood?

■ Who is hurt by this trend and who gains?

■ What is the environmental impact of replacing the smaller houses with bigger ones?

How Do I Manage the Sources I Find?

Once you have your research question, begin gathering sources, assessing their relevance and considering how you might use them. We recommend that you not gather a massive pile of materials to look through later. Instead of one long round of gathering sources, think of this stage as alternating between gathering and reading, note-taking, and reflecting on what you have, and then returning to find more sources as you follow up on leads and questions you encounter. Reading sources as you gather them allows you to develop more interesting research questions and refine your focus. It also helps in developing an understanding of how sources relate to each other and therefore a sense of the big picture you will need to make your own contribution to the topic. Some sources will also direct you to others as you consult the footnotes and bibliographies they provide.

To manage the sources you uncover during this stage, develop a research log, make copies of sources to annotate, and maintain a working bibliography so you can cite sources fully as you draft your project.

Create a Research Log

See Chapter 19, pages 383–84, for help with avoiding accidental plagiarism.

Keeping track of the sources you consult and the notes you take from them is crucial to avoiding plagiarism and writing a successful research project. Maintaining a research log can help you work more efficiently by making it easier for you to keep track of sources and by helping you to avoid having to retrace your steps.

A research log should contain the following:

■ Your research question, which you might revise as you move through the research process.

■ Ideas and questions that occur to you while browsing and reading.

■ Search terms you used, added as you find new terms.

■ Notes about catalogs and indexes you searched on any particular day.

■ A working bibliography with *complete bibliographical information about each source and notes about what the source contains,* why it is credible and worthy of your and your readers' trust, and how you might use it. See more on working bibliographies on pages 332–34 in this chapter.

Your research log could be a notebook, a computer file, or a series of file folders, or it could be housed online in an electronic source management tool like *Zotero*. You may have folders for different kinds of notes (such as search terms or responses to readings).

Make Copies of Sources

Many sources can be downloaded and stored on your computer. However, we advise that you also print out electronic sources and make photocopies of print sources as well. With paper copies you will be able to read more critically, marking up and annotating the more difficult sources. Making copies also helps you avoid problems when sources are no longer available, as when someone else checks out the book you need or an online source is taken down or moved. Student researchers may also need to submit copies of their sources with their project.

BEST PRACTICES   Storing Copies of Your Sources

1. When photocopying a printed source, be sure to get all the information you will need later: Avoid cutting off page numbers. Be sure to photocopy not only the chapters or sections of print sources that will help answer your research question but also the title page and copyright page for books, the front cover or table of contents for magazines and journals, and the top portion of newspaper pages (where the name of the newspaper, the date of publication, and the edition are located). You will need the information on these portions of your sources in order to cite your source fully and accurately.

2. Clip or staple your printed copies, label them clearly, and keep them in a file folder or binder.

3. For electronic magazine and journal articles, save PDF files, rather than HTML files, whenever possible. PDF files include the source's page numbers and illustrations, which you will need when creating your works cited list (sometimes called a references list or bibliography). HTML files include the text but not the page numbers from the original article. The pages will not match up with the pages of the original.

4. Keep all electronic copies of articles in a file folder; label the files and folders clearly so you know at a glance what it contains. Doing so will save you a good deal of time and trouble later.

5. Bookmark your online sources. Keep a list of websites you want to return to in an Internet browser's Bookmarks or Favorites folders. Make one file for all your bookmarks on a single project. Library databases usually also provide some means for storing links to sources, bibliographic information, and even notes on the source. Check the tools or visit the database vendor's website to learn more.

Keep a Working Bibliography

A working bibliography is a list of the publication information for your potential sources, including books, articles, websites, and any other type of source. Keep a separate entry in your working bibliography for each source you might possibly use. The entries in a working bibliography are the same as those in the works cited page or references page that you will eventually include in your final draft. The working bibliography, however, keeps track of all potential sources and all of the sources that you've read regardless of whether you actually use them in the research project itself. It should also include an annotation with notes about the content of the source and your personal responses, such as how you might use the source and how different sources compare or contrast on the same topic or issue.

To save yourself time later on, construct your working bibliography in the appropriate documentation format (see Chapter 20, pages 385–410, for MLA style, and Chapter 21, pages 411–34, for APA style). Doing this will reduce the time and effort required at the end of the project. It will also prevent you from having to track down books and articles you no longer have or search for bibliographic information that you did not know you needed (such as volume numbers or reprint dates).

Citation software like *Zotero* (free on the Web) and *RefWorks* and *EndNote* (sometimes available through your library's webpage or through your school's computer center) can help you format your citations. Be aware, however, that citation software is not perfect. Be sure to check the format against the models in this book or in the style guide you are using in your course before submitting your research project.

Table 15.1 shows the essential information needed for the most common categories of sources.

Annotate Your Working Bibliography

As you skim, evaluate, and read potential sources, annotate your working bibliography by explaining how the source addresses your research question and how you might use the source in your paper. Entries might include the following information:

- **Genre, or Type, of Writing** Is it, for example, an informational article or an argument, an opinion column or an article in a scholarly journal, a book review or an abstract?

- **Author's Credentials** Is the author a reporter, a journalist, or a professor? What are the author's areas of expertise, educational background, credentials, and affiliations?

- **Use of Source** How would you use the source? To answer your research question, provide background information, stimulate thought, represent an alternative viewpoint?

Print Sources	Electronic Sources
Book • Author(s), full name • Book title, subtitle • City where published • Publisher • Year published	**E-book** • Author(s), full name • Book title, subtitle • City where published • Publisher • Year published • Website title if found online (e.g., *Google Book Search* or *Bartleby.com*) • Date of access
Selection from a book or anthology • Author(s), full name • Article or essay title • Book title, subtitle • Editor's name (or editors' names) • City where published • Publisher • Year published • Inclusive page numbers of the article	**Selection from an online book or anthology** • Author(s), full name • Article or essay title • Book title, subtitle • Editor's name (or editors' names) • City where published • Publisher • Year published • Inclusive page numbers of the article (if fixed) • Website title if found online (e.g., *Google Book Search* or *Bartleby.com*) • Date of access

Magazine article
• Author(s), full name
• Article title
• Title of the periodical
• Date of publication (day, month, and year for weekly or biweekly magazines, month and year for monthly magazines)
• Page numbers on which article appears
	E-zine or online journal article
	• Author(s), full name
	• Article title
	• Website title (e.g., *TheAtlantic.com, TIME.com*)
	• Site sponsor (e.g., The Atlantic Monthly Group, Time Inc.; look for this at the bottom of the webpage)
	• Date of publication (day, month, and year). (Skip this information if the name of the Web site is similar to the sponsor's name.)
	• Name of the database (e.g., Academic OneFile)
	• Date last accessed
	• For an article accessed through a database, also include the following:
	  • Name of the database (e.g., Academic OneFile)
	  • Date last accessed

TABLE 15.1

Basic Citation Information for Working Bibliography Entries

TABLE **15.1**
continued

Print Sources	Electronic Sources

Journal article
• Author(s), full name
• Article title
• Journal title
• Volume and issue numbers
• Date of publication (year)
• Article page numbers (inclusive)
	Online journal article
	• Author(s), full name
	• Article title
	• Journal title
	• Volume and issue numbers
	• Date of publication (year)
	• Article page numbers; use *n.p.* ("no page numbers") if not available or permanent
	• Date last accessed
	• For an article accessed through a database, add the following:
	  • Name of the database (e.g., Academic OneFile)
	  • Date last accessed

Newspaper article • Author(s), full name, if listed • Article title • Newspaper title (include city name if not included in title) • Date of publication (day, month, and year) • Edition (such as late edition), if specified • Section name or number, if paginated separately • Page numbers on which article appears	**Online newspaper article** • Author(s), full name, if listed • Article title • Newspaper website title (e.g., *NYTimes.com, LATimes.com*) • Site sponsor (e.g., The New York Times Company, Los Angeles Times; look for this at the bottom of the webpage). (Skip this information if the name of the Web site is similar to the sponsor's name.) • Date of publication (day, month, and year)
	Webpage, website, discussion list, blog • Author(s), full name • Webpage or post title, or subject line (if any) • Title of website, discussion list, or blog • Edition, version (if any) • Site sponsor • Date of publication (day, month, year or whatever is available) • Date last accessed

Student Example: Working Bibliography

Below is an example from a student's working bibliography. The research question was: Is there a difference in the experience of reading online versus reading in a printed book? This entry is for an article in an online journal.

- **Author(s):** Not given
- **Article title:** "Bye Bye Books"
- **Journal title:** *Wilson Quarterly*
- **Volume, issue numbers:** 33:2
- **Publication date (year):** 2009
- **Article page number(s):** 69
- **Date last accessed:** Aug. 8, 2009
- **Database:** Academic OneFile

Notes: This unsigned review article in a journal published by Woodrow Wilson International Center for Scholars assesses two essays in other magazines. The essay by Christine Rosen in *The New Atlantis* magazine is relevant to my question. (The other is not—it's about libraries.) The most interesting point is that Rosen thinks that reading printed books and reading online sources are creating two different classes of people, one with book-reading abilities and the other without. The people with only screen-reading abilities have more dopamine, blocking activity in the part of the brain that "controls judgment and measures risk." Both adults and children who read online books wind up becoming more interested in using the technology than in deep reading. I could use this source to argue that the switch is making people less thoughtful. It doesn't have many facts or references about the dopamine studies, but I could go to Rosen's original article for more of her argument. Rosen is a respected writer and editor.

The advice so far should give you an overview of the research process and how it unfolds. In the next chapter, we take you more deeply into the many options for finding good sources.

CHAPTER 16

Finding Sources

ONE OF THE PURPOSES OF A RESEARCHED WRITING PROJECT IS TO INTRODUCE YOU TO THE WIDE ARRAY OF RESOURCES available to anyone who wants to learn more about virtually any topic. An Internet search engine like Google is just one of many resources. Public, college, and government-sponsored libraries and websites offer resources for finding everything from general information to specialized data and scholarly articles. In addition to finding information, you may want to generate your own through interviews, experiments, and observations. This chapter shows you how to stretch your research skills and take advantage of the variety of resources that will help you find not just any sources but the best sources for your project.

How Do I Conduct a Keyword Search?

No matter what kind of index or database you are searching, you will need to think about the words to use. Begin by thinking of *terms that people commonly use to name or describe your topic*. These are known as **keywords** in searching. Keyword searches are good when starting research because databases look for them not only in titles but anywhere in the text of an article.

Develop a List of Keywords as You Find Them

Start generating a list of keywords by examining your research question for words that name and describe your topic. Add words you encounter when reading as well as synonyms or related

"McMansion" describes a large house of cheap construction. Typical of a McMansion, the house on the left lacks architectural details except on the front.

Courtesy of Carolyn Channell

concepts, and soon you will have a list of words with which to begin. For example, in Chapter 4, we mentioned a student whose topic was the replacement of older homes in her neighborhood by huge new ones. Julie Ross began her search with the term "teardowns," which she had picked up in neighborhood discussions. She also thought of "neighborhood preservation." As she did preliminary research, she uncovered two more terms she would not have thought of on her own: "McMansions" and "mansionization," which describe the houses built after the tearing down. An abridged version of Ross's completed essay appears in Chapter 4, pages 57–60.

List your keywords in your research log. You will add to this list as your reading takes you more deeply into your topic. Using research to find more keywords is just one example of the ways research is like a branching tree. One good search term leads to more.

See pages 330–35 in Chapter 15 on keeping a research log.

Know How to Narrow or Broaden Your Search

Keywords should be specific to your topic, such as the word "teardowns" in the search described above. If the student had begun her search with a word like "houses" or "neighborhood," she would have found hundreds of irrelevant sources. On the other hand, a term like "McMansion" might be too specific as a starting point and yield few results.

- **Combining Search Terms** Most search engines and library databases use what are called Boolean, or logical, operators to narrow or broaden your search. The operators AND and NOT narrow your search, and the operators OR and the wildcard character—usually an asterisk (*) or a question mark (?)—broaden your search. Table 16.1 shows how these operators work.

- **Advanced Searching** Search engines like Google and online indexes and databases such as those on your library's website offer an advanced search option to help you do more precise searching. In Google, Advanced Search is especially helpful in filtering the vast amounts of material on the Web. By going to the Google Advanced Search screen you can choose webpages by keywords, phrases, and possible alternatives to your keywords. You can also filter out pages with words that you know would be irrelevant to your search, and you can limit the search to certain languages, reading levels, websites, or domains. Figure 16.1 shows an example of an advanced search in Google.

See pages 354–55 in Chapter 17 for more about domains.

Boolean Operator	Search Results
AND	Narrows your search. Use to find sources that cover two different concepts. Example: (gas-powered cars) AND (electric-powered cars)
OR	Broadens your search. Use to search for sources using one or more synonyms. Example: (electric cars) OR (fuel cell cars)
NOT	Narrows your search. Use to eliminate irrelevant material. Example: (gasoline-powered cars) NOT (natural-gas powered cars)
*	Broadens your search. Use to search multiple versions of a term (photograph, photographs, photographic, photography) simultaneously. Example: Civil War AND photograph*

TABLE 16.1

Use Boolean Operators to Narrow or Broaden a Search

FIGURE **16.1**

Advanced Search in Google

© Google and the Google logo are registered trademarks of Google Inc., used with permission.

The screen above shows a Google Advanced Search narrowed to find sources about the costs of negative political campaign advertisements, eliminating all commercial sites known as "dot-com" sites, and written at an intermediate reading level.

Keywords versus Subject Words

Many databases will give you the option of searching by keywords as well as subject words. What is the difference? The subject word option limits the search to the vocabulary preferred by the database; it is less forgiving if you do not know whether the database prefers the word "car" or "automobile," just to give an example. However, most databases provide a thesaurus tool that will direct you to the preferred terms. Once you know the right subject words to search by, the results are going to be good sources, highly relevant to your topic.

What Resources Can I Find through My College Library?

The Internet has not caused libraries and librarians to become extinct. In fact, librarians are more necessary than ever as technology keeps adding to the reserves of information available online.

The library's home page is the gateway to all the resources available to you in print and online, including films, audio recordings, artworks, and other media. The

FIGURE **16.2**

Example of a College Library Home Page

example home page in Figure 16.2 gives you an idea of the resources available at one school library; notice the options available under the tab titled "Library Resources."

How Do I Find Reference Works through My College Library?

To many people, research suggests books, but the library online catalog offers other great resources to inspect before heading across campus to cart home a load of books. For example, consider beginning with **reference works.** Reference works can be books or websites but regardless of the media, *they are compilations of information organized for easy reference.* They are therefore excellent entries into any topic. Too often, students overlook reference works or are unaware of their existence, except for the common encyclopedias.

General Reference Works

Before digging into more detailed books and articles, you can get entry-level knowledge on a topic through general reference works such as encyclopedias, dictionaries, and almanacs. Some examples of general reference works are

> *Oxford English Dictionary*
>
> *The World Almanac and Book of Facts*
>
> *Encyclopædia Britannica*
>
> *Wikipedia*

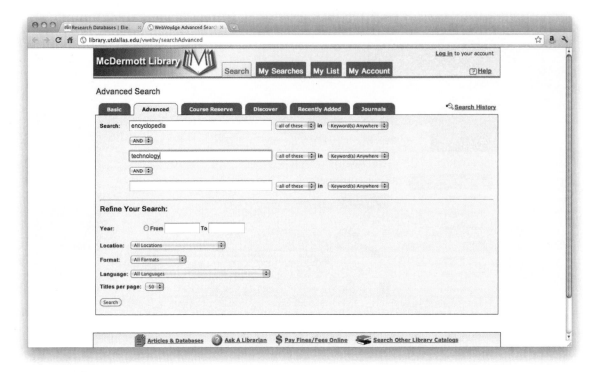

FIGURE **16.3**

Example of a Search for a Specialized Encyclopedia

Many professors prefer that you use general reference works only as starting points for increasing your background knowledge about a topic. General reference works are seldom cited in college writing because the information there is **common knowledge.** That does not mean that everyone knows it; common knowledge is technically defined as *information easily available to anyone from at least three sources.* In the case of *Wikipedia,* many professors advise students to double-check its information because, although it is usually accurate, it is a group-sourced work to which anyone can contribute. For more about *Wikipedia,* see Chapter 17, Evaluating Sources, pages 350–56.

Specialized Reference Works

In contrast to general reference works, libraries also offer more specialized reference works, and these are excellent sources for college papers. You can find them on a wide range of topics, as is evident from these sample titles: *The Almanac of New York City, Encyclopedia of 20th-Century American Humor,* and *Encyclopedia of Multimedia Technology and Networking.* Many are available online through the library, and those that are in print are easy to find. Reference books do not circulate, so you can count on finding them on the shelf.

To find them, do an advanced search in the library's online catalog. As illustrated in Figure 16.3, simply combine your keyword(s) with the term "dictionary," "encyclopedia," "atlas," or "almanac" to find these works online or in your library.

FIGURE **16.4**

Example of an Online Bibliography

Source: NASA

Bibliographies

Bibliographies are lists of sources on a topic. You can often find them in the back of books, where authors list works that they have consulted or that other readers may wish to consult to get more information. You can also search for bibliographies in your library's catalog using the method described above for specialized encyclopedias, or ask your librarian if there are research guides on the subject of your research. Many will be bound books, but increasingly bibliographies are available online, as in Figure 16.4.

How Do I Use a Library Catalog to Find Books and Other Resources?

Your library's home page will have a link to the library catalog, which is an index of all the library's holdings in all media: print, film, digital, and so on. The home page in Figure 16.5 shows what you can expect to find.

Two main categories of resources are books and audiovisual materials.

- **Books** You can search for books by subject, author name, title, keyword, and call number, as shown in the advanced search screen in Figure 16.6.
- **Audiovisual Materials** Audiovisual materials are also found through the catalog and sometimes through a link on the library's home page.

FIGURE **16.5**

Example of a Quick Search in a Library Catalog

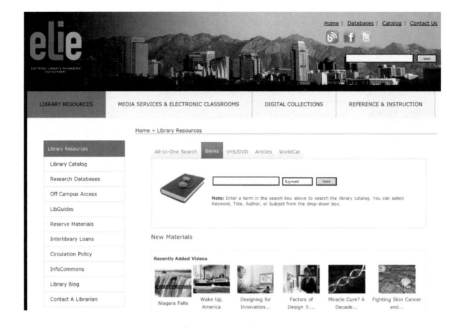

FIGURE **16.6**

Example of an Advanced Library Search

How Do I Use Library Databases to Find Periodicals?

A periodical is any publication that appears on a regular schedule. Newspapers are usually published daily, magazines weekly or monthly, and scholarly journals quarterly. While you can find periodicals through a Web search, the best route to finding reliable articles is through your library's online databases, which are typically accessed through the library's home page. Look for a link under categories like "Find," "Search," or "Research," or look for labels like "articles," "databases," "e-resources," or "online resources."

Thousands of databases are available to researchers, and libraries subscribe to a range, both general and subject-specific. Some of the most popular databases are listed in Table 16.2.

A library's databases will often be listed alphabetically, by title and by subject area, and by popularity. Other search options may also be available, as illustrated below.

Anatomy of a Database Search

Finding articles in subscription databases is a multistep process.

Step 1: Search. Choose one of the databases, and type your keywords in the search field. Advanced search options allow you to narrow or broaden a search. (See Table 16.1 to learn more about Boolean searching.) In a hypothetical search, we wanted to find out if reading literature made people more empathetic. In an

Database	Useful for accessing . . .
Academic OneFile	Articles in both popular and scholarly periodicals for a broad range of disciplines
Academic Search Complete	Articles in both popular and scholarly periodicals for a broad range of disciplines
LexisNexis Academic	Articles from newspapers around the world
ERIC (Education Resources Information Center)	Resources on education from a wide range of sources
JSTOR	Indexes more than 1,000 academic journals and more than 1 million images, letters, and other primary sources, most of them in the humanities and social sciences
MLA International Bibliography	Indexes articles on topics in literature and languages
ProQuest	Indexes a mix of scholarly journals, trade publications, magazines, and newspapers
PsycARTICLES	Articles on topics in psychology
Web of Science	Articles on topics in the sciences

TABLE 16.2

Popular Library Databases

FIGURE **16.7**

**Example of Results
of an Advanced
Search**

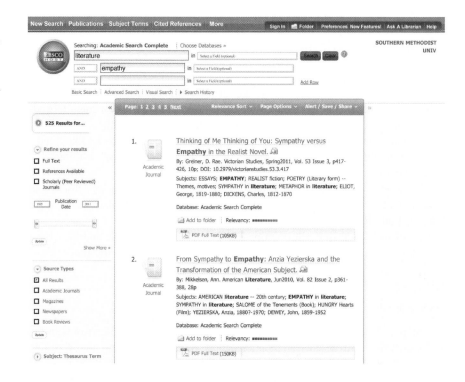

advanced search of Academic Search Complete, we combined the keywords "literature" and "empathy" to get the results shown in Figure 16.7.

Step 2: Survey the results of your search. Figure 16.7 shows some of the titles this search turned up. Some things to note are

Details of the search query appear at the top of the page.

Each entry tells you if the article is available in full text online, and if so, whether in HTML or PDF files.

Results may be filtered further by publication type or by date.

Step 3: Open and examine the entries. Click on a title to find out more about that source. A typical article entry will include useful information such as an abstract of the article and links to related subjects (see Figure 16.8).

How Do I Use the Web to Find Reliable Websites and Online Journals?

The Internet provides access to a vast and ever-changing assortment of files: commercial advertising, personal webpages and blogs, newspapers and magazines, videos and podcasts, images, archives, university projects, government documents, and on and on. In short, the Internet is an unfiltered mass of information. However, it can be an excellent source of free, high-quality information if you know how to use the search engines efficiently and assess the reliability of your results carefully.

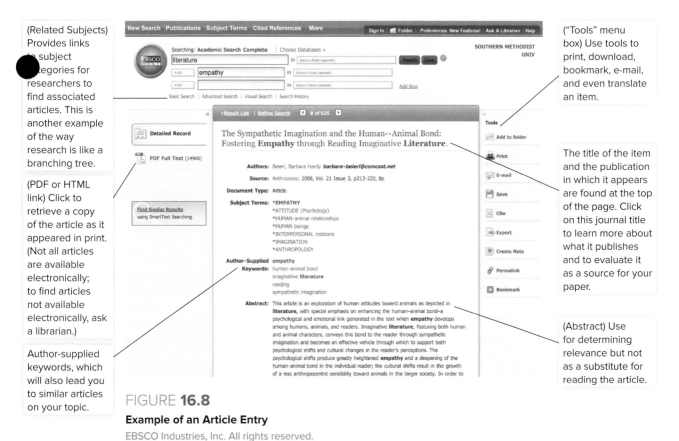

(Related Subjects) Provides links to subject categories for researchers to find associated articles. This is another example of the way research is like a branching tree.

(PDF or HTML link) Click to retrieve a copy of the article as it appeared in print. (Not all articles are available electronically; to find articles not available electronically, ask a librarian.)

Author-supplied keywords, which will also lead you to similar articles on your topic.

("Tools" menu box) Use tools to print, download, bookmark, e-mail, and even translate an item.

The title of the item and the publication in which it appears are found at the top of the page. Click on this journal title to learn more about what it publishes and to evaluate it as a source for your paper.

(Abstract) Use for determining relevance but not as a substitute for reading the article.

FIGURE **16.8**

Example of an Article Entry

CONCEPT CLOSE-UP — Why Care Is Needed in Internet Searching

While the Internet is a great resource, researchers should see it as a complement to the library rather than a substitute, for several reasons:

- Because anyone can publish online, Web sources must be assessed carefully.

- The quantity of information can be overwhelming. The Internet is so large—estimated to contain more than 11 billion webpages—that one can easily waste valuable time sifting through the mass.[1]

- Many excellent sources are available for free through libraries, but you may have to pay to access them on the Internet.

See the criteria for evaluating websites in Chapter 17, pages 353–56.

Use Web-Based Databases and Search Engines

Whether you use Google, Bing, Yahoo!, Exalead, or another online search engine, an ordinary Internet search casts a wide net, often yielding an overwhelming list of unfiltered websites. To narrow your search, try the suggestions below.

---

1. Maurice de Kunder. "The Size of the World Wide Web (The Internet)." *WorldWideWebSize* *.com*. 25 Oct. 2011, www.worldwidewebsize.com/.

Advanced Search Options

See Figure 16.1, page 338, for an example of a Google Advanced Search.

Search engines have an advanced search option that allows you to narrow your search by combining terms. Earlier in this chapter, we discussed how Advanced Search in Google helps refine a search. Most other search engines and databases offer similar advanced search options that allow you to combine terms, search by author, and limit your results to specific media and time frames.

Scholarly Searches on the Internet

Some databases on the Internet, such as Google Scholar, specialize in indexing scholarly publications. Google Scholar is a cross-disciplinary index to journal articles, theses, books, abstracts, and legal sources. The sources are highly credible, coming from academic presses, professional organizations, research centers, and university websites. In Google Scholar, sources are arranged in descending order according to those most cited by other academics.

While Google Scholar can help you locate good sources, be aware that not all the results of your search will be available for free. Many scholarly journals require that you subscribe or pay a onetime fee for single articles. However, if you are enrolled at a school that subscribes to the journal or publishing house, you will have free full-text access through your school library. Many library online resources pages contain a link to Google Scholar so students can use it to search their own library's resources.

Online Periodicals (Newspapers, Journals, and Magazines Not Published in Print)

Articles in some scholarly journals, such as *Kairos: A Journal of Rhetoric, Technology, and Pedagogy,* and magazines, such as *Slate* (www.slate.com), are "born digital" (online only). As such, these sources may or may not be indexed in your library's databases. If you are having trouble finding sources in periodicals that are online-only, ask your school librarian for help. Online periodicals, such as your campus newspaper, are usually searchable by author.

Audiovisual and Archived Materials

Resources available online include the following:

- **Smithsonian Institution** (www.si.edu/researchcenters/). This is a searchable website of the Smithsonian's holdings, museums, encyclopedia, and research projects. You can find podcasts at the Smithsonian Institution site at www.si.edu/podcasts/.
- **Library of Congress** (www.loc.gov). This is also a searchable website. Go to www.loc.gov/library/libarch-digital.html to search the digital collections.

Online Reference Works and Bibliographies

You can find some specialized reference works available free online by searching in the same way we advised searching your library's catalog. In a Google Advanced Search, for example, you could type "encyclopedia" and one or more of your keywords.

An excellent source of online bibliographies is available through the Library of Congress website at www.loc.gov/rr/program/bib/bibhome.html.

How Do I Find Interactive Online Sources?

Many intelligent discussions take place on blogs, e-mail discussion groups, podcasts, and comment threads in online journals. Online communication can provide you with timely and stimulating debate on a topic. Although the style of this writing is less formal than in published work, these writers often have professional credentials and may be considered experts in their field. Always evaluate interactive sources carefully, however; sources in which anyone can join the conversation or in which participants remain anonymous are unlikely to be reliable. Below is a list of source types that may be useful in a college research project:

- **E-Mail Discussion Lists** People subscribe to these lists to participate in conversations on topics of interest. For a good list of groups in the humanities and social sciences, go to H-Net: www.h-net.org/lists/.

- **Blogs** For academic blogs in the humanities, social sciences, sciences, and many other disciplines and subject areas, go to Academic Blogs wiki at academicblogs .org/index.php?title=Main_Page. Nearly all online versions of newspapers have opinion blogs by their columnists. You can also google respected authors and scholars to see if they publish a blog by inserting the author's name (in quotation marks) and adding the word "blog."

How Do I Generate My Own Information?

Sometimes a research question will take you out of the library and into the world—into "the field" as researchers call it—to observe some aspect of the world around us: people and other living things, places, nature, buildings, social behavior, institutions, media, and anything that can be observed, measured, drawn, recorded, photographed, or filmed.

The need for field research arises when a researcher simply cannot answer her or his research question with existing sources. Perhaps the research question involves traffic flow in a village center, but the city has collected no traffic data. Or the question examines employee responses to changes in health care coverage, but no one has surveyed the workers yet. In such cases, the researcher may need to perform his or her own field research.

The methods for performing field research depend upon the researcher's question and the type of information available to answer that question. Can the information be observed? A researcher could observe and record information about traffic flow in a village center. Can the information be collected? In the case of employee responses to changes in health care coverage, the researcher might conduct surveys or even interview individuals.

Field research is a time-consuming and challenging venture. For example, how many days of traffic would the researcher need to observe—or how many employees would need to be surveyed—before readers would consider the field research

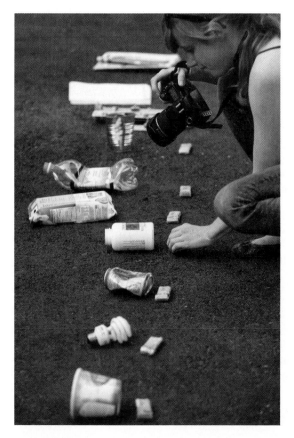

This photograph illustrates part of an experiment conducted through Massachusetts Institute of Technology that began when one woman in Seattle asked the question: "Where does my trash go when I toss it out?" Students attached electronic transmitters to trash in order to trace its journey to its ultimate destination.

© Kevin P. Casey/The New York Times/Redux

complete and accurate? Guidance about research methodology is beyond the scope of this chapter, but it should be required reading for those planning a serious field research project. We offer some brief advice about conducting observations, surveys, and interviews.

Observational Studies

Depending on your topic, firsthand observations can be useful in developing a response to your research question.

Earlier, we described one student's research topic, the tearing down of old homes and their replacement with newer, larger ones. To do research for the project, the student walked the streets of her own neighborhood, noting specifics and taking photographs. More dramatically, a writer can observe undercover, like the anthropologist who posed (with the university's approval) as "Rebekah Nathan," a first-year student living in the dorms and attending classes. Her book, *My Freshman Year* (Cornell UP 2005), aims to give professors an understanding of college from the student's perspective.

Surveys

You may be able to get information on some topics, especially if they are local or campus-related, by doing a survey. Be forewarned, however, that it is difficult to conduct a reliable survey questionnaire. First, there is the problem of designing a clear and unbiased survey instrument. If you have ever filled out an evaluation form for an instructor or a course, you know how problems of clarity can arise. An evaluation might ask whether an instructor returns papers "in a reasonable length of time"; what is "reasonable" to some students may be too long for others.

Second, there is the problem of getting a representative response, that is, a response that represents the whole group the survey is intended to represent. A survey of undergraduates taken at the entrance to the library in the evening might have vastly different results from one taken at the gym in the afternoon.

Surveys can be useful, but seek additional advice on how to design and administer them. You might consult a book like T. L. Brink's *Questionnaires: Practical Hints on How to Avoid Mistakes in Design and Interpretation* (Heuristic Books 2004.)

Interviews

Depending on your topic and research question, personal interviews can be a wonderful source of information. Many people in your community, in your workplace, or at your school are experts on specific topics—from city leaders, to environmental activists, to bank presidents. Most will happily share what they know.

Interviews require time from people's often busy schedules, so it is only polite to ask well in advance for their participation, explain what you will be asking them, and give them an estimate of how much of their time you will need. Once you have determined possible sources, begin a courteous round of phone calls and carefully composed e-mails, continuing until you connect with the right person. If necessary, let the person know that you are willing to conduct the interview by e-mail or phone as well as face-to-face.

Prepare for the interview by having questions ready; if you want to record it, be sure to gain permission. Begin the interview by acknowledging the value of the person's time. Tell the person about your research project but withhold your own position on controversial matters. Take careful and complete notes, including the spelling of the person's name as well as the person's title and credentials. Later, follow up with a thank-you note or e-mail. If multiple people in your class are researching the same topic, avoid flooding any one person with requests for interviews. One or two students could conduct the interview and report to the class, or the interview could take place in the class either in person or through live chat or video.

We suggest that you evaluate sources, covered in Chapter 17, as you do your research rather than making evaluation a separate step. You might spend a day gathering possible sources, and then, before going on to more databases and indexes, look over the ones you have at hand. Evaluating can be as simple as checking a website's home page for information about the credibility of its author or sponsor, or it can be a more time-consuming process of skimming or reading an article or book. Considering the credibility, focus, and angle of the sources you find will help you decide if they are a good fit with your proposed research question and the scope of your project.

For more about how to do interviews, see Chapter 6, Creating Profiles, pages 104–05.

CHAPTER 17

Evaluating Sources

OF THE HUNDREDS OF POTENTIAL SOURCES THAT TURN UP IN A SEARCH, how do you select the ones that will be the best for your project? This is an important question because, like a gourmet dish, your paper will be only as good as the ingredients that go into it. Asking two questions will help you make smart choices: (1) How useful will a source be in helping me achieve my purpose for writing? (2) How credible or reliable are the contents of the source? These two questions are equally important. Although we take them up separately here, you should have both of them in mind as you inspect each possible source.

How Do I Decide If a Source Is Useful?

For a source to be useful, it has to fit well with your topic and purpose. The contents need to be relevant to your research question. You cannot always make that determination from the title alone, but there are other ways to predict usefulness. If an article abstract is available, read it; if one is not, skim the article for subheadings or major subdivisions of the content. For a book, read the introduction, preface, or book jacket; skim the index at the back to see what topics are covered. If a book looks promising, you might want to read a couple of reviews to find more about its coverage and the author's angle on your topic.

Below are a few more questions to ask yourself for determining the usefulness of a source.

- **Is the source's angle on your topic a good fit for your purposes?** For example, a search on the topic of bullying in schools might turn up articles on specific kinds, such as bullying of children with autism or bullying of immigrants. You may decide that you want to take your research in that direction, but be aware that doing so may make other sources you already have irrelevant to the new angle. Also, many databases and search engines will turn up articles and websites from foreign countries. Research from and about foreign countries may or may not be relevant to your topic. The point is: Be aware and make an informed decision.

- **Does the source offer the kinds of information you need in order to accomplish your purpose?** Do you need case studies, experts' analyses of a situation, or arguments on an issue? Do you need statistics or other kinds of data? How in-depth is the information? Does the source go beyond the level of what is considered common knowledge—that is, information readily available from multiple other sources? For any source that looks promising, do a preliminary reading and take some notes about how and where it could contribute to your research project.

■ **If your topic requires up-to-date information and expert opinions, is the source current enough?** There is no "date of expiration" on a source, and you may want to use a classic or historic work, but if your topic needs recent sources, do enough research to find them before settling on a source that may no longer be relevant.

■ **Is the source a good fit with your ability, not just to read but to read critically on your chosen topic?** Sources for college research projects should be challenging, but if a source is so specialized or technical that you have to skip over parts of it, you may not be able to write confidently and clearly about the ideas and information in it. Titles can often clue you to levels of difficulty. For example, a database search for articles on school bullying turned up a title that contained the phrase "longitudinal consequences of adolescent bullying perpetration." If a title contains unfamiliar concepts, chances are the article will too.

See Chapter 2, pages 12–17 for an explanation of critical reading.

How Do I Decide If a Source Is Reliable?

The reliability of a source is as important as its usefulness. A source that your readers will not respect and find credible is not a useful one. A reliable source will provide you with credible information, authoritative opinions, and responsible research.

Journals and books that are published by universities can usually be assumed to be reliable. If a book or journal is published by a university press, it has gone through a process known as "peer review," which means it has been critiqued and approved by other scholars working on the topic. You may trust that the books and journals available through your college or university library are credible because they have been selected by librarians and professors.

However, you will also find many sources from publications more broadly available to the public, such as books from popular presses, magazines, and materials on the Internet. Making responsible choices from these more popular sources requires careful scrutiny and critical thinking. For any source, the following questions will help you decide if you should use it.

Who Is the Author?

Information about the author is one of the best clues to a source's credibility. Whether your source is a book, an article, or a website, you should be able to find some information about the author's credentials, such as

■ Educational background, advanced degrees

■ Professional affiliations, honors, and awards

■ Other publications

Information about the author should not be difficult to find. It is usually printed as a headnote or footnote in articles and in the back pages of books and anthologies. For Internet sites, a tab titled "About Me" or "Biography" provides a link to this important information. Consider whether the person's education and affiliations would indicate that he or she is an authority on the subject. Be suspicious if you cannot find information about an author on the source itself.

If the author is a journalist rather than a scholar or professional in the field of your research, you should consider the credibility of the publication itself, as described below.

Who Published the Source?

Every book, periodical, primary source, and website has a person or organization responsible for its existence. That person or group may be a university press, a government agency, or an organization with an agenda to push or a product to sell. Sometimes a publisher's goals might conflict with the purported topic in a way that may lessen the credibility of the information. To determine the credibility of publishers, ask the following questions:

- **Is the publisher well recognized and respected, such as a major city's newspaper or a newspaper with nationwide circulation?** For books, is the publisher an established house or has the author self-published the book? If the latter, you need to look further into his or her credentials.

- **Who is the sponsor behind the publication?** Is it an institution, like the Smithsonian? Is it an independent research center or a university?

- **Does the publication list its editorial board, including members' credentials?**

- **What other types of articles or other authors does this publisher publish?**

- **What is the purpose or goal of the publication?** You can often find the mission statement of magazines and newspapers near the masthead inside, and websites also provide descriptions of their purpose through an "About" link on the home page. If you are using a library database like Academic Search Complete, the journal or magazine title in the detailed record is a link that takes you to information about the publication, including bias, audience, and topics typically covered.

How Recent Is the Source?

We mentioned this criterion earlier in the chapter, but the date of a source's publication is as important to its credibility as it is to its usefulness. Especially in the social science and science disciplines, information that is more than five years old may well be outdated by more recent research. Although older sources may provide a history of the subject, more recent sources provide more credible information.

How Good Are the Source's Sources?

Just as your instructor expects you to provide documentation for information in your writing, you can expect to find documentation in your sources. When a source includes facts, information, statistics, or quotations, the author should tell you where that information came from. Naming one's sources gives scholarly credibility to work and helps readers in their own research, a professional courtesy. Even if a source does not include footnotes, endnotes, or a list of works cited, you should find specific references to books, articles, and experts woven into the body of the writing.

Will Your Readers Find the Source Authoritative?

Your search may turn up books, articles, and websites aimed at readers of high school age or younger. The information may be perfectly correct, but in making the topic

FIGURE **17.1**

Government Website Dedicated to Prevention of Bullying

www.Stopbullying.gov

accessible, writers may provide a simplified, less specific treatment than they would give to an older readership. Or the audience for the source may simply be the general public. The information in such sources is often common knowledge. In a paper for a college class, you need to go beyond common knowledge to information that justifies citing your source.

Clues to audience are the level of vocabulary and specialized terminology as well as visual elements such as graphics. In Figure 17.1, the titles, links, and visuals, including an embedded video, should clue you to the fact that this government website on bullying is aimed at the general public. This government website gives basic information and does not acknowledge its sources since the information is common knowledge.

Figure 17.2 shows the first page of a bibliography of current academic research on bullying, assembled by faculty at the Curry School of Education at the University of Virginia. Any of the sources listed here would be appropriate for a research paper. More help with evaluating websites follows.

How Do I Evaluate a Website?

No one oversees the reliability or truth of material posted on the Web. Anyone can post almost anything, so users have to take the responsibility for assessing credibility unless the source is a digital version of a reliable print source. All of the questions listed above are relevant to evaluating both print and online sources; however, the questions below are specific to evaluating websites.

FIGURE **17.2**

University Website with a List of Scholarly Research on Bullying

Courtesy of Rector and Visitors of the University of Virginia

What Is the Domain Name Extension?

You can use a website's URL (uniform resource locator) to help you judge reliability. Every URL ends with a period followed by an abbreviation indicating its domain. Some of the more common domain types are

- **Commercial (.com and .net).** "Dot-com" and "dot-net" sites include businesses and their publications and other commercial publications. Magazines on the Web usually are dot-com sites, as are many personal webpages and blogs.

- **Nonprofit organizations (.org).** Most nonprofit organizations use the dot-org extension. These organizations include charities and advocacy groups, such as Autism Speaks (www.autismspeaks.org), which supports research, fund-raising, and general awareness of the facts about autism. Be aware, though, that use of the dot-org extension is open to anyone. On its own, the fact that a website ends in .org does not guarantee that the site is operated by a nonprofit organization or that it is reliable.

- **Educational institutions (.edu).** The "dot-edu" extension is associated with schools, colleges, and universities, including the pages and e-mails of individuals associated with these institutions.

- **Government agencies (.gov and .mil).** "Dot-gov" sites are useful for getting the latest information about any aspect of American government and its agencies. The U.S. military has its own extension, "dot-mil."

■ **Foreign countries (for example, .ca or .uk).** These examples are the domain abbreviations for Canadian and United Kingdom sites, but all countries outside the United States have URLs ending in an abbreviation for the name of the country.

In general, sources located on educational (.edu) and government (.gov or .mil) sites are most likely to be reliable. However, an article posted on a website ending in .edu could be the paper of a first-year student or even a student in high school, so you always need to look further into the source. Sources with other domain name extensions, such as .org, .com, .net, or .biz, should be carefully evaluated to determine if they are credible.

Who Is the Publisher of the Website?

A website that serves as the official online presence of a reputable commercial or non-profit organization is also likely to be reliable. You will need to use critical thinking and reading skills to determine which websites are legitimate. One way to verify that the website is legitimate and reliable is to consider how you arrived at the URL; being directed to a website by a source you already trust indicates that the site is reliable. For example, if the *New York Times* publishes the URL for a company in an article, that's an indication that the website is official and credible. Printed material produced by an organization will also usually include the URL of the organization's website.

The definitive way to determine whether the site is the official arm of the entity it purports to represent is to perform a WHOIS Lookup on the domain and verify that the registration information is real contact information for the organization. Go to www.whois.net and enter the domain name in the WHOIS Lookup box. You can verify that the contact information returned by the lookup corresponds to the organization's real contact information by using phone books or other directories. Be wary of any site for which information about the registered owner is not available.

What Is the Purpose or Agenda of the Website?

Websites of reputable institutions and organizations will provide information about the sponsoring person, organization, or body, as well as their mission and funding, on a page with a name like "About Us," "Philosophy," or "Biography." Links to these pages should be available on the home page, which is usually easily accessible by a link on every page on the site.

Does the Author Have Appropriate Credentials?

If articles on a website are signed, check to see if the author has credentials that would ensure he or she has some authority on the topic. If the article is unsigned, the credibility rests on that of the publisher.

Has the Website Been Updated Recently?

Look for the date of the most recent update, commonly located at the bottom of the page. If no one has updated a website in more than a year, it may be abandoned or at least neglected. Avoid websites that offer undated information.

Has the Author Cited Sources for His or Her Information?

Has the author documented his or her sources with links or with footnotes and a works cited or references list? If there are links, do they work? Do the links take you to high-quality sources?

FIGURE **17.3**

This hoax website fooled at least one professional writer who included it as a legitimate source. What clues indicate that it is satire?

Is the Website Possibly a Hoax?

It is always possible that on the face of things, a website will appear legitimate but actually be satirical or deceitful (see Figure 17.3). You should not be fooled if you have carefully answered the above questions and used some common sense. Having a slightly skeptical attitude is good insurance against fraud.

CHAPTER 18

Incorporating Source Materials

SOURCE MATERIALS ARE INTEGRAL TO RESEARCHED WRITING. Reading sources generates questions, helps you find an angle, and gives you information and ideas for developing your paper. While some sources will make major contributions and others play lesser roles, all the sources taken together form a foundation for writing with your own voice and purpose. As you read about your topic, a big picture starts to take shape, and your knowledge and confidence grow. Eventually, you are ready to enter the conversation, asserting your own thesis and bringing in sources to develop and support it.

What Does It Mean to Enter the Conversation?

Beginning research is like entering a conversation on your topic. When you write using sources, you join a conversation that includes ideas from the sources you cite, your interpretation of what these other voices are saying, your presentation of your own views, and the responses of people who read your completed paper.

BEST PRACTICES Read While You Research

Take time to read *while* you research. Reading is a part of research, not something you do after you have gathered up a stack of sources. The following are good reasons to read the sources as you find them:

1. **One good source leads to another.** Writers will refer to others who have written on your topic. You will find these references in the body of a reading and/or in a bibliography at the end.
2. **You will gradually learn the angles and range of opinions on your topic,** so when it is time for you to form your own thesis, you will be operating with full knowledge of the conversation already out there.
3. **You will be able to compare the sources,** deciding which have the best information and arguments to use in your paper.

Reading while you research can start lightly with skimming, getting a quick overview of the genre, author, and angle of each potential source. Following are some questions you could ask while skimming, or previewing, sources. Chapter 2 (pages 12–31) gives you more information about how to preview sources and how to read them critically if you decide to use them in your writing.

© Indeed/Getty Images, RF

How Does Informal Writing Engage Me in the Conversation?

When you are involved in an oral conversation, you listen to what others have to say, you respond, and you ask questions. In much the same way, while you are reading, you should not simply read to hear what a writer is saying but think about it, respond to it, and question it. Writing informally helps you engage with sources by preserving your responses and questions before, during, and after you read.

How Do I Annotate to Engage with a Source?

Annotating means taking notes on the source itself—in the margins, between the lines, or on sticky notes if you prefer not to mark up your copy. Annotating supports critical reading, as explained in Chapter 2, in the Art of Questioning box on pages 20–21. When annotating, you interact with the source, firming up your understanding of what it says as well as what it implies. Students who mark up their sources have better comprehension than those who don't and therefore are able to use sources more competently.

Annotations support research by helping form the big picture of the conversation on your topic, especially if you mark up passages with notes about how author "X" compares with authors "Y" and "Z" on similar points. Annotations can point to places in a text that offer leads to other sources you might want to consult.

The reading that follows is a newspaper article on the topic of fast versus slow reading. Informative newspaper articles are good starting points for research because they present new research in an accessible style and they name people who have written on your topic, thus providing you with leads for further research.

Our annotations show common kinds of notes readers make to themselves in the margins to help make good use of a source.

The full text of Newkirk's argument can be found online at www.ascd.org/publications/educational-leadership/mar10/vol67/num06/The-Case-for-Slow-Reading.aspx.

R E A D I N G **18.1**

New Hampshire Professor Pushes for Return to Slow Reading

HOLLY RAMER

Holly Ramer is a writer for the Associated Press news service. This article appeared in several major newspapers in June 2010.

1 Slow readers of the world, uuuuuuuu. . .niiiiite!

2 At a time when people spend much of their time skimming websites, text messages and e-mails, an English professor at the University of New Hampshire is making the case for slowing down as a way to gain more meaning and pleasure out of the written word.

3 Thomas Newkirk isn't the first or most prominent proponent of the so-called "slow reading" movement, but he argues it's becoming all the more important in a culture and educational system that often treats reading as fast food to be gobbled up as quickly as possible.

Look for the article by Newkirk.

4 "You see schools where reading is turned into a race, you see kids on the stopwatch to see how many words they can read in a minute," he said. "That tells students a story about what reading is. It tells students to be fast is to be good."

This is quotable.

5 Newkirk is encouraging schools from elementary through college to return to old strategies such as reading aloud and memorization as a way to help students truly "taste" the words. He uses those techniques in his own classroom, where students have told him that they've become so accustomed to flitting from page to page online that they have trouble concentrating while reading printed books.

6 "One student told me even when he was reading a regular book, he'd come to a word and it would almost act like a hyper link. It would just send his mind off to some other thing," Newkirk said. "I think they recognize they're missing out on something."

Important: Clarifies definition of slow reading. Also, the last part is quotable.

7 The idea is not to read everything as slowly as possible, however. As with the slow food movement, the goal is a closer connection between readers and their information, said John Miedema, whose 2009 book "Slow Reading" explores the movement.

Look for this book by Miedema.

8 "It's not just about students reading as slowly as possible," he said. "To me, slow reading is about bringing more of the person to bear on the book."

Miedema, a technology specialist at IBM in Ottawa, Ontario, said little formal research has been done on slow reading, other than studies on physical conditions such as dyslexia. But he said the movement is gaining ground: the 2004 book "In Praise of Slow: How a Worldwide Movement Is Changing the Cult of Speed" sprang from author Carl Honore's realization that his "rushaholism" had gotten out of hand when he considered buying a collection of "one-minute bedtime stories" for his children.

Another possible source.

In a 2007 article in *The Chronicle of Higher Education,* the executive humanities editor at Harvard University Press describes a worldwide reading crisis and calls for a "revolution in reading."

Another possible source. Author is Lindsay Waters.

"Instead of rushing by works so fast that we don't even muss up our hair, we should tarry, attend to the sensuousness of reading, allow ourselves to enter the experience of words," Lindsay Waters wrote.

Though slow, or close reading, always has been emphasized at the college-level in literary criticism and other areas, it's also popping up in elementary schools, Miedema said.

Mary Ellen Webb, a third-grade teacher at Mast Way Elementary School in Durham, N.H., has her students memorize poems upward of 40 lines long and then perform them for their peers and parents. She does it more for the sense of pride her students feel but said the technique does transfer to other kinds of reading—the children remember how re-reading and memorizing their poems helped them understand tricky text.

Here is an example of how to teach slow reading.

"Memorization is one of those lost things, it hasn't been the 'in' thing for a while," she said. "There's a big focus on fluency. Some people think because you can read quickly . . . that's a judge of what a great reader they are. I think fluency is important, but I think we can err too much on that side."

This assumption might be shared by my readers.

It's all about balance, said Patti Flynn, an assistant principal in Nashua, N.H., and mother of a 10-year-old girl.

Her school has offered, and her daughter has participated in, numerous reading challenges that reward students for reaching certain milestones—a pizza party for a class that reads 100 books, for example. Though such contests may appear to emphasize speed rather than reading for pleasure or comprehension, they also are good incentives for children who weren't motivated to read, she said. The challenges have encouraged parents to make reading a priority at home, Flynn said.

This woman has a slightly opposing view.

"The goal shouldn't be to be whipping through a certain number of pages, the goal should be to make sure kids are gaining some conceptual understanding," she said.

Her daughter, Lily, said she considers herself a "medium-speed" reader and had to increase her speed to finish about 10 books for her classroom's 100-book challenge. But she said she enjoyed the process and feels like she understood and remembers what she read.

"It was fun," she said.

9

10

11

12

13

14

15

16

17

18

19

Holly Ramer. "New Hampshire Professor Pushes for Return to Slow Reading." The Associated Press, 17 June 2010. Reprinted by permission.

How Can a Research Log or a Notebook Help Me Engage with My Source?

Although marginal annotations can include personal responses, it is better to use a notebook or file on your computer to write more expanded informal responses. The more you write to interact with your sources before you use them in your own writing, the more comfortable you will be when it comes time to weave their voices and ideas into your paper. Following are some examples of the kind of background writing that helps you rehearse your use of sources. Performing these actions immediately after reading a source will save you time later because you will have generated raw material for some of your draft.

THE ART OF QUESTIONING — What Do I Think about What the Source Is Saying?

Assert your own voice by freewriting in your research log or writer's notebook in response to questions such as the following:

- What do I agree with here, and why? What do I know that causes me to agree?

- What do I disagree with here, and why?

- What would I like to know more about, checking for the accuracy of the writer's information?

- What other context or perspective might be possible on the views expressed here?

- What other sources or writers have I found that speak on the same topics, and how do these sources compare?

Below are some example notebook entries in response to Ramer's article:

I wonder how college students would respond to being asked to memorize poems and read aloud, as Newkirk has his students do.

Notes can pose a question.

I agree with the teacher who says there is too much emphasis on speed. If students learn to read everything fast, they read their own writing too fast to critique and catch their errors.

Notes can agree or disagree with a writer or speaker.

In Newkirk's own article, he disapproves of pizza parties and silly stunts like teachers wearing pajamas to school just to reward kids for reading huge numbers of books. He would disagree with this principal.

Notes can show agreement or disagreement between sources.

This reading reminds me of how Nicholas Carr ("Is Google Making Us Stupid?") compares digital reading to jet skiing and deep reading to scuba diving.

Notes can show your observations of similarities between sources.

How Do I Draw Connections between Sources?

To use your sources well, you must not use each in isolation, taking them up one at a time. You will need to blend them, a critical thinking skill known as **synthesizing,** which means *bringing together.* A good research paper uses multiple sources in any one section, even any one paragraph. (Synthesis is covered in Chapter 9, Comparing Perspectives, pages 168–200.)

In a good research paper, the writer weaves material from multiple sources into a coherent whole.

© Tony Sweet/Digital Vision/Getty Images, RF

As you read a second source, a third, a fourth, and so on, use informal writing to note where authors talk about the same topics. Notice places where they agree or disagree. It is possible that sources will contradict each other; this too, is worth noting and pursuing in further research.

Many kinds of informal writing can help you manage the job of synthesis: We have already suggested annotations and notebook entries. You could also create a chart, like the one shown on page 189 in Chapter 9. All of these methods can help you with the difficult task of organizing ideas across sources.

The example notes that follow illustrate how writers can use their notebooks to make connections between points in multiple sources. The student paper in Chapter 20, pages 404–10 shows how these notes helped the writer synthesize his sources.

S T U D E N T E X A M P L E **Notes**

Note: Three English professors bring up this idea: Education and books should help us escape the hectic pace of life and slow down and reflect on our lives.

Mark Edmundson, English professor, U. Va.
Says students "skate fast over the surfaces of life." But "To live well, we must sometimes stop and think, and then try to remake the work in progress that we currently are. There's no better place for that than a college classroom where, together, we can slow it down and live deliberately, if only for a while." (no pages)

Mark Edmundson

Thomas Newkirk, English professor, U. of New Hampshire
Schools need to take a stand for an alternative to an increasingly hectic digital environment where so many of us read and write in severely abbreviated messages and through clicks of the mouse. He says "there is real pleasure in downshifting, in slowing down. We can gain some pleasures and meanings no other way." (no pages)

A good way to draw connections between sources is to paraphrase and directly quote passages from different sources that touch on similar points. The highlighting here shows specific points that run across the three sources.

_____

Mark Bauerlein, English professor, Emory U.

Says that reading should be a relief from stress and a way to help us put our lives into better perspective: "Books afford young readers a place to slow down and reflect, to find role models, to observe their own turbulent feelings well expressed, or to discover moral convictions" (58).

Writing informally to note where sources converge in their thinking, or where they diverge, will help you put them together in a plan of your own. The next sections of this chapter address the many ways you can employ sources, working them gracefully into your own writing and documenting them correctly.

What Roles Can Sources Play in My Writing?

As you prepare to start drafting, think of the ways you can use your sources. Remember that sources are integral to the construction of your thinking and the development of your ideas. Bring your sources in as you draft, and cite them correctly so you do not have to find the needed bibliographic information later. Consider the many contributions sources make to academic and workplace writing:

1. Sources provide the background knowledge you need in order to know if your research question is important or already settled.

2. Sources provide awareness of the climate of opinion on an issue, so you can explain opposing views.

3. Sources provide detailed information that makes any kind of writing specific and interesting. Your readers may need background information, concept explanations, and examples that illustrate your topic.

4. In an argument, sources provide evidence and opinions that the writer may use for support.

5. The sources we use not only provide evidence and opinions but also give legitimacy to our writing. Without sources, writing appears untrustworthy.

6. Using a range of sources shows the writer has inquired thoroughly into a topic and considered a wide spectrum of evidence and opinion in order to arrive at a thesis.

What Are My Options for Bringing in Source Material?

To incorporate source information into a paper or project, a writer has three options: direct quotations, paraphrases (also called indirect quotations), and summaries. In the first method, words are taken exactly as they appear in the source, with any alterations noted. In the second, paraphrase, the source material is reworded, and in the third, source material is both reworded and shortened. Each method is appropriate to specific circumstances; making the right choice depends on your purpose as well as the content of the material you plan to include.

Using Direct Quotations

Direct quotations are an efficient way to present material from a source. However, of the three options, direct quotation is the one you should use least. A great deal of source material is not worth quoting directly, and overuse of direct quoting can create a patchwork of voices in your paper, drowning out your own voice. It can also create a choppy, incoherent style if you don't set quotations up with enough context from the source. A good rule of thumb is that no more than 10 percent of a paper should be direct quotations: 100 words in a 1,000-word paper. So when should you use them?

Reserve direct quotations for the words of people whose credentials and opinions will lend weight to your paper or for the words of sources you want to dispute or analyze. You might also use direct quotations for

- Strongly or uniquely worded statements of opinion where capturing the colorful voice of the speaker matters to the point you are making.

- Literary turns of phrase, such as metaphors and analogies, where the style is part of the message.

- Highly technical language, such as professional jargon, where no easy translation is possible.

The example passage below makes good use of a direct quotation.

Appropriate Use of Direct Quotation to Present an Opinion from a Source

Mark Bauerlein, an Emory University professor of English, believes teenagers have stunted their intellects by limiting their use of the Internet and other information technology to peer-to-peer socializing. Although he has called them "the Dumbest Generation," he says, "These kids have just as much intelligence and ambition as any previous cohort, but they exercise them too much on one another. They are building youth culture into a ubiquitous universe, and as ever youth culture is a drag on maturity" (22).

Bauerlein, Mark. "Generation Text." *America,* 12 October 2009, americamagazine. org/issue/710/new-media/generation-text.

Using Paraphrases

Paraphrases are more common in professional researched writing than direct quotations. Unlike quoting, paraphrasing and summarizing let you maintain your role as the paper's dominant voice. Also, readers find direct quotations distracting when there is no good reason for using someone else's exact words instead of your own.

Paraphrase Facts or Background Information

Paraphrase when presenting information such as facts found in reference books, websites, and newspaper articles where the writer is a reporter or journalist, not an expert whose credentials would bolster your paper's credibility. Rewriting an informative passage in your own words may seem like extra work, but it is better to make the effort than to use direct quotations for passages that simply provide information. The following box gives advice on how to write a good paraphrase.

BEST PRACTICES   Writing Paraphrases

Follow these steps to create your own paraphrase:

1. Read the entire source or section. You cannot write a good paraphrase of a passage you have taken out of context. Surrounding sentences will provide information essential for understanding the sentence you are paraphrasing; to make the idea clear to your readers, you will need to set up the context so that your readers will understand how the passage fits into the source.

2. Read the passage and surrounding sentences several times, including surrounding text, until you understand it and its context. Annotate it. Look up any words that are even slightly unfamiliar to you.

3. Put the text away so you will not be able to look at it while you try to say it in your own way. Recall the main ideas, and try to put each one into your own words and your own wording. A paraphrase must not be an echo of the original's sentence patterns with synonyms plugged in. That is really a form of plagiarism since it involves "stealing" the author's sentence pattern. You may want to break up complex sentences into shorter, simpler ones that make the idea easier to comprehend.

4. If the passage refers to or depends on surrounding material for meaning, put that information into your paraphrase. For example, you may need to replace a pronoun with a noun for clarity.

5. Do not feel that you must find a substitute word for every ordinary word in the passage. For example, if a passage has the word *children,* don't feel you have to say *kids.*

6. Go back and check your paraphrase against the original to see if you have accurately represented the full content of the original passage. Make adjustments as needed.

See Chapter 19, pages 383–84, for examples of plagiarism in poorly written paraphrases.

A paraphrase should not retain the same syntax, or sentence patterns, as the original, even if the vocabulary is different. A paraphrase that imitates the original sentence is technically plagiarism and does not improve comprehension of the ideas. A good paraphrase is likely to be as long as, or even longer than, the original passage, especially if it expresses the same meaning.

Below is an example of a passage from a draft in which the writer uses a long direct quotation. Note that the quoted material is not memorable in style. The wording is not worth reproducing as a direct quotation.

> Food writer Mark Bittman argues that people should take a more sustainable approach to eating: "To reduce our impact on the environment, we should depend on foods that require little or no processing, packaging, or transportation, and those that efficiently convert the energy required to raise them into nutritional calories to sustain human beings" (19).

A revised version uses all of Bittman's point but not any of his exact wording. As you see here, paraphrasing allows you to keep your own voice, vocabulary, and style in the writing. When you paraphrase, you "own" the material, explaining it as you understand it.

> Food writer Mark Bittman believes people need to take a sustainable approach to eating. We should shrink our environmental food footprint by choosing locally grown foods that require minimal processing and packaging. And, in order that energy not be wasted in the production of junk food, he says we should choose nutritious foods that give us a good return in energy for the energy it takes to produce them (19).
>
> Bittman, Mark. *Food Matters: A Guide to Conscious Eating.* Simon & Schuster, 2009.

In the two examples below, the draft passage uses a direct quotation to present purely factual information, while the revised version uses a paraphrase of the basic information in the quoted material. Writers should avoid direct quotations of facts.

Draft Version: Inappropriate Use of a Direct Quotation

> Human invention of laws resulted from the need to regulate water use in dry areas such as the Tigris-Euphrates Valley. According to Michael Mares, "our very system of written laws dates back to Hammurabi, king of Babylonia from 1792 to 1750 B.C., whose first laws were written to deal with the use of water for agricultural purposes" (xxix).

In the revision below, the information has been paraphrased.

Revised Version: Appropriate Use of Paraphrase

> The human invention of law began under King Hammurabi, who ruled Babylonia from 1792 to 1750 B.C. In the arid region of the Tigris-Euphrates Valley, the Babylonian people needed laws to regulate their use of water, a precious commodity for the development of agriculture (Mares xxix).
>
> Mares, Michael A. *Encyclopedia of Deserts.* U of Oklahoma P, 1999.

A paraphrase must completely rework the wording and sentence patterns of the original passage. Students can commit plagiarism inadvertently if they do not double-check paraphrases for too much similarity to the wording of the source.

For additional guidance on paraphrasing, see Chapter 19, pages 383–84, and Chapter 2, page 24.

Blend Direct Quotations with Paraphrases

A good way to avoid overly long quotations and to blend your own voice with some key phrases from a source is to embed the quotable bits into paraphrases, as shown in the example below. When you blend paraphrase and direct quotation so that the quoted words are integral to your own sentence, no punctuation is needed to set off the quoted words.

> Bauerlein disdainfully describes the world of thirteen- to seventeen-year-olds as a "dynamic 24/7 network" in which "teen activity accrues more and more significance" as the events of the day "are recorded and circulated" (22).

Using a Summary

When you are working with the extended ideas of one of your major sources, you may need to include more than a few quotations and paraphrases in your paper to do the idea justice. In books, it is common to find passages that summarize the entire argument of a source, often with some discussion woven in. Therefore, it is reasonable in some cases to devote one to two paragraphs to a summary, depending upon the length of your paper and the relevance of the source. If you do choose to summarize, make sure that the summary contains only content relevant to your paper and that you comment upon the relevance of the source.

The following Best Practices box gives advice on the steps necessary to writing a good summary. Summary writing is also covered in Chapter 2, pages 26–27.

BEST PRACTICES Summarizing a Source

In your notebook, first write down the author, title, and other source information you'll need for your works cited list (for MLA—Modern Language Association) or list of references (APA—American Psychological Association). Then follow these suggestions for writing summaries.

1. Read and annotate the entire source, noting the main points and the key supporting points.
2. For long texts, break them into subdivisions. Working with one subdivision at a time, write paraphrases of the main ideas in each. Try working from memory as you write, and check the original later for accuracy. Decide which specific facts would be appropriate to include, depending on the purpose of your summary.
3. Make sure that your sentences restate the points; do not just describe the original passage, as in "The author talks about. . . ." Instead, say what the author's point is.

4. You may include brief direct quotations, but avoid quoting whole sentences. That is not efficient.

5. Do not try to include all of the figurative language and tone of the original. Write the summary in your own voice, not in imitation of the author's voice and style.

6. Keep your summary objective; reserve your commentary for follow-up if you use the summary as part of your paper.

7. Edit your summary to reduce repetition and to combine points into single sentences where possible.

A good summary restates the author's points rather than simply describing what the author does. It provides enough detail so that the readers of the summary have something close to the experience of reading the original, but in a more concise version.

Below we offer a passage from a source that is represented in summary form in the student example paper in Chapter 20 on pages 404–10. If the passage is long and difficult, as is the one below, it helps to annotate it with notes to yourself, as we demonstrate here, before attempting to draft the summary.

Refresh memory on Socrates: 469–399 B.C. Philosopher who engaged the young men of Athens in debating philosophical questions about virtue and truth. Felt the unexamined life is not worth living.

This section of the reading introduces the question of how well young people know themselves, really, versus how others have defined them.

This paragraph acts as a transition into the role of college in finding identity.

Original Passage with Annotations from "Dwelling in Possibilities" by Mark Edmundson

If Socrates looked out on the current dispensation, what would he see? He'd see the velocity and the hunger for more life, faster, faster—sure. But given his interests, he'd notice something else, too. He'd see that by the time students get to college, they have been told who they are and what the world is many times over. Parents and friends, teachers, counselors, priests and rabbis, ministers and imams have had their say. They've let each student know how they size him up, and they've let him know what they think he should value. Every student has been submitted to what Socrates liked to call *doxa,* common sense, general belief.

And a student may be all the things the people who raised her say she is; she may want the things they have shown her are worth wanting. She may genuinely be her father and mother's daughter. But then again, she may not.

I think he means the order of things, how things are on campuses.

The source of orthodox?

Socrates encouraged questioning common beliefs, for which he was seen as stirring up trouble.

Here, the author is suggesting that reading the great authors helps students see beyond the common views they may have grown up believing.

The primary reason to study Blake and Dickinson and Freud and Dickens is not to become more cultivated, or more articulate, or to be someone who at a cocktail party is never embarrassed (but can embarrass others). The ultimate reason to read them is to see if they may know you better than you know yourself. They may help you to cut through established opinion—*doxa*—about who you are and what the world is. They may give you new ways of seeing and saying things, and those ways may be truer for you than the ones that you grew up with. Genuine education is a process that gives students a second chance. They've been socialized once by their parents and teachers; now it's time for a second, maybe a better, shot. It's time—to be a little idealizing about it—for Socrates to have a turn.

This is clever. He knows that some people read books for superficial reasons, for the status.

Should college change you, and make you question prior beliefs?

This section shows why students should read the great writers for wisdom and new understandings of the world.

After noting the major subdivisions and writing paraphrases of them, the student put the paraphrases together smoothly to make the summary below. (The bibliographic information for this essay by Mark Edmundson appears in the works cited list of the student's paper, on page 410.) Note how the following summary also makes use of several direct quotations to convey some of the original language of the source.

Summary

Edmundson imagines that if Socrates were around today, he would worry about the same thing Edmundson worries about—the fast pace of college students' lives and how well they really know themselves and the world. All through their years of school, they've been influenced by adults in their lives—parents, teachers, and clergy—who have told them how to define themselves and interpret the world. Edmundson says these interpretations may be true, but then again, they may not. That is why education and books are important. They challenge "established opinion" and what seems like "common sense" but may not be true. Thus, books give students new perspectives about themselves and the world that may be truer for them than what they had always been told was true.

How Do I Acknowledge, Integrate, and Cite My Source Materials?

When using source information, whether factual data or the opinions and arguments of other people, writers must acknowledge each source and integrate the material smoothly into their own surrounding text. In scholarly and professional writing, they must also cite their sources.

Mark Edmundson. "Dwelling in Possibilities." *Chronicle of Higher Education,* 14 Mar. 2008, chronicle.com/article/Dwelling-in-Possibilities/7083.

Acknowledging sources means *giving credit to a source for paraphrased ideas, direct quotations, and any information that is not common knowledge.* Acknowledging can include citing, as discussed below, but in some genres that do not include documentation, just mentioning a name serves as an acknowledgment. To fail to acknowledge a source is to steal from it, to plagiarize. In magazines, newspapers, trade books, and online writing, authors must acknowledge their sources of information. Authors who do not are considered unethical and irresponsible.

Integrating sources means *blending in source material alongside your own words* so that your paper flows, with no gaps in thought or expression. Smooth integration requires writing in your own voice and signaling readers when you introduce others' words and ideas.

Citing sources (also called documenting) means *providing written information about a source's author, title, date, and place of publication,* in some cases including when and how you found the source. Documentation is not a standard feature in the popular press, but it is usually required in academic articles and scholarly books. While there are many documentation styles, this book covers the two most common ones: those of the Modern Language Association and American Psychological Association.

The following paragraph demonstrates the basic elements of acknowledging, integrating, and citing sources. It uses the MLA documentation form.

Integrates the source material by leading into the history of zombie films.	The modern zombie movie has been around for almost forty years and, like other genres, it has gone through periods of feast and famine. According to film scholar Darryl Jones, the genre was born in 1968 with the release of George A. Romero's *Night of the Living Dead* (161), in which a motley group of people, led by an African American antihero named Ben (Duane Jones), must spend the night in a besieged country house, waiting for the authorities to arrive. When the county militia finally does show up, its first response is to shoot and kill Ben, the only survivor of the supernatural abattoir. The violence and graphic images in this low-budget horror film were unprecedented at the time, and the movie functions largely as a metaphor for the atrocities of Vietnam and racism. Called "hippie Gothic" by film theorist Joseph Maddrey (51), *Night* protests the war by graphically confronting audiences with the horrors of death and dismemberment and by openly criticizing those who use violence to solve their problems. The politically subversive film gained a cult following and eventually made more than $30 million worldwide ("Business Data for *Night*").

Left margin annotations:
- Integrates the source material by leading into the history of zombie films.
- Documents, or cites, the source by giving the page number.
- Integrates the source by paraphrasing factual information rather than overrelying on direct quotations.

Right margin annotations:
- Acknowledges the source by giving the expert's full name on first mention, along with some identification or credentials.
- Integrates the upcoming source by setting up the context of social unrest in the 1960s.
- Unique words taken from a source must be in quotation marks.
- Citations can be placed before the end of a sentence to show precisely what was taken from the source.
- Documents, or cites, the source of this information by title because there is no author.

Works Cited

"Business Data for *Night of the Living Dead*." *Internet Movie Database*. amazon.com, 3 May 2006, www.imdb.com/title/tt0063350/.

Jones, Darryl. *Horror: A Thematic History in Fiction and Film*. Arnold, 2002.

Maddrey, Joseph. *Nightmares in Red, White and Blue: The Evolution of the American Horror Film*. McFarland, 2004.

Kyle Bishop. "Dead Man Still Walking: Explaining the Zombie Renaissance." *Journal of Popular Film and Television*, vol. 37, no. 1, 2009, pp. 16–25.

What Are the Options for Acknowledging Sources?

Acknowledging means giving credit. The first time you introduce an important speaker, give the person's first and last name; thereafter, use last names only. Give credentials such as publications or university affiliations.

Acknowledge Sources with Short Phrases or Sentences

You can acknowledge a source in a short phrase, known as a signal phrase because it signals the connection between the material and its source. You can also use a complete sentence to acknowledge a source. (The examples below include citations in MLA form.)

The two introductory phrases below, each followed by a comma, provide the name and expertise of the source. (Citations will be explained briefly in this chapter on pages 376–77 and in detail in Chapters 20 and 21.)

Signal Phrase to Identify a Source

According to Maryanne Wolf, a reading expert from Tufts University, "Typically when you read, you have more time to think" than when you look at images or listen to stories (qtd. in Dzubow).

You should also use signal phrases to acknowledge paraphrased material from a source.

According to Maryanne Wolf, a reading expert from Tufts University, reading is an activity that allows the brain more time for thinking than does listening to a story or watching it in a movie or television show (qtd. in Dzubow).

In this example, Wolf is not the author of the source. See Chapter 20 (page 388) and Chapter 21 (page 415) for how to cite sources used by your sources, known as indirect sources. Dzubow is an online source, so no page number is available.

Even if you have paraphrased the words or ideas of a source found in your source, MLA requires that you use "qtd. in" in your parenthetical citation.

You can also acknowledge sources with a complete sentence. In this case, however, you must use a colon rather than a comma between your words and those of the source. The colon is needed here to prevent a comma splice. A comma splice before a quotation is a common punctuation error.

Complete Sentence to Identify a Source

Maryanne Wolf, director of the Center for Reading and Language Research at Tufts University, explains why reading is more stimulating to the brain than hearing speech or looking at images: "Typically when you read, you have more time to think" (qtd. in Dzubow).

In this example, the complete sentence provides more context for the quotation than would a simple signal phrase, making a smooth transition between the quotation and the preceding discussion of the mental benefits of reading.

Vary the Placement of Acknowledgments

To add variety to your writing style, you can place the acknowledgment of a source before the material, after it, or in the middle.

Acknowledgment before a Source

In an *Atlantic* article, Nicholas Carr, an expert on information technology, describes how using the Internet has changed his reading style: "Once I was a scuba diver in the sea of words. Now I zip along on the surface like a guy on a Jet Ski."

Acknowledgment after a Source

"Once I was a scuba diver in the sea of words. Now I zip along on the surface like a guy on a Jet Ski," writes information technology expert Nicholas Carr in an *Atlantic* article about the effects of the Internet on people's reading styles.

Acknowledgment Surrounded by a Source

"Once I was a scuba diver in the sea of words," says information technology expert Nicholas Carr in an *Atlantic* article. "Now I zip along on the surface like a guy on a Jet Ski."

Use a Variety of Verbs to Indicate Acknowledgment

Using the word "says" to lead into quotations becomes repetitive. Think about how you are using the quotation and which verb would best describe the function of the quotation. Here are some options for changing things up:

admits	finds	points out
argues	holds	remarks
claims	insists	shows
comments	maintains	states
contends	observes	suggests

Follow Conventions When Choosing Verb Tenses to Use When Acknowledging Sources

It is customary to use present tense when leading into a quotation or paraphrase from a text you are using as a source. Use past tense only when referring to a past action, as in this example:

> In the 1940s, Edmund Wilson declared that "detective stories [are] simply a kind of vice that, for silliness and minor harmfulness, ranks somewhere between smoking and crossword puzzles."

The author refers to Wilson's action of speaking.

How Can I Integrate Source Material into My Writing?

Integrating sources means blending them smoothly into your own writing. If you've ever received a paper back from your instructor and found the comment "choppy" or "needs to flow" in the margins, then you can understand the difficulties writers face when they bring outside material into their own writing. Making ideas flow can be tricky enough when they are all your own ideas, so adding other voices can make it even trickier.

Researched writing sounds choppy and even incoherent if the writer has not led into quotations, anchored them with a signal phrase, and followed up on quotations with some commentary. Even paraphrases need some setting up, and if your paraphrase is not specific enough, your reader will have trouble getting the point.

BEST PRACTICES   Guidelines for Integrating Sources

Source material should not be dropped into a researched paper like items into a shopping cart. Your paper does not simply contain the sources; it is constructed using the sources.

- Organize around your own points; use sources to develop those points in depth.

- Cite as you write. Do not try to draft without including your source material, correctly worked in and cited.

- Lead up with enough explanation to show your readers how the source fits into your discussion.

- When presenting an authority's viewpoint, introduce the person first, with full name on first mention and any relevant credentials or affiliations. This formality is more common in MLA style than in APA.

- When quoting directly, anchor the words from the source to the surrounding text with a phrase or sentence that introduces the speaker. You should also indicate how the quotation relates to the surrounding text.

- Prefer paraphrase to direct quotation when presenting factual information. Keep direct quotations to approximately 10 percent of your paper.

- Follow up by commenting on the ideas or information to show how the source relates to a point of your own.

Avoid Dropped-In Quotations

Direct quotations need to be set up, not dropped into your paper. Provide enough of the original context to fit the quotation coherently into your paragraph. You may need to paraphrase some of the surrounding sentences from which the quotation was taken. If you have not done so already, you may need to introduce the speaker of the words, along with his or her credentials if the speaker is an important writer or authority. If the author is a staff writer, it is sufficient simply to put the last name in a parenthetical citation.

In the following example, the student did not do enough to connect the speaker's words to the idea in the preceding sentence.

> Some people claim that reading on computer screens is the same as reading on paper. "Are you not exercising the same cognitive muscles because these words are made out of pixels and not little splotches of ink?" (Johnson).

The revised version below does a better job of setting up and integrating the quotation.

> Some people claim that reading on computer screens is the same as reading on paper. In an online newspaper column titled "Dawn of the Digital Natives," Steven Johnson, a best-selling nonfiction author, asks his readers, "Odds are that you are reading these words on a computer monitor. Are you not exercising the same cognitive muscles because these words are made out of pixels and not little splotches of ink?"

Set Off Long Quotations in Block Style

See Chapter 20, page 388, and Chapter 21, page 415.

The two main documentation styles differ slightly on the rules for block quotes, but they agree that it is necessary to set off longer quotations in order to distinguish them from your own words, as in the example below.

> When the Nielsen researchers used an eye tracker to see how people read on the Internet, they discovered a surprising pattern that creators of websites need to know:
>> The pattern looks like the capital letter F. At the top of the page, users read all the way across, but as they proceed their descent quickens and horizontal movement shortens, with a slowdown around the middle of the page. Near the bottom of the page, the eyes move almost vertically, forming the lower stem of the F shape. . . . Whatever content businesses want to communicate to visitors better not be concentrated in the lower-right portions of the screen, Nielsen advised. (Bauerlein 144)

> For block style quotes only, the period at the end of a sentence precedes the parenthetical citation.

For an overview of the guidelines for formatting quotations in both APA and MLA styles, see Table 18.1.

TABLE **18.1**

Formatting Quotations

Length	Spacing
MLA If a quotation extends to more than four lines in your paper, use the block form. **APA** If a quotation is forty words or longer, use the block form.	**MLA** Begin a new line and indent it one inch (ten spaces) from the left margin. If you are quoting only one paragraph or part of one, do not indent the first line any farther. If the quotation runs more than one paragraph, indent the first line of each new paragraph by three spaces. **APA** Begin a new line and indent it one-half inch (five spaces) from the left margin. If the quotation runs more than one paragraph, indent the first line of each new paragraph by one-half inch (five spaces).

Guidelines for Both MLA and APA	
How to space it	Double space the quotation. Do not add extra spacing at the top or bottom.
How to cite it	With block quotations, any parenthetical citation follows the final punctuation mark.
How to treat internal quotations	Internal quotations within block form quotes receive the standard double quotation marks.
How to lead into long quotations	Depending on the context, you may need no punctuation between your lead-in or attributive tag and your quotation; however, it is common to lead in with a full sentence and a colon.

To Delete Parts of Direct Quotations, Use Ellipses

Sometimes a direct quotation goes into more detail than is necessary for your purpose or contains references or transitional expressions that had a purpose in the original passage but would only be confusing to your readers. When you remove these words from a quotation, you replace them with ellipses. An ellipsis is a series of three spaced periods. When removing words from the end of a sentence, you add a fourth period.

This is the original passage from Steven Johnson's book *Everything Bad Is Good for You:*

> Tools like Google have fulfilled the original dream of digital machines becoming extensions of our memory, but the new social networking applications have done something that the visionaries never imagined: <u>they are augmenting our people skills as well, widening our social networks, and creating new possibilities for strangers to share ideas and experiences.</u>

If you wanted to use only the underlined section of the passage, you should remove the transitional expression "as well" since it no longer serves the purpose of relating the two points in the original passage.

> Some people think that because online communication is not face-to-face, it is causing a decline in our social skills. But Steven Johnson argues that the social networking sites "are augmenting our people skills . . . , widening our social networks, and creating new possibilities for strangers to share ideas and experiences" (124).

In most cases, writers use ellipses to remove passages that are too detailed or irrelevant to the purpose of their own paper.

Use Square Brackets to Change Wording for Clarity and Grammatical Correctness

You can change quotations to make them fit more smoothly into your sentence, provided that you use square brackets around the words you alter. If you take words out and replace them with words in brackets, the brackets will signal to the reader that you have made a substitution, so there is no need for an ellipsis.

Sometimes you need to change the tense of verbs, as in this example from the student paper that appears on pages 404–10 in Chapter 20. The original passage by University of Virginia professor Mark Edmundson quoted Ralph Waldo Emerson and read

> The idea is to keep moving, never to stop. . . . "In skating over thin ice," Emerson says, "our safety is in our speed." . . . Skate fast over the surfaces of life and cover all the extended space you can, says the new ethos.

In the passage from a student's paper, below, to combine his own words smoothly with the quoted passage, the student writer had to change the form of the verb *skate:*

> Too many students are connected to everything and everyone but themselves, as Edmundson says, "[skating] fast over the surfaces of life," depending on energy drinks or someone else's Adderall.

You can also use brackets to alter a word to make a quotation clearer in the context of your sentence, as in the following example. Steven Johnson's book contained this sentence about one drawback of the Internet compared with books:

> But it is harder to transmit a fully fledged worldview.

To fit Johnson's words into his own sentence, the writer had to change the article *a* to *the:*

> Steven Johnson admits in his book *Everything Bad Is Good for You* that the Internet is not so good at "training our minds to follow a sustained textual argument" (187) or to "transmit [the] fully fledged worldview" of another person (186).

Avoid Stringing Sources Together with No Commentary

In the following example, the author has used many short quotations without showing enough of their original context and how the quotations connect with each other. The result is a paragraph that contains *words* from the sources but not enough of the *ideas* from the sources, as in the revised example below.

> Native Americans have always shared a strong traditional relationship with the Earth. To the Native American, the Earth is "sacred and itself a spiritual entity" (Kidwell, Noley, and Tinker 127). The Earth was not thought of as merely real estate, but rather a "gift from the Creator given for the care of creation" (Kidwell, Noley, and Tinker 127). As Jerry H. Gill says, "The Native American seeks to fit in with nature rather than alter it" (175). Native Americans view the Earth as their "mother" and the sky as their "father" (Momaday 33). This is why a plan to build a gondola ride into the Grand Canyon has met opposition from the Hopi, Zuni, and some Navajo people. The contractors of the Grand Canyon Escalade Project seek to build the tramway and other tourist attractions near the confluence of the Colorado and Little Colorado rivers, an area that these tribes see as a place of their emergence from the earth and sky (Cart). As one Navajo said, "This is the heart of our Mother Earth. This is a sacred area. It is going to be true destruction" (Yellowhorse qtd. in Nagourney).

A revised version introduces the important authorities used as sources and fills in the gaps with more explanation of the origin story and its relationship to the goal of conserving and respecting the Confluence area as a sacred place.

> Native Americans have traditionally shared a strong spiritual relationship with the Earth. Historians and theologians Clara Sue Kidwell, Homer Noley, and George "Tink" Tinker explain that while the Native Americans do not worship the Earth, they do see it as alive, "a spiritual entity" given by the Creator "for the care of creation" (127). For this reason, the Native Americans have a conservation ethic toward the land, wanting to preserve the gift as it was made by the Creator. As sociologist Jerry H. Gill says, "The Native American seeks to fit in with nature rather than alter it" (175). Further, the Earth is seen as sacred because many tribes believe that they emerged from worlds below or above. The Kiowa-American

author N. Scott Momaday explains that the Native Americans' "investment" in the Earth begins with a concept central to their worldview: "The earth is our mother. The sky is our father" (qtd. in Momaday 33). For these reasons, a plan to build a gondola ride into the Grand Canyon has met opposition from the Hopi, Zuni, and some Navajo people. The contractors of the Grand Canyon Escalade Project seek to build the tramway and other tourist attractions near the confluence of the Colorado and Little Colorado rivers, an area that these tribes see as a place of their emergence from the earth and sky (Cart). Renae Yellowhorse, a Navajo woman, told a reporter, "This is the heart of our Mother Earth. This is a sacred area. [The development] is going to be true destruction" (qtd. in Nagourney).

How Do I Document My Sources?

Documentation is a two-step process. The first step, which appears in the paper itself and is therefore called an in-text citation, is to identify the author (or title if there is no author) and the page number if one is available. Acknowledgment of an author by name does some of the work of citing but not all of it.

The second step, which appears at the end of the paper, is to provide a full bibliography, an alphabetical list of sources (articles, books, websites, and so on) that are referenced in the paper. This bibliography is called a list of works cited (MLA) or a list of references (APA). In academic writing, every source quoted or paraphrased must appear in the bibliography. These lists appear at the ends of books, articles, and sometimes chapters.

The important point to make here is that when a project calls for documentation, you must have two matching citations: one in the text of your paper and its partner in the list of sources at the back. For every source used in the paper, there must be an item on the list at the back. For every item on the list, there must be a corresponding reference to it in the body of your paper.

Chapter 20, pages 385–410, covers in-text citing and works cited lists in MLA style. Chapter 21, pages 411–34, covers in-text citing and reference lists in APA style.

How Do I Incorporate Sources without Losing My Own Voice?

To wrap up our advice on incorporating source materials, we want to remind you of the importance of keeping your own voice and perspective in your writing. When a writer brings other people's voices into a paper, one danger is those sources may try to dominate the conversation and determine how the paper develops. The source authors are often, after all, experts on the topic. However, your job as the writer is to politely control the conversation.

Imagine that writing a research paper is like hosting a dinner party. You need to plan the meal and invite the guests. Your sources are like guests who should not monopolize the conversation or take over the dinner. In a paper, you are in charge, organizing around your goals and presenting your perspective. Your thesis drives the paper; your sources are there to help support your points.

Maintain Your Own Angle and Plan

Writers sometimes feel intimidated about asserting their own voices in a conversation of published experts. When you encounter this situation, ask these questions:

- What are my angle and purpose?
- How does this source's information serve my angle and purpose?
- What is the smallest amount of information that I need from this source to make my point?

The following example, illustrating APA documentation style, shows how nutritional scientist Sera L. Young kept her voice in a paper about how attitudes have changed over time on a peculiar type of human behavior. Notice how the writer's tone differs from the tone of her sources' quoted words. Notice also how little of each source's words she needs to convey her point.

> Earth-eating, or geophagia, has always incited strongly negative reactions. Even scientists have done little to conceal their "disgust" for such a "vile habit" (Cragin, 1835) and denounce geophagists: "[W]ith the tenacity of ignorance these people cling to their filthy habits" ("The clay eaters," 1897, p. 150). Positive or even neutral regard for geophagia has only emerged in the last few decades. Yet the grounds for the proclamation of geophagia as "good" or "bad" are limited, even today.
>
> Young, Sera L. (2007). A vile habit? The potential biological consequences of geophagia, with special attention to iron. In J. MacClancy, J. Henry, & H. Macbeth (Eds.), *Consuming the inedible: Neglected dimensions of food choice* (pp. 67–79). New York, NY: Berghahn Books.

By maintaining a neutral tone, Young shows the contrast between her modern perspective and the outdated attitudes of the sources' voices. Also note that Young has successfully acknowledged her sources, integrated their words smoothly into her own sentences, and cited both in text and in a bibliographic entry at the end.

Chapters 20 and 21 continue our advice about how to cite sources in the text of your papers and in the works cited (MLA) and references (APA) lists at the end of the paper.

CHAPTER 19

Using Sources Responsibly

RESEARCHERS BUILD THEIR WORK ON FOUNDATIONS LAID BY OTHERS. However, the structure falls apart when a researcher steals material. Whether on purpose or not, using another person's work without acknowledging or giving credit to the source is theft.

Word processing software and the Internet have made it easy to copy and paste the words and visual images found in sources. The interactive nature of creative content on the Internet makes borrowing and mashing up seem perfectly acceptable. However, *anytime you put your name on something and claim it as your own work, borrowing without acknowledging is plagiarism*. Universities, the business world, and the law take it very seriously.

Writers who steal not only lose the reader's trust, but they also often face criminal charges. Cases of copyright infringement often make the news, and they damage the careers of popular novelists, song writers, newspaper reporters, and sometimes even professors who have been careless while taking notes or been too trusting of assistants' research skills.

By citing your sources, you earn your readers' respect. Readers are more likely to accept your views if you project good character, what the ancient rhetoricians called *ethos*. Honesty is part of good character. Part of writing honestly is distinguishing your ideas from the ideas of others. Therefore, *when in doubt, always cite*.

What Is Plagiarism?

Ethical use of sources requires paying careful attention to the texts of sources, whether written, audio, video, or works of art. Failure to acknowledge sources is plagiarism.

Intentional plagiarism occurs when a student knowingly submits work containing the words, ideas, images, or other intellectual property of another person without acknowledging and citing the source of the material. Note that plagiarism does not have to consist of word-for-word copying of another person's work. Rewording another person's ideas without acknowledging the source of the ideas is every bit as much plagiarism as copying and pasting material from a source into your paper.

Many professors and institutions regard unintentional or accidental plagiarism as seriously as the intentional kind and give it the same penalties. Unintentional plagiarism occurs when a researcher has been sloppy about note-taking and paraphrasing, not realizing that even a single phrase or word group taken verbatim needs quotation marks and a citation. It occurs when a researcher fails to distinguish an opinion found in a source from common knowledge or common facts, which may not need to be cited, as we will explain below. Unintentional plagiarism may not be as unethical as intentional plagiarism, but it is nevertheless serious and can result in an "F" for a paper.

In college, punishment for plagiarism can include failure in the course or even suspension or expulsion from the university. Many universities will indicate on a student's transcript if there has been an honor violation, something that potential employers will see.

When Do I Need to Cite My Sources?

The point of using sources is to combine other people's ideas and knowledge with your own, and the point of citing sources is to distinguish between your sources' knowledge and your own knowledge and ideas. Specifically, acknowledging (giving credit) and citing (with appropriate documentation) are required in the situations described below.

Cite and Quote Exact Words, Phrases, and Sentences

It is easy to understand that you need to put quotation marks around whole sentences that you take from one of your sources. For example, a complete sentence from a book is cited below.

> Yale law Professor Steven L. Carter is concerned about the future of democracy. Noting that many people vote without bothering to inform themselves on the issues, he argues, "Living in a democracy requires hard work that we seem less and less willing to do" (17).

If you wanted to take just a few words from this sentence, the words that express Carter's opinion of Americans' voter apathy, you would still have to enclose the words in quotation marks, as in the example below.

> Yale law Professor Steven L. Carter is concerned about the future of democracy. Noting that many people vote without bothering to inform themselves on the issues, he argues that Americans "seem less and less willing" to carry out the "hard work" of responsible citizenship (17).

Cite Ideas Found in Your Sources

See Chapter 18, pages 365–67, for guidance on paraphrasing.

Even if you rework someone else's writing into a paraphrase, *if you use someone else's idea, then you need to cite the source because ideas are intellectual property.* When you paraphrase, you must also acknowledge the source, or you are plagiarizing.

Cite Paraphrased Ideas from Your Sources

It is a standard practice for writers to draw upon the work of others, including both the information they have gathered and the ideas they have formulated. Whether you quote them directly or put them into your own words, you need to give credit to the source, so you do not appear to be claiming these ideas as your own.

The following passage comes from a *Wall Street Journal* blog post on the rise of incivility in business settings. The post was written by Sue Shellenbarger. Note that she opens with her own point but develops it with the research of an authority, Robert

Stephen L. Carter. *Civility: Manners, Morals, and the Etiquette of Democracy.* Basic Books, 1999.

Putnam. Shellenbarger paraphrases the research in her own words and acknowledges Putnam as the source by naming him.

> TV also shifted the center of gravity of society from the public park and the bowling alley to the privacy of our own homes, as couch potatoes in front of a giant screen. Over time, the single screen in the living room migrated into separate TV screens in each bedroom. Families retreated from other families, and then family members eventually retreated from one another. The political scientist Robert Putnam, in *Bowling Alone*, his magisterial account of the decline of civic engagement, found that time in front of the TV screen is the most powerful single characteristic accounting for the long-term decline in the time devoted to civic activities.

Cite Ideas That Coincide with Your Own

You may encounter ideas in sources that coincide with your own. For example, suppose you think that optimistic people do better in life than pessimists. This is a belief you have concluded from observations of family and friends—and perhaps your own attitudes in meeting challenges. Then you read Gregg Easterbrook's book *The Progress Paradox,* and on page 223 you see the following:

> Lisa Aspinwall, a psychologist at the University of Utah, has shown that as a group, the optimistic do better in life than the pessimistic. . . . [O]ptimists . . . are actually better at overcoming negative experiences because they can bounce back rather than be dragged under.

Easterbrook is acknowledging Aspinwall as his source. Easterbrook is your source, but do you need to cite the source of something you could have said on your own? If you do not use Easterbrook's exact words, is it plagiarism to use Aspinwall's opinion without acknowledging Aspinwall's research and citing Easterbrook's book?

A classic book on research, *The Craft of Research,*[1] advises you to take the cautious approach and cite: "In the world of research, priority counts not for everything, but for a lot. If you do not cite that prior source, you risk having people think that you plagiarized it, even though you did not" (203). You do not have to check to see that all of your own ideas are not already out there; however, if you encounter one of your own in a source, you should acknowledge that source. This also strengthens your case: Not only do you believe optimists tend to be more successful in life, but others think so too.

Cite Even a Single Significant Word or Phrase

Verbatim use of some words and phrases cannot be avoided; it would not be necessary to put quotation marks around common words and phrases, such as *fifth-graders* and

---

1. Wayne C. Booth, Gregory G. Colomb, and Joseph M. Williams. *The Craft of Research.* 2nd ed., U of Chicago P, 2003.

Jeffrey D. Sachs. *The Price of Civilization: Reawakening American Virtue and Prosperity.* Random House, 2011.

Gregg Easterbrook. *The Progress Paradox.* Random House, 2004.

proper nouns like *White House* or *Secretary of State John Kerry.* However, *when a single word expresses a writer's opinion or judgment, it should go in quotation marks and the source should be acknowledged.*

For example, in this passage from Steven L. Carter's book *Civility,* the word "diabolical" is significant enough to merit a citation:

> As for the automobile itself, it seems an almost diabolical tool, in the traditional sense of the word—a thing of the devil, made to bring out the worst in us.

In your paper, you might put the idea into your own words, acknowledge Carter as the source, and quote the single word.

> Under the cover of anonymity within their cars, drivers become not just uncivil but, as Steven Carter puts it, even "diabolical" once behind the wheel (7).

Cite Factual Information That Is Not "Common Knowledge"

Facts that can be easily obtained through multiple sources such as reference books, Google searches, and standard textbooks do not have to be cited. A rule of thumb is that *if the reader could fact-check your information in at least three easily accessed sources, it can count as common knowledge.*

Common knowledge generally includes factual information not in dispute, such as dates or authors of books. For example, a historical date like the bombing of Pearl Harbor on December 7, 1941, is common knowledge. However, the equally important historical date September 6, 1941, when Japanese leaders decided to take the country to war, is not common knowledge, so it is information that must be documented.

If you already knew something that shows up in your research, that is a good indication it is common knowledge, but also consider whether your *readers* would already know it. If your readers know less about your topic than you do, it is good to cite the source, especially if the information might surprise them. Citing sources is a courtesy to readers who may want to pursue their interest in your topic.

It is also not necessary to cite the exact source location for commonly known quotations, such as Martin Luther King Jr.'s declaration "I have a dream," or commonly available sources, such as the *Declaration of Independence.* Again, the rule of thumb here is that if readers could easily find a copy of the document, it is not necessary to cite it. However, the motto for research remains important: *When in doubt, cite your source.* You can also consult your professor for advice on when to cite.

Cite Debatable or Unique Information

Some information is disputed or still open to debate. For example, some research has shown that

S. L. Carter. *Civility: Manners, Morals, and the Etiquette of Democracy.* Basic Books, 1999.

gas and oil production using hydraulic fracturing, known as fracking, is more likely to pollute groundwater than traditional methods such as mining. However, other studies show no greater levels of pollution caused by fracking.

If information is not generally agreed upon, then the source of the information should always be cited. When in doubt, imagine one of your readers asking, "But how do you know that?" If readers can pose this question, it is best to point them to a source.

Cite Charts, Artwork, and Graphics

Any time you include artwork, photographs, graphics, charts, diagrams, maps, and other audiovisual materials that you got from another source rather than creating the image yourself, you must acknowledge and cite the source.

How Can I Avoid Plagiarizing?

It is easy to avoid blatant forms of plagiarism, such as buying a paper, having someone write your paper for you, or copying and pasting from the Internet into your paper without acknowledging the source. You simply choose not to do it.

However, writers can accidentally plagiarize if, for example, they are careless when taking notes and fail to place quotation marks when they copy something from a source into their notes and then transfer that passage into their paper. Writers are responsible for double-checking paraphrases against the original passage. *Make sure the words and sentence patterns are your own to avoid accidental plagiarism.*

Consider the example of accidental plagiarism below.

Original Passage from *iBrain* by Gary Small and Gigi Vorgan[2]

Our high-tech revolution has plunged us into a state of *continuous partial attention,* which software executive Linda Stone describes as continually staying busy—keeping tabs on everything while never truly focusing on anything. . . . When paying continuous partial attention, people may place their brain in a heightened state of stress. They no longer have time to reflect, contemplate or make thoughtful decisions. Instead they exist in a sense of constant crisis—on alert for a new contact or bit of exciting news or information at any moment. Once people get used to this state, they tend to thrive on the perpetual connectivity. It feeds their ego and sense of self-worth, and it becomes irresistible.

In the example below, too many words and phrases have been taken directly from the source. *This is plagiarism even though the authors and the page have been cited.*

Irresponsible (Plagiarized) Paraphrase or Short Summary

Our high-tech revolution has put us into a state of continuous partial attention. According to software executive Linda Stone, this is a state of continually staying

---

2. Gary Small and Gigi Vorgan. *iBrain: Surviving the Technological Alteration of the Modern Mind.* HarperCollins, 2008.

Some features of good paraphrasing to note: The paraphrase is set up with the authors' names and credentials; the sentences are new, some longer, some shorter. The words "continuous partial attention" are quoted the first time they appear to show that those are the words of the source. It would be optional to use quotation marks the second time since the term has been established as a technical phrase.

busy—paying attention to everything while never really focusing on anything. In continuous partial attention, people place their brain in an increased state of stress or constant crisis, without time to reflect or make thoughtful decisions. They are always on alert for exciting tidbits of news. Once they get accustomed to this state, they thrive on being constantly connected because it feeds their ego and gives them a sense of self worth (Small and Vorgan 18).

Responsible Paraphrase or Short Summary

According to Gary Small and Gigi Vorgan, authors of the book *iBrain,* technology has caused some people to experience "continuous partial attention," a state in which people divide their attention among many things at once but never really focus their mind on any one thing at a time. They are always seeking the next exciting piece of information. Small and Vorgan say continuous partial attention is stressful because it leaves people with no time to reflect. But it is also addictive, because once people get used to it, they like the feeling of self-importance they get from being connected at all times (18).

The best way to avoid an inadvertent plagiarism problem is to pay close attention whenever you are using material from sources:

See Chapter 2, pages 24–27, on paraphrasing and summarizing.

See Chapter 18, pages 369–77, on using and documenting sources.

- Take careful notes.
- If you ever cut and paste from an online source into a draft with the intention of reworking the passage into a quotation or summary/paraphrase later, highlight or shadow the entire passage in some bright color so it will stand out as writing that is not your own.
- Summarize fairly and accurately.
- Paraphrase by putting ideas fully into your own words and sentences.
- Choose quotations that accurately depict ideas in the source and carefully use quotation marks to indicate use of exact wording.

CHAPTER 20

Documenting Your Sources: MLA

THE MODERN LANGUAGE ASSOCIATION (MLA) STYLE OF DOCUMENTATION IS USED IN THE ARTS AND HUMANITIES—in particular, by researchers in the fields of language and literature. MLA documentation uses in-text parenthetical citations that are matched to a list of works cited at the end of the paper. This chapter covers the basics of using MLA documentation style. You can find detailed explanations of MLA guidelines for documenting your sources and formatting your papers in the *MLA Handbook,* 8th edition.

How Do I Make In-Text Citations Using MLA Style?

When you quote from, summarize, or paraphrase the work of someone else—and when you provide information that is not common knowledge—cite your sources in the text by providing the author's last name and, if available, the exact page number(s) where the quoted or paraphrased material was found. If the author's name appears in your signal phrase (for example, "As Smith said"), omit it in the parenthetical citation. All in-text citations must match the citations in your works cited list. The examples that follow illustrate the most common ways to cite sources in the text of your papers.

See Chapter 18, pages 365–69, for guidance on summary and paraphrase.

For an explanation of what is considered common knowledge, see Chapter 19, page 382.

Direct Quotation with Source Named in Signal Phrase

As part of his argument that popular culture makes us smarter, Steven Johnson argues, "The rise of the Internet has challenged our minds in three fundamental and related ways: by virtue of being participatory, by forcing users to learn new interfaces, and by creating new channels for social interaction" (118).

> **Punctuation Alert:** Use a comma between a signal phrase and the opening of a quotation that is a complete sentence.

> **Punctuation Alert:** Close direct quotations before parenthetical citations. Place a period after the parenthetical citation unless you have a block quotation (see page 388).

Direct Quotation with Source Named in Parentheses

Popular culture can be mentally stimulating. The Internet, for example, "has challenged our minds in three fundamental and related ways: by virtue of being participatory, by forcing users to learn new interfaces, and by creating new channels for social interaction" (Johnson 118).

Steven Johnson. *Everything Bad Is Good for You.* Penguin Group USA, 2006.

> **Punctuation Alert:** In MLA style, there is no comma between the name of the author and the page number. Do not use the word *page* or any abbreviation for it.

Summary or Paraphrase with Source Named in Parentheses

Reading is unlike other natural human functions of seeing, moving, speaking, and thinking. Reading is an invented cognitive function, and understanding how it works illustrates the amazing plasticity of the brain (Wolf and Barzillai).

When you are citing online sources with no page numbers and no numbering of paragraphs, as in the example above, you will not be able to cite a page. You also do not need to cite a page if the source is only one page long or if you are referring to it in its entirety.

Source with Two Authors

If your source has two authors, give both last names.

In their book *iBrain,* Small and Vorgan claim that Internet use can be addictive, as people get a rush of the brain chemical dopamine when they turn on their computers (48–49).

For three authors or more, give the first author's name followed by the abbreviation *et al.* (not in italics, but ending with a period).

The nativist opposition to immigration in the 19th century was fueled by the rising numbers of immigrant voters who cast their votes against temperance, antislavery, and other reforms favored by the Protestant native-born majority (Maier et al. 481).

Two or More Works by the Same Author

When you are citing more than one work by an author, you need to specify which one you are referring to; do this by using shortened versions of the titles:

Mark Edmundson believes that people should read good literature with the hope or goal of being influenced by it ("Narcissis Regards"). He argues that this goal is especially important for college students because college reading opens doors to ideas different from the ones students grew up with ("Dwelling" 28).

Two or More Authors with the Same Last Name

If you have sources by two or more authors with the same last name, use initials for first names in parenthetical references (or full names if the initials are also the same). In your discussion, you should use full names the first time you mention an author.

Although some researchers (C. Smith) have found that this particular gene plays a significant role in promoting cancer cell growth, others (R. Smith) have not been able to discover a link.

Organization or Agency as Author

Treat an organization or government agency the same way you would treat an individual author; the name may be used in a signal phrase or in a parenthetical reference. Try to introduce long names in a signal phrase. If you use the name in a parenthetical citation, you may shorten or abbreviate it, but be certain that it matches the reference list entry. For example, in parentheses you may use Natl. Public Radio instead of National Public Radio.

Work with No Author or Editor

If no author or editor is named, use the title of the work in both in-text citations and works cited entries. If the title is long, abbreviate it. Begin the title or its abbreviation with the first word that is not an article *(the, a, an)* because your works cited list will be organized alphabetically according to the first significant word in the title. The following example is from a page on a website.

> The Law School Aptitude Test (LSAT) measures ability to read and comprehend in-depth texts with insight, to draw "reasonable inferences" from readings, and to analyze and evaluate the reasoning of others' arguments ("About the LSAT").

More than One Source in a Parenthetical Citation

If you have more than one source to cite for a piece of information, list them alphabetically, separated by a semicolon:

> Several researchers believe that reading books puts the brain to work in ways that reading on the Internet does not (Bauerlein; Wolf and Barzillai).

Reference to an Entire Work; Work with No Page Numbers

> Mark Bauerlein's *The Dumbest Generation* argues that people under thirty are not taking full advantage of the Internet's resources for gaining knowledge.

When you do not have page numbers to cite because you are referring to an entire work, try to put the author's name in the text of the sentence rather than in parentheses. The works cited list would contain full bibliographic information for this source. A reference to a source with no page numbers is treated in the same way.

Use of Quotation Marks within a Quotation

In the source from which the following example comes, "truth" appeared in quotation marks. When you quote the entire passage yourself, *truth* should have single quotation marks:

> According to Wolf and Barzillai, "[Socrates] worried that the seeming permanence of writing would delude young people into thinking that they had learned the 'truth,' when they had just begun the search for it."

Punctuation Alert: In the above example, "he" was used instead of "Socrates" in the source. You need to substitute Socrates because otherwise your reader would not know who "he" was. Use square brackets to substitute proper names for pronouns that have no clear reference in your own sentence.

Maryanne Wolf and Mirit Barzillai. "The Importance of Deep Reading." *Educational Leadership, vol. 66, no. 6, 2010,* pp. 32–37.

Long Quotations (Block Quotations)

For direct quotations that will be more than four lines in your paper, omit quotation marks and display the quotation as a block of text set in from the left margin by one inch. Double-space the entire block quotation. In a block quotation, the final period precedes the parenthetical citation. Here is an example of a block quotation:

> In his best-selling book, *The Dumbest Generation,* Mark Bauerlein describes the studies of Jacob Nielsen, who runs a consulting group that designs Web pages for corporations. This group does eye-tracking studies to show how people read on computer screens. The researchers' conclusion was "They *don't*" (qtd. in Bauerlein 143). The eye tracker revealed a surprising pattern that creators of Web sites need to know:
>
> > The pattern looks like the capital letter F. At the top of the page, users read all the way across, but as they proceed their descent quickens and horizontal movement shortens, with a slowdown around the middle of the page. Near the bottom of the page, the eyes move almost vertically, forming the lower stem of the F shape. . . . Whatever content businesses want to communicate to visitors better not be concentrated in the lower-right portions of the screen, Nielsen advised. (Bauerlein 144)

Indirect Source (a Source Your Source Used)

Sources quote and document their own sources. How do you treat a source within a source? First, do not cite anything that you have not consulted yourself. Second, use *qtd. in* (not italicized) for "quoted in" and cite the source in which you found the quotation. In the example below, the student's source was an article by William Major.

> Students today are always connected, always in touch. When a professor asked his students to give up cell phones for a few days, they responded as if he had asked them to take off their clothes (Major). In contrast to Thoreau, who wrote, "I never found the companion that was so companionable as solitude," (qtd. in Major), today's students seem more frightened by than enthusiastic about the possibilities offered by solitude.

> **Punctuation Alert:** As in the example above, use double quotation marks around direct quotes. If your quotation itself contains words or phrases that should be in quotation marks, put these in single quotation marks. *Do not use quotation marks around block quotations* unless they are themselves quotations (dialogue from a novel, for example).

A Work in an Anthology

Cite the author of the individual work, not the editor or compiler of the anthology.

> In "Toadstools," the narrator suspects that the food in supermarket aisles "hold[s] stories of other people's houses" (Nguyen 130).

A Multivolume Work

If your citation requires page numbers, list volume number, followed by a colon and the page numbers. If you are not referring to specific pages, then use the abbreviation for volume: vol. 2.

> In his narrative history of the Civil War, Shelby Foote devotes the chapter "Beleaguered City" to the Battle of Vicksburg (323-427; vol.2).

Work of Literature or Classic Work

Because works that are out of copyright (such as nineteenth-century novels) can be found in many editions, citing a page number alone will not help your reader. Along with the page number, provide chapter numbers, section numbers, or even paragraph numbers if that is the only way the work is divided. Use abbreviations for parts of books.

> Elizabeth Bennet expresses her recognition of her own pride and prejudice to her sister: "I have courted prepossession and ignorance, and driven reason away. . . . Till this moment I never knew myself" (Austen 136; ch. 36).

> **Punctuation Alert:** Use a semicolon after the page number and before any additional material.

Poetry is cited by line numbers. The first time you cite a poem, use the word *line* or *lines;* after that, give just the numbers.

> He did not touch the shroud, or raise the fold
> That hid my face, or take my hand in his,
> Or ruffle the smooth pillows for my head:
> He did not love me living; but once dead
> He pitied me; and very sweet it is
> To know he still is warm though I am cold. (Rossetti, lines 9–14)

> **Punctuation Alert:** Use a comma after the author's name if what follows is not a number.

Use Arabic numerals to cite act, scene, and lines (if needed) from a play; use periods to separate them.

> The warrior Fortinbras has the final words in *Hamlet:* "Take up the bodies; such a sight as this / Becomes the field, but here shows much amiss. / Go, bid the soldiers shoot" (5.2.386–88).

Jane Austen. *Pride and Prejudice.* Vol. 3, 1813.
Christina Rossetti. "After Death."
William Shakespeare. *Hamlet.*

> **Punctuation Alert:** If you are using fewer than four lines of poetry, use a slash (virgule) to separate lines; the slash is preceded and followed by a space.

Religious Texts

Do not italicize the name of sacred texts in your sentences: the Bible, the Koran, the Bhagavad Gita. However, the names of specific editions should be in italics. In parenthetical references, abbreviate the names of biblical books, and separate chapter and verse with periods. The titles of biblical books are not italicized.

> The translation in the *New Oxford Annotated Bible* reads: "Now the manna was like coriander seed, and its appearance like that of bdellium. The people went about and gathered it, and ground it in mills or beat it in mortars, and boiled it in pots, and made cakes of it; and the taste of it was like the taste of cakes baked with oil" (Num. 11.7–8).

How Do I Make Entries in the Works Cited List Using MLA Style?

Your works cited list should include complete bibliographic information for all sources you refer to in your paper. The examples in this section indicate how to cite the kinds of sources commonly used in first-year writing assignments.

General Guidelines for Your Works Cited List

All the guidelines described below are illustrated in the example research paper at the end of this chapter, pages 404–10.

- The first word of each entry on the works cited list must match the in-text citation. If you refer, for instance, to Edward Hoagland's essay on aging in your paper, there should be an entry in the works cited list that begins with "Hoagland, Edward."

- Put *all* entries in alphabetical order according to the first word in each entry. Usually the first word will be the lead author's or editor's last name or—if no author is named—the first word in the title not including articles *(a, an, the)*.

- Do not number the entries.

- Double-space within and between entries.

- Begin each entry at the left margin and indent all subsequent lines by one-half inch. The hanging indent feature of your word processing program will help you.

- Italicize titles of books, periodicals (such as magazines and journals), films, and other major works like websites and blogs.

- Put quotation marks around titles of articles and essays from periodicals or books of collected works (such as anthologies) and around pages or posts found on a website.

- Capitalize all words in titles and subtitles except for articles *(a, an, the),* coordinating conjunctions *(and, or, but),* and prepositions. Always capitalize the first and last word of a title, regardless of its part of speech.

- Include subtitles of works. Separate them from the title with a colon.

New Oxford Annotated Bible. Num. 11.7–8.

■ If some publication information is not given, use the following abbreviations (not italicized) in place of the missing data: *n.p.* for "no place" or "no publisher," *n.d.* for "no date," and *n. pag.* for "no pagination."

Printed Books

Your entries for printed books should contain the following:

1. Name of author or editor, last name first, followed by a period (unless no author or editor is listed)
2. Title of the work, italicized, followed by a period
3. Publisher, followed by a comma
4. Year of publication, followed by a period

In the works cited list, do not cite page numbers for chapters or portions of books. Do include page numbers for items in an anthology or collected set of works.

> Last name, First name. *Title*. Publisher, date.

Book by a Single Author

> Urrea, Luis Alberto. *The Devil's Highway: A True Story.* Little, 2004.

Two or More Books by the Same Author

Instead of repeating the author's name in your works cited list, give the name in the first entry only. For subsequent works, use three hyphens in place of the name, followed by a period. Arrange the works in alphabetical order according to the first word in the title of the work, excluding articles *(a, an, the)*.

> Obama, Barack. *The Audacity of Hope: Thoughts on Reclaiming the American Dream.* Crown, 2006.
> ———. *Dreams from My Father: A Story of Race and Inheritance.* 1995. Three Rivers, 2004.

Note: For reprinted works, include the original date of publication immediately following the title, as in the second citation above.

Book by Two Authors

Put the name of the lead author first, beginning with his or her last name. Begin with the first name for the second author. Use commas between names.

> Small, Gary, and Gigi Vorgan. *iBrain: Surviving the Technological Alteration of the Modern Mind.* HarperCollins, 2008.

> Suárez-Orozco, Carola, Marcelo M. Suárez-Orozco, and Irina Todorova. *Learning a New Land: Immigrant Students in American Society.* Belknap-Harvard UP, 2008.

If the title page shows an imprint (for example, Belknap, an imprint of Harvard University Press, in the citation above), include both it and the publisher's name, separated by a hyphen.

Book by Three or More Authors

Use only the first author's name and the Latin abbreviation *et al.* (not italicized), meaning "and others."

> Chambers, Mortimer, et al. *The Western Experience.* 9th ed., McGraw, 2007.

In the works cited list, use a comma between the author's first name and *et al.* The parenthetical in-text citation would read (Chambers et al. 2007), with no comma.

Book by a Corporate Author or Government Agency

Treat the corporation or agency as an author.

> Modern Language Association. *MLA Handbook for Writers of Research Papers.* 8th ed., MLA, 2016.

If you abbreviate publisher names, use abbreviations that your readers will understand.

Book with No Author or Editor

Begin the citation with the title. In the works cited list, ignore articles *a, an,* and *the* when placing entries in alphabetical order; the following example would be alphabetized under *New.*

> *The New York Times Guide to Essential Knowledge: A Desk Reference for the Curious Mind.* 3rd ed., St. Martin's, 2011.

Later Edition of a Book

Directly after the title, add the edition number without italics. Use numerals; abbreviate *edition.*

> Williams, Joseph M. *Style: Ten Lessons in Clarity and Grace.* 9th ed., Pearson, 2007.

Reprinted Book

Include the original date of publication before current publication information.

> Adams, Henry. *The Education of Henry Adams: An Autobiography.* 1918. Houghton, 1961.

Translation

For a translated work, follow the title of the work with the name of the translator, followed by a comma and current publication information. Include this information before current publication information.

> Vargas Llosa, Mario. *The Bad Girl.* Translated by Edith Grossman, Farrar, 2007.

Preface, Introduction, Foreword, or Afterword Not by the Book's Author or Editor

Start the entry with the name of the author of the part of the book; then provide the name of the section, followed by the title of the book. Use the word *By* before the author of the book. If the book is a reprint, include the original date of publication. Indicate the inclusive page numbers for the part of the book you used as your source.

> Bellow, Saul. Foreword. *The Closing of the American Mind.* By Allen Bloom, Simon & Schuster, 1987, pp. 11–18.

If the section has a title of its own, use the following format:

> Mochulsky, Konstantin. "Dostoevsky and *The Brothers Karamazov.*" Introduction. *The Brothers Karamazov.* By Fyodor Dostoevsky. Translated by Andrew R. MacAndrew. 1970, Bantam, 2003, pp. xiii–xxii.

Scholarly Edition

Important works are often published in scholarly editions, and the scholarship of the editor (on the text, introduction, and footnotes, for example) might be what you cite in your paper. Use the following format if most of your citations are to the work itself:

> Melville, Herman. *Moby Dick.* 1851. Edited by Tony Tanner. Oxford UP, 2008.

Use this format if most of your citations are to the editor's work:

> Tanner, Tony, editor. *Moby Dick.* By Herman Melville. 1851. Oxford UP, 2008.

Anthology or Edited Compilation

Place a comma after the editor's name, and add editor.

> Shreve, Susan Richards, editor. *Dream Me Home Safely: Writers on Growing Up in America.* Houghton, 2003.

Work in an Anthology

For works in collections of essays, poetry, and short stories, put the author of the individual work first, followed by its title in quotation marks, and then the title of the collection in italics. The editor's name follows. Note that entries for works in anthologies do cite the inclusive page numbers of the selection.

> Nguyen, Bich Minh. "Toadstools." *Dream Me Home Safely: Writers on Growing Up in America,* edited by Susan Richards Shreve, Houghton, 2003, pp. 129–132.

The MLA rule for inclusive page numbers is to include all digits for numbers 1–99 but only the last two digits of the second number when the range starts at 100 or higher (unless more are needed for clarity): 23–67, 79–102, 107–23, 1859–75, 1859–917.

Two or More Works from the Same Anthology

If you are using more than one selection from an anthology, you will need at least three entries in your works cited list, one for the entire work, opening with the name of its editor, and one for each of the items, opening with the name of its author. The editor's last name follows the title of the selection and refers your readers to the entire book; it is followed by the inclusive page numbers of the selection. Place each entry in its alphabetically determined spot on the works cited list, as illustrated below.

> Griffith, Patricia. "The Spiral Staircase." Shreve, pp. 73–81.
> MacDonald, Michael Patrick. "Spitting Image." Shreve, pp. 112–22.
> Shreve, Susan Richards, editor. *Dream Me Home Safely: Writers on Growing Up in America.* Houghton, 2003.

One Volume of a Multivolume Work

Directly after the title of the work, indicate the volume number you used.

> Foote, Shelby. *The Civil War: A Narrative.* Vol. 2. Random, 1963.

More than One Volume of a Multivolume Work

After the title, indicate the total number of volumes in the work. If the work was published over multiple years, indicate the range of years.

> Foote, Shelby. *The Civil War: A Narrative.* 3 vols. Random, 1958–74.

Book That Is Part of a Series

Open with the name of the series and a series number for the work if available. End with the name of the series. Do not italicize the series title.

> Horning, Alice, and Anne Becker, editors. *Revision: History, Theory, and Practice.* Parlor, 2006. Reference Guides to Rhetoric and Composition.

Signed Article in a Reference Book

Cite the name of the author, the title of the entry, the title of the reference work, name of the editor, and publication information. Do not include page numbers if entries are arranged in alphabetical order in the reference book itself.

> Zangwill, O. L. "Hypnotism, History of." *The Oxford Companion to the Mind,* edited by Richard L. Gregory. Oxford UP, 1987.

Unsigned Article in a Reference Book

Open with the title of the entry. Include page numbers if entries do not appear in alphabetical order.

> "A Technical History of Photography." *The New York Times Guide to Essential Knowledge: A Desk Reference for the Curious Mind.* St. Martin's, 2004, pp. 104–12.

Edition of a Religious Text

Italicize the title and provide names of editors and/or translators and the publication information.

> *The New Oxford Annotated Bible with Apocrypha.* New Revised Standard Version. Edited by Michael D. Coogan et al. 4th ed., Oxford UP, 2010.
>
> *The Bhagavad Gita: According to Paramhansa Yogananda.* Edited by Swami Kriyananda. Crystal Clarity, 2008.

Art Reproduction

Treat art found in books in the same way you treat selections found in edited collections. Open the entry with the artist's name, followed by the title of the work and the date it was created, if available. Before you list publication information, indicate where the original work of art may be found.

> O'Keeffe, Georgia. *Light /17: Evening Star, No. V.* 1917. McNay Art Museum, San Antonio. *O'Keefe and Texas.* By Sharyn R. Udall. The Marion Koogler McNay Art Museum, 1998, p. 51.

Articles in Print Periodicals

Your works cited entries for articles in print periodicals should contain the following:

1. Author's name, followed by a period
2. Title of the article, followed by a period, all in quotation marks
3. Title of the periodical, italicized, followed by a comma
4. Volume number (if given); issue number (if given)
5. Date (if given), followed by a comma
6. Inclusive page numbers, followed by a period

Article in a Journal with Volume Numbers

Put the volume number (for example, "71" in the example below), a period, and the issue number (if there is one) after the title of the article. Put the year in parentheses.

> Last name, First name. "Article Title." *Journal Title,* vol., issue, date, pages.

> Bracher, Mark. "How to Teach for Social Justice: Lessons from *Uncle Tom's Cabin* and Cognitive Science." *College English,* vol. 71, no. 4, 2009, pp. 363–88.

Some journals are not published by volume. In this case, use issue number only.

Article in a Monthly Magazine

Last name, First Name. "Article Title." *Magazine Title,* date, pages.

Abbreviate all months except May, June, and July.

Walter, Chip. "First Artists." *National Geographic,* Jan. 2015, pp. 32–57.

Article in a Weekly Magazine

Levy, Ariel. "Nora Knows What to Do." *The New Yorker,* 6 July 2009, pp. 60–69.

Article in a Newspaper

Last name, First name. "Article Title." *Newspaper Title,* date, edition, pages.

Give the day, month, year, and edition if specified; use abbreviations. Give section and page number. If pages are not consecutive, put a plus sign after the first page number.

Keller, Julia. "Sticks and Stones and Presidential Speeches." *The Chicago Tribune,* 23 Jan. 2011 final edition, sec. 4, p. 4.

Yoon, Carol Kaesuk. "Reviving the Lost Art of Naming the World." *The New York Times,* 11 Aug. 2009, natl. ed.: D1+.

If the page number does not include the section number or letter, indicate the section in another way: for example, sec. A, sec. 6, Arts and Entertainment sec. If the city is not named in the newspaper title, add it (not italicized) in brackets after the title, but before the date: *Times Union* [Albany], 13 Jan. 2011.

Editorial in a Newspaper—No Named Author

If no author is named, begin the citation with the title.

"Poverty-Busting in Dallas." Editorial. *Dallas Morning News.* 19 Jan. 2015, p. A20.

Letter to the Editor of a Newspaper or Magazine

Add *Letter* (not italicized) following the author name to indicate a letter to the editor.

Black, Antony. Letter. *Economist,* 22 Jan. 2011, p. 20.

Lyon, Danny. Letter. *New Yorker,* 19 Jan. 2015, p. 3.

Review

Open with the name of the reviewer and the title of the review, if there is one. Add the abbreviation *Rev. of* (not italicized) for "review of," followed by the title of the work being reviewed, and its author or performer.

Hofferth, Sandra. "Buying So Children Belong." Review of *Longing and Belonging: Parents, Children, and Consumer Culture,* by Allison J. Pugh. *Science,* vol. 324, no. 5935, 26 June 2009, p. 1674.

Advertisement in Print Medium

Open with the name of the item or service being advertised.

> Canon. Advertisement. *National Geographic,* Jan. 2015, p. 3.

Digital Sources

When the information is available, your works cited entries for digital sources should contain the following:

1. Name of author, editor, performer, or translator, followed by a period
2. Title of work, followed by a period
3. Title of website, followed by a comma
4. Publisher or sponsor of the site, followed by a comma
5. Date last updated (or n.d), followed by a comma
6. The URL (without "http://"), followed by a period.

> Last name, First name. "Title of article or page." *Title of website,* Sponsor/publisher, date of update, URL.

Example Entry for Entire Website

See Figure 20.1. Begin with the title of the site if there is no author named. If the source no longer exists, provide the date of your last access to it.

> *Pew Hispanic Center.* Pew Research Center, 2015. www.pewhispanic.org/.

Example Entry for a Webpage or Document Found on a Website

> Author. "Title of Page." *Title of Site,* Sponsor, date of publication, Location (URL).

This format for an individual webpage or document, such as the one displayed in Figure 20.2, is the basis for many different types of MLA works cited entries, including news stories on television network sites, documents in online archives, online video and audio, and even online performances. Some of the variations on this format follow.

Personal Website

If the site has no title, use *Home page* or some other descriptive title, not italicized. If there is no sponsoring organization, use *N.p.* (not italicized) to indicate no publisher.

> Alexie, Sherman. Home page. Falls Apart Productions, 2015, fallsapart.com/.

Books Accessed Online

Begin as you would for any book, but after the publication information, include the online library or retrieval service, and the URL.

> Austen, Jane. *Pride and Prejudice.* 1895. *Project Gutenberg,* www.gutenberg.org/files/1342/1342-h/1342.htm.

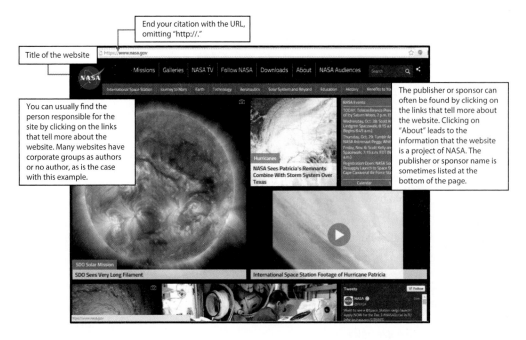

End your citation with the URL, omitting "http://."

Title of the website

You can usually find the person responsible for the site by clicking on the links that tell more about the website. Many websites have corporate groups as authors or no author, as is the case with this example.

The publisher or sponsor can often be found by clicking on the links that tell more about the website. Clicking on "About" leads to the information that the website is a project of NASA. The publisher or sponsor name is sometimes listed at the bottom of the page.

FIGURE **20.1**

Example of a Website or Independent Online Work

Source: NASA

URL of the website.

Publisher of the website.

Date of publication.

Author of article, if available, will typically appear below, the title of the article.

Title of the overall website.

Title of article.

FIGURE **20.2**

Webpage or Document Found on a Website

Source: NASA

Use the digital publication date. If the Web source gives print data for the edition used, include it.

> Austen, Jane. *Pride and Prejudice.* Vol. 3 1813. Interactive Media, 2012. *Google Books,* books.google.com/books?id=aFbCdW8CcuAC&printsec=frontcover& dq=pride+prejudice&hl=en&sa=X&ved=0ahUKEwjfl-Oyo_3LAhXKPCYKHawX A5QQ6AEIJjAA#v=onepa.

For books published before 1900, the publisher's name is not needed.

Article in an Online Journal

Follow the print format, but add the URL. The following periodical is published annually, so it has a volume number only.

> O'Dwyer, Kathleen. "Nietzsche's Reflections on Love." *Minerva—An Internet Journal of Philosophy,* vol. 12, 2008, pp. 37–77, minerva.mic.ul.ie/vol12/ Nietzsche.pdf.

If no pages are given, use *n. pag.* (not italicized).

Article Accessed through a Library Subscription Database

Give print information and then database information. Italicize the database name.

> Wolf, Maryanne, and Mirit Barzillai. "The Importance of Deep Reading." *Educational Leadership, Academic Search Complete.* vol. 66, no. 6, 2009, pp. 32–37.

Article in an Online Magazine

> Wilson, A. N. "Leo Tolstoy, Russia's Thunderous Prophet." *Real Clear Politics,* The Slate Group. 20 Nov. 2010, http://www.realclearpolitics.com/2010/11/20/ leo_tolstoy_russia039s_thunderous_prophet_246117.html.

Article in an Online Newspaper

Put the website in italics; follow with the name of the sponsor or publisher, not italicized.

> Hotz, Robert L. "Creative Destruction on a Cosmic Scale: Scientists Say Asteroid Blasts, Once Thought Apocalyptic, Fostered Life on Earth by Carrying Water and Protective Greenhouse Gas." *The Wall Street Journal.* Dow Jones & Company, 14 Aug. 2009, www.wsj.com/articles/ SB125020578491030557.

Editorial in an Online Newspaper or Magazine

Cite as you would online articles in periodicals, but add the designation *Editorial.*

> "Pre-K Must Be Texas Priority." Editorial. *San Antonio Express-News,* Hearst Newspapers, 16 Jan. 2015, www.expressnews.com/opinion/article/Your-Turn-Jan-15-6015616.php.

Online Letter to the Editor

Open with the author of the letter and the designation *Letter*.

> Talley, Penelope. Letter. *San Antonio Express-News,* San Antonio Express-News.
> Hearst Newspapers, 14 Jan. 2015, www.expressnews.com/opinion/article/
> Pre-K-must-be-a-Texas-priority-6021304.php.

Online Review

Use *Review of* (not in italics) to introduce the title of the book being reviewed. If the review has a title of its own, include it.

> Garner, Dwight. "Engagements with History Punctuate a Lifetime in Books." Review
> of *Outside Looking In,* by Garry Wills, *The New York Times,* 2 Nov. 2010,
> mobile.nytimes.com/2010/11/03/books/03book.html?.

Article in an Online Reference Work

If unsigned, open with the title of the article. When alphabetizing, ignore opening articles *(a, an, the)*.

> "The Philosophy of Dance." *Stanford Encyclopedia of Philosophy.*
> Metaphysics Research Lab, Stanford U, 12 Jan. 2015, plato.stanford.edu/
> entries/dance/.

Blog Entry

Put the title of the post in quotation marks and the blog title in italics.

> Jerz, Dennis. "Writing School Papers: Does Your First Version Say It All?" *Jerz's
> Literacy Weblog,* 12 Jan. 2015, learningenglish.voanews.com/content/
> writing-school-papers/2569201.html.

Government Document on the Web

> United States Congress, Senate Special Committee on Aging. *Social Security
> Modernization: Options to Address Solvency and Benefits Adequacy.* 111th
> Cong., 2nd sess. S. Rept. 111–187. 13 May 2010. Government Printing Office,
> 2010. 111th Congress, 2nd session, Senate Report 111-187.www.congress.
> gov/111/crpt/srpt187/CRPT-111srpt187.pdf.

Broadcast or Published Interview

Open with the names of the interviewee or interviewees, followed by the title of the interview, if there is one; if not, provide the interviewer's name.

> Fahim, Kareem. "How Does Al-Quaida Continue to Grow?" Interview by
> Arun Rath, *All Things Considered,* Natl. Public Radio, WBUR, Accessed
> 10 Jan. 2015.

Discussion Groups and Online Forums

MLA suggests that postings to online forums and discussion groups are not appropriate sources for research papers and does not provide a format. But there might be a reason for you to cite them in a paper that examined Internet communication, for example.

> Perlstein, Arnie. "A Novelist's Progress." Message to Austen-L. 26 Jan. 2011, www.
> pemberley.com/janeinfo/austen-l.html.

Wiki

> "Herman Melville." *Wikipedia.* Wikimedia Foundation, 13 Jan. 2015, en.wikipedia.org/
> wiki/Herman_Melville.

E-Mail Message

> Crusius, Timothy. "Procedural Suggestions." Received by Carolyn Channell,
> 9 April 2016.

Other Sources

Online Book

Use the format for a print book, modifying as necessary.

> Hawes, Elizabeth. *Camus: A Romance.* Grove, 2009. Kindle.

Motion Picture

Begin with the title of the film followed by the director and performers.

> *The King's Speech.* Directed by Tom Hooper, performance by Colin Firth, Geoffrey
> Rush, and Helena Bonham Carter, Weinstein, 2010.

Television

For an individual episode:

> "Cleaning House." *How I Met Your Mother.* Created by Pamela Fryman, directed by
> Steven Lloyd. CBS. WBBM, Chicago, 28 Sept. 2010.

For a series:

> *Monk.* Created by Andy Breckman, performance by Tony Shalhoub, Jason Gray-
> Stanford, Ted Levine, and Traylor Howard. USA Network. 2002–2009.

Play or Other Live Performance

> *In the Heights.* By Lin-Manuel Miranda. Directed by Thomas Kail. Choreographed by
> Andy Blankenbuehler. Richard Rodgers Theatre, New York. 9 Jan. 2011. Dance
> performance.

Add a description of the performance if not otherwise obvious. If you want to emphasize an individual's contribution, use this format:

> Sher, Bartlett, director. *South Pacific.* By Richard Rodgers and Oscar Hammerstein II, performance by Kelli O'Hara and Paulo Szot. Vivian Beaumont Theater, Lincoln Center, New York. 3 Apr. 2008.

Musical Composition and Sound Recording

If your emphasis is on the work, start with the composer. If it is on the performance, start with the conductor or performers. Song names are in quotation marks; longer works are italicized. Add the production company and release date.

> Baez, Joan, performer. "Simple Twist of Fate." By Bob Dylan. *Diamonds and Rust.* A&M, 1988.
> Barenboim, Daniel, conductor *Symphony No. 5.* By Gustav Mahler. Chicago Symphony Orchestra. Rhino, 2006.
> Cooder, Ry. *Paradise and Lunch.* Reprise, 1990.

Podcast

Cite as you would a radio program.

> "Fearless." Narrated by Lulu Miller and Alix Spiegel. *Invisibilia.* Natl. Public Radio, 16 Jan. 2015.

Cartoon

Designate the cartoon genre, as these examples show.

> Batiuk, Tom. "Funky Winkerbean." Comic strip. *The Chicago Tribune* 19, Jan. 2011, p. 12.
> Wilson, Gahan. Cartoon. *The New Yorker* 24, Jan. 2011, p. 24.

Work of Visual Art

For works of visual art, state artist, title (italicized), date of composition (or n.d.), the work's medium, the location (such as the museum, gallery, collection), and city.

> Seurat, Georges. *A Sunday on La Grande Jatte.* 1884, Art Institute, Chicago.

If your source comes from the Web, use the following format:

> Seurat, Georges. *A Sunday on La Grande Jatte.* 1884, School of the Art Institute, Chicago, www.artic.edu/aic/collections/artwork/27992.

Map

> Olivebridge, New York. Map, *Mapquest,* www.mapquest.com/us/ny/olivebridge-282894452.

A map from a book would be cited this way:

> "The Pusan Perimeter, August 4, 1950." Map, *The Coldest Winter: America and the Korean War.* By David Halberstam. Hyperion, 2007, p. 165.

Use this form only if the map was your only source from the book; otherwise, list the entire book under works cited and indicate in a signal phrase that you are referring to a map.

Oral Presentations

This category includes papers presented at professional conferences as well as readings, speeches, and keynote addresses. Use quotation marks around titles.

> Laurence, David. "The Condition of the Modern Languages in Higher Education: What the Data Tell Us." Rocky Mountain Modern Language Association Conference, Albuquerque, 15 Oct. 2010. Address.

Pamphlet

Set up works cited entries for pamphlets and brochures as if they were books.

> Museum of Indian Arts and Culture. *Turquoise—Water—Sky: The Stone and Its Meaning.* New Mexico Department of Cultural Affairs, 2014.

Use *n.p.* (no italics) if no place of publication is listed; use *n.d.* (no italics) for "no date."

Legal Sources

Open citation with the title of the act or case, followed by numerical details.

> Griswold v. Connecticut. 381 US 479. Supreme Court of the US. 1965. *FindLaw.* Thomson Reuters, 2011, caselaw.findlaw.com/us-supreme-court/381/479.html.

The names of legal cases are italicized in your text: *Griswold v. Connecticut.*

Personal Interview

Give the name of the person interviewed, and the date it took place.

> Amsel, Stephanie. Personal interview. 20 Oct. 2014.

SAMPLE RESEARCH PAPER **MLA Style**

1"

½" ⎡ 1"

Van Buskirk 1   Header

Put your name and the page number at the right top corner of every page.

Kyle Van Buskirk

Professor Channell

English 1302

April 25, 2010

Identifying information (double spaced)

Double space between date and title

The Benefits of Slow Reading Lost in Our Fast-Paced Culture

Double space between title and 1st line

½" For many young adults today, reading anything in depth almost seems like an

ancient pastime. In English class, high school students will search online for the Cliff

Notes rather than actually read the book. When we want news, instead of read-

ing newspapers, we check the headlines on MSNBC. Doing research, we surf the

Internet. A study of computer activity in the British Library found that researchers

skim and "bounce" from site to site. "It almost seems that they go online to avoid

reading in the traditional sense," concluded the authors of the study (qtd. in Carr).

People have lost sight of the many benefits of reading because we live in such a

fast-paced, technology-driven culture. We have become too impatient to read.

Carr is quoting the authors of the study, but Carr is the source. Use the abbreviation for "quoted in" for indirect sources.

Our pace of life makes everything that takes time seem like a burden. Even

sitting down to drink a cup of coffee takes too long, so we use the drive-through at

Starbucks. What people do not realize is that life is short, and it will be shallow and

unsatisfying if we refuse to slow down to think and reflect. Reading books pro-

vides us with that opportunity, enriching our lives in the long run, but also giving us

many immediate, practical benefits.

Some people claim that we read just as much as ever, only we do it on com-

puter screens. In an on-line newspaper column titled "Dawn of the Digital Natives,"

Steven Johnson, a best-selling nonfiction author, asks his readers, "Odds are that

you are reading these words on a computer monitor. Are you not exercising the

Lead into an opinion by first introducing the person who holds that opinion, giving full name on first mention and some identification or credentials.

1"

Van Buskirk 2

same cognitive muscles because these words are made out of pixels and not little splotches of ink?"

But there is evidence that on-line reading and on-paper reading are not the same. In his best-selling book, *The Dumbest Generation,* Mark Bauerlein describes the studies of Jacob Nielsen, who runs a consulting group that designs Web pages for corporations. This group does eye-tracking studies to show how people read on computer screens. The researchers' conclusion was "They *don't*" (qtd. in Bauerlein 143). The eye tracker revealed a surprising pattern that creators of Web sites need to know:

> The pattern looks like the capital letter F. At the top of the page, users read all the way across, but as they proceed their descent quickens and horizontal movement shortens, with a slowdown around the middle of the page. Near the bottom of the page, the eyes move almost vertically, forming the lower stem of the F shape. . . . Whatever content businesses want to communicate to visitors better not be concentrated in the lower-right portions of the screen, Nielsen advised. (Bauerlein 144)

This study gives scientific evidence that on-line readers could be missing a lot of content. But if people do not read books, they also miss out on important mental exercise.

Even though Steven Johnson defends screen reading as making "Digital Natives" highly informed, he admits in his book *Everything Bad Is Good for You* that the Internet is not so good at "training our minds to follow a sustained textual argument" (187) or to "transmit [the] fully fledged world view" of another person (186). Johnson writes a blog to exchange ideas with readers, but he writes books to present his arguments in full.

Can we get the benefits of book reading from watching the movie version of a novel or listening to an audio book while we drive? According to reading experts, we cannot. Oprah Winfrey, who has promoted book reading on her TV

Use block form for quotations of more than four lines of type. Double-space as normal before, after, and within block quotations.

Period ending a block quotation goes before the parenthetical citation.

Work quotations into a paraphrase to present key ideas concisely. Use square brackets where you have had to alter a quotation to fit it into your sentence.

Use ellipses to show where parts of quotations have been deleted. An ellipsis is a series of three spaced periods. The first period here is not spaced because it ends the sentence before the deleted portion.

Van Buskirk 3

show, published an article in her magazine *O* about the mental benefits of reading. Reading gives your brain more of a neurobiological workout than hearing speech or looking at images (Dzubow). Maryanne Wolf, director of the Center for Reading and Language Research at Tufts University, explains why: "Typically, when you read, you have more time to think. Reading gives you a unique pause button for comprehension and insight. By and large, with oral language—when you watch a film or listen to a tape—you don't press pause" (qtd. in Dzubow). In a more technical article, Wolf explains that experienced readers' brains have developed "streamlined" circuits that allow them to go far beyond just decoding the words. As they read, experienced readers can also "question, analyze, and probe" and "go beyond the wisdom of the author to think their own thoughts," a process that involves "all four lobes and both hemispheres of the brain" (Wolf and Barzillai 34). Reading gives our brains a workout, but because on-line readers click on links and allow their eyes to jump around in the F-shaped pattern described earlier, they are not developing these critical reading skills.

However, even when a person sits down with a book, he or she may not take the time to hit the pause button and read deeply. In an article for *Atlantic Monthly* titled "Is Google Making Us Stupid?" Nicholas Carr, who writes about information technology, describes how switching to the Internet as his main source of information has changed his style of reading. He went from loving to read long books to having to struggle to pay attention to them: "I get fidgety, lose the thread, begin looking for something else to do. I feel that I am always dragging my wayward brain back to the text." Carr has lost the ability to immerse himself in a book. As he describes it, "Once I was a scuba diver in the sea of words. Now I zip along the surface like a guy on a Jet Ski."

One would think that schools would encourage reading for pleasure, but too often they encourage reading for speed. This bothers Thomas Newkirk, Professor of English at University of New Hampshire. He criticizes the Accelerated Reading Program, which awards points for numbers of books read, and standardized

---

Use a colon before a direct quotation if you lead into it with a complete sentence instead of a phrase.

Cite the source of paraphrased information that is not common knowledge.

Grade 12 in 2005

Reading scores range from 0 to 500.

FIG. **1**

Average Reading Scores by Frequency of Reading Fiction Books or Stories Outside School

Source: United States, Department of Education, National Center for Education Statistics, reported in United States, National Endowment for the Arts, *To Read or Not to Read: A Question of National Consequence,* Nov. 2007, 71, www.arts.gov/sites/default/files/ToRead.pdf.

testing "in which reading is always 'on the clock.'" A slow reader himself, Newkirk says fast readers miss out on a lot, just as riders on high-speed European trains miss out on the details of the scenery and see the distant landscape as a blur. Newkirk says that "there is real pleasure in downshifting, in slowing down. We can gain some pleasures and meanings no other way." The pleasure is not just a result of going slow, explains John Miedema, who wrote a book on slow reading. "To me," he says, "slow reading is about bringing more of the person to bear on the book" (qtd. in Ramer). This is what people mean when they say they "got into" a book. Getting lost in a book is fun.

Setting aside time to read for pleasure also pays off in practical ways. Students who read for pleasure have distinctly higher reading comprehension scores and better writing scores. Fig. 1 shows the correlation between twelfth graders' reading scores and the amount of time they spend reading fiction for fun.

Van Buskirk 5

Fig. 2 shows the results of a slightly older study on writing ability. Students who read every day scored almost thirty points higher than those who did almost no reading for fun.

Reading for pleasure is also a way of improving mental wellness. Most students live at too fast a pace. We are distracted and stressed, constantly worrying about the next quiz, test, project, or research paper. Bauerlein believes leisure reading provides relief from stress and helps us put our lives into perspective. He explains, "Books afford young readers a place to slow down and reflect, to find role models, to observe their own turbulent feelings well expressed, or to discover moral convictions" (58). Slowing down to think is necessary in college, when students are making important decisions about their morals, goals, and identity.

Likewise, Newkirk argues that schools should encourage slow reading to show students "an alternative to an increasingly hectic digital environment where

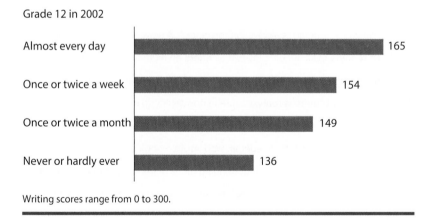

Grade 12 in 2002

Almost every day — 165
Once or twice a week — 154
Once or twice a month — 149
Never or hardly ever — 136

Writing scores range from 0 to 300.

FIG. **2**

Average Writing Scores by Frequency of Reading for Fun

Source: United States, Department of Education, National Center for Education Statistics, reported in United States, National Endowment for the Arts, *To Read or Not to Read: A Question of National Consequence,* Nov. 2007, p. 72, www.arts.gov/sites/default/files/ToRead.pdf.

Van Buskirk 6

so many of us read and write in severely abbreviated messages. . . ." Encouraging slow rather than fast reading would be one way to help students keep their lives in balance. Even before the Internet, media critic Neil Postman argued that a "major role" for schools "is to help conserve that which is necessary to a humane survival and threatened by a furious and exhausting culture" (qtd. in Newkirk). In other words, reading quality literature at a leisurely pace helps to keep us human.

Another English professor, Mark Edmundson, at the University of Virginia, is also concerned that the lifestyle of college students is too hectic. He sees that his students are always connected through their cell phones and laptops, working too hard, playing too hard, and taking ADD drugs to keep going. Edmundson worries that the fast pace of his students' lives keeps them from really knowing themselves and reflecting on the world. He imagines that Socrates would worry that today's students do not slow down enough to question what they have been told is true, what Socrates referred to as "*doxa,* common sense, general belief". All through their years of growing up, adults in their lives—parents, teachers, and clergy—have told them how to define themselves and interpret the world. Edmundson says these interpretations may be true, but then again, they may not. That is why education and books are important. Edmundson wants professors to slow their classes down: "to live well, we must sometimes stop and think, and then try to remake the work in progress that we currently are."

> Use summary to present a large section of a source, citing pages for paraphrases as well as where brief quotations help to preserve the voice of the source's author.

We do a disservice to ourselves when we do not take time to read slowly. In addition to preparing us for success in our careers, deep reading helps us put our lives into perspective. Too many students are connected to everything and everyone but themselves, as Edmundson says, "[skating] fast over the surfaces of life," but not thinking about where we are going and why." Reading books for leisure helps to connect us with our own lives because books contain wisdom, not just more information, which we are already drowning in. To read for wisdom, we have to slow down the pace.

> Use brackets when changing verb tenses to make them fit grammatically into your sentence.

Van Buskirk 7

Works Cited

Bauerlein, Mark. *The Dumbest Generation: How the Digital Age Stupefies Young Americans and Jeopardizes Our Future.* Tarcher-Penguin, 2008.

Carr, Nicholas. "Is Google Making Us Stupid?" *TheAtlantic.com*, July-Aug. 2008, www.theatlantic.com/magazine/archive/2008/07/is-google-making-us-stupid/306868/.

Dzubow, Lauren. "Watch This. No. Read It!" *Oprah.com,* Harpo Productions, June 2008, www.oprah.com/health/How-Reading-Can-Improve-Your-Memory.

Edmundson, Mark. "Dwelling in Possibilities: Our Students' Spectacular Hunger for Life Makes Them Radically Vulnerable." *The Chronicle of Higher Education,* 14 Mar. 2008, chronicle.com/article/Dwelling-in-Possibilities/7083.

Johnson, Steven. "Dawn of the Digital Natives." *guardian.co.uk.* Guardian News and Media Ltd., 7 Feb. 2008, www.theguardian.com/technology/2008/feb/07/internet.literacy.

---. *Everything Bad Is Good for You: How Today's Popular Culture Is Actually Making Us Smarter.* Riverhead, 2005.

Newkirk, Thomas. "The Case for Slow Reading." *Educational Leadership,* vol. 67, no. 6, 2010, www.ascd.org/publications/educational-leadership/mar10/vol67/num06/The-Case-for-Slow-Reading.aspx.

Ramer, Holly. "NH Professor Pushes for Return to Slow Reading." *Seattle Times,* 17 June 2010, www.seattletimes.com/nation-world/nh-professor-pushes-for-return-to-slow-reading/.

United States. Natl. Endowment for the Arts. *To Read or Not to Read: A Question of National Consequence.* Nov. 2007, www.arts.gov/sites/default/files/ToRead.pdf.

Wolf, Maryanne, and Mirit Barzillai. "The Importance of Deep Reading." *Educational Leadership,* vol. 66, no. 6, 2009, pp. 32–37. *Academic Search Complete,* search.ebscohost.com.proxy.libraries.smu.edu/login.aspx?direct=true&db=a9h&AN=36666622&login.asp&site=ehost-live&scope=site.

CHAPTER 21

Documenting Your Sources: APA

THE AMERICAN PSYCHOLOGICAL ASSOCIATION (APA) STYLE OF DOCUMENTATION is used not only in the field of psychology but also in education, anthropology, social work, business, and other behavioral and social sciences. In APA documents, it is common to find authors referred to by their last name only rather than their full names, as in Modern Language Association (MLA) documents.

Like MLA style, APA documentation requires that a writer acknowledge the source of all direct quotations, paraphrased and summarized ideas from sources, and information that is not common knowledge. Citing is a two-step process that includes a brief in-text reference to the author and date of publication and a longer entry with complete bibliographical information in the reference list at the end of the article or book.

How Do I Make In-Text Citations Using APA Style?

For direct quotations and paraphrases of information that is not common knowledge, the basic in-text citation provides the last name of the author of the source, directly followed by the year the source was published. Citing page numbers is required for direct quotations and highly specific data but not for summarizing or paraphrasing ideas found throughout a text. The following examples show options for citing in text.

Summary or Paraphrase with One Author Named in Your Sentence

The playground is a space where gender identities are constructed. Paechter (2007) argues that boys who are physically passive on the playground move into the marginal spaces occupied by girls and younger children and thus become stigmatized by other boys as effeminate.

Summary or Paraphrase with One Author Named in Parentheses

The playground is a space where gender identities are constructed. Boys who are physically passive on the playground move into the marginal spaces occupied by girls and younger children and thus become stigmatized by other boys as effeminate (Paechter, 2007).

> **Punctuation Alert:** Place a comma between the author's name and the date of publication.

The parenthetical citation does not include page numbers because the information is a summary.

Direct Quotation with Author Named in the Sentence

According to Yoon (2009) anthropologists have found that people around the world create remarkably similar categories when labeling plants and animals, a phenomenon known as folk taxonomy. Yoon finds consensus about such categories as trees, vines, and bushes especially interesting "since there is no way to define a tree versus a bush" (p. D4). In naming the world around them, people appear "unconsciously to follow a set of unwritten rules" (p. D1).

Use the abbreviations *p.* or *pp.* (not in italics) for page references. Also cite figure numbers, table numbers, or other parts of a book if they are the source of specific information.

> **Punctuation Alert:** Close direct quotations before parenthetical citations. Place periods after the parenthetical citation unless you have a block quotation (see page 415).

Direct Quotation with Author Named in Parentheses

Unless the author is named in a sentence, all references in parentheses must include the last name and the year.

Anthropologists have found that people around the world create remarkably similar categories when labeling plants and animals, a phenomenon known as folk taxonomy (Yoon, 2009). Consensus about such categories as trees, vines, and bushes is especially interesting "since there is no way to define a tree versus a bush" (Yoon, 2009, p. D4). In naming the world around them, people appear "unconsciously to follow a set of unwritten rules" (Yoon, 2009, p. D1).

Source with Two Authors

Give both authors' last names each time you refer to the source. If you name them as part of your sentence, use *and* to join them.

Wolf and Barzillai (2009) describe the cognitive work of the reading brain.

If you name them in parentheses, use an ampersand (&).

Reading is very much unlike our other natural human functions of seeing, moving, speaking, and thinking. Reading is an invented cognitive function, and understanding how it works illustrates the amazing plasticity of the brain (Wolf & Barzillai, 2009).

Source with Three or More Authors

For three, four, or five authors, give all authors' last names in your first reference to the work. Write out "and" when the list is part of your sentence. Subsequent references should give only the first author's last name followed by the abbreviation *et al.* (not in italics).

C. K. Yoon. "Reviving the Lost Art of Naming the World." *New York Times* 11 Aug. 2009: D1+. Print.

First Reference

Radeloff, Hammer, and Stewart (2005) studied the impact of housing density on forests in the midwestern United States.

Later References

Radeloff et al. (2005) argue that rural sprawl has more impact on forests than urban sprawl because even though rural sprawl is less dense, its effects are spread over larger areas that once were forests.

For six or more authors, give only the first author's last name, followed by *et al.* (not in italics).

Mottron et al. (2007) studied locally oriented perception in children with autism.

More than One Publication by an Author in the Same Year

When you are citing more than one publication by an author with the same year of publication, label the years *a, b, c,* and so on (not italicized); the letter *a* would be assigned to the publication that comes first alphabetically. See the reference list example on pages 420–421.

Developmental psychologists often focus on the stresses of adolescence rather than on the positive aspects of that stage of life (Steinberg, 2005a, 2005b).

Punctuation Alert: Works by the same author are separated by commas.

Two or More Authors with the Same Last Name

Include identifying initials before each last name.

S. Young (2007) complains that scientists study earth-eating, or geophagia, only from the standpoint of their own disciplinary interests. Thus, there is no "global perspective of all the possible benefits and all the possible negative consequences of geopaghia" (p. 67).

Organization or Agency as Author

Spell out the name the first time you use it.

According to the National Collegiate Athletic Association (2015), the Academic Progress Rate is a way to measure academic performance for college and university sports teams.

If the name is long and has a familiar abbreviation, you may use that in subsequent citations.

(NCAA, 2015)

Sera L. Young. "A Vile Habit? The Potential Biological Consequences of Geophagia, with Special Attention to Iron" in J. MacClancy, J. Henry, & H. Macbeth (Eds.), *Consuming the Inedible: Neglected Dimensions of Food Choice*. New York, NY: Berghahn Books, 2007. 67. Print.

Always spell out brief names or names that do not have familiar abbreviations.

Work with No Author or Editor

If no author or editor is named, use the title of the work in both in-text citations and reference list entries. If the title is long, abbreviate it in the text but not on the reference list. Use double quotation marks around the title of an article, a chapter, or a webpage in your discussion, but not in the reference list. Italicize the title of a periodical, book, or report. The example below shows a webpage.

> The Law School Aptitude Test (LSAT) measures ability to read and comprehend in-depth texts with insight, to draw "reasonable inferences" from readings, and to analyze and evaluate the reasoning of others' arguments ("About the LSAT," 2015).

More than One Source in a Parenthetical Citation

If you have more than one source for the same information, include all sources in the parenthetical citation, in alphabetical order, as they would appear in the reference list. Use a semicolon to separate sources by different authors.

> (Steinberg, 2005a, 2005b; Stewart, 1987)

Work with No Page Numbers (Including Webpages and E-Books)

If online material, e-books, or even print material is unpaged and you need to cite a specific passage, use chapters, paragraphs, headings, or whatever other indicators will help readers find the passage.

> According to Friend (2009), "Extraordinary oddities of conduct are tolerated among Wasps so long as you show up for Christmas" (Chapter 4, para. 78).

If the chapters have further numbered subdivisions, include them. For example,

> (Section 5, para. 4)

Reprinted Works

When you cite a work that has been republished, give both the original date and the date of the version you are using. The in-text citation for the example on page 418 would be (Obama 1995/2004). The date of original publication comes first, although on the reference list the date following the author's name will reflect the edition you used (2004, in this case).

Citations within Quotations

You will often find that your source cites other sources. Do not put these sources on your reference list unless you also read them and used them in your paper. When quoting, include the citations as they appear in the passage you are quoting.

T. Friend. *Cheerful Money: Me, My Family, and the Last Days of Wasp Splendor.* Hachette Book Group, 2009. Print.

Hunters seldom wear protection for their hearing, resulting in hearing loss among practitioners of the sport, as Flamme et al. (2010) explain:

> Firearm impulse sound exposure contributes to the poorer hearing ability and hearing handicap evident in sports hunters when compared to nonhunters (Taylor & Williams, 1966; Stewart et al., 2002). Nondahl et al. (2000) calculated a 7% increase in the likelihood of having a marked high-frequency hearing loss for every 5 years of hunting.

Long Quotations

For direct quotations of forty or more words, omit quotation marks and display the quotation as a block of text set in from the left margin by one-half inch (in the same place as a new paragraph's opening). Double-space the entire quotation. See the example above on citations within quotations.

> **Punctuation Alert:** With block quotations, place the final period before the parenthetical citation.

Indirect Sources

A good researcher relies on primary sources. But if your only source for information was cited in another source, use this format.

. . . as noted by Conley (as cited in McMaster, 2009).

Include McMaster on your reference list, not Conley.

Work in an Anthology

If you are citing a selection from an anthology, list the author of the selection. If you are citing the collection as a whole, list the editor or compiler of the book.

Classics and Religious Works

When you are citing a work whose original publication date is not known or is not relevant, show the date of the version you are using—(Defoe, 2005 version), for example, for a modern version of *Robinson Crusoe,* first published in 1719. For a translation of a classical work, show the date of translation (Sophocles, trans. 1911). Religious works are cited only in the text, not in the reference list. Instead of page numbers, cite books, chapters, verses, lines, and so forth. Use standard abbreviations for biblical books: Num. 11.7–8, for instance.

A Multivolume Work

Cite all the years of publication if you are referring to the entire work.

(Foote, 1958–1974)

If you have used all the volumes but are citing from just one, include the volume number.

(Foote, 1958–1974, Vol. 2, p. 165)

An Entire Website

When your source is an entire website, cite it in the text by providing the uniform resource locator (URL), but do not provide a reference list entry.

> The PsychCentral website, sponsored by mental health professionals, offers news, information, and support group hosting for people interested in or affected by mental health disorders (http://psychcentral.com).

Personal Communications

Personal communications such as letters and interviews are not listed in the reference list; they are cited in text as in the following example.

> Carolyn Coman described her use of storyboarding to focus on the emotional impact of significant scenes in her fiction (C. Coman, personal communication, August 15, 2009).

Note that the names of months are not abbreviated in APA style and that month precedes day.

How Do I Make Entries in a Reference List Using APA Style?

This section includes examples of how to cite the most common kinds of sources in papers using the APA style of documentation.

General Guidelines for Your Reference List

- Begin the list on a new page and center the word *References* at the top. (Do not italicize.)
- The first word of each entry must match the in-text citation.
- Put all entries, regardless of genre and medium, in alphabetical order according to the author's (or editor's) last name, followed by the initials of the author's first name or names. Use an ampersand before the last author's name.
- If no author is named, use the first word in the title that is not an article (*a, an, the*). See page 418 for an example.
- Do not number the entries.
- Double-space within and between entries.
- Begin each entry at the left margin and indent all subsequent lines by one-half inch. The hanging indent feature of your word processing program will help you do this.
- Italicize titles of books and periodicals.
- Do not enclose titles of articles in quotation marks, although you do use quotation marks for article titles when you refer to them in text.

- Capitalize only the first word of titles and subtitles of books and articles; however, capitalize all proper nouns in any title or subtitle (for example, a person's name).

- Capitalize the full names of periodicals, journals, and newspapers.

- Use city and state, unless the state is included in the publisher's name (Albuquerque: University of New Mexico Press). Use postal abbreviations for state names (New Haven, CT).

- In general, when the entry ends with something other than a publisher's name or page number, such as the DOI (digital objective identifier), URL, accession number, or original publication date, there is no end punctuation.

See the list of examples for more help with citing specific kinds of sources.

Printed Books

Your entries for printed books should contain the following:

1. Name of author (or editor) in inverted order, followed by a period (unless no author or editor is listed)
2. Date of publication in parentheses, followed by a period
3. Title of the work, in italics, followed by a period
4. City and state of publication, followed by a colon
5. Publisher, followed by a period

Last name, Initial(s). (Date). *Title*. City, State: Publisher.

Book by a Single Author

Paechter, C. F. (2007). *Being boys, being girls: Learning masculinities and femininities*. New York, NY: McGraw-Hill.

Use a brief form of the publisher's name. Do not include words like *Company, Corporation, or Inc.* Words like *Books* and *Press* should be retained. Do not use abbreviations.

Two or More Books by the Same Author

List the works in order of publication, with the earliest first. Repeat the author's name for each entry.

Obama, B. (2004). *Dreams from my father: A story of race and inheritance*. New York, NY: Three Rivers. (Original work published 1995)
Obama, B. (2006). *The audacity of hope: Thoughts on reclaiming the American dream*. New York, NY: Crown.

Book by Two or More Authors

List all authors by last name and initials, separated by commas. Use an ampersand (&) before the final name. If a work has up to seven authors, list them all. If there are more than seven, list the first six, then an ellipsis (three spaced dots), then the last author. (See the example for a journal article on page 423.)

> Booth, W., Colomb, G., & Williams, J. (2003). *The craft of research* (2nd ed.). Chicago, IL: University of Chicago Press.
> Small, G., & Vorgan, G. (2008). *iBrain: Surviving the technological alteration of the modern mind.* New York, NY: HarperCollins.

Book by a Corporate Author or Government Agency

Treat the corporation or agency as an author. If the author and publisher are the same, put "Author" after the place of publication.

> American Psychological Association. (2010). *Publication manual of the American Psychological Association* (6th ed.). Washington, DC: Author.

Book with No Author or Editor

Start with the title of the work. Use "Anonymous" only if that is what the title page says.

> *The Chicago Manual of Style.* (2010). Chicago, IL: University of Chicago Press.

Later Edition of a Book

Put the edition number in parentheses after the title.

> Williams, J. M. (2013). *Style: Ten lessons in clarity and grace* (11th ed.). New York, NY: Pearson Longman.

Reprinted Book

Indicate the original date of publication in parentheses.

> Obama, B. (2004). *Dreams from my father: A story of race and inheritance.* New York, NY: Three Rivers. (Original work published 1995)

Note: The in-text citation should include both dates, with the original publication date first (1995/2004).

Anthology or Compilation

Between the editor's name and the date, put the abbreviation for editor(s) in parentheses, followed by a period.

> MacClancy, J., Henry, J., & Macbeth, H. (Eds.). (2007). *Consuming the inedible: Neglected dimensions of food choice.* New York, NY: Berghahn Books.

Selection in an Anthology or Compilation

For articles in edited works, put the author of the individual work first, followed by the year of publication, and then the title of the article, followed by the word *In* and the editor or editors' names (not in inverse order) and the title of the collected work. The inclusive pages of the selection follow the title of the book, in parentheses. End the citation with place and name of publisher.

> Young, S. (2007). A vile habit? The potential biological consequences of geophagia, with special attention to iron. In J. MacClancy, J. Henry, & H. Macbeth (Eds.), *Consuming the inedible: Neglected dimensions of food choice* (pp. 67–79). New York, NY: Berghahn Books.

Note that APA style for inclusive numbers uses all digits.

Translation

Put the translator's initials and last name, followed by the abbreviation for translator in parentheses after the book's title.

> Ariès, P. (1965). *Centuries of childhood* (R. Baldick, Trans.). New York, NY: Vintage Books. (Original work published 1962)
> Sophocles. (1911). *Oedipus Rex* (J. E. Thomas, Trans.). Clayton, DE: Prestwick House. Retrieved from http://www.gutenberg.org/wiki/Main_Page

For classical works, such as *Oedipus Rex,* cite the date of translation in your text: (Sophocles, trans. 1911). This example also illustrates the format for a book retrieved online.

Preface, Introduction, Foreword, or Afterword Not by the Book's Author or Editor

Open the entry with the name of the author of the part of the book; then put the date in parentheses and write out the name of the section written by this author. Follow with author or editor, title, and publication information for the entire book.

> Gore, A. (2008). Foreword. In B. McKibben (Ed.), *American earth: Environmental writing since Thoreau.* New York, NY: Library of America.

Multivolume Work

Directly after the author, indicate the inclusive dates of the volumes. After the title of the work, indicate in parentheses the number of volumes.

> Churchill, W. (1956–1958). *A history of the English-speaking peoples* (Vols. 1–4). London, England: Cassell.

One Volume of a Multivolume Work

If the individual volumes in a multivolume work have their own titles, use the following format when only one of them should be included in your reference list.

> Churchill, W. (1957). *A history of the English-speaking peoples: Vol. 3. The age of revolution.* London, England: Cassell.

If the volume does not have its own title, then put the volume number in parentheses after the title, as when citing all volumes.

Signed Article in a Reference Book

Include inclusive page numbers for the entry in parentheses after the title of the book.

> Zangwill, O. L. (1987). Hypnotism, history of. In R. L. Gregory (Ed.), *The Oxford companion to the mind* (pp. 330–334). New York, NY: Oxford University Press.

Unsigned Article in a Reference Book

Open with the title of the entry.

> A technical history of photography. (2004). In *The New York Times guide to essential knowledge: A desk reference for the curious mind* (pp. 104–112). New York, NY: St. Martin's.

Articles in Print Periodicals

Your reference list entries for print periodicals should contain the following:

1. Name of author (or editor) in inverted order, followed by a period (unless no author or editor is listed)
2. Date of publication in parentheses, followed by a period
3. Title of the article, not in italics, followed by a period
4. Title of the periodical, in italics, followed by a comma (and, for a journal, further publication information)
5. Inclusive page numbers, followed by a period

Article in a Journal with Volume and/or Issue Number

> Last name, Initial(s). (Date). Title of article. *Title of Periodical, vol. no*(issue), pages.

Put a comma after the journal title, followed by the volume number in italics; then (with no space) put the issue number, if one is needed, in parentheses, followed by a comma and inclusive page numbers. For journals, use the issue number *only* if the journal is paged by issue, not by volume.

> Bracher, M. (2009). How to teach for social justice: Lessons from Uncle Tom's Cabin and cognitive science. *College English, 71*, 363–388.
> Wolf, M., & Barzillai M. (2009). The importance of deep reading. *Educational Leadership, 66(6)*, 32–37.

Multiple Publications by the Same Author in the Same Year

Use letters to distinguish works by the same author in the same year; assign the letters according to the alphabetical order of the titles of the works.

> Steinberg, L. (2005a). Cognitive and affective development in adolescence. *Trends in Cognitive Sciences, 9*, 69–74.

Steinberg, L. (2005b). *The ten basic principles of good parenting.* New York, NY: Simon & Schuster.

Article in a Monthly Magazine

For magazine articles, do not use *p.* or *pp.* Instead, put the volume number in italics followed by the issue number in parentheses, a comma, and page numbers. Because magazines are paged by issue, the issue number is required.

Mooney, C. (2008, July). Climate repair made simple. *Wired, 16*(7), 128–133.

Article in a Weekly Magazine

Include the day as well as the month and year.

Gladwell, M. (2009, October 19). Offensive play: How different are dogfighting and football? *The New Yorker,* 50–59.

Article in a Newspaper

Give the day, month, year, and edition if specified. For newspaper articles, use the abbreviations *p.* and *pp.* (not italicized) before the page number. List all page numbers if the article appeared on discontinuous pages.

Yoon, C. K. (2009, August 11). Reviving the lost art of naming the world. *The New York Times,* pp. D1, D4.

Do not abbreviate the names of months. Include articles at the beginning of periodical titles.

Newspaper Article with an Anonymous Author

Start with the title of the article. When alphabetizing, ignore opening articles *(a, an, the).*

Nuns' numbers dwindling. (2015, January 25). *Dallas Morning News,* p. 4A.

Editorial in a Newspaper—No Author Given

Put the genre (editorial) in square brackets. Unlike citations for other periodicals, those for newspapers have *p.* or *pp.* before the page number or numbers.

Poverty-busting in Dallas [Editorial]. (2015, January 19). *Dallas Morning News,* p. 20A.

Letter to the Editor of a Newspaper or Magazine

Put the genre (letter to the editor) in square brackets. If the letter appears in a newspaper, use the abbreviation *p.* and *pp.* (not italicized) before the page number; if it appears in a magazine, this is not required.

Schlosberg, J. (2015, January 26). Clickbait [Letter to the editor]. *The New Yorker,* p. 5.

Review

Open with the name of the reviewer, the date, and the title of the review, if there is one. Put "Review of," followed by the item being reviewed, in square brackets.

> Denby, D. (2011, January 24). Man up. [Review of the films *The Green Hornet,* dir.
>   M. Gondry, and *The Dilemma,* dir. R. Howard]. *The New Yorker,* 82–83.
> Hofferth, S. (2009, June 26). Buying so children belong [Review of the book
>   *Longing and belonging: Parents, children, and consumer culture* by A. J.
>   Pugh]. *Science, 324,* 1674.

Although *Science* is a scholarly journal, it is published weekly; APA style treats it and similar journals like a magazine.

Advertisement in Print Medium

Open with the sponsor of the advertisement, followed by the date of publication, its title, and the page number.

> New York City Ballet. (2015, January 26). [Advertisement]. *The New Yorker,* 5.

Sources on the Internet

Your reference list entries for Internet sources will vary according to the kind of source: online periodical, database, reference work, public service site, government site, and so on. Each entry should contain the following:

1. Name of author (or editors) in inverted order, followed by a period (unless no author or editor is listed)

2. Date of publication in parentheses, followed by a period

3. Title (including a format description in square brackets for unusual sources), followed by a period

4. Retrieval path, often a DOI or URL, or a database name and accession number (if available)

Other information may be included, such as periodical titles and page numbers, where available.

> Last name, Initial(s). (Date). Title [Label if needed]. Retrieval path.

Website

Do not list entire websites in the reference list. Give the URL in your discussion. See the example on page 416.

Webpage

> Tartakovsky, M. (2010). Asperger's syndrome. http://psychcentral.com/lib/
>   aspergers-syndrome/0004226

If the source is something unusual, such as a lecture, a data file, or a video, put that in square brackets after the title.

Journal Article Retrieved Online—with DOI

Because URLs often change, a new method of locating online materials has been developed. Increasingly, you will find that articles have an alphanumeric identification string, usually located near the copyright date in the article. You can also find it in the bibliographic information in the library's full-record display. Always use the DOI, if available, instead of the URL from which you retrieved the online article. Use the format for a print journal. Conclude the entry with the DOI. There is no space between the colon and the number when giving a DOI.

> Mottron, L., Mineau, S., Martel, G., St.-Charles Bernier, C., Berthiaume, C., Dawson, M., . . . & Faubert, J. (2007). Lateral glances toward moving stimuli among young children with autism: Early regulation of locally oriented perception. *Development and Psychopathology, 19,* 23–26. doi:10.1017/S0954579407070022

Note the treatment of more than seven authors. The first six are listed; an ellipsis follows, and then the last author is named. This article has ten authors.

Journal Article Retrieved Online—without DOI

Follow the format for a print article. Follow with "Retrieved from" and the URL for the journal home page.

> O'Dwyer, K. (2008). Nietzsche's reflections on love. *Minerva—An Internet Journal of Philosophy, 12,* 37–77. Retrieved from http://www.ul.ie/~philos/

Source Accessed through a Database

Cite books and periodicals according to the guidelines already given. Include the name of the database only if you think it would be difficult to find the source in any other way. In that case, at the end of the citation, add "Retrieved from" and the database name. Give the accession number, if there is one, in parentheses. Put information identifying the genre in square brackets after the title.

> Van der Woude, G. (2002). *Harriet Tubman integrated unit* [Classroom guide]. Retrieved from ERIC database. (Accession No. ED476397)

Article in an Online Magazine

Conclude the entry with "Retrieved from" and the URL for the home page of the magazine. Use the DOI if there is one.

> Vanderbilt, T. (2011, January 13). Streetcars vs. monorails. *Slate.* Retrieved from http://slate.com

Article in an Online Newspaper

Use the URL for the home page of the newspaper if the article can be found by searching the site, as is usually the case.

> Hotz, R. L. (2009, August 14). Creative destruction on a cosmic scale: Scientists say asteroid blasts, once thought apocalyptic, fostered life on earth by carrying

water and protective greenhouse gas. *The Wall Street Journal.* Retrieved
from http://online.wsj.com/home-page

Article in an Online Encyclopedia or Reference Work

If the entry is unsigned, open with its title, as in the first example below.

The philosophy of dance. (2015, January 12). In E. N. Zalta (Ed.), *Stanford
Encyclopedia of Philosophy.* Retrieved from http://plato.stanford.edu/
entries/dance/

Botstein, L. (2005). Robert Maynard Hutchins and the University of Chicago.
In J. Reiff, A. D. Keating, & J. R. Grossman (Eds.), *Encyclopedia of
Chicago.* Retrieved from http://www.encyclopedia.chicagohistory.org/
pages/2190.html

Use the URL that will get you to the specific article.

Abstract

Sweeten, G., Bushway, S. D., & Paternoster, R. (2009). Does dropping out of school
mean dropping out into delinquency? *Criminology, 47,* 47–92. Abstract
retrieved from http://www.ncjrs.gov

Blog Post

Give the title of the post and the URL for the post but not the title of the blog.

Agapakis, C. (2010, December 8). Making blind mice see [Web log post].
Retrieved from http://scienceblogs.com/oscillator/2010/12/making_blind_
mice_see.php

Published or Broadcast Interview

Include the format in which the interview was published and follow the style for that
format.

Fahim, K. (2015, January 10). Interview by Arun Rath [Web]. Retrieved from
http://www.npr.org/2015/01/10/376381082/how-does-al-qaida-continue-
to-grow

Discussion Groups and Online Forums

Begin with the author of the post, the date, the title, the genre in brackets, and the
retrieval path.

Mendez, J. O. (2014, October 27). First-year seminars and academic advising
[Online forum comment]. Retrieved from http://dus.psu.edu/mentor/2013/08/
first-year-seminars-academic-advising/

Bracketed labels could also include:

[Discussion list message]
[Newsgroup posting]

Video on the Internet

Open with the producer of the video.

> Hirsh, M. (2010, December 16). Richard Holbrooke: A friend to journalists [Video file]. Retrieved from http://www.youtube.com/watch?v=IeGGGEUsCI0

Other Kinds of Sources

E-Book

> Friend, T. (2009). *Cheerful money: Me, my family, and the last days of Wasp splendor* [Kindle version]. Retrieved from Amazon.com

Indicate the type of e-book file. If there is a DOI for the e-book file, include it at the end.

Films

> Gonzalez, A. (Producer & Director). (2014). *Birdman or (The unexpected virtue of ignorance)* [Motion picture]. United States: Fox Searchlights Pictures.

List the producer and the director, the studio, and the country of origin.

Television Program (Episode from a Series)

> Fryman, P. (Writer), & Lloyd, S. (Director). (2010). Cleaning house [Television series episode]. In C. Bays, P. Fryman, R. Greenberg, & C. Thomas (Executive Producers), *How I met your mother.* New York, NY: CBS.

If you want to cite the entire series, list the creators and producers first, along with inclusive dates.

Live Performance

> Rickson, I. (Director). (2014, November 28). *The river* [Live performance]. Circle in the Square, New York, NY.

Musical Compositions and Sound Recordings

> Cooder, R. (1990). *Paradise and lunch* [CD]. New York, NY: Reprise.
> Mahler, G. (Composer), & Barenboim, D. (Conductor). (2006). *Symphony no. 5* [Recorded by Chicago Symphony Orchestra]. [MP3]. New York, NY: Rhino. Retrieved January 21, 2011, from Amazon.com

Podcast

> Palca, J. (Narrator). (2011, January 13). *Rock-munching mollusks a model for artificial bones* [Audio podcast]. Retrieved from http://www.npr.org

Map

> Google Maps. (2015, January 21). Kingsville, Texas [Road map]. Retrieved from http://maps.google.com/

For a map in a book or article, cite the map number or page number in your text and indicate in your signal phrase that you are referring to a map.

Visual Art

> Seurat, G. (1884). *A Sunday on La Grande Jatte* [Painting]. Art Institute, Chicago, IL.

Give the medium and the location. If you cite a work of art in a book, indicate what you are referring to (painting, sculpture, etc.) in your text and list the entire book in the reference list.

Dissertation or Thesis Retrieved from a Database

> Neland, L. S. (1989). *Correlates of marital satisfaction in chemically dependent women* [Doctoral dissertation]. Retrieved from ProQuest. (AAT 9007511)

Unpublished Dissertation or Thesis

> Pendleton, R. (2005). *Teaching biography: History as lives, lives as history* (Unpublished master's thesis). University of Rochester, Rochester, NY.

Paper Presented at a Professional Conference

> Jones, S. L., and Yarhouse, M. A. (2009, August 9). *Ex-gays? An extended longitudinal study of attempted religiously mediated change in sexual orientation.* Paper presented at the meeting of the American Psychological Association, Toronto, Canada.

Legal Sources

> Griswold v. Connecticut, 381 U.S. 479 (1965).
> Patient Protection and Affordable Care Act, Public Law 111-148, 124 Stat. 119-1025 (2010).

Your in-text citations should italicize the names of court cases.

Wikipedia Entry

> Sigmund Freud. (n.d.). In *Wikipedia*. Retrieved January 28, 2011, from http://en.wikipedia.org/wiki/Sigmund_Freud

Because APA requires publication dates (not dates of update), *n.d.* is usually used for Wikipedia entries. The retrieval date is given because the material you cite is likely to change over time on Wikipedia.

Personal Communications

Personal communications such as interviews and letters are not included in the list of references in APA style. However, you need to cite them in the text as described on page 416.

S A M P L E   R E S E A R C H   P A P E R   **APA Style**

Running head: POPULARITY'S DOWNSIDE

1

Use your title, but not your subtitle, as a running head on every page. Number all pages, starting with title page.

Popularity's Downside:

Valuing Quantity over Quality in Friendship

Audra Ames

Southern Methodist University

Center the title, author, and name of college or university in upper half of page.

POPULARITY'S DOWNSIDE   2

½"   1"

1"

Do not indent
first line of
abstract.

1"

Abstract   Heading (centered), new page

Adolescents commonly value popularity over having a few high-quality friends, as

they see popularity as a mark of status. However, making popularity one's main

goal causes young people to miss out on the benefits of real friendship because

the values and behavior required for popularity conflict with those that would

allow true friendships to form. True friendship encourages personal growth and

deep intimacy while an obsession with popularity encourages aggression, mean

competition, and conformity to peer group preferences. It also causes young peo-

ple to keep personal problems to themselves and to become self-absorbed to the

point of narcissism. Young people with poor self-image and values may seek the

security of groups whose friendship can be destructive, but most settle for super-

ficial friendships that are not harmful, but do not promote personal growth or offer

the deep rewards of true friendship. Popularity itself is good but should be seen

as a means for finding potential friends with whom to form deep relationships.

Keywords: popularity, competition, peers, friendship

Abstract is
an objective
summary of
the main points
in the essay or
article.

Abstract
should be
between
150 and 250
words.

POPULARITY'S DOWNSIDE   3

Popularity's Downside:

Indent 5
spaces or 1/2"   Valuing Quantity over Quality in Friendship

Double space
between title
and opening of
the essay.

⟵⟶ In middle school, junior high, and high school, social hierarchies are very impor-

tant, with the top rungs of the ladder usually occupied by cheerleaders, athletes,

and the physically attractive people. There is a high correlation between these

sources of status and being popular. Popularity itself is a source of status. Even after

high school, some people want to continue to play the popularity game; they seek

quantity of friends, not quality in friendships. Studies show that this is a mistake.

Having large quantities of friends is not as worthwhile as having a few high quality

friendships. Real friendships are based not on status and hierarchies but on shared

interests and equality. Making popularity one's main goal causes young people

to miss out on the benefits of real friendship because the values and behavior

required for popularity conflict with those that would allow true friendships to form.

Thesis states
the main point
derived from
the findings of
the research.

The Value of Friendship

Subheads are
bolded and
centered.

High-quality friendships have been described as relationships in which

people are willing to put aside some of their own self-interests to invest attention

in each other's goals and personal growth. Friendships support mutual growth.

Relationships with friends are not static and unchanging because friends keep

each other moving forward, as described by Csikszentmihalyi (1997): "We try new

things, activities, and adventures; we develop new attitudes, ideas, and values; we

get to know friends . . . deeply and intimately" (pp. 81–82). Similarly, Berndt (2004)

found that "friendships are higher in quality when friends feel free to disclose their

most intimate thoughts and feelings to each other" (p. 1). With true friends, no one

feels the need to hide who they are, or what they really think and feel, or fear

being seen as weak if they confide about insecurities and doubts.

The rewards of friendship are great; studies have shown that people's

most positive experiences occur with friends, and this is "especially true for

1"

1"

POPULARITY'S DOWNSIDE   4

adolescents" (Csikszentmihalyi, 1997, p. 81). Growing up is just easier with a good friend. Studies have found that having a close friend and being in a reciprocated friendship helps children of middle-school age adjust to their changing environment with less stress and depression (Dittmann, 2004).

How Popularity Conflicts with Friendship

However, a problem for many adolescents is the importance of popularity over having a few quality relationships. A study of middle school girls found that although they highly valued friendship as a source of trust and intimacy, "friendship was seldom a serious contender with popularity when girls had to choose" (Merten, 2004, p. 362). Similarly, Closson (2009) found that clique members were willing to give up their personal preferences in friends to comply with the leaders' preferences. He concluded that "the desire for popularity may be stronger than the desire for a stable, high-quality friendship in early adolescence" (p. 429).

It seems that young people are torn between their desire for friendship and their desire for status. Studies confirm what most people know from personal experience: Social status is "a central aspect of daily life" for young adolescents (Closson, 2009, p. 407). The desire for status conflicts with the desire for friendship because young people choose to associate with those who can help boost their status rather than those who share their interests and goals. Csiksentzmihalyi (1997) argued that "friendships are expected to provide mutual benefits, with no external constraints that might lead to exploitation" (p. 82). The desire for status puts constraints on the choice of friends, and young people might act friendly to someone simply for the social benefits that person brings.

Too much concern for popularity can keep young people from discussing personal problems, and thus getting the benefit of a peer's sympathy and support. In his study of junior high girls, Merten (2004) noted that true friendships encouraged sharing of all experiences (inclusion), while the desire for popularity caused girls to exclude from conversations any experiences that might cause them to be judged as weak. In friendships, Merten saw girls "respecting and valuing each other's experiences, rather than having the demands of popularity select which experiences were worthy of inclusion in a relationship" (p. 364). Basically, the girls seeking popularity had to filter what they said around their popular friends in order to not have a vulnerability exploited. Popularity is accompanied by a fear of vulnerability. If you show weakness, you are picked apart or criticized for it.

The Downside of Popularity

The fact is that popularity is associated with some bad traits, such as aggression and gossip. Even within cliques, Closson (2009) found that members act aggressively to gain and keep status, and this happened most frequently in cliques that were recognized as having high status within the school:

> Compared to members of lower status cliques, those in perceived popular cliques used more instrumental relational aggression. Some researchers have suggested that peer-directed relational aggression may be used intentionally to damage another peer's social reputation, thereby . . . maintaining or increasing one's status within the clique by decreasing the social position of others. (p. 428)

Closson (2009) also found that popular people were described by their peers as "cool, nice, and funny yet also conceited, exclusionary, and mean" (p. 408). But conceited people are not usually happy because they are too self-absorbed.

A desire for popularity inspires narcissism, which can be described as overly high self-esteem and self-absorption. Narcissistic people are "looking for happiness by way of what they can draw toward themselves, rather than what they can share with others" (Schumaker, 2007, p. 175). People who are obsessed with being popular are buying into a system that almost rules out the possibility of real friendship because as Merten (2004) found, "Popularity was based on hierarchy, public recognition, and self-interest [while] friendship was based on equality . . ." (p. 363). The main focus of popularity seems to be popularity in itself, and especially the attributes that go along with being popular, like physical attractiveness (p. 363). It is not surprising that narcissism has been connected with aggressive behavior, including bullying. Schumaker (2007) described narcissists as aggressive, with a tendency to bully (p. 168). When their self-esteem is threatened, narcissists put others down in order to build up their egos again.

Sometimes people can be popular in another way that creates malignant growth. They can be popular with the wrong crowd, and this can inspire aggressive, antisocial behavior. Interactions with a certain group of people may change a person or encourage violence and aggression, so that the person is more willing to commit unlawful, harmful acts in order to impress his peers. Berndt (2004) summarized studies related to "the three A's of friendship: adjustment, attachment, and aggression." In one study done on aggression in children, surprising data was collected. "Students higher in relational aggression actually had higher quality friendships, perhaps because these students needed friends to join them in attacking or excluding their victims" (Berndt, 2004, p. 2). These relationships are of high quality, but only because peers bond over acts of violence, which does not create a stable, high quality life. An extreme example of destructive friendship would be gangs, in which individuals support each other in a kind of "malignant growth" (Csikszentmihalyi, 1997, p. 82).

Putting Popularity in Its Place

More commonly, people of all ages settle for superficial "friendships" that are more like high school cliques. Csikszentmihalyi (1997) describes these groups as "safe cocoon[s]" for people not seeking to change: "The superficial sociability of teenage peer groups, suburban clubs and coffee klatches, professional associations, drinking buddies, gives a soothing sense of being part of a like-minded set of people without demanding much effort or growth" (p. 82). Having a large circle of acquaintances is not a bad thing if people do not see it as sufficient for the real happiness of true friendship.

One argument in favor of popularity is that it enables people to find friends and to be friends: Nangle, Erdley, Newman, Mason, and Carpenter (2003) found that popularity laid the groundwork for children with good social skills to find potential friends from a large "pool" of others with similarly good social skills (p. 551). Most important, these researchers found that young people with good

POPULARITY'S DOWNSIDE   7

social skills were able to form deep and long-lasting close friendships. Popularity is not a substitute for real friendship, just a stepping stone to it.

Conclusion

When you have a few good quality friendships versus a lot of acquaintances, you are able to explore, challenge and push yourself into becoming a better person. Equally important is the social support of a good friend. Studies have shown that the most frequent complaint of people dealing with an emotional crisis is that they do not have any true friends to turn to (Csikszentmihalyi, 1997, p. 83). People that do not have social support when they experience a rough patch are more likely to become depressed. Young people need to make it through adolescence with an appreciation for real friendship, and not give in to an immature obsession with popularity as a status symbol. Overall, quality over quantity in friendship is a much more successful route through all of one's life.

POPULARITY'S DOWNSIDE   8

References

Berndt, T. J. (2004). Friendship and three A's (aggression, adjustment, and

attachment). *Journal of Experimental Child Psychology 88*(1), 1–4.

doi:10.1016/j.jecp.2004.03.004

Closson, L. M. (2009). Aggressive and prosocial behaviors within early adolescent

friendship cliques: What's status got to do with it? *Merrill-Palmer Quarterly:*

Journal of Developmental Psychology, 55, 406–435. doi:10.1353/

mpq.0.0035

Csikszentmihalyi, M. (1997). *Finding flow: The psychology of engagement with*

everyday life. New York, NY: Basic Books.

Dittmann, M. (2004, July). Friendships ease middle school adjustment. *American*

Psychological Association. Retrieved from http://www.apa.org/monitor/

julaug04/friendships.aspx

Merten, D. E. (2004). Securing her experience: Friendship versus popularity.

Feminism & Psychology, 14, 361–365. doi:10.1177/0959-353504044635

Nangle, D. W., Erdley, C. A., Newman, J. E., Mason, C. A., & Carpenter, E. M. (2003).

Popularity, friendship quantity, and friendship quality: Interactive influences on

children's loneliness and depression. *Journal of Clinical Child and Adolescent*

Psychology, 32, 546–555. doi:10.1207/S15374424JCCP3204_7

Schumaker, J. F. (2007). *In search of happiness: Understanding an endangered*

state of mind. Westport, CT: Praeger Publishers.

Include the issue number if a journal is paginated by issue.

Begin references on a separate page.

If your source has a digital object identifier, it is not necessary to give the URL or the date of access.

Include information about databases for on-line articles only if the article is rare and not easily found in several databases.

For a journal paginated by volume, it is not necessary to give the issue number.

If a source has one to seven authors, list all in the order given. Use an ampersand (&) before the final name.

INDEX